# RHETORICAL TRADITIONS AND BRITISH ROMANTIC LITERATURE

# RHETORICAL TRADITIONS AND BRITISH ROMANTIC LITERATURE

EDITED BY

DON H. BIALOSTOSKY

AND

LAWRENCE D. NEEDHAM

INDIANA UNIVERSITY PRESS
*Bloomington and Indianapolis*

© 1995 by Indiana University Press
All rights reserved

No part of this book may be reproduced or utilized in any form or by any means, electronic or mechanical, including photocopying and recording, or by any information storage and retrieval system, without permission in writing from the publisher. The Association of American University Presses' Resolution on Permissions constitutes the only exception to this prohibition.

The paper used in this publication meets the minimum requirements of American National Standard for Information Sciences—Permanence of Paper for Printed Library Materials, ANSI Z39.48-1984.

Manufactured in the United States of America

**Library of Congress Cataloging-in-Publication Data**

Rhetorical traditions and British romantic literature / edited by Don H. Bialostosky and Lawrence D. Needham.
  p.   cm.
Includes bibliographical references (p.   ) and index.
ISBN 0-253-31180-2 (alk. paper)
  1. English literature—19th century—History and criticism—Theory, etc.  2. English literature—18th century—History and criticism—Theory, etc.  3. Romanticism—Great Britain.  4. English language—Rhetoric.  5. Poetics.  I. Bialostosky, Don H.
II. Needham, Lawrence D.
PR457.R4558  1995
821.009'145—dc20                                         94-19475

1 2 3 4 5 00 99 98 97 96 95

# CONTENTS

ACKNOWLEDGMENTS — vii

Introduction — 1

## Part I. Sophistic Rhetoric

I. The Method of *The Friend* — 11
   *Jerome Christensen*
II. "Comparing Power" — 28
   Coleridge and Simile
   *Susan J. Wolfson*
III. De Quincey's Rhetoric of Display and *Confessions of an English Opium-Eater* — 48
   *Lawrence D. Needham*

## Part II. Classical Rhetoric

IV. Romantic Prose and Classical Rhetoric — 65
   *John R. Nabholtz*
V. Wordsworth's *Cintra* Tract — 79
   Politics, the Classics, and the Duty of the Poet
   *Richard W. Clancey*
VI. The Oratorical Pedlar — 94
   *Bruce E. Graver*
VII. Wordsworth's *Poems, in Two Volumes* (1807) and the Epideictic Tradition — 108
   *David Ginsberg*
VIII. The Case for William Wordsworth — 122
   Romantic Invention versus Romantic Genius
   *Theresa M. Kelley*

|     |     |
| --- | --- |
| IX. The Invention/Disposition of *The Prelude*, Book I<br>    Don H. Bialostosky | 139 |
| X. Romantic Aversions<br>    Apostrophe Reconsidered<br>    *J. Douglas Kneale* | 149 |
| XI. Shelley and the Ciceronian Orator<br>    *Stephen C. Behrendt* | 167 |

## Part III. Biblical Rhetoric

|     |     |
| --- | --- |
| XII. Prophetic Form<br>    The "Still Better Order" of Blake's Rhetoric<br>    *Leslie Tannenbaum* | 185 |
| XIII. Robert Lowth's *Sacred Hebrew Poetry* and the Oral Dimension of Romantic Rhetoric<br>    *Scott Harshbarger* | 199 |

## Part IV. Enlightenment Rhetoric

|     |     |
| --- | --- |
| XIV. The New Rhetoric and Romantic Poetics<br>    *James Engell* | 217 |
| XV. The Conversable World<br>    Eighteenth-Century Transformations of the Relation of Rhetoric and Truth<br>    *Nancy S. Struever* | 233 |
| XVI. Jeanie Deans and the Nature of True Eloquence<br>    *Marie Secor* | 250 |
| Appendix<br>    Wordsworth and the Rhetorical Tradition in England (1944)<br>    *Klaus Dockhorn*<br>    TRANSLATED BY *Heidi I. Saur-Stull* | 265 |
| SELECT BIBLIOGRAPHY | 281 |
| CONTRIBUTORS | 300 |
| INDEX | 302 |

# ACKNOWLEDGMENTS

Preparation of this volume was facilitated by the assistance of Lori Demers and Chris Herr and support from the Department of English Colloquium in Rhetorical Theory at the University of Toledo. The select bibliography was prepared and citations were regularized by Rosa Eberly at Pennsylvania State University. Sue Bialostosky assisted with proofreading. Publication has been subsidized by an internal faculty award from the Research and Graduate Studies Office of the College of Liberal Arts at Penn State. We are grateful for this good help and generous support.

We are also grateful for permission to reprint revised versions of the following essays and chapters:

Don H. Bialostosky. "The Revival of Rhetoric and the Reading of Wordsworth's *Prelude*." *Wordsworth, Dialogics, and the Practice of Criticism*. Cambridge: Cambridge University Press, 1992. Pp. 200–231.

Jerome Christensen. "The Method of *The Friend*." *Coleridge's Blessed Machine of Language*. Ithaca: Cornell University Press, 1981. Pp. 186–269.

James Engell. "The New Rhetoricians: Psychology, Semiotics, and Critical Theory." In *Psychology and Literature in the Eighteenth Century*. Ed. Christopher Fox. New York: AMS Press, 1987. This article was also revised as chapter 8 of Engell's *Forming the Critical Mind: Dryden to Coleridge*. Cambridge: Harvard University Press, 1989. Pp. 194–219.

Earlier versions of J. Douglas Kneale's essay appeared in *ELH* 58 (1991): 141–65 and *The Mind in Creation: Essays on English Romantic Literature in Honour of Ross G. Woodman*. Ed. J. Douglas Kneale. Montreal: McGill-Queen's University Press, 1992. Pp. 91–105.

Nabholtz, John R. "Romantic Prose and Classical Rhetoric." *Wordsworth Circle* 11 (1980): 119–26.

Nancy S. Struever. "The Conversable World: Eighteenth-Century Transformations of the Relation of Rhetoric and Truth." In *Rhetoric and the Pursuit of Truth: Language Change in the Seventeenth and Eighteenth Centuries*. Ed. Brian Vickers and Nancy S. Struever. Los Angeles: William Andrews Clark Memorial Library, 1985. Pp. 79–119.

Leslie Tannenbaum. *Biblical Tradition in Blake's Early Prophecies*. Princeton: Princeton University Press, 1982. Pp. 25–54.

Susan Wolfson. "'Comparing Power': Coleridge and Simile." In *Coleridge's Theory of Imagination Today*. Ed. Christine Gallant. New York: AMS Press, 1989. Pp. 167-95.

# INTRODUCTION

That rhetoric declined as Romanticism rose is the commonest of commonplaces, a story seemingly agreed to by all parties. Traditionalist Brian Vickers rehearses it: "rhetoric . . . was still growing when the first generation Romantics abruptly cut it off" (*Classical Rhetoric in English Poetry* 58); postmodernists John Bender and David E. Wellbery repeat the tale: "Romanticism . . . set the paradigm for the postrhetorical production, interpretation, and historiography of literature, and in this sense brought on the second death of rhetoric" (*The Ends of Rhetoric* 15). Historian of literary criticism M. H. Abrams tells the story persuasively as the shift from "pragmatic" to "expressive" critical orientations at the turn of the eighteenth century; historian of rhetoric Wilbur Samuel Howell marks the end of rhetoric at the same turn. Anthologists of the rhetorical tradition Patricia Bizzell and Bruce Herzberg go so far as to elide the Romantic period altogether in *The Rhetorical Tradition,* moving directly from selections representing Enlightenment rhetoric to those characterizing twentieth-century rhetoric. Having omitted Longinus from their selection of ancient rhetorical theorists (he finds his place in another editor's companion volume, *The Critical Tradition*), they give his Romantic revivers and redactors no place among the modern ones. Thus does the commonplace story become institutionalized in substantial anthologies designed for distinct courses that legitimate and reproduce the separate fields of rhetoric and literary studies and shape the expectations of their professors.

Those whose expectations have been formed by these commonplaces will experience the dissonance of an oxymoron in the title of this collection. Though Morse Peckham as early as 1969 was decrying in the wilderness the opposition between rhetoric and Romanticism, they will not have had ears to hear him. Nor, we think, will they have heard the significance of John R. Nabholtz's demonstration (reprinted here) of the importance of rhetoric in the educations of the major male Romantic writers or of Richard E. Matlak's seminal demonstration of rhetorical patterns in the shaping of what has been taken to be a prototypically original Romantic lyric, Wordsworth's "Tintern Abbey," or of Lee M. Johnson's discovery of similar patterns in Wordsworth's sonnets.

They may have noticed Jonathan Arac's recognition that modern criticism of *The Prelude* has been shaped by a German philological tradition deeply informed by the history of rhetoric, but will they have followed the path he traces that leads from two of our most persuasive expositors of the poem, Herbert Lindenberger and Geoffrey Hartman, comparatists both, to Erich Auerbach's and Ernst R. Curtius's knowledge of rhetoric? And will they have pressed beyond those familiar, translated philologists to the previously untranslated scholar both Lindenberger and Hartman cite, Klaus Dockhorn, selections from whose "Wordsworth and the Rhetorical Tradition in England" (1944) appear here in English for the first time?

They may have read one or another of the several previously published essays or chapters we have chosen to reprint here—Jerome Christensen's examination of Coleridge's response to the sophists, for example, or James Engell's reading of Romantic poetics in light of eighteenth-century Scottish new rhetoric—but they are not likely to have come across all of them, published as they were in diverse contexts under diverse heads, or to have seen in them, as we have and hope the readers of this book will, a common rediscovery of the relevance of rhetoric to the understanding of Romantic poetry and prose. These eight previously published essays, along with the eight essays we publish here for the first time, make a strong statement about the fruitfulness of informing our inquiries into Romantic literature with a knowledge of rhetorical traditions.

Our readers will probably have seen the strongest recent linking of Romanticism and rhetoric, Paul de Man's *Rhetoric of Romanticism,* but they will probably not have linked it with rhetorical traditions, even its own distinctively French one, but with a contemporary deconstructive rhetoric of tropes. Deconstructive rhetoric as it has been brought to Romanticism by de Man and his followers has at least reconnected the terms our title features, but it has also, for a time, preempted the field of investigation and perhaps even prevented studies based upon more comprehensive and varied rhetorical traditions from achieving recognition. For those whose first encounter with rhetoric has been with this deconstructive variety, much that we include here under this rubric will look like something else, not "rhetoric" as they know it.

Our collection aims to foster recognition of and inquiry into rhetoric in British Romantic literature, but it holds that such recognition is best achieved not by fixing in our mind's eye a single idea of rhetoric, be it de Man's deconstructive one or Brian Vickers's classicist one. Neither of them can recognize the other's rhetoric *as* rhetoric. Recognition and inquiry are best cultivated, we believe, by familiarizing ourselves with the family resemblances that connect and separate concurrent rhetorical enterprises and link them to others over time in "traditions" or genealogies. Any verbal practice anyone calls rhetorical belongs in this field of inquiry along with practices not so named but nonetheless somehow strikingly like them. We affirm with Wordsworth the power of "similitude in dissimilitude" as "the great spring of the activity of our minds" and deliberately bring into play versions of rhetoric like and unlike one another as well as like and unlike earlier and later exemplars of the art. We believe that these resemblances and differences will provoke others to further thought and inquiry that will enrich their understanding of both rhetoric and Romanticism.

The plural rhetorical traditions we invoke to organize the essays in this volume are neither arbitrary nor essential but partake of the provocative iden-

## Introduction 3

tity in difference we wish to cultivate. Part I explores two Romantic writers' affinities with the sophistic rhetorical tradition that has also informed some recent deconstructive versions of rhetoric. In the opening essay Jerome Christensen argues that Coleridge introduces method as the surety of truth in response to the proliferation of "sophistical argument" that followed the French Revolution and the ascendancy of the market economy. Another chapter in the contest between rhetoric and philosophy, Coleridge's attack on sophistry reproduces strategies of scapegoating and exclusion that gave birth to philosophy in the first place. That Coleridge's method ultimately is a "charm" against sophistry managed by the sleight-of-hand of figuration suggests the affinity of the Philosopher, who is the Friend, with his itinerant, hireling opposite, the Sophist. Extending Christensen's understanding of figuration to Coleridge's poetry, Susan J. Wolfson argues that despite his espousal of principles of unity and identity, Coleridge was aware of the mediation of figural language in his poetic practice, at times foregrounding the rhetorical strains—employed for neither embellishment nor instruction but for imaginative pleasure alone—of apparently organic designs. Pursuing lines initiated by Christensen and Wolfson, Lawrence Needham demonstrates how De Quincey draws on the sophistic rhetorical exercise of developing opposing theses to establish the ethos and authority of the new man of letters in *Confessions of an English Opium-Eater*. He shows how De Quincey's imaginative rhetoric of display derives from Renaissance and classical declamation and sophistical paradox.

The next and longest part, "Classical Rhetoric," opens with John R. Nabholtz's survey of the classical rhetorical educations of the major male Romantic poets. Richard W. Clancey further specifies Wordsworth's rhetorical education and shows how the rhetorical models of Horace and Demosthenes influence the tone and stance of one of Wordsworth's overtly rhetorical performances in prose, *The Convention of Cintra*. Bruce E. Graver discovers a similar influence in one of Wordsworth's least appreciated long poetic works, *The Excursion*. Graver shows how Cicero's *De Oratore* shapes the overall genre of the work, provides a model of the good orator that Wordsworth imitates in the character of the Wanderer, and informs the rhetorical genres of the Wanderer's speeches, deliberative, forensic, and epideictic. David Ginsberg demonstrates the importance of the last of these genres, mediated by the Renaissance tradition of epideictic verse, for understanding the short lyrics from Wordsworth's 1807 *Poems, in Two Volumes*.

The next three essays illustrate the value of the three principal offices of classical rhetoric—invention, disposition, and style—for the understanding of Romantic poetry and poetics. Theresa M. Kelley reconsiders Romantic discussions of poetic originality in the light of Wordsworth's use of the classical topics of invention. Don H. Bialostosky, following Richard Matlak's earlier argument on "Tintern Abbey," shows how a classical paradigm for the disposition of parts in the oration can account for the structure of the first book of *The Prelude*. J. Douglas Kneale rehabilitates our historical understanding of one classical stylistic figure, the apostrophe, to answer less historically informed accounts of it in recent criticism and to demonstrate consequences of this rehabilitation for reading Wordsworth's poetry.

Stephen C. Behrendt, in the final essay of part II, shows the powerful influence of the classical tradition on another Romantic writer, Percy Bysshe Shelley, demonstrating Shelley's strong sense of the nature and function of oratory as Cicero conceived it and analyzing Shelley's attempt to blend that classical rhetorical model with another derived from the New Testament figure of Jesus Christ. Shelley, Behrendt argues, "was attempting to entwine and update these two strains of rhetorical tradition in a new, heterogeneous rhetoric suited to the volatile times of Regency England and to the vexing diversity of audiences that had evolved in the wake of the spread of literacy."

Biblical rhetoric is the focus of part III. In its first essay Leslie Tannenbaum shows how the eighteenth-century divine Thomas Howes discovered argumentative and persuasive design in the "irregular" order of the Scriptures. His image of the prophet as orator, who moved audiences through exhortation, admonition, and invective, was taken up by William Blake and influenced Romantic writers such as Wordsworth, Coleridge, and Shelley when they presented themselves to their audiences. Next, Scott Harshbarger traces the influence of another eighteenth-century writer, Robert Lowth, whose pronouncements on the inspired, sublime language of scriptural authors, Homer, and eighteenth-century bards stimulated interest in the expressive power of natural, primitive discourse, such as Wordsworth exhibits in his *Lyrical Ballads*.

The secular strain of eighteenth-century rhetoric informs our final section, part IV. In it James Engell links Romantic interest in the power of expressive, "natural" language to eighteenth-century New Rhetoricians, who, in the practice of criticism, studied the connection between states of mind and language. Their psychological and linguistic approach to the study of literature influenced subsequent theory and practice of reading and writing. Like Engell, Nancy S. Struever emphasizes the significance of the arts of criticism in the belletristic tradition of rhetoric, demonstrating their relevance to the discursive arts of conversation. Using Jane Austen's novels as her examples, she argues that the practice of reading, writing, and speaking created a discourse community whose conversation fulfilled the epideictic function of displaying the good and beautiful in the service of inculcating the proper behavior of a privileged class. Finally, Marie Secor demonstrates the importance of the concept of eloquence, as defined by the Scottish New Rhetoricians, to understanding the meaning and formal features of Scott's *Heart of Midlothian*.

The four rhetorical traditions we distinguish here are not mutually exclusive. Wolfson's account of Coleridge is indebted to classical as well as sophistic terms. Behrendt's Shelley is a Biblical as well as classical rhetorician. Kneale's philological recovery of apostrophe is turned to the purposes of deconstructive reading. The new rhetoric in its several guises remains powerfully informed by the old, just as the old is revived and revised to serve the purposes of the new. Nevertheless these divisions distinguish important communities of interest and emphasis and open richer lines of inquiry into Romantic appropriations of rhetoric than a monolithic account of rhetoric would.

By emphasizing the rhetorical identity in difference of the work we are collecting, we hope not only to advance inquiries into the arts and models that informed the art of the Romantic period but also to provoke rethinking of the contemporary institutional arrangements that depend upon the separation of rhetoric from the category of "literature" that the Romantics helped to invent. A new investigation of the relationship between Romanticism and rhetoric may lead to a rapprochement between the literary and rhetorical branches of English studies (as well as between English and Rhetoric departments) whose separation was founded upon and is sustained by the commonplace story of the end of rhetoric and the rise of literature in the Romantic period.

We are not concerned, however, to tell another grand literary historical narrative to replace the old one and establish new departmental boundaries. We would rather loosen the hold of that story and open the field to interdisciplinary inquiries that were prematurely closed by its hegemony. We want to rethink the story of the relationship between Romanticism and rhetoric as it is told in standard historical accounts of the subject, not reimpose a new standard account of that relationship.

Those accounts have been bedeviled by many of the shortcomings revisionist historians of rhetoric find in traditional histories of rhetoric. They assume that rhetorics occur through the agency of great men producing great books and identify rhetoric with systematic treatises on the subject. They also assume a ruling temporal design of progress toward, or regress from, an ideal or perfect rhetoric (usually classical rhetoric) and identify rhetoric with one unchanging traditional form. And they assume that theories about writing match the practices of writing and that statements about writing are disinterested and not rhetorical. These assumptions, singularly or in tandem, have supported the idea of the fundamental incompatibility of rhetoric and Romanticism.

Thus the critical commonplace that locates the demise or death of rhetoric during the Romantic period is attributable, in part, to the failure of critics to draw the useful distinction De Quincey makes between a *rhetorica docens* and a *rhetorica utens*, between a rhetoric codified in a tract for the purposes of training students and rhetoric as a practice and applied technique employed to promote individual and group interests. That Romantic writers did not produce a systematic treatise on rhetoric has been taken to indicate their lack of interest in rhetorical issues and practices; the absence of evidence is interpreted as evidence of absence. De Quincey's "On Rhetoric" can be considered the exception to the rule, though only with some stretching—it is hardly a systematic treatise. It is also the exception that proves the rule: its idiosyncratic nature as a product of genius points to the difficulty (if not the logical inconsistency) of considering a Romantic "rhetoric" to be anything more than justification for an individual author's original practice, which, by definition, cannot and should not be replicated.

In the absence of formal rhetorics there has been little attempt to supplement accounts of rhetoric and Romanticism with texts that are not tracts on rhetoric but that discuss language, style, and communication or performatively demonstrate rhetorical strategies and techniques. In the first instance, we have in mind texts that approach a systematic exposition of at least one aspect of the arts of discourse—Coleridge's "Essays on Method," Hazlitt's "On Nicknames," De Quincey's "Style," "Language," "Conversation," and, of course, "Rhetoric"—as well as essays that broach serious issues concerning language use and instrumental communication—Wordsworth's discussion of *epideixis* in his essays on epitaphs, Hazlitt's discerning recognition of techniques of identification and tactics of exclusion in his disquisitions on party spirit, De Quincey's understanding of the uses of mystification and his elaboration of a rhetoric of secrecy and disclosure in his treatment of secret societies. In the second instance, we have in mind the panoply of Romantic prefaces that accommodate and challenge their intended audiences in creating the taste by which Romantic literature is to be enjoyed and, as will become evident, some of the prose pieces and poems analyzed in this collection.

The belief that rhetoric and Romanticism are incompatible is based not only on the absence of formal rhetorics written by Romantic authors but also on the perceived decline in classical study by the early nineteenth century. From a long view, looking back over the whole of the nineteenth century, this assessment is essentially correct; classical education for a relatively privileged few gave way to state-sponsored public instruction with the result that the "universality of the *res publica litteraria* was shattered by the proliferation of vernacular reading publics, and the classical *traditio* ceded its preeminence to national historical traditions" (Bender and Wellbery 14). Yet, as demonstrated by even a cursory examination of the evidence—class notes, texts, curriculum, and practices, which some of our contributors treat exhaustively—the Romantic writers we consider were immersed in classical study and familiar with classical rhetoric. One scholar has put the matter succinctly: "Despite the apparent decline in the reputation of classical rhetoric and in particular its figures by the early nineteenth century, there remained a considerable knowledge of traditional rhetorical issues and practices, conveyed either by elementary and university school training or, more broadly, by way of contemporary imitations and even critiques of classical models and texts" (Kelley, "'Fantastic Shapes'" 227). The influence of that knowledge on the practice of Romantic literature is one burden of this collection.

That influence manifests itself superficially, though not insignificantly, through allusions and citational references that identified members of a writerly coterie and their work. Such references remind us that despite political and commercial revolutions (or because of them), polite learning and the study of belles lettres and the classics persisted, even among new middle-class professionals, some of whom selectively emulated genteel values and practices as marks of distinction. It is hardly revolutionary anymore to note a conservative impulse in Romantic literature and its writers, many of whom belonged to or were affiliated in some fashion with aristocratic culture. Perhaps more fundamentally, familiarity with traditional rhetorical issues and models provided a starting point from which to accommodate writing to new occasions and writing situations. At minimum, classical rhetoric provided a frame of reference from which to begin those investigations into language use and figures of speech and thought that were part of Romantic literary experimentation. At most, classical models provided architectonic structures for inclusive Romantic writing, the application of which involved creative imitation through adaptation, reformulation, extension, even parody. In many cases, imitation and originality were not opposed but cooperative matters.

Yet, even were it granted that classical rhetoric suffered a significant decline in reputation by the early nineteenth century, that in itself would not argue for the absence of rhetoric in Romantic literature. To maintain such a position would be to assume a virtual identity between classical rhetoric and rhetoric and conflate the two, as Bender and Wellbery tend to do in their account of the demise of rhetoric following the advent of modernity. Their acute analysis attributes the progressive attenuation of classical rhetoric to the forces of modernity—the rise of nationalism, the ascendancy of print culture, the growth of science—which eventually effaced all rhetoric until the emergence of rhetoricality under Modernism. For our part, our collection insists on the diversity and durability of traditional rhetoric; it comprised many strands which, themselves the outgrowths of "traumatic" sociopolitical pressures, were capable of withstanding similar ones. Our collection also insists on its flexibility; it had adjusted itself all along to writing and, since the Renaissance at least, had adapted itself to print culture and vernacular reading publics. In addition, our collection identifies alternate rhetorical traditions that addressed whatever exigencies traditional rhetorics were incapable of meeting, such as the rise of evangelicalism, which drew upon Biblical and religious rhetoric, or the emergence of psychology, which influenced and was influenced by "new" eighteenth-century rhetorics. The death of classical rhetoric did not mean the death of all rhetoric.

Among new exigencies demanding a full arsenal of verbal resources was the emergence of a new scene of writing that followed the decline of patronage and the rise of market forces as factors determining a writer's career. The needs of the marketplace, the demands and requirements of publication, the professionalization of writing, and a new reading public stimulated fresh thinking about the production and reception of discourse and heightened interest in rhetorical matters, including strategies of securing literary property and cultural authority. To cite just one example, in order to succeed, the professional man of letters had to be his own patron and publicist, had to present himself to a reading public to his best advantage. In rhetorical terms, this entailed a keen appreciation of ethos and a profound concern for strategies of self-presentation—hence the proliferation of Romantic prefaces that involved the writer in attack, defense, insinuation, and the like. The rise of the author, usually considered fatal to rhetoric, presented the male Romantic writer with new challenges: how to authorize himself and legitimize his writing in a competitive market through literary "puffing" and the "Kill"—the verbal arts of invective, eristic, polemic, and logomachy. Such self-display and self-promotion are reminiscent of the tactics of the Sophists and may explain the hesitancy of historians of rhetoric to place Romantic writers in the marketplace and political arena, though the identification of Sophist and Romantic writer at times seems inescapable. Both struggled for power and authority at moments of heightened political and cultural ferment, with their success—and livelihood—dependent on their ability to captivate a fickle public through the pleasures and enchantments of language embodied within several literatures of power. (Of course, in keeping with their concern for effective self-fashioning, Romantic authors selected other precursors and personae for their projects, including, as we shall see, the Ciceronian orator and Biblical prophet.)

Finally, the hesitancy of historians of rhetoric to consider political, cultural, or material factors when discussing rhetoric and Romanticism has been due to their willingness to accept at face value what Romantic authors have said about writing. For example, they have accepted uncritically pronouncements about Romantic genius that place the author outside lines of dependency and relationship—and beyond the concerns of rhetoric. This easy acceptance is based on assumptions that theories about writing match practices of writing and that statements about writing are objective and disinterested. The disinterestedness of writing is, of course, a fundamental tenet of Romantic ideology and its acceptance has led to a paradoxical state of critical affairs. By ignoring the various sociopolitical and economic factors affecting the production and reception of Romantic discourse, historians of rhetoric have been curiously ahistorical in their accounts of rhetoric and Romanticism, and in disregarding considerations of a new rhetorical situation surrounding the Romantic scene of writing, they have been strangely arhetorical. What is demanded to provide a more accurate and resolute focus on rhetoric—and what some of our contributors have gestured toward by referencing the Convention of Cintra, the Porteous Affair, and Peterloo or by evoking the contemporary scene of writing—is careful attention to the contexts of Romantic literature, leading, we believe, to an increased awareness of its rhetoricity and of the importance of traditions of rhetoric to its full understanding and appreciation.

# Part I
# Sophistic Rhetoric

# I

# THE METHOD OF *THE FRIEND*

## Jerome Christensen

Although few would now agree, Coleridge always thought of the collection of essays called *The Friend*—published serially in 1809, then revised for republication in 1818—as a more important work than the hastily composed *Biographia Literaria*. Its professed aim, to refer men's opinions to and anchor men's behavior in their absolute principles, was the central project of Coleridge's career as philosopher, moralist, and social critic. This essay charts the odd twists and turns that Coleridge writes himself into and out of as he follows that itinerary in the revised version of *The Friend*.

Coleridge begins *The Friend* of 1818 as he had its earlier incarnation, by exemplifying the hazards that beset the oracular moralist in the "Fable of the Madning Rain." Having sounded this note of mingled caution and pathos, Coleridge proceeds to expand on the moral dangers of bluntly communicating the truth in a long introductory section wherein he contrasts an appropriately discreet communication with the irresponsible truth telling of the French Encyclopaedists, who, by indiscriminately broadcasting technically correct but circumstantially inadequate notions, stripped truth of the reserve essential to the preservation of its moral force. Rather than jeopardize himself or his reader, Coleridge forsakes the stances of oracle and philosophe to write as the Friend—friend to truth, friend to the reader's reason.

The Friend honors the reserve that is the warrant and safeguard of true principle—honors it, one might say, to the point of obsession. The Friend lavishes chapter after chapter of *The Friend* on baroque justifications of his protracted deferral of the promised establishment of those absolute principles that would be perspicuous to reason and a reliable guide to conduct. Delay is promptly renewed at the beginning of each essay. But it is not as though nothing is getting done. The Friend's justification takes in a world of matters—political, cultural, and social; it also does duty as a defense of his tortuously obscure style, which, in its turns and counterturns, its haltings and dizzying inwardnesses, is, he maintains, the proper medium for the apprehension of the truth in its sublimity.

As I hope to show, however, by annexing truth to a particular style, the

Friend arouses suspicion that the sense of a profound truth residing apart but eventually accessible may be simply an effect of that style. Indeed, because the Friend's periodic style so plausibly evokes the place and feel of truth, indulgence in the exquisitely meditated cadences of the Friend's periodic style may on balance be a more serious hazard to the pilgrim soul than the naked impieties of Jacobin rhetoric.

In his "Essays on Method" the Friend defends his moral authority by first ritually casting out the sophists, archetypal enemies of all principle, and by laying claim to dialectic as the conflicted but unerring discourse of reason. But the selections from Shakespeare that the Friend uses to illustrate method improvidently devour his thesis, and the chiasmus with which he figures method wantons with the antithetical division between true philosophy and specious rhetoric. The truth that the Friend successfully communicates (with what moral consequences we must stay ignorant) is the figure of the Friend, of whom, as of Coleridge, it may be said that the philosopher is in the sophist, the sophist in the philosopher.

*The Friend* begins with a scenario for a recognition scene. "What is that," the Friend asks, "which first strikes us, and strikes us at once, in a man of education? And which, among educated men, so instantly distinguishes the man of superior mind, that (as was observed with eminent propriety of the late Edmund Burke) 'we cannot stand under the same arch-way during a shower of rain, *without finding him out?*'" The Friend dismisses as distinguishing marks "the weight or novelty of his remarks" and "any unusual interest of facts communicated by him," as well as "any peculiarity in his words and phrases" (*Friend* 448). He concludes that there "remains but one other point of distinction possible; and this must be, and in fact is, the true cause of the impression made on us. It is the unpremeditated and evidently habitual *arrangement* of his words, grounded on the habit of foreseeing, in each integral part, or (more plainly) in every sentence, the whole that he then intends to communicate. However irregular and desultory his talk, there *is* method in the fragments" (*Friend* 449).

Intention's proper discourse, method is the projective logic that relates an original purpose to its ultimate end. The virtue of thought, method exhibits "the first merit, that which admits neither substitute nor equivalent [which] is, that *every thing is in its place*" (*Friend* 449). There is no substitute or equivalent for method because method is the principle by which substitutes and equivalents are legitimately made.

Abstractly considered, method would appear to be one of many arts of discourse, an important skill, certainly; laborious to acquire and difficult to practice, perhaps; but generally accessible to the willing student. The Friend, however, does not consider method abstractly; he discovers it in the man, for whom it is not the acquisition of a course of study but the fruit of a genial development.[1] "METHOD," according to the Friend, "becomes natural to the mind which has been accustomed to contemplate not *things* only, or for their own sake alone, but likewise and chiefly the *relations* of things, either

## The Method of The Friend

their relations to each other, or to the observer, or to the state and apprehension of the hearers" (*Friend* 451). What becomes natural to the man of superior mind is to be able to traverse a network of relations (between himself and things, things themselves, things and his hearers) that is the discourse by which he is recognized and in which he comes to recognize himself—not only the occasionally fragmentary self that appears but the whole self that he then intends to communicate.

Method may distinguish the superior mind, but it does not constitute that mind. The Friend insists on "the necessity of a mental Initiative to all Method" (*Friend* 469), "the leading Thought" (*Friend* 455) and "master-light" (*Friend* 468), without which any arrangement is merely artificial. To exemplify such "artificial arrangement" the Friend invokes the vast classificatory system of Linnaean botany, which, when examined, reduces to "the mere verbal definition" of sex, a technical convenience that has been abstracted from "the central idea of vegetation itself" (*Friend* 468, 467). Lacking an initiative of its own, Linnaean botany could only conceive of vegetables without vegetation, with the ironic consequence that the science of growing plants has become the most lifeless and mechanical of all contemporary systems, "a mass enlarging by endless appositions, but without a nerve that oscillates, or a pulse that throbs, in sign of *growth* or inward sympathy." The book of nature, the Friend laments, has become the "dictionary" of the Encyclopaedists (*Friend* 469).

Against such "blind and guideless industry" the Friend counterposes the work of the "philosophic seer" whose vision is armed by "the knowledge of LAW [in which] alone dwell Power and Prophecy, decisive Experiment, and, lastly, a scientific method" (*Friend* 470). Such philosophical scientists can be found among the English chemists, whose luminous example excites comparison with Shakespeare and quotation from Milton:

> If in SHAKESPEARE we find nature idealized into poetry, through the creative power of a profound yet observant meditation, so through the meditative observation of a DAVY, a WOOLASTON, or a HATCHETT;
>
> > By some connatural force
> > Powerful at greatest distance to unite
> > With secret amity things of like kind,
>
> we find poetry, as it were, substantiated and realized in nature . . . (*Friend* 471)

The forebears of these chemists include Plato, Bacon, and particularly Kepler, who "seemed born to prove that true genius can overpower all obstacles. If he gives an account of his modes of proceeding, and of the views under which they first occurred to his mind, how unostentatiously and *in transitu,* as it were, does he introduce himself to our notice: and yet never fails to present the living germ out of which the genuine method, as the inner form of science springs up!" (*Friend* 485).

The organic metaphor is, of course, no accident; nor is it arbitrary, for the method we acknowledge in the work of man corresponds to the organization which it is our instinct to find in nature, and in "a self-conscious and thence reflecting being, no instinct can exist, without engendering the belief of an object corresponding to it. . . . Least of all can this mysterious predisposition exist without evolving a belief that the productive power, which is in nature as nature, is essentially one . . . with the intelligence, which is in the human mind above nature" (*Friend* 497–98). Correspondents reflect a transcendent unity and imply with an unignorable force that the law of nature as of science is in "act and substance" finally spiritual: "It is the idea of the common centre, of the universal law, by which all power manifests itself in opposite yet interdependent forces . . . that enlightening inquiry, multiplying experiment, and at once inspiring humility and perseverance will lead him to comprehend gradually and progressively the relation of each to the other, of each to all, and of all to each" (*Friend* 511). Such is the "mid-channel" of the stream of truth, the method of method, which has "its bed, its banks, and its line of progression" (*Friend* 512). And though nothing of certainty can be said about the connection between the knowing of the mind and the being of nature, the coincidence between the method of science and the general, beneficent teleology of nature prepares the mind to accept the conclusion that this method must derive its initiative from a genius who is united with but different from his effects and continuous in his changes, as from a divine author whose existence is predicated in the very statement of its possibility and who manifests himself as the masterlight of all conception.

Though proposed as a discursive movement that naturally integrates differences within a progressive continuity, method is only natural because it is opposed to unnatural and hostile artifice. The Friend exposes the alien artificer in his essay "On the Origin and Progress of the Sect of Sophists in Greece," which prefaces the section on method.[2] Unlike the title "philosopher," which originally identified a true "lover of wisdom," "sophist" signified "one who professes the power of making others wise, a wholesale and retail *dealer* in wisdom—a wisdom-monger. . . . In this and not in their abuse of the arts of reasoning, have Plato and Aristotle placed the *essential* of the sophistic character" (*Friend* 436).

Further aspects of that character appear in further echoes of Plato and his disciple Aristotle, rivals allied in their steadfast contempt for the sophist. For the former he was "one who hires himself out or puts himself up at auction"; for the latter his generic character was the "baseness of motives joined with the impudence and delusive nature of the pretense." Just less important than this "pretense of selling wisdom and eloquence" in distinguishing the sophists was their "itinerancy," their ceaseless traversal of Greece from the provincial towns and villages to Athens, "their great emporium and place of rendezvous" (*Friend* 437). Each stop on the sophist's route was merely an opportunity for him to market his impressive rhetorical techniques. "Some of these," according to the Friend, "applied the lessons of their art in their own persons, and traded for gain and gainful influence in the character of demagogues and public orators; but the greater number offered themselves as instructors, in the art of persuasion and temporary impression, to as many as would come up to the high prices, at which they rated their services" (*Friend* 438).

Using rhetoric to make the worse cause appear the better or to raise a demagogue in the guise of a statesman is, doubtless, a vicious practice, but at least in either case vice implies virtue, and the rhetorician conveys by his very immorality the antithesis between good and evil. That inversion can be eventually exposed and the proper relations restored by the authoritative application of true method. But the base motives of the sophist are fundamentally more subversive than that, for the sophist is not motivated by ambition for power and prestige but by money, which is for him *the* base motive, one that can be substituted for all others, into which all others can be successfully transformed, to the corruption of all virtue:

> *Hireling hunters of the young and rich,* they offered to the vanity of youth and the ambition of wealth a substitute for that authority, which by the institutions of Solon had been attached to high birth and property, or rather to the moral discipline, the habits, attainments and directing motives, on which the great legislator had calculated (not indeed as necessary or constant accompaniments, but yet) as the regular and ordinary results of comparative opulence and renowned ancestry. (*Friend* 438–39)

The viciousness of sophistical substitution can be gauged by the disruptions it caused in the calculations of Solon, who had methodically devised a state in which high birth and property were the natural signs of authority, signs which it was presumably the interest of those with authority to maintain. But in their willingness to accept a sophistical, delusive substitute for their inheritance, the Athenian youths abandoned reason and prudence. They were ambitious for wealth, but to have sacrificed property and position to that ambition was perversely to relinquish the sensible ends in order to indulge in the blind means. Sophistical exchange seems to abstract wealth from its source in value into pure motive: what ones does not have, what one can desire. In opting for the sophist, Athenian youths chose unnaturally, of course, but the uncanny unanimity of their deviance would seem somehow to have naturalized the unnatural. The dynamics of that bizarre substitution ferment in the very metaphor with which Plato snags the sophists, "hireling hunters of the young and rich"—a trope that in turning its trick on the sophists presumes its own scandal: that the young would sacrifice all that belongs to them in order to hire their hunters.

According to the Friend, the appearance of the sophists in Athens, during the aftermath of the Persian War, came at a time when the "light and sensitive Athenians" were caught up in "the giddiness of sudden aggrandizement" (*Friend* 438) and were dangerously susceptible to sophistical advances. We recognize symptoms of the French disease, already infecting the English, in this description of an Athens ripe for corruption: "The restless spirit of republican ambition, engendered by their success in a just war, and by the romantic character of that success, had already formed a close alliance with luxury in its early and most vigorous state, when it acts as an appetite to enkindle, and before it has exhausted and dulled the vital energies by the habit of enjoyment" (*Friend* 439). The French, light-headed and susceptible, succumbed to just such vicious habits of enjoyment and have since paid the price. One would hope that, left to themselves, the level-headed English, anchored by the gravity of their ancient institutions and their weighty traditions, could resist the rare dizziness that follows upon ambition's sudden success. The sophists represent the futility of that hope; the Friend's meditation on sophistic power displays his seasoned awareness that men, as moral agents, are never left to themselves. To contemplate the possibility of the sophists is to have already admitted them within the walls: "But this corruption was now to be introduced into the *citadel* of the moral being, and to be openly defended by the very arms and its instruments, which had been given for the purpose of preventing or chastising its approach" (*Friend* 439). The weightiness of institutions and traditions is little protection against a "*sleight-of-word* juggler" (*Friend* 437) who teases gravity into playing his own game. The sophist owes his success to his wizardly ability to turn aggression into the appearance of defense, a withstanding that gives him a kind of standing equivalent to the principles he has supplanted.

When the Friend examines the means by which the sophists accomplished their sensational turnabout, he attributes it to their strategy of sensualizing the understanding. Like their modern type, the hirelings of the British press, the sophists' arguments may not have been true or reasonable or even persuasive in themselves, "yet the principles so attacked were brought into doubt by the mere frequency of hearing *all* things doubted, and the most sacred of all now openly denied, and now insulted by sneer and ridicule" (*Friend* 439).

> Religion, in its widest sense, signifies the act and habit of reverencing THE INVISIBLE, as the highest both in ourselves and in nature. To this the senses and their immediate objects are to be made subservient, the one as its organs, the other as its exponents: and as such therefore, having on their own account no true *value*, because no inherent *worth*. They are a *language*, in short: and taken independently of their representative function, from *words* they become mere empty *sounds*, and differ from *noise* only by exciting expectations which they cannot gratify—fit ingredients of the idolatrous *charm*, the potent Abracadabra, of a sophisticated race, who had sacrificed the religion of faith to the superstition of the senses, a race of animals, in whom the presence of reason is manifested solely by the absence of instinct. [*Friend* 440]

The sophistication of the race is accomplished by abstracting words from their true source in the invisible and manufacturing a language of empty sounds that can be hypnotically jingled like idolatrous charms for the superstitious.

As synonym for sophistical rhetoric and sophistic sound the Friend offers "language," and one way of placing the sophist is to describe his habitat as that traverse where language is first differentiated, where noise takes on the slightest resistant obscurity, which endows it with the simulacrum of meaning.

# The Method of The Friend

The charm (excitement and power) of sophistical rhetoric is the charm of ornament.

> To shape, to dye, to paint over, and to mechanize the mind, he [Plato] resigned, as their proper trade, to the sophists, against whom he waged open and unremitting war. For the ancients, as well as the moderns, had their machinery for the extemporaneous mintage of intellects, by means of which, *off-hand*, as it were, the scholar was enabled to *make a figure* on any and all subjects, on any and all occasions. (*Friend* 473)

Shaping, dyeing, and painting over are the ornamental arts by which the offhanded sophistic craftsman transfigures the mind into the machine of language. Like the poet whose personifications dramatize a scandalous impropriety, the sophist who makes figures on all subjects (the subjects of a sovereign reason) transgresses the sacred distinction between persons and things; he not only mints the intellects of others, he is "himself" only the figure, the ornamental equivalent of empty sounds, made on his own invisible subject. Moreover, the sophist seems insensible of any trespass and immune to loss; because he performs his legerdemain offhandedly, the sophist extends nothing of his that could be wounded or severed by reason's harsh dictate.

Given that the sophist is capable, at no cost to himself, of minting intellects in mimicry of those powers that are reserved to God alone and accepting that his rhetoric demoralizes any reasonable attempt to trap him in an antithetical framework that would disarm him and restrain his criminal enterprise, the problem of how to discriminate the counterfeiter's artifice from the genius's method becomes embarrassingly acute and explains the Friend's reaffirmation of the single Platonic criterion of wage earning: selling wisdom is the sole visible sign by which the sophist can be identified and by which his appeal to otherwise noble and blameless youths can be understood, thereby erasing the scandal of their voluntary victimage. Ambitious for gain, the sophist sells the ability to make money to those who have been secretly afflicted by the same greed. The exchange of a coin signals avarice and permits the Platonic philosopher to indict the unauthorized minter of intellects for violating the sovereign's law. The coin is the mark of the greedy counterfeiter. It signifies not only the sophist's essential vice but also that there is an essence to sophistry that can be retrieved from the labyrinth of evanescent differences, echoes, and reflections and that confirms the essentiality of the philosopher's gold.

The case of Philosophy versus the Sophist is not merely a historical curiosity for the Friend. The successful prosecution of the sophist is urgent to an Englishman who lives in a culture where, as in the languidly skeptical Athens following the Persian War, traditional values have lost their presumptive authority and where "arguments," as the Friend has commented earlier, "are the sole current coin of intellect." Because there is "no royal mintage for arguments," it is often frustratingly difficult to tell the difference between "the honest man's intellectual coin" and the "light or counterfeit." Despite confusing signs and even willful error, however, the Friend insists that there are criteria that enable the truth seeker to discriminate between the true worth of a superior mind and the sham sense of an impostor; these evidences may be "only *conjectural* marks; yet such," he claims, "as will seldom mislead any man of plain sense, who is both honest and observant" (*Friend* 277–78). For the Friend the conjectural mark is the sign of method, the discourse of a superior mind. His supposition of method as the "rock of refuge" presupposes the displacement of the insidious sophist and requires a hermeneutics of conjectural marks that can assure the honest and observant reader that what he recognizes as method is the real thing and not a base simulacrum.

In the *Biographia* the recognition of Wordsworth's genius is followed by an attempt to deduce the imagination that is eventually rescued in chapter XIII from foundering by the man of the letter. The "Essays on Method" begin with a recognition scene also, but here the enthusiastic hypothesis of the man of method is not followed by an attempt at rigorous theoretical validation. Instead the Friend substitutes exemplification and commentary for deduction; he deploys characters from Shakespeare as the figures of the presence and absence, range and nuance, of method.

The Friend first cites the conversation between Falstaff and Mrs. Quickley in *Henry IV, Part II* (i. 74–86), which he uses to portray the shallow mind whose thought, lacking hooks, eyes, or any principle of progression, is at the mercy of a verbal association that confuses the idea at hand with a flurry of remembered incidents. Mrs. Quickley's speech, the voluble rehash of a sensualized understanding, exemplifies "the absence of Method, which characterizes the uneducated, [and which] is occasioned by an habitual submission of the understanding to mere events and images as such, and independent of any power in the mind to classify or appropriate them" (*Friend* 451). But it is equally significant that in the eddying of this speech, which of all other possible Shakespearean examples (mentioned are the clown in *Measure for Measure* and the Nurse in *Romeo and Juliet*) the Friend chooses to reproduce, Mrs. Quickley tosses up, like foam on the current, the pointed *topos* of the true king—a *topos* central to both *Henry IV* and *The Friend*. Mrs. Quickley recalls a moment when Falstaff was punished by Hal for insulting the king with a crude simile, a presumption that might seem to have been authoritatively answered by the application of an appropriate penalty, except that the recording angel registers the punishment without being impressed by the presumption, thus mooting the authority of Hal's lesson. Mrs. Quickley recalls Hal's punishment of Falstaff for presumptuously dragging the king down to a base level in common tavern conversation as if it were just another incident in the anarchic whirl of her seamy establishment, more fuel for the engine of her tongue—of as much interest or meaning as "the round table, by a seacoal fire." Not only, then, has the king been abused by Falstaff's reaching simile, the abuse is itself debased by Mrs. Quickley's promiscuous recollection: kings make no special difference in her immethodical mind and in her spindrift world. Tavern life endangers Hal because it attracts him into a democratic

*The Method of* The Friend                                                                 19

carnival of circumstance that would sever him from his natural sovereignty not only by force of habit but also by the gibbering of an idle tongue.

As counterexample to Quickley and as illustration of genial method, the Friend chooses the passage from *Hamlet* where the Prince describes to Horatio the events that occurred during his interrupted voyage to England. Although Hamlet's discourse is oceans apart from the landlady's, once again the issue of method attracts the theme of sovereignty.

> "HAM. Sir, in my heart there was a kind of fighting
> That would not let me sleep: methought I lay
> Worse than the mutines in the bilboes. Rashly
> And prais'd be rashness for it—*Let us know,*
> *Our indiscretion sometimes serves us well,*
> *When our deep plots do fail: and that should teach us*
> *There's a divinity that shapes our ends,*
> *Rough-hew them how we will.*
> HOR. That is most certain.
> HAM. Up from my cabin,
> My sea-gown scarf'd about me, in the dark
> Grop'd I to find out them; had my desire;
> Finger'd their pocket; and, in fine, withdrew
> To my own room again: making so bold,
> *My fears forgetting manners* to unseal
> Their grand commission; where I found, Horatio,
> A royal knavery—an exact command,
> *Larded with many several sorts of reasons,*
> *Importing Denmark's health, and England's too,*
> With ho! such bugs and goblins in *my* life,
> That on the supervize, no leisure bated,
> No, not to stay the grinding of the axe,
> My head should be struck off!
> HOR. Is't possible?
> HAM. Here's the commission.—Read it at more leisure."
>                                                  Act v. sc. 2. (*Friend* 451–52)

The Friend relies on his first set of italics to alert the reader to Hamlet's testimony of a continuity between the methodical shaping of divinity and the rough-hewn ends of man. Coleridge praises Hamlet's narration for the way "the events, with the circumstances of time and place, are all stated with equal compression and rapidity, not one introduced which could have been omitted without injury to the intelligibility of the whole process" (*Friend* 452). Nothing added injures but something omitted halts: "If any tendency is discoverable, as far as the mere facts are in question, it is the tendency to omission: and, accordingly, the reader will observe, that the attention of the narrator is called back to one material circumstance, which he was hurrying by, by a direct question *from the friend* to whom the story is communicated, 'HOW WAS THIS SEALED?'" (*Friend* 452, italics added). Horatio's query recalls the omission that shatters Hamlet's continuity, the one material circumstance that has the deepest spiritual import. The seal, we know, is the signature of the king, the unequivocal representative of his ruling arm, the certain mark of a sovereign authority beyond conjecture. Although in Denmark the seal has fallen into the hands of the usurper, the sovereign symbolism of the seal is unaffected, for its meaning is subject to neither the vagaries of politics nor the virtues of a particular individual. If the seal were to be debased by the usurper's mounting to power, it would by default absolve him of usurpation by proving that what he has seized had no intrinsic worth, was not the authentic property of the sovereign after all. Hence it is the logic of the seal, which is the logic of sovereignty recognized by both Claudius and Hamlet, that, for the sake of intelligibility, requires the death of the Prince; in the hands of the usurper the seal must mean the decapitation of the true king. That death had been sealed by the time the ship disembarked, and throughout his transit Hamlet was caught in what seems a fatal dilemma: he had the choice of reverence or rebellion, of submitting to the proscription of the seal or breaking it. The logic of the seal dictates that either decision must mean his death, since the sealed message is an order for execution and the unauthorized rupture of the seal is itself punishable by death. Recounting his own adventure, however, Hamlet seems insensible of the dilemma; he rushes past it in the exuberance of his telling as Mrs. Quickley had hurried past Falstaff's punishment. Horatio arrests that exuberance by questioning the errant tendency in Hamlet's otherwise methodical narrative, the single omission that explains its life.

Until Horatio's question Hamlet had been the exemplar of method; but the Friend comments on the following passage, where Hamlet tells how he altered the commission of Claudius in order to command the death of Rosencrantz and Guildenstern, that the Prince is "ever disposed to generalize, and meditative to excess" (*Friend* 452). Hamlet, of course, like Coleridge himself, is renowned for his abstruser musings, but I would suggest that Hamlet's meditative excess is objected to here not because it occludes action but because it reveals too much about an action that has the fascination of the breaking of a taboo. To put it even more pointedly, Hamlet's excess is the excess of Hamlet the man who is left over, first, after the crunch of the dilemma that should have killed him and, second, after the awful question "HOW WAS THIS SEALED?" which should have subdued meditation and silenced speech forever. Unmoved, the Prince answers: "Why, even in that was heaven ordinant." But this time the Friend withholds his applauding italics from an exculpatory piety that flirts with blasphemy by confusing heavenly ordinance with inordinate desires: "I had my father's signet in my purse, / Which was," the Prince continues, "the model of that Danish seal: folded the writ up in the form of the other; / Subscribed it; gave't the impression; placed it safely, / The changeling never known" (*Friend* 453). Hamlet's ploy to escape his dilemma has been to produce, as if from nowhere, the model of Claudius's seal, which until then had been the presumptive original. What had been taken to be the original is disclosed by Hamlet to be a copy of a model which, though passed from father to son and symbolic of the unbroken genealogy of authority, has its sole value for Hamlet in that it can duplicate its own replica. By forging with the original, Hamlet has not only imitated the mark of his uncle's supposed sovereignty but also mimicked Claudius's usurpation in a finer tone. By the mere self-saving frequency of his repetition of the seal, the desperate Hamlet has certified the so-called usurper's employment of the seal as just another pretext for power or survival, purposes which in both *Hamlet* and *The Friend* come to the same thing. By replicating the seal, in effect substituting the original for itself, the king has turned his signet, the one infallible sign of his sovereignty, into an instrument of forgery with which he or anyone can offhandedly mint the impression of a king. Hamlet does commit regicide and parricide but "only" figuratively: the king and father are not killed *because* they are king and father but *by* conceiving of them as figures, manipulable by the ingenious conjurer who acts from no Oedipal instigation but according to motives that combine power and survival in differentials too subtle to stage. By betraying his father's seal as the self-unraveling clue of sovereignty, the putative heir has divulged that not only is there no royal mintage for arguments, there is not even a royal mintage for monarchs.[3] The seals of king and usurper are identical, each the counterfeit of the other. The marks of no signet satisfy our conjectures into the truth of a character who, like the Friend's Hamlet, lavishes the mind with his essential excess.

Hamlet's insouciance regarding his forgery is matched by his unsettling lack of remorse or even polite regret for the demise of the false friends Guildenstern and Rosencrantz. He makes some attempt to dismiss their fate as the organic consequence of their actions when he claims that "their defeat doth by their insinuation grow," but he concludes by sophisticating their deaths into a necessary by-product of the machinery of the seal, a mark of its intelligibility: *"'Tis dangerous when the baser nature comes / Between the pass and fell incensed points / Of mighty opposites."*

In Hamlet, then, we see method in "undue preponderance," the proof that "when the prerogative of the mind is stretched into despotism, the discourse may degenerate into the grotesque or the fantastical" (*Friend* 455). And in the penultimate passage that the Friend quotes from the play, Hamlet himself comments on the dissolution of the sovereign prerogative into not just despotism but the baser elements from which it had been magically raised. Madly methodical, he "explains" his melancholy disposition by a trope that unravels sovereignty in an entropic regress halted only by a terminus that pointedly jests at conclusions:

> "To what base uses we may return, Horatio! Why may not imagination trace the noble dust of Alexander, till he find it stopping a bung-hole? HOR. It were to consider too curiously to consider so. HAM. No, faith, not a jot; but to follow him thither with modesty enough and likelihood to lead it. As thus: Alexander died, Alexander was buried, Alexander returneth to dust—the dust is earth; of earth we make loam: and why of that loam, whereto he was converted, might they not stop a beer-barrel?

>     Imperial Caesar, dead and turn'd to clay,
>     Might stop a hole to keep the wind away!" (*Friend* 455)

In the method of *The Friend* the base use of the signet returns Hamlet to this meditation on baseness, which conceives of the difference between the elemental clay and the imperial monarch as only a matter of turns on a figurative path that the wayward mind at once both tracks and forges. In the madness of his method Hamlet hangs suspended between the mighty points of king and clay, his eddying life sustained only by the improper power of substitution for which he exchanged sovereignty of throne and soul. That power is his seal.

The last quotation from Shakespeare in the chapter is offered as another perversion of method, to show that if "the excess [of thought and imagination] lead to Method misapplied, and to connections of the moment, the absence, or marked deficiency, either precludes Method altogether, both form and substance: or . . . retains the outward form only." But that which is proposed as a version of immethod (the empty, outward form of method) is at the same time a comment on the preceding illustrations; it is Polonius's explanation to Gertrude of her son's madness:

>     "My liege and madam! to expostulate
>     What majesty should be, what duty is,
>     Why day is day, night night, and time is time,
>     Were nothing but to waste night, day and time.
>     Therefore—since brevity is the soul of wit,
>     And tediousness the limbs and outward flourishes,
>     I will be brief. Your noble son is mad:
>     Mad call I it—for to define true madness,
>     What is't, but to be nothing else but mad!
>     But let that go.
>     QUEEN. More matter with less art.
>     POL. Madam! I swear, I use no art at all.
>     That he is mad, tis true: tis true, tis pity:
>     And pity tis, tis true (a foolish figure!
>     But farewell it, for I will use no art.)
>     Mad let us grant him then! and now remains,
>     That we find out the cause of this effect,
>     Or rather say the cause of this defect:
>     For this effect defective comes by cause.
>     Thus it remains, and the remainder thus
>     Perpend!"
>                     *Hamlet,* act ii. scene 2. (*Friend* 456)

The Queen demands more matter after an address that has, in truth, been all matter, in which the definitions of majesty, duty, day, night, and time have been abandoned as so much dead weight, and whose self-evidential nature is epitomized in the final tautology "True madness" is "to be nothing else but mad." At the queen's insistence, Polonius demonstrates the art of significance by methodically differentiating the base tautology as a chiasmus which is its best commentary: "That he is mad, tis true: tis true, tis pity: / And pity tis, tis true. . . ." Polonius has promised to use no art, and, indeed, the "tautegorical" chiasmus[4]—identity doubled and spaced; a base nature between points that are, at least on the face of the page, opposed—is the merest art, tautology's own "progressive transition" (*Friend* 457) toward significance. The art is in the matter, the matter in the art. The friendly councillor has watched his charge closely and has reproduced well the method of his madness.

Polonius's chiasmus, with its baroque redoubling, may be, as he says, "a foolish figure," but the same figure is employed with deeper seriousness and deployed with greater effect in the address of William Sedgwick to the Parliament's Army, a speech which the Friend gives place of precedence at the head of the final section of his essays, rescuing it "from oblivion, both for the honor of our forefathers, and in proof of the intense difference between the republicans of that period, and the democrats, or rather demagogues of the present (*Friend* 411). Sedgwick's speech to his comrades was a futile attempt to dissuade them from their intent to execute the defeated and imprisoned Charles. He argues that regicide under such and indeed any circumstances is a kind of suicide, for on the sanctity of the monarch depends the religious fidelity of the people, which is in turn the soul of both state and individual, and the only sure foundation of the parliamentary cause. Sedgwick's defense of the king, in which the argument to withhold the ax for the sake of a greater truth is inseparable from a style of stately reserve, is the organic expression of the values that the seventeenth century symbolizes for the Friend; its vital seed is a chiasmus. "The king is in the people, the people in the king" represents the richly ceremonious interchange of a diversified yet united nation. By bringing king and people together in the chiasmus, Sedgwick affirms their union while maintaining their difference; the repetition and inversion of terms is a transitive movement carried out within a horizon of identity that disarms extremes of their antithetical point. In this commonwealth the head of the king is the capital that produces all interest, makes possible all economy. In this nation the king may not abuse his prerogative by ruling according to fiat; nor may the people confuse vox *populi* with vox *dei*. The chiasmus states that king and people are each essentially inside the other; the chiasmus formulates an existential distribution of powers and grants a delimited place to each outside the other. Each term in Sedgwick's chiasmus is the soul of the other's body.

Yet merely to state the figurative principle of Sedgwick's address is to ignore the pathos of its expression. At one and the same time Sedgwick claims to state a truth that is independent of the imagination of men and yet yields to the imagination's restless desire for a sensible figure to represent the manifest self-evident truth. Thus, although he warns of a danger to come, he contemplates it as a catastrophe completed; for the chiasmus figures to the imagination what is no longer fully present to the reason: to imagine the dissolution of the symbol is to represent it within an allegory that presupposes the breach of its monolithic integrity. The death of the king—Charles, any king, all kings—depends not on scaffold, guillotine, or gibbet, awaits not the sinister stratagems of desperate men, but lies in the conception of sovereignty as subject to the actions and arguments of men in the discourse of history—a conception that does not murder but memorializes. When we look back at the seventeenth century, we find a speaker minting the gold that will float an insolvent sovereign, trying to give currency to that which has lost its value. When we hearken to Sedgwick's words, we hear an echo of the Friend's own accents, inflections, and intonations.

For the amicable chiasmus is the figure of method. The chiasmus expresses the transitive integration of opposites by impressing it on the page: "And this is METHOD, itself a distinct science, the immediate offspring of philosophy, and the link or mordant by which philosophy becomes scientific and the sciences philosophical" (*Friend* 463). The discovery of method corresponds to the religious strength of a "true *efficient* conviction of moral truth," which is, in discursive terms, "the implication of doctrine in the miracle and of miracle in the doctrine, which is the bridge of communication between the senses and the soul" (*Friend* 431). In its limitless fecundity, method connects Shakespeare and Plato, "the philosophic poet to the poetic philosopher" (*Friend* 472), identifies the continuity between the deductive Plato and the inductive Bacon, "the Athenian Verulam and the British Plato" (*Friend* 488), and synthesizes poetry and science, as when we find the correspondent to the "observant meditation" of Shakespeare that produces "nature idealized into poetry" in the "meditative observation" of the British chemists by which "poetry, [is] as it were, substantiated and realized in nature" (*Friend* 471). The "self-unravelling clue" of method will lead the investigator to comprehend "gradually and progressively the relation of each to the other, or each to all, and of all to each" (*Friend* 511). Link, mordant, bridge, infinitesimal elementary body, solution of continuity—method morally communicates between soul and sense, reason and understanding, God and world, king and subject, author and book. Partaking of both poles, distinct from either, method is both the crossing plank from one side of the stream to the other and the eddy where circulates the proprieties of intention and act: *a* in *b*, *b* in *a*. Translucent, provisional, faultlessly deferential to the truth it serves—method follows the track of the chiasmus.

We imagine the itinerant sophists condemned to pass like night from land to land, hungry for a fee, dependent on the reputation that precedes them and the letters of introduction which they bear, peddling their virtuosity from one town to the next, whereas Plato unostentatiously introduces himself in transition, while all the time residing in one place—in the dialogues that are both his proper figure and the eternal property of philosophy. It is in the interest of philosophy to fear the sophist, to raise the specter of "open and unremitting war," and to mark its own allies with the hypnotic brilliance of a glittering eye,[5] for the light of that eye obscures the powerful mechanics of method and that vision of a bloody defensive struggle justifies centuries of inkshed. But the sophists, if sophists there were, have been bought out long ago. Their wares could not compete with the power of Plato's method both to comprehend and to exclude them. For though the sophists may have had the ability "to shape, to dye, to paint over, and to mechanize the mind," even "to make a figure on any and all subjects," Plato's method enabled him to resign such dealings to them "as their proper trade," to resign, that is, to the sophists what belongs to them and them alone, thereby endowing their very impropriety with a philosophical propriety. If the danger of the sophists is that they exchange knowledge for money, money that, as Karl Marx stated, "appears as a *disruptive* power for the individual and for the social bonds" because it "changes fidelity into infidelity, love into hate, hate into love, virtue into vice, vice into virtue, servant into master, stupidity into intelligence and intelligence into stupidity" (193), philosophy appears as the power to make a figure of the sophists; the power, that is, to identify their inversions, to contain their disruption, and even to confer an instructive value on their subversion by means of the superior virtue of method's friendly chiasmus.

Plato could buy out the sophists and even make them slave for him because his method is the money of the mind,[6] a fund more fecund than nature itself, minted from the basest nature of all, black marks on a white page. If there were a royal mintage for arguments, it would be indistinguishable from Plato's, and he who owns the mint can afford to scoff at those who work for hire. Thus Plato does not lose anything by exchanging his inherited wealth and position for the writing of Socrates' speech, because in so doing he removes his self and philosophy from an economy of loss and gain: Socrates' method is the method of Plato. The history of philosophy, as we have been told, is a series of footnotes to Plato, which is to say, no history at all. What passes for history is the interest generated by Plato's initial reserve, truth's notional debt: once the blessed machine is set in motion, all play with the counters supplied; all profit from keeping the game going because it's the only game in town.

It is surely the only game in *The Friend,* where method is that "connatural force, / Powerful at greatest distance to unite / With secret amity things of like kind." When the robust style and the home truths of *Paradise Lost* make their last appearance in the prose of the nineteenth-century moral essayist (*Friend* 471), they emerge not as challenge, prohibition, or warning, not even as legacy, but as one more likening in a green and pleasant island of likeness. As if by a connatural force working across a great distance, Milton's method—like Plato's, like Shakespeare's, like Kepler's, like Bacon's, like Sedgwick's—has become the Friend's own: the Friend is in the method, the method in the Friend. Extremes meet in the chiasmus: it is the "charm" (*Friend* 449) that can communicate moral principles while preserving the sovereign principal because it substitutes for family romance an amicable exchange.[7] Yet that substitution by which principle's matter is shaped into artful discourse chastens and subdues the sovereign it serves as well as the sophist it suppresses. As in Sedgwick's speech before the court of history, as in Hamlet's secret replication of the royal seal, so in the Friend's essays, the figure that methodizes the king moots sovereignty. As Socrates mirrors Plato in the dialogues, so all versions of the king—God and genius, prince and usurper—when subjected to the quicksilver medium of the chiasmus, mirror the motile Friend, figure to figure, preface to preface.

The Friend's surprising and strenuous efforts to work up the sophists into a credible, traumatic threat to the living body of thought describe an anxiety *for* the sophist, the other who must be without for the self to be within, the wily counterfeiter who would by his fraud validate the Platonic signature, the opponent whom one can withstand and thereby confirm one's standing. True philosophy may be "Truth without alloy and unsophisticated," but Plato and the Friend show that philosophy must be sophisticated in order to prove its value as gold. Subjected to method, the supposed sophist, like his Platonic adversary, never appears in his own right. "We found no such order. The men indeed and the name we found. . . . It is nothing more or less than a practical pun" (*Friend* 273) that would turn those poor fellows Protagoras and Thrasymachus into the supposed febrile hunters of the young, whom they are supposed to represent. Plato, as well as the Friend after him, puns the sophists into something like life in order to paint over his chrematistics into the appearance of an economy of loss and gain.[8] The philosopher values the sophists for the continuing interest they can generate. As the figure of Bonaparte, "genuine offspring of the old serpent," drives the marvelous economy of the British state, so does Callicles, "Napoleon of old" (*Friend* 443), fuel the blessed machine of philosophy. We come only as close to the face of the hypothetical sophists as we come to the face of the hireling, itinerant, periodical writer who is the Friend and whose amity, unconstrained by the awful decorum imposed by the Oedipal tragedy, "by its own moods interprets, everywhere / Echo or mirror seeking of itself, / And makes a toy of Thought." The flow of amity "turns the obstacle into its own form and character and as it makes its way increases its stream"; no more than England or truth or an enchanted spot within a waste of sands does any island of likeness in that stream afford a firm place to stand. The secret ministry of method carries on its getting and spending—political, philosophical, and erotic—unhelped by any awful sovereign, unhindered by any rebellious subject.

Secret ministry, secret amity—the force that unites all within an island of likeness partakes of the same essential and functional obscurity that the Friend has attributed to the difficult style, a powerful obscurity, whether it be the impressive congestion of perpending periods, or the chiasmus that paints over matter into art and philosophy into discourse, or, to shave it further, whether it be the merest resistance that is brute nature's profession of significance. To reduce my argument drastically would be to ask the pointed question "Is not *The Friend,* then, the Friend alone?" Yet to reduce a text, to reduce a reading of a text, is not so easy as that; to follow the "self-unravelling clue" is not, is precisely never, to undo. To state that *The Friend is* the Friend alone is not to summon the humanist's cherished nightmare of solipsism. To note that *The Friend is* the Friend merely figures Coleridge's blessed machine of language;

for the blessedness, insofar as it can be tracked down, subsists in that mechanical addition of the italics that mark the Friend with an eminence, however marginal, that he alone could never have, that grant him a title, a prerogative, and a discourse. From base letters the secret ministry of the compositor makes book of the Friend, turns identity into amity, figure into author.

## NOTES

1. The strongest case for the centrality of "The Essays on Method" in Coleridge's criticism is made by J. R. de J. Jackson, *Method and Imagination in Coleridge's Criticism.*

2. As the editor notes, much of the Friend's account of the origin and progress of the sophists has been taken without attribution from Wilhelm Gottlieb Tenneman's *Geschicte der Philosophie.* It is the equivocal fulfillment of a project that Coleridge set for himself in 1803: "I do not think, that as yet the whole of the *crime,* the cause, nature & consequences of *Sophistry* has been developed. Try it dear Coleridge!" (*Notebooks* 1: 1511). For a recent evenhanded account of both the sophists and the various ways their origin and progress have been interpreted, see W. K. C. Guthrie, *A History of Greek Philosophy* (3: 3–319).

3. Cf. the republican Tom Paine's comments on Pitt's and Fox's debate on the question of the Regency: "Among the curiosities which this contentious debate afforded was that of making the Great Seal into a King; the affixing of which to an act, was to be royal authority. If, therefore, Royal Authority is a Great Seal, it consequently is in itself nothing (*The Rights of Man* 1: 152–53).

4. A Coleridgean coinage: "*taute*gorical (i.e. expressing the *same* subject but with a difference) in contra-distinction from metaphors and similitudes, that are always *alle*gorical" (*Aids to Reflection* 199).

5. The Ancient Mariner, of course, "hath his will" by means of the force of his "glittering eye" (lines 13–16). So, finally, does the patient Stranger in *The Sophist,* whose wandering inquiry into absolutely reliable criteria of sophistry is supervised by the authoritative eye, emblem of the divine genealogy that he upholds and claims to represent. Responding to a question about the origin of natural life, Theaitetos says, "Owing perhaps to my youth, I often move from one opinion to the other; but here and now, looking into your eyes and believing you to hold that the things in question are of divine origin, I too am convinced" (*The Sophist* 221). The vacillation of Theaitetos, of sophistry and philosophy, is restrained by the master's eye. Cf. Coleridge's experiments with double touch, in Jerome Christensen chap. 2.

6. Marc Shell uses the phrase "money of the mind" to describe Plato's fear of what may be the true economy of Socratic thought *(Economy of Literature).* I suspect that what fear is evident (Shell gives no clearcut examples) is merely the canny pretense of a lack of financial sophistication.

7. Cf. Walter Pater's characterization of Coleridge's work as "the production of one who made way ever by a charm" (68).

8. Shell, following Aristotle, distinguishes between chrematistics and true economy. "The tyrant," he explains, "is defined as a chrematistical profit-making ruler interested only in selfish ends. On the other hand, the statesman is defined as an economist who dispenses or disposes but does not make a profit" (91–92). Cf. Aristotle, *Politics* 1257b.

# II

# "COMPARING POWER"
## COLERIDGE AND SIMILE

*Susan J. Wolfson*

> "The Beautiful is the perfection, the Sublime the suspension, of the comparing Power."
>
> —Coleridge, quoted in Raysor

### Unity versus "the Shape of Formal Similes"

In the midst of complaining to Sotheby about Bowles's "perpetual trick of *moralizing* every thing"—his inability "to see or describe any interesting appearance in nature, without connecting it by dim analogies with the moral world"—Coleridge insists that a "Poet's *Heart & Intellect* should be *combined, intimately* combined & *unified,* with the great appearances in Nature—& not merely held in solution & loose mixture with them, in the shape of formal Similes" (Sept. 10, 1802; *Collected Letters* 2: 864). To Coleridge, similes and their mode of dim analogy expose only a "formal" species of relation, opposite and inferior to the organic and consubstantial principles of unity that he would gloss with a passage from Plotinus at the close of chapter 6 of *Biographia Literaria:* "in order to direct the view aright, it behoves [*sic*] that the beholder should have made himself congenerous and similar to the object beheld. Never could the eye have beheld the sun, had not its own essence been soliform" (1: 114–15). So accustomed are we to this Romantic poetics of unity that readers such as Herbert Lindenberger are moved to argue that "distinctions between tenor and vehicle, crucial as they are to the understanding of Renaissance and metaphysical verse, are of little avail" to reading the Romantic rhetoric of interaction in which "the literal becomes figurative and then literal again" (69). It is from Coleridge, in fact, that W. K. Wimsatt draws his paradigm of "the Structure of Romantic Nature Imagery," a poetics "making less use of the central overt statement of similitude which is so important in all rhetoric stemming from Aristotle and the Renaissance" and, instead, working tenor and vehicle "in a parallel process out of the same material"; in such a structure, Wimsatt argues, "the element of tension in disparity is not so important as for metaphysical wit. The interest derives not from our being aware of disparity where likeness is firmly insisted on [he has in mind the metaphysical conceit], but in an opposite activity of discerning the design which is latent in the multiform sensuous picture" (109–10).

One may agree with Lindenberger and Wimsatt about the pervasiveness of this feature in Romantic rhetoric yet still be interested in those moments where the poetry resists such conflations of tenor and vehicle or even aggravates a disparity—not as an exercise of metaphysical wit but as a critical probing into the poetics of unity. For all his vehemence about Bowles's tricks of simile, Coleridge himself turns to the figure in a poem of the same year as the letter to Sotheby, *Hymn before Sun-rise, in the Vale of Chamouni*. Coleridge begins with an apostrophe to an object named as present, then shifts to a memory, a mental prospect:

> O dread and silent form! I gazed upon thee,
> Til thou, still present to my bodily eye,
> Didst vanish from my thought: entranced in prayer
> I worshipped the INVISIBLE alone. (13–16)[1]

Coleridge's poetic form poses a tentative relation between "I" and object: line 16 is organized to allow "alone" a reference both to "I" and "the INVISIBLE." But since "INVISIBLE" is a negative, the syntax may link only mutual isolations. To evoke a deeper relation, a more tentative rhetoric appears:

> Yet thou meantime, wast working on my soul,
> E'en like some deep enchanting melody . . . (17–18)

In replacing a crisis of visible form and invisible presence with a simile of deeper melodies to the spirit, Coleridge uses "like" both expressively and dramatically: it is a provisional figure, which in its rhetoric and its reflexive relation to the hymn's own melody, represents the effort of poetic making.

The importance of comparison as a provisional figure shapes Coleridge's revisions as he expands this simile into an analogously "constructed" rhetoric, analogy itself:

> Thou, the meanwhile, was blending with my Thought,
> Yea, with my Life and Life's own secret joy:
> Till the dilating Soul, enrapt, transfused,
> Into the mighty vision passing—there
> As in her natural form, swelled vast to Heaven! (19–23)

In this syntactic dilation, "As" blends subject into object, but it also concedes their difference, and so evokes the absences that occasion the present-tense apostrophes. Coleridge's gloss of these lines repeats this double work. He describes himself "gazing on the Mountain till as if it had been a Shape emanating from and sensibly representing her own essence, my Soul had become diffused thro' 'the mighty Vision'" (*Collected Letters* 4: 974). The ambiguous referent of the *as if* clause sustains the sensation of unity: "it" seems at first to be "the Mountain" (a self-involved "Shape" to which the poet's gaze is superfluous); when the referent is clarified as the poet's own "Soul," the effect is less to cancel than to augment the first suggestion.

A display of comparing power in the poetics of harmony is delicately calibrated in *Frost at Midnight,* where the restraint strengthens the sentiment. Reeve Parker has described this as a poem whose many sets of "companionable forms" test the possibility of an "adequate symbology in the natural world" (132). An early manuscript (ca. 1796) shows Coleridge using simile in this test, but in ways that qualify even as they elaborate the harmonies famously figured in the conclusion of the published text:

> Or whether the secret ministry of cold
> Shall hang them up in silent icicles,
> Quietly shining to the quiet moon,
> Like those, my babe! which ere tomorrow's warmth
> Have capp'd their sharp keen points with pendulous drops,
> Will catch thine eye, and with their novelty
> Suspend thy little soul; then make thee shout,
> And stretch and flutter from thy mother's arms
> As thou wouldst fly for very eagerness. (MS. 4°, *Poems* 242–43)

"Like" works in two different but complementary ways. Filling out the quiet harmonies, it gives the icicles imagined only in general the feel of an imminent event—one, moreover, in which their pendulous form is reflected in the captured eye and suspended soul of his babe. The last line completes the figure by contracting its implied "as if" to the quasi-simile *as:* "As thou wouldst fly." Its internal image, "flutter," furthermore, reverberates in the poem's larger text of comparisons: the poet finds a "companionable form" (15–16) for himself in a fluttering film on the grate, which evokes a boyhood memory of the "fluttering *stranger*" on a school-house grate (25–26), which recalls another, earlier memory of churchbells and a fantasy also conveyed by simile, their sounding "Most like articulate sounds of things to come" (33). As the poetry links these diverse times, it also displays how habits of comparison shape these links in a self-aware rhetoric of temporality. Even the simile that concludes the manuscript version concedes through certain indicators—*ere, will, then*—the dissolution of the babe's happy elation in a flux of form in which hanging icicles will become "pendulous drops" and then, inevitably, another form altogether.

If Coleridge's simile-making is symbolic of anything, it is of his contradictory reflections on language in general. As a philosopher and theorist, he often sounds logocentric, insisting on imagination as a power of harmony and the agent of its poetic symbolism. So idealizing is this discourse that Earl Wasserman confesses a critical "embarrassment" in trying to conceive how its theoretical "symbolism" could be reified in poetic practice or define "a process for the transformation of images into symbols" ("The English Romantics" 30). Coleridge's poetic process confirms the problem, for it is less often an achievement of unity than a matter of fragments, disjunctions, and revisions. Even some of his prose hymns to symbol—such as that of *The Statesman's Manual*—bear contradictions. The theory is articulate enough: "True natural philosophy is comprized in the study of the science and language of *symbols*," he insists, adding that "by a symbol I mean, not a metaphor or allegory or any other figure of speech or form of fancy, but an actual and essential part of that, the whole of which it represents" (79). Symbols are "consubstantial with the truths, of which they are the *conductors*" (29) and are distinguishable in this respect from the "disjunction of Faculty" in allegory (*Notebooks* 4053)—and in simile, too, for "similitudes . . . are always *all*egorical, that is, expressing a different subject" across "a resemblance" of figures (*Aids to Reflection* 199).[2] These distinctions involve more than literary figures; in positing ontological stability and epistemological continuity, they bear on entire modes of thought and imagination:

> with particular reference to that undivided Reason, neither merely speculative or merely practical, but both in one . . . contra-distinguish[ed] from the Understanding, I seem to myself to behold in the quiet objects, on which I am gazing, more than an arbitrary illustration, more than a mere *simile,* the work of my own Fancy! I feel an awe, as if there were before my eyes the same Power, as that of the REASON—the same Power in a lower dignity, and therefore a symbol established in the truth of things. (*Statesman's Manual* 72)

Yet the distinctions are as precarious as they are insistent: to set forth this "undivided" mode of apprehension, Coleridge resorts to a language of division and opposition, invoking a quasi- or dilated simile, *as if,* to illustrate. The syntax of hypothesis abets the rhetoric of simile by straining the connection so arranged.[3]

What simile keeps visible is the difference from which language is produced. "Hard to express that sense of analogy or likeness of a Thing which enables a Symbol to represent it so that we think of the thing itself—and yet knowing that the Thing is not present to us.—Surely on this universal fact of words & images depends by more or less mediations the *imitation* instead of *copy* . . . that difference . . . that likeness not identity," Coleridge muses in 1804 (*Notebooks* 2: 2274). Such moods pose the issue that a modern critic of rhetoric, Jacques Derrida, would address with an analysis of writing as a dangerous supplement: if writing "represents and makes an image," he argues, this happens "by the anterior default of a presence. . . . The supplement is *exterior,* outside of the positivity to which it is super-added" (*Of Grammatology* 145, his italics). Coleridge's alertness to this poetics of addition not only competes with the symbology that theorizes presence and incorporation; it makes this symbology seem a compensatory desire—thus Paul de Man's sense of the elevation of symbol over allegory as a "defensive strategy," a "tenacious self-mystification" of the impossibility of identity or identification (*Blindness* 208). Yet in this defensiveness, Coleridge's rhetoric may not be as mystified as de Man claims: recall his famous antipathy to "marble-peach" modes of art that, feigning likeness, subvert the value of "Imitation [a]s the mesothesis of Likeness and Difference." "The Difference," he insists, "is as essential to it as the Likeness, for without the Difference, it would be Copy or Fac-simile."[4] So when de Man asks whether one can take a "continuity between depth and surface, between style and theme, for granted," or whether "this is the most problematic issue with which the theory of poetry [has] to deal" (*Blindness* 23), one answer is that this debate is already in motion in Coleridge's poetics of simile. For here, the play of simile in representation not only puts representation itself into question but focuses on the agency of poetic making in its projects.

With this double motion, Coleridge taps a latency in the classical conception of *verisimile,* a quasi-oxymoron that mediates a potential polarization (into either a naïve poetics of presence or a skeptical concession to device) with the "metaphorical ambiguity of 'resemblance to' (reflection) and 'semblance' (illusion) of reality." It is revealing of Coleridge's intellectual tuning to this doubleness that H. R. Jauss (whom I quote) uses "willing suspension of disbelief" to gloss the aesthetic power so enabled (4–5). Coleridge's theoretical prescience, as well as his alertness to what is ambiguous or unstable in precursive traditions, helps explain why he can be so readily cited to prefigure deconstructive as well as organicist methods of reading. This double legacy, which neither can nor should be resolved, is continuously negotiated in Coleridge's poetics of simile. Because the structure of simile works with disparity, testing likeness against difference, it has a figurative capacity to set the power of language to construct, connect, and refer, against its potential for exposing absence, supplement, and difference. And because it does this in one figure, it can explore the interaction of these energies. In theorizing and writing a poetics of simile, Coleridge finds himself investigating the very processes that define poetic form.

## The Poetics of Disjunction

Coleridge's ambivalence about simile emerges from a traditional condescension to the figure. In *Jerusalem,* Los's proclamation—"I must Create a System, or be enslav'd by another Mans"—involves a pledge that elevates this poetic and political imperative over lesser cognitive enterprises: "I will not Reason & Compare: my business is to Create" (*Complete Poetry* 10: 21–22).[5] Whatever his other revolutionary impulses, Blake shared this discrimination with classical rhetorics, whose hierarchy of figures routinely views simile as a device of secondary elaboration, a figure for embellishment or a sometimes useful device for instruction, persuasion, communication, or other such effect. Aristotle regards simile chiefly this way, and he does not trust it, preferring the method of direct, logical correspondence in metaphor to the strenuous comparison sometimes required by the structure of the simile (see *The "Art" of Rhetoric* 3.10.2–5 and Freese's note).[6] Quintilian, too, worries about relying on simile to "illuminat[e] our descriptions . . . to help our proof." "In employing [this] form of ornament," he cautions that "anything . . . selected for the purpose of illuminating something else must itself be clearer than that which it is designed to illustrate"; it is "quite unsuitable for an orator to illustrate something quite plain by . . . obscure allusions" (VIII: 3. 72, 73–74). One must also attend to propriety; indeed, Quintilian advises, the best way to refute a simile in debate is to "lay stress on [the] extreme dissimilarity" *(dissimilia)* of what is being compared (V: 13. 24). Coleridge echoes these precepts, defining metaphor as more integrative—"Substitute a simile for the thing, it resembles, instead of annexing it, and it becomes a metaphor" (*Lectures 1808–1819* 2: 101)—and less inclined to extravagance than simile: "The purpose of a Metaphor is to illustrate something less known by a partial identification of it with some other things better understood, or at least more familiar" (*Aids to Reflection* 312). In the work of "resemblance," metaphor has always been the definitive trope, observes Derrida, and "the magnetizing effect of similarity" (versus difference) in its organization "presuppose[s] a symbolist position" ("White Mythology" 13).

Derrida's postmodern critique is pointed toward a metaphysical deconstruction, but it is linked to Coleridge's Romanticism in its reading of figures for play as well as purpose. It is a revealing feature even of traditional commentary that simile could register against its protocol this way, producing disruptively exotic comparisons that, while a liability in argument, may enhance oratory. Even in forensics, Quintilian is willing to admire the effect of simile in making speech "sublime, rich, attractive or striking, as the case may be. For the more remote the *similitudo* is from the subject to which it is applied, the greater will be the impression of novelty and the unexpected which it produces" (VIII: 3. 74). This view was echoed in the eighteenth century by Kames; and even Johnson, who despite his famous complaint about the farflung combinations of metaphysical wit, proposed (in his own simile about simile) that if "simile may be compared to lines converging at a point," the effect "is more excellent as the lines approach from a greater distance."[7]

Coleridge's more habitual tendency as critical reader, however, is to attribute wide breaches of tenor and vehicle to the extravagance of Fancy, "bring[ing] together images which have no connection natural or moral, but are yoked together by the poet by means of some accidental coincidence."[8] He thus invests the notion of a *"leading Thought"* to bring "things the most remote and diverse in time, place, and outward circumstance . . . into mental contiguity and succession," and echoes the view that "the more striking" links will be "the less expected" (*Friend* 1: 455). Yet if this sounds more like the problem itself, Coleridge's poetry shows a figurative interest in the consequence. For while in theory, Imagination is preferable to Fancy, and symbol to simile and allegory, in practice, Fancy and its forms of comparison prove a resource for representing those very orders of thought that symbol would overcome: the tentative, the provisional, the uncertain, the ambiguous. In *Dejection,* for example, the poet recalls a time when

> . . . all misfortunes were but as the stuff
> Whence Fancy made me dreams of happiness:
> For hope grew round me, like the twining vine,
> And fruits, and foliage, not my own, seemed mine. (78–81)

Representing this illusion in the rhetoric of "like" is apt, for the gap between tenor and vehicle is also a gap between the self and its imagined properties. The false surmise of misfortune as the stuff of anticipated happiness takes the form of analogy; the erroneous reading of hopeful projections as actual property shapes a simile whose vehicle exposes a categorical difference between "me" and the delusively fruitful vine.

Such gaps between tenor and vehicle trouble interpretive attention, but not without calling it forth. In *Christabel* we hear that Geraldine "sank, belike through pain" as she was carried across the threshold, and then that she "rose again, / And moved, as she were not in pain" (129, 133–34); asleep, Christabel "seems to smile / As infants" do, or "Like a youthful hermitess" (317–20), while Geraldine "belike hath drunken deep / Of all the blessedness of sleep" (375–76); the next morning she looks "as one that prayed" (462), while Christabel looks at Sir Leoline "like a thing, that sought relief" (593). Comparison is the rhetoric that Coleridge summons in *The Rime of the Ancient Mariner* to show the processes by which a chance event gets read into significance:

> At length did cross an Albatross,
> Thorough the fog it came;
> As if it had been a Christian soul,
> We hail'd it in God's name. (63–66)

"As if" expresses a desire to bring ideas and images, words and things, into relation. At the same time, its form exposes a fiction, a willed association of event and information. Here, as throughout *The Rime,* Coleridge deploys *as if* to convey the sense-making needs that motivate and qualify various ventures of interpretation.[9]

This pressure intensifies when Coleridge subverts the explanatory protocol of simile by implicating its writing in contexts in which all explanations seem problematic. *The Rime* effectively concludes with similes that not only obscure their tenors but also signify by reversing the classical decorum of instruction. The Mariner's summary figure for himself deploys a simile whose vehicle expands, without clarifying, his opacity of knowledge: "I pass, like night, from land to land . . ." (586). Although he claims that this global errancy has a mission, to "teach" his "tale," the irony is exposed by the final simile: the thwarted Wedding-Guest who is forced into audience "went like one that hath

# Coleridge and Simile

been stunned, / And is of sense forlorn" (621–23). Among the few things that may be said to be clear in *The Rime* is Coleridge's use of simile to alienate the world of the poem from any grid of shared, harmonious experience.

The poem's single epic simile produces a dark parody of the ideal of shared experience that is the classical basis of the trope.[10] Released from his spell, the Mariner

> look'd far-forth, but little saw
> Of what might else be seen.
>
> Like one, that on a lonely road
>   Doth walk in fear and dread,
> And having once turn'd round, walks on,
>   And turns no more his head:
> Because he knows, a frightful fiend
>   Doth close behind him tread. (449–56)[11]

That Coleridge gives the simile its own stanza endows it with a weird independence from the narrative, making the state of mind it conveys seem as detachable and free floating as the wandering Mariner himself. This is the quality that Mary Shelley imports when she has Frankenstein voice these same lines to express "the load that weighed upon [his] mind" as he walks the streets, hoping "to avoid the wretch whom [he] feared every turning of the street would present to [his] view" (54). As often as Coleridge invests poetic language with the work of intelligible relation, he summons simile, as Shelley's allusion helps us see, to evoke sensations in which the project of relation recoils, to turn round a circle of subjectivity impervious to clarification.

## "Satisfying . . . the Desire for Resemblance"

The anarchic and fundamentally self-reflexive energy in simile limned in Coleridge's free-floating stanza is also part of the figure's legacy. Pope felt he had to defend Homer's similes from the charge of being "too exuberant and full of circumstances," of exposing a failure of imagination to "confine itself to that single circumstance upon which the comparison is grounded." The self-generating expansions of Milton's similes were similarly controversial, provoking complaints about decorum or calling for careful defense.[12] What the debate exposes is the protocol that traditionally keeps simile in rein, namely, its reference to a conceptual ideology. The frame is what underwrites and supports the explanatory and pedagogic claim of simile, and with sufficient tenacity in rhetorical tradition to give acts of comparison an almost architectonic organization in the psychology, epistemology, and metaphysics of analogy.

However various Coleridge's play with simile, when the comparisons expand to analogy, the stakes are raised: "language is analogous, wherever a thing, power, or principle in a higher dignity is expressed by the same thing, power, or principle in a lower but more known form" (*Aids to Reflection* 199). In poems of such "intricate analogical ingenuity" and so "implicitly informed by ... unobtrusive analogical gesture" as *This Lime-tree Bower my Prison* (the language is Reeve Parker's),[13] the similes are correspondingly charged. Comparative syntax virtually plots this poem's drama of mind. We first hear its speaker in a hyperbolic sulk, lamenting his loss of

> Beauties and feelings, such as would have been
> Most sweet to remembrance even when age
> Had dimm'd mine eyes to blindness. (3–5)

This querulous simile has an oddly tentative structure: the present account of what is "lost" gets compared to a future frustration, making this a simile whose vehicle is conceived only as hypothesis. Coleridge brilliantly accommodates this peculiarity by expanding the whole figure into "blindness"—and, by implication, inviting the compensatory acts of imagination that come into play as the visual field recedes. In this prospect of absence, negation, and invisibility, simile emerges as the agent of restoration.

This conversion begins with the next comparison, in which the poet envisions his friend Charles "struck with deep joy," standing "as I have stood, / Silent with swimming sense" (37–39). This turn of sympathy across time and space through the comparison of "as" propels the verse from the original sensation of deprivation into a moment of spiritual participation, whose present tenses and capacious participles suggest a shared experience as well as a projected fantasy. Together they

> gaze till all doth seem
> Less gross than bodily; and of such hues
> As veil the Almighty Spirit, when yet he makes
> Spirits perceive his presence. (40–43)

This second "as" (42) enhances the poetics of participation by translating the "such as" that had earlier signified absence and isolation ("such as would have been / Most sweet") into a term of "presence" and relation. The repetition not only aligns the poet's gesture of friendly sympathy with how "the Almighty Spirit" relates to human "Spirits"; it also raises the syntax of relation to a principle of divinely sanctioned generosity (Hosea reports that the Lord "used similitudes" to speak to the Israelites [12: 10]). Coleridge extends this rhetoric to express his sensation of renewal:

> A delight
> Comes sudden on my heart, and I am glad
> As I myself were there! (43–45)

The exclamation gains force by seeming to absorb its subjunctive *as (if)*, which admits absence, into a comparison of present experiences of gladness.

Wordsworth's remark that "in lyric poetry the subject and simile should be as much as possible lost in each other" finds no better satisfaction than in Coleridge's subtle transformations of the figure in this poem.[14]

Poems such as *On observing a Blossom on the First of February 1796* suggest that comparison is nearly synonymous with any exercise of thought—or of writing. Contemplating a "Flower that must perish!" the poet spins comparisons with the campy ease of a Shakespearean sonneteer: "shall I liken thee / To some sweet girl . . . Nipp'd by consumption mid untimely charms? / Or to Bristowa's bard . . . ? or . . . Shall I compare thee to poor Poland's hope?" (9–16). While the language with which Coleridge judges this activity— "Dim similitudes / Weaving in moral strains" (19–20)—echoes his complaint about Bowles's "dim analogies," it is complicated by the way the verb of agency, *weaving,* summons and puns its Latin participle, *textus.*[15] The effect is to cast similitudes, dim and idle though they seem, as figures for any writer's method. They may even be this poet's restoration, for in this weaving, he says, he has found relief "From anxious Self, Life's cruel taskmaster!" (21). The exercise of invention, the interrogative syntax, and the sheer act of accumulation organized by nothing more crucial than an equalizing "or" are recreation in a life that holds other tasks: on this occasion, one thought is as good as another, and patent simile liberates language into play. As Byron proposes in *Don Juan,* "what you will;— / My similes are gathered in a heap, / So pick and chuse—" (6. 68). For Coleridge's poet, the activity of simile-making turns out, ironically, to fulfill the harmonizing functions of the symbol:

> the warm wooings of this sunny day
> Tremble along my frame and harmonize
> The attempered organ. (22–24)

The poem ends, appropriately, with a simile that is about its own processes of reading the perishable flower: "even saddest thoughts / Mix with some sweet sensations, like harsh tunes / Played deftly on a soft-toned instrument" (24–26).

The exposure of this process is the figurative plot of conversation in the earliest version of *The Eolian Harp.* It opens by dallying with self-mocking, Bowlesian moralizing about nature as a storehouse of "Meet emblems" for Innocence, Love, and Wisdom. The "artificiality of the construct" impedes the "fusion of tenor and vehicle in a properly symbolic style." As Tilottama Rajan says, it thwarts "the imaginative realization of a symbolic landscape instinct with the signatures of consciousness" ("Displacing" 471). I would suggest that this impediment is calculated in order to foreground the process of signature itself. The initial emblemizing is merely a more formulaic version of the emblemizing that unfolds from "And that simplest Lute . . . hark!" Both the conjunctive "And" and its placement in the same metrical line that concludes the playful emblemizing draw the ensuing similes—"How by the desultory breeze caress'd, / Like some coy maid half yielding to her lover . . .

such sweet upbraiding, as must needs / Tempt to repeat the wrong!" (10–17)—into the fictive trajectory of the initial "emblems." The only difference is the air of spontaneous invention that displaces conventional readings. The acknowledged artificiality is part of the pleasure of invention, and the poet happily indulges it:

> Such a soft floating witchery of sound
> As twilight Elfins make, when they at eve
> Voyage on gentle gales from Fairy-Land,
> Where Melodies round honey-dropping flowers,
> Footless and wild, like birds of Paradise,
> Nor pause, nor perch, hovering on untam'd wing! (20–25)

As the play of simile becomes ever more involuted, each vehicle spinning a new tenor, Coleridge checks it with a softly satiric self-consciousness. Expanding only along the axis of fantasy, or even, as the last vehicle suggests, patently prelapsarian idyll, the terms are finally self-reflexive: the motion ascribed to those birds of Paradise wittily mirrors the simile-maker's own activity—his enthusiastic and nearly untamed leaping from simile to simile. Even as the famous effusion, "O! the one Life within us and abroad," solicits symbol, the shift from idle play into this enthusiastic declaration is too subversively abrupt. The textual status of these lines, in fact, is more related to simile than to symbol: far from organic to the original composition, they were added much later, as if a superinduced gloss.[16]

The original text stays committed to simile, not only in its visual figures but also, as the next verse paragraph reveals, in its rhetorical ones:

> And thus, my Love! as on the midway slope        [34]
> Of yonder hill I stretch my limbs at noon,
> Whilst through my half-clos'd eye-lids I behold   [36]
> The sunbeams dance, like diamonds, on the main,
> And tranquil muse upon tranquility;
> Full many a thought uncall'd and undetain'd,
> And many idle flitting phantasies,
> Traverse my indolent and passive brain,
> As wild and various as the random gales            [42]
> That swell and flutter on this subject Lute!
>     And what if all of animated nature
> Be but organic Harps diversely fram'd,
> That tremble into thought, as o'er them sweeps
> Plastic and vast, one intellectual breeze,
> At once the Soul of each, and God of all? (34–48)

The "as" of line 34 is a circumstantial marker (like the synchronic, syntactically parallel *Whilst* of 36) of the postures that court such flitting phantasies. But its verbal repetition at line 42 links the posture of the thinker with the play of his thoughts, his physical with his metaphysical receptivity. The stretch

# Coleridge and Simile

of "as" across these senses corresponds to the several hoverings in this scene of mental play: the poet is midway on a slope, at midday, with half-closed eyes, making similes ("sunbeams dance, like diamonds") that mediate first between fantasy and nature and then boldly animate nature itself as a vehicle for "thought." In some early versions of this passage, Coleridge began the pivotal "And what if . . . ?" stanza with an introductory "Or," as if to distinguish its surmise about the unifying principle of diverse framings from the flitting fantasies preceding it (*Poems* 102). Yet one draft not only retains "And" and keeps the surmise in the same verse paragraph, it also bears a simile: "And what if All of animated Life / Be but as Instruments diversely fram'd?" (MS. R; *Poems* 520). Both the verse form of the paragraph and the rhetorical form of the simile keep the speculation affiliated to other idle plays of thought. Working against the Platonic tradition of hypothetical play as a vehicle for truths, "as" resists making special claims for its tenor. As Demetrius remarks in *On Style,* simile is the "less risky expression."[17] If Coleridge's subsequent erasure of "as" accelerates his surmise, his "what if?" still confronts a reproof from his companion (however undecidable the irony), and this is a scene that every text retains.

In these forms, Coleridge is more prone to skepticism about figures than to a poetics of blithe equivalence. He is aware of how analogical reading, traditionally vested as ontologically informed, may weave relations neither predicated on nor legislated by rational, analogical order. The term *dim similitude* tends to signal dubious explanations. As the poet of *The Destiny of Nations,* for instance, declares his own belief that "Properties are God" (36), he describes another line of reflection taken by those who

> boldlier think
> That as one body seems the aggregate
> Of atoms numberless, each organized;
> So by a strange and dim similitude
> Infinite myriads of self-conscious minds
> Are one all-conscious Spirit. (39–44)

The method of "similitude" dims the analogical argument it would shape and the chiasmus it would anchor. One doesn't quite know how to take the irony of this same voice resorting to simile over the course of the poem to explicate its own dim or obscure apprehensions. The perplexity is Coleridge's as well: even as he notes that "different means to the same end seem to constitute analogy," he has to admit that "analogy always implies a difference in kind & not merely in degree" (Dec. 12, 1804; *Notebooks* 2319).

## "Suspending the Power of Comparison"

The "difference" that simile, for better or worse, always implies helps explain the pervasive interest in Romantic poetics in events that call the power of comparison into question or suspend it altogether, canceling its efforts in the sensation of a totalizing unity. For Coleridge, the most intense apprehensions occur as the exercises of mind figured in and by similes are shown to be not only inadequate but impossible: if the "beautiful . . . in its highest perfection sustains while it satisfies the comparing Power," the "sublime" appears "in relation to which the exercise of comparison is suspended."[18] This suspense infuses his report of "a storm of wind" over the Lake of Ratzeburg, accompanied "during the whole night" by "the thunders and howlings of the breaking ice." Such sounds, Coleridge says, are "more sublime than any sight can be, more absolutely suspending the power of comparison, and more utterly absorbing the mind's self-consciousness in its total attention to the object working upon it." The power of comparison returns only in aftermath, and only with the return of visual coordinates: "On the evening of the next day, at sun-set, the shattered ice thus frozen, appeared of a deep blue and in shape like an agitated sea" (*Friend* 1: 367). In the ice-skating episode from Book 1 of *The Prelude* that he appends to this report, we see Wordsworth's sympathy with this drama of comparing activity. Its similes describe action and sensation that are still in the realm of the familiar, but about to be propelled into alien registers of sensation:

> I wheel'd about,
> Proud and exulting, like an untir'd horse
> That car'd not for its home. . . .
> The leafless trees and every icy crag
> Tinkled like iron. (*Friend* 1: 369)

Even in these structures of comparison we see Wordsworth's resistance to the merely picturesque "habit" of "giving way / To a comparison of scene with scene" (*Prelude* 11: 156–58). Like Coleridge, his imagination is tuned more deeply to events that baffle comparison. And his investment is the same: "whatever suspends the comparing power of the mind & possesses it with a feeling or image of intense unity, without a conscious contemplation of parts, has produced that state of the mind which is the consummation of the sublime" (*Prose* 2: 353–54).

Crucial in Wordsworth's aesthetic is his trusting of this suspense to an abundant recompense—a possession from without by a sensation of "intense unity." Yet more often than not, it is the phase of transfer, rather than the consummation devoutly to be wished, in which he and Coleridge apprehend the sublime. This intermediary mental exertion produces a language of shifting comparisons—some potent, others potential and flickering, others patently inadequate, and often releasing the bridging rhetoric of "as if" to mediate between comparisons acknowledged as inadequate and apprehensions that defeat all comparison. The effort at comparison, even as the mind is drawn "to the point of total attention to the object working on it," generates the sensation and the aesthetics of the sublime. This tension between willful imagining and rapt absorption is more interesting to Coleridge than the immediacy of a dream. Although dreaming too "consists in a suspension of the voluntary and therefore of the comparative power," it differs from the workings of "illusion" which solicit the cooperation, rather than the cooptation, of voluntary imagination: "in sleep we pass at once by a sudden collapse into this suspension of Will and the Comparative power: whereas in an interesting Play, read or represented, we are brought up to this point . . . gradually, by the Art . . . and with the consent and positive Aidance of our own Will" (*Lectures* 2: 266).

In the art of poetry, this positive aidance is the work of simile in releasing the aesthetics of the sublime. For both Coleridge and Wordsworth, the effort to shape a simile at the limits of imagination confirms the sublime, and the sensation of mental power on the verge of suspense is as crucial to the effect as the overwhelmed state of mind that follows. Thus Wordsworth admires one of the notoriously dilated similes in *Paradise Lost:* focusing on how it images as it evokes a sublime suspense, he praises both the descriptive integrity of the vehicle and its "reference to the motion and appearance of the sublime object to which it is compared":[19]

> As when far off at sea a fleet descried
> *Hangs* in the clouds . . .
>
> . . . so seemed
> Far off the flying Fiend.

With a similar interest in suspense, Coleridge cites another passage of *Paradise Lost* in which shifting seemings and similes do not cancel comparison but leave the mind "hovering between images . . . unfixed and wavering" among intangible options, to yield a "sublime feeling of the unimaginable." It is Milton's "fine description of Death" (*Lectures* 2: 495–96):

> . . . black it stood as Night;
> Fierce as ten Furies, terrible as Hell,
> And shook a dreadful Dart; what seem'd his head
> The likeness of a Kingly Crown had on . . .

The first simile shows what Coleridge senses in comparisons conscripted into the sublime: "as Night" at once poses an image of blackness and evokes a massively impenetrable, all-encompassing effect—Death stood as a figure of Night. This effect is intensified by the next two similes, "Fierce as ten Furies, terrible as Hell," each vehicle as opaque as the tenor it would explain. As a total trope of representation, Milton's similes show comparative power being overtaken by the unimaginable, an effect starkly fulfilled in the devastating image toward which these all build: "what seem'd his head / The likeness of a Kingly Crown had on."

In the aesthetics of the sublime, simile is the trope of representational inadequacy. But insofar as this inadequacy taints verbal power per se, simile emerges as the subscript of all figures, shadowing even that to which it is typically opposed, the symbol and its claim of presence. Staging this consequence in *Religious Musings,* Coleridge begins with a potent simile, one that appears to offer the most affirmative of associations:

> This is the time, when most divine to hear,
> The voice of Adoration rouses me,
> As with a Cherub's trump: and high upborne,
> Yea, mingling with the Choir, I seem to view
> The vision of the heavenly multitude.... (1–5)

But in the company of a tentative *seem,* the simile strains, and soon statements of presence are yielding to notes of absence. Referring to "the Great / Invisible (by symbols only seen)" (9–10), the poet concedes a gap between what the senses apprehend and what is, at best, qualitatively different, "invisible."

This is de Man's "rhetoric of temporality," exposing the "translucence" of the symbol as a "reflection of a more original unity that does not exist in the material world" (*Blindness* 192). But it is Coleridge's rhetoric, too, in moments when his symbolic figures occupy a language that thwarts, defers, and conceals, as much as it seems to present, reveal and unite the material word and world. One may rephrase this, as de Man has, to say that as symbolism becomes more enmeshed in distance, difference, and noncoincidence, it tends toward allegory: "symbol and allegory alike ... have a common origin beyond the world of matter," both designating a "transcendental source" (192). Allegory unveils what symbol veils, mystifies, and suppresses—the inevitable distance of the sign "in relation to its own origin" that consigns all language to "the void of this temporal difference" (207). For Derrida, this is the general situation of language, which not only "always implies within itself the distinction between signifier and signified" but exposes the latter as "always already in the position of the signifier" (*Of Grammatology* 11, 73).

The capacity of allegory to expose difference and distinction in both rhetoric and history suggests why Coleridge is drawn to it as a poetic mode and uses it to intensify such striking similes as the one from *Constancy to An Ideal Object* that Cleanth Brooks has admired: the poet imagines that his "Fond thought" will receive "life-enkindling breath" only "when, like strangers shelt'ring from a storm, / Hope and Despair meet in the porch of Death"— when, that is, the temporal prospect to which both Hope and Despair refer is no more. In Brooks's poetics, this simile "has something of the paradoxical quality of metaphysical poetry and it comes to the reader with a fine rhetorical shock," whose "reverberations of meaning ... expand and deepen the total import."[20] It is suggestive that not only the New Critic Brooks but even the New Historicist Jerome J. McGann find common ground with the deconstructive interests of de Man and Derrida in Coleridge's poetics of allegory. Whether the issue is "rhetorical shock" (Brooks), "temporal difference" (de Man), or "ideas and institutions" (McGann), allegory as a poetical form that Coleridge "associated with a divided or alienated consciousness" was "peculiarly adapted to expose and explore critically the world of illusions, divisions, and false-consciousness," and was troublingly attractive to an imagination "always subject to a negative dialectic of 'apparation and evanishment'" (McGann 96–97).[21]

A turn to simile as a figure enacting the very perplexities that it seeks to resolve is the dramatic climax of *Constancy to an Ideal Object*. Here Coleridge shows a poet using an extended simile to fill the space between the presence of a "she" as an object of thought and the absence that makes her only a figure of thought. The poet begins by addressing a "yearning Thought that liv'st but in the brain" (4):

> ... still thou haunt'st me; and though well I see,
> She is not thou, and only thou art she,
> Still, still as though some dear embodied Good,
> Some living Love before my eyes there stood
> With answering look a ready ear to lend,
> I mourn to thee.... (11–16)

If the repeated "still" equivocates between duration and position, "as though" intensifies the equivocation by shifting self-consciously into a fully imagined hypothesis, a presimilitic maneuver in the drama of this poem. Hans Vaihinger, a careful reader of the synonym *as if,* observes that while *as* is "clearly an equating of two terms," *if* "affirms that the condition is ... unreal or impossible" (258–59): as the "case is posited ... its impossibility is frankly stated" (93). Yet even with this concession, the proposal entertained by *as if* "is still formally maintained" (92–93). The syntax of Coleridge's "as though ... before my eyes there stood" (13–14) is similarly poised. Echoing the "and though" that resigns itself to actual absence and difference (11), "as though" also yearns for correspondence in the figures of poetry.

The actual simile of *Constancy,* one of the most complexly beautiful passages in Coleridge's poetry, structures the poem's final paragraph in terms of such equivocation and implies the dependence of language itself on such dialectics of absence and presence. Coleridge's poet asks of his "Fond Thought":

> And art thou nothing? Such thou art, as when
> The woodman winding westward up the glen
> At wintry dawn, where o'er the sheep-track's maze
> The viewless snow-mist weaves a glist'ning haze,
> Sees full before him, gliding without tread,
> An image with a glory round its head;
> The enamoured rustic worships its fair hues,
> Nor knows he makes the shadow, he pursues! (25–32)

This chiasmus, both mirroring and revising the negative chiasmus of "She is not thou, and only thou art she," answers its question with a simile, a correlative figure for ambivalent constancy to an uncertain object. Appealing to an extraordinary natural phenomenon, the poet can imply relation between his constancy and the rustic's worship, and at the same time use the form of simile as a figure of knowing irony. This irony writes the simile as self-consciously textual. Its imagery, Arden Reed remarks, points "to its own status as a linguistic construction": weaving is "a metaphor for texuality or poetic language"; the mist, "besides figuring a text . . . is also the blank sheet a text is written on"; "the woodman's shadow inscribes a figure on the fog"; he is "surrounded by, indeed trapped in, his own linguistic and imagistic net" (97). Coleridge's placement of the comma in the last line marks this entrapment: as punctuation, it stresses the rustic's delusion; and figurally, it supplants a phantom "that" that would designate the object of pursuit as a self-made shadow.

Part of the poignancy is the verging of the poet's simile on the rustic's delusion, even as ironic detachment is signaled. Coleridge's note to the poem is similarly prone: the "phenomenon" is one "which the author has himself experienced. . . . The beholder either recognises it as a projected form of his own Being, that moves before him with a Glory round its head, or recoils from it as a Spectre" (*Poems* 456). As with some of his other glosses, Coleridge's explanation overproduces, for neither of the alternatives that its two comparisons offer coincides exactly with the situation of the rustic, who neither recognizes the image as a glorified self projection nor recoils from it as a disembodied other. And the simile-weaver escapes glossing, too, for his wistful comparison, though it uses rather than identifies with the unwitting rustic, cannot quite distill projection from delusion. His simile bends the alternatives into a figure that both tests and ironizes about the affinity of poet's constancy with the rustic's blind self-enamoration. Without having to answer the question, "And art thou nothing?" the poet lets a rustic's phantom displace a desired "thou" and its equations to thought ("She is not thou, and only thou art she"), using the simile to put before himself and us a figure that simultaneously credits and resists the attraction of ideal objects. If, as Rajan writes, this is a poem that "gives itself and does not give itself to its own illusions," simile emerges as the privileged rhetoric of this painful dilemma.[22]

To Lord Monboddo, who prefers "figurative words only by way of ornament," similes mark an unsophisticated linguistic culture whose speakers, "not being able to express a thing by its proper name . . . are naturally driven to tell what it is like" (3: 41). To modern theorists, this is the situation of all linguistic culture. Coleridge sensed the vital dependence of poetic voice on these very perceptions of difference. In the ideal of a symbol's simultaneity and unity, voice is redundant, silenced, absorbed; but simile stirs with a productive difference, even a Derridean "differance": "without the possibility of differance," proposes Derrida, "the desire of presence [against absence] would not find its breathing-space. . . . Differance produces what it forbids, makes possible the very thing that it makes impossible" (*Of Grammatology* 143). This breathing-space and its latent power of inspiration are both the occasion and the subject of one of Coleridge's notebook entries from 1806. His revisions show him trying to generate a simile, first with the concentration of *like*, then with the more expansive expressive potential of *as:*

> ~~Like the soft-eyed Hart (Hind)~~
> Lur'd by her Hunter ~~with the Shepherd's Pipe~~ Flute,
> ~~Whose music~~ voyaging the twilight ~~wind~~ breezes
> ~~Like~~ As the shy Hind, the soft-eyed gentle Brute,
> Now moves, now stops, approaching by degrees
> At length emerg~~inge~~es from the sheltring Trees,
> Lur'd by her Hunter with the shepherd's Flute
> Whose music travelling on the twilight Breeze
> When all beside was mute,
> She ~~lov'd to hear~~ oft had heard unharm'd & ever loves to hear,
> She, fearful Beast! but that no Sound of Fear. (*Notebooks* 2951)

A tidied-up text of the last eight lines, in fact, appears in E. H. Coleridge's edition of the poems under the singular title, *A Simile*. Not only has the poet elaborated a simile but even more remarkably, he lets the vehicle expand without apparent purpose or tenor of argument. As a scenario of danger from a charming device of insidious intent, it courts reading as a critique of the rhetoric of simile. But Coleridge's elaboration is not so critically pointed. It is indulged for independent imaginative pleasure, an exercise recorded only as a potential resource whose tenor, as if in defiance of the danger it hints at, is unknown and scarcely inevitable.

This indulgence, far from consigning Coleridge's attraction to simile to the trivial motions of an unfocused imagination, displays the vital involvement of his writing with a figure whose form defers even the most urgent demands of allegorizing or referential utility. The vehicle that is pure vehicle, the image that resists the totalizing forms of narrative or idealized symbol, is a compelling demonstration of how poetry can be generated (and in this case, suspended) by its rhetorical structures. Coleridge's persistent turns and returns to simile are the signature of an imagination always given to reading its world, in various degrees, in textures of *like* and *as*.

## NOTES

1. I follow the text of the *Morning Post*, Sept. 11, 1802; the variants are given in *Poems* 377–78.

2. Hartley also finds common ground between simile and allegory in the poetics of likeness: "If the Likeness extend to many Particulars, the Figure becomes implicitly a Simile, Fable, Parable, or Allegory ... all Instances of natural Analogies improved and set off by Art" (*Observations* 1: 292 and 297). These designs of likeness also spell difference, however: "the ubiquitous urge to find some moral or subjective analogue," as Earl R. Wasserman remarks about the eighteenth-century penchant for analogizing, "reveals the anxiety to internalize the external and integrate the spiritual with the phenomenal. The resort to analogy only dodges the problem, since it both pretends to a relation between subject and object and yet keeps them categorically apart" (20–21).

Coleridge suggests as much when he complains about the co-presence of analogical perception and simile in Bowles.

3. For a comprehensive discussion of this figure, see Hans Vaihinger.

4. July 1, 1833; *Table Talk* 1: 408. Addressing this discrepancy between theoretical value and discursive and poetic practice, John Gatta, Jr., notes that "the inherently binary structure of the allegorical mode" offers Coleridge a counterpart for "a sensibility peculiarly disposed toward dualistic vision and 'desynonymizing,' toward the development of binary distinctions" (75)—such as those between Reason and Understanding, Imagination and Fancy, Imitation and Copy, and—not a little ironically—Symbol and Allegory.

5. Los's system does not escape the forces of enslavement, however; Los simply avoids the powerless position. That he speaks thus "in fury & strength" and, it seems, tyranny—"Obey my voice & never deviate from my will" (29)—suggests the energy of Blake's opposition to strictures of comparison. Annotating Reynolds's statement in the *Discourses* that "it is the same taste which relishes a demonstration in geometry, that is pleased with the resemblance of a picture to an original, and touched with the harmony of musick," Blake counters, "Demonstration Similitude & Harmony are Objects of Reasoning" (*Complete Poetry* 659).

6. Jacques Derrida remarks that "classical theory of metaphor" tends to treat the figure "as an 'economical' way of avoiding 'extended explanations': and, in the first place, of avoiding simile" ("White Mythology" 20). For Aristotle's centrality in ancient theories of comparison, see Marsh H. McCall, Jr., 24ff.

7. The force of simile depending on the difference and "dissimilitude" of its components, Kames advises, "a resemblance between objects of different kinds, and a difference between objects of the same kind, have remarkably an enlivening effect" (1: 279). Johnson is quoted by James Whaler (1071).

8. *Table Talk* 1: 489–90 (June 23, 1834); cf. "Fancy ... the bringing together Images dissimilar in the main by some one point or more of Likeness" (*Lectures 1808–1819* 1: 67).

9. I discuss the ambiguities of interpretation Coleridge dramatizes in the poem and extends to the reader in my essay "The Language of Interpretation in Romantic Poetry."

10. For relevant discussions, see Viktor Pöschl (esp. 81), Thomas Vogler (9), George Whalley (767–68), and L. D. Lerner (297–98).

11. For this simile and the lines that introduce it, I follow the 1798 text (as given by R. L. Brett and A. R. Jones) because this is the one that Shelley quotes in *Frankenstein* (vol. 1, chap. 4). The concentration of the simile on a single effect makes it more Miltonic than Homeric: comparing the Miltonic simile to the "similitudes" of Homer and Virgil, Addison, for instance, sees Milton working "his simile till it rises to some very great idea, which is often foreign to the occasion that gave birth to it" (*Spectator* no. 303; *Works* 3: 209).

12. Pope, Preface to *The Iliad* (*Works* 255). It is suggestive that as a gloss on the potential of the Miltonic simile for overwhelming singleness of effect with a multiplicity of elaboration, Whalley summons Coleridge: "This, in Coleridgean terms, could be described as a movement from Imagination to Fancy" (768).

13. Reeve Parker (64, 27). Parker does not study the poem's similes in this respect but focuses on how analogy gives Coleridge "the grammar for the language of symbols": Coleridge's "creative intelligence" reveals "a strong analogical bent," animated by general sense of "the common ground of nature and mind in One Life" and "ultimately conceived in terms of Christian emblemism" (47, 52).

14. To Alaric Watts, Nov. 16, 1824; *Letters, Later Years* 1: 284. One may note Jean-Pierre Mileur's point about the deferral and evasion implied by the "imaginative and temporal distance" that conditions "the privileged insight," and share his interest in how a suggestion of something withheld as well as revealed makes "the manifesta-

tion of this spirit . . . only a figure," but still wonder whether his "only" too unequivocally deconstructs Coleridge's poetics (44). For even if this event is "only a figure" (how can it be otherwise in a poem?), Coleridge's simile allows the language of "manifestation" to organize and comment on all the other versions of figuring by "as" in the speaker's mind, and to do so in ways that suggest how these figures themselves present meaningful terms of participation.

15. Barthes meditates on the etymology in "From Work to Text" in *Image-Music-Text* (159).

16. See *Poems* 101: the lines "O! the one Life within us and abroad, / Which meets all motion and becomes its soul, / Rhythm in all thought, and joyance every where—" (26–29) were first published in 1828.

17. Quoted in McCall 143. For an alert study of Coleridge's various versions and revisions of these lines, see Paul Magnuson, who also feels that the draft encloses the surmise as part of a series of equally "idle flitting phantasies," "merely one figure among other[s]" (8).

18. John Shawcross 341; cf. T. M. Raysor 533. In this respect, both Coleridge and Wordsworth echo Kant, who denominates the sublime as that which is "not only great, but absolutely great in every point of view (great beyond all comparison)" (*Critique of Judgment* 86). For a good discussion of Coleridge's debts to Kant on his articulation of the sublime, and especially on the principle of comparison, see Raimonda Modiano 101–37.

19. *Paradise Lost* 2.636–43; Wordsworth's italic (*Prose* 3: 31). It is revealing of the expansions to which the structure of epic simile is felt to conduct that the one that Wordsworth singled out for praise seemed a nearly Satanic excess in the eyes of some of the more orthodox pre-Romantics: Zachary Pearce agrees with Richard Bentley that this passage showed Milton's undisciplined habit of "wandring into some unresembling Circumstance; which has no relation to his Comparison" (Bentley in Pearce, 66–67).

20. Cleanth Brooks, "Metaphysical Poet" 153–54. As Patricia Ward has remarked, in practice Coleridge "employs allegory as a critical principle much more vigorously than he does the symbol," and in "discussing the language of poetry [he] seems more concerned with the fancy and arbitrary figures than with symbols" (30). One may add that as a practicing poet he also remains engaged with allegory: throughout the career we find such figures as Faith, Hope, Charity, Death, Love, Fear, Patience; *To An Unfortunate Woman Whom the Author Had Known in the Days of Her Innocence* appears as "Allegorical Lines" in manuscript (*Poems* 172) and in two letters (*Collected Letters* 1: 314, 315) and is termed "an *allegory*" in a third (3: 322); and certain late poems, notably *Time, Real and Imaginary, The Pang More Sharp Than All,* and *Love's Apparition and Evanishment,* carry subtitles designating them as allegories—the last one, Coleridge says, revised to give "greater *perspecuity* in the Allegory" (6: 952, his emphasis) and renamed "an allegorical Romance" from "a Madrigal" (6: 954). He also refers to that figure of the sublime itself, Milton's death, as "half person, half allegory" ("Apolgetic Preface to 'Fire, Famine, and Slaughter,'" *Poems* 599), titles an early prose piece *An Allegoric Vision* and calls the opening essay of *The Friend* an "allegory" (1.9).

21. Jerome J. McGann observes that the "negative pattern" developed by these "allegorical deconstructions" of "the most fundamental objects of the mind . . . grew more firmly rooted in the poetry even as Coleridge's prose developed a more confident ideological focus"; to McGann, what makes "these sorts of ideological losses and surrenders" so "powerful and terribly moving" is the fact that "their vehicular form is a poetic one" (97–98).

22. Tilottama Rajan, *Dark Interpreter* 204. Cleanth Brooks, although with a different theoretical emphasis, notes something similar even in the figure of analogy: within the limitations of language, he remarks, the poet "has no one term. . . . He must work by contradiction and qualification . . . by analogies" (*Urn* 9).

# III

# DE QUINCEY'S RHETORIC OF DISPLAY AND *CONFESSIONS OF AN ENGLISH OPIUM-EATER*

*Lawrence D. Needham*

In the course of his ruminations on style, Thomas De Quincey interposes a question that opened a window on a new field of inquiry for stylistics.

> Did the reader ever happen to reflect on the great idea of *publication?* An idea we call it; because even in our own times, with all the mechanic aids of steam-presses, & c., this object is most imperfectly approached, and is destined, perhaps, for ever to remain an unattainable ideal.... One condition of publication defeats another. Even so much as a general publication is a hopeless idea. Yet, on the other hand, publication in some degree, and by some mode, is a *sine qua non* condition for the generation of literature. Without a larger sympathy than that of his own personal circle, it is evident that no writer could have a motive for those exertions.... (10:231-32)[1]

A professional man of letters who recognized the need to publicize himself, a writer and editor who struggled with deadlines and intractable print media, De Quincey was one of the first commentators on style to discuss techniques of publicity in relation to the literary expression of given authors and periods. The thesis of "Style," relating publication to reading and writing practices, has been called "striking" and "original" (Hudson 211); it is paradoxical as well, for De Quincey argued that "one condition of publication"—the multiplication of books through improved technology—defeated the object of publication—to make something known publicly to the understanding and the eye—in growing progression. In short, as readers increased and presses multiplied, books, "increasing in a still greater proportion ... left as the practical result an average quotient of publicity for each book, taken apart, continually decreasing." A chilling observation for an author was the probability that "many books were never opened" and were left "absolutely without a reader" (10:232).

De Quincey responded to a scene of writing in which the proliferation of printed materials threatened his emergence as a man of letters by developing a rhetorical practice exploiting elements of surprise and novelty—especially paradox—to "fix the reader's attention" (7:206) on his prose and his genius. Though recognizing that "every year buries its own literature," he understood as well that "every month, every day indeed, produces its own novelties, with the additional *zest* that they are novelties" (233). He actively pursued the fresh perspective or unusual point of view, holding that "to think reasonably upon any question" was not a "sufficient ground for writing upon it," unless he were "able to offer some considerable novelty" (6:2)—hence, for example, his novel approach to style in its relation to publicity and his interest in developing the paradox that "engines of publication" were both instrumental and detrimental to the idea of publication.

De Quincey's taste for novelty and paradox—core elements of his discursive practice—also is evidenced in "Rhetoric," which not only delineates his conception of rhetoric as the "art of aggrandizing and bringing out into strong relief, by means of various and striking thoughts, some aspect of truth" (10:92) but instantiates it through a performance rife with unusual perspectives, one-sided estimations, and exaggerated claims. Ironically, his exhibition—meant "to fix the attention" of his contemporaries—has succeeded in consternating twentieth-century critics, many of whom agree with René Wellek that it's a "curious theory of rhetoric" best forgotten (269). His art of intellectual display has been praised for originality or damned for idiosyncracy—and in most cases dismissed. Part of the difficulty lies with critics who have refused to read "Rhetoric" on its own terms, as a bravura performance of verbal display. Even so judicious a critic as Frederick Burwick, who cautions readers to "keep in mind that De Quincey attempted only an informal commentary and not a systematic treatise on rhetoric" (xi), laments his "lack of systematic development . . . in his account of the history of rhetoric" and his failure to provide a formal account of the philosophical relationship between "aspects of his theory" (xlii). De Quincey's "excursive review" of rhetoric has been criticized for what it omits, or imperfectly recalls, or distorts through selective memory, objections that fail to take into account De Quincey's thesis, supported by arguments giving it "colourable support" (10:86) that the rhetorician "exhibits his art by giving an impulse to one side, and by withdrawing the mind so steadily from all thoughts and images which support the other as to leave it practically under the possession of a one-sided estimate" (10:91). Supporters and detractors alike have objected to its lack of a real interest and persuasive purpose; Wilbur Samuel Howell argued that De Quincey's rhetoric is "so attenuated, so unreal, so far divorced from actual experience, so completely devoid of connections with the urgent issues of politics and law, that we can only wonder why De Quincey would think it worthwhile . . . for any serious-minded person to bother with it in any theoretical or practical way" ("De Quincey" 412). Finally, De Quincey's rhetoric of display has been dismissed or overlooked as an anomaly or curiosity, written at a cultural moment when rhetoric was dead and presenting no clear connectedness to the rhetorical tradition, excepting the relations De Quincey perversely or mistakenly establishes in his "capricious" history of the subject. The one critic who, in writing a revisionist history of rhetoric, has taken De Quincey's rhetoric seriously has found it necessary to invent a genealogy for him, placing De Quincey in an imaginary line including Montaigne, Vico, and Derrida.[2]

To proceed as De Quincey did—that is, contrarily and paradoxically, shouting, "Here, reader, are some extraordinary truths, looking so very like falsehoods that you would never take them for anything else if you were not invited to give them special examination" (7:206)—I will argue that De Quincey's conception of rhetoric is not anomalous but constitutes his interpretation of an important (if a sometime discredited or repudiated) strand of a multiplex rhetorical tradition. With precedent in the practice of the first Sophists, his art of developing theses copiously, with an eye toward novelty and paradox, borrows from Cicero and Quintilian and is informed by his understanding of classical declamation, which influenced the seventeenth-century poetry and prose he so much admired. Furthermore, I hope to suggest that far from being divorced from actuality, De Quincey's rhetoric of display constitutes his response to the very real demands of publication and the exigencies of the marketplace.

For some commentators, De Quincey's assertion that his view of rhetoric coincides with Aristotle's has been enough to discredit his purchase on rhetorical tradition and his place in the history of rhetoric. David Masson, editor of *The Collected Writings of Thomas de Quincey,* appended a three-page footnote by way of elucidating and clarifying De Quincey's "imperfect recollection of the contents and substance of Aristotle's Treatise on Rhetoric" (10:82); other commentators have overlooked his references to Aristotle, perhaps in response to De Quincey's mischievous comment that "all parties may possibly fancy a confirmation of their views in Aristotle" (10:83) or in reaction to his explicit intention to offer a novel perspective on Aristotle so startling and unheard of that "we question, indeed, whether any fulminating powder, descending upon the schools of Oxford, would cause more consternation than the explosion of that novelty which we are going to discharge" (10:84-85). Nonetheless, De Quincey's discussion of Aristotelian rhetoric, however exaggerated and misleading at points, offers key insights into understanding his own art of rhetoric, if only by way of studying its deviations from its illustrious predecessor.

Surprisingly, some of De Quincey's views on Aristotelian rhetoric are supportable and cannot be dismissed out of hand—for example, his understanding that the province of rhetoric is *doxa,* not *episteme,* and his conviction that, at base, rhetoric is an inventional art, involving the capacity for observing or discovering available arguments. Other views are questionable, inaccurately paraphrasing Aristotle's notions of rhetoric to suite De Quincey's "one-sided estimate." For example, De Quincey renders Aristotle's well-known definition of rhetoric—the "ability, in each [particular] case, to see the available means of persuasion"³—as "the finding such arguments for any given thesis as, without positively proving or disproving it, should give it a colourable support" (10:85-86). His modifications are significant: substituting arguments for available means of persuasion, he eliminates emotional and ethical appeals as "extraessential" (10:92), establishing, by default, mind play as the end of rhetoric; in substituting "colourable support" for persuasion, he intimates the suggestion he develops later that the end of rhetoric is momentary assent. More important, for my purposes, in substituting "any given thesis" for "in each particular case," he removes rhetoric from a concern with "the determinate cases of real life" (10:94) and signals his understanding of, and participation in, another line of the rhetorical tradition.

The precedent I allude to was the Roman practice of declaiming on any given subject in *utramque partem*—on each and every side. Comprised of two kinds—*suasoriae* and *controversiae*, which were intended to give a student practice in deliberative and forensic oratory, respectively—Roman declamation gradually was divorced from the practices of courts and assemblies and pursued in and of itself, for pleasure and approbation. As the practice of declamation became a matter of public display, test cases of law were romanticized and elaborated beyond the circumstances of everyday concerns and appeared to be designed not so much to weigh the validity of laws or policies or to test a student's grasp of legal questions but to test the skill and ingenuity of the declaimer. A subject, or *thema*, was announced, and the *declamator*, working with a challenging set of circumstances, argued a position with the purpose of achieving an artful exhibition of subject and speaker. Novelty, variety, and copiosity characterized successful declamation, and a performer was expected to display considerable resourcefulness; as Bonner notes, "the same speakers often debated the same theme both for and against, in Latin and then in Greek, and it was a sign of ability to adopt the more difficult side" (51).

The rift between declamatory display—once considered practice for public life—and effectual oratory grew so large that success in one endeavor often was a liability in the other. The distinction between rhetors in schools and drawing rooms and speakers in courts and assemblies became a commonplace of critics of declamation, who cited the impractical nature of rhetorical training and the excesses of the schools for the degeneracy of oratory. Seneca, for example, contrasts *scholastici* and *novi declamatores*, whose *scholastica*, or school orations, were presented for applause, with an earlier generation of speakers whose private rehearsals prepared them for the courts and assemblies. As Bonner notes, critics of declamation, with precedent in Cicero, "constantly stress the difference between the training-ground of the schools and the battleground of real life, and between the *rhetor* and the *orator*" (43).

It is precisely this discrimination De Quincey relies on when he makes his startling claim that "amongst the greater orators of Greece there is not a solitary gleam of rhetoric" (10:94). Its most famous orator, Demosthenes, was not a great rhetor because the exigencies of the moment—particularly the demands of the audience, likened to a "wasp always angry" or a lunatic "always coming out of a passion or preparing to go into one" (10:326-27)—forced him "to curtail his arguments, and rarely indeed to pursue a theme with the requisite fulness of development or illustration" (10:327). Along similar lines, De Quincey argues that, excluding Edmund Burke, the exception proving the rule, a rhetor could not possibly emerge in contemporary popular assemblies because deliberative and forensic proceedings were so "vulgarized" by detail and weighted down by the "technicalities of law" and the "intricacy of facts" that they offered no scope for invention (10:99). For De Quincey, the orator is an impassioned speaker who strives to achieve tangible, practical outcomes when engaging with the "impassioned realities in the forum or in the senate" (10:324); the rhetor, on the other hand, is a calculating artificer who aims "at an elaborate form of beauty which shrinks from the strife of business" and can "neither arise nor make itself felt in a tumultuous assembly" (10:93). As the art of invention that pursues thoughts "through a maze of inversions, evolutions and harlequin changes" (10:97), rhetoric finally is, in De Quincey's phrase, an "eloquentia umbratica" (10:93), an experience "won in the shade" by a "umbraticus doctor," or "mere scholastic student" (10:324-25) with the leisure and opportunity to pursue a species of fantastic art.

It is no accident that De Quincey's "mere scholastic" student, or chamber rhetorician, who "declaimed in the closet" (10:324), calls to mind the *scholastici* mentioned by Seneca and others, for, as "Rhetoric" makes clear, De Quincey was familiar with those authors traditionally associated with the practice and criticism of Roman declamation—Ovid, Livy, Lucan, Seneca, Quintilian. In fact, De Quincey closely identified the art of rhetoric with the practice of declamation. For example, when mentioning Ovid's *Metamorphosis* as "a chef-d'oeuvre" of rhetoric (10:95), he notes in particular the contest for the arms of Achilles—a set piece of declamatory practice—as the prime example of an unrivaled Roman rhetoric. Believing that one found "the true El Dorado of rhetoric" in the literature of Rome (10:95), he singles out for special attention the two Senecas and seems to have in mind the elder Seneca (author of *Controversiae* and *Suasoriae*) when he mentions a "peculiar [Roman] rhetoric," "such as Seneca's," which produced a body of rhetorical composition without parallel in Greek literature (10:254).

The peculiarities of Roman declamation are exaggerated in Seneca, who offers his readers fragments of declamations to showcase what he takes to be the declamation's essential parts. He divides his study into *sententiae, colores,* and *divisiones*. The *sententiae* were pointed comments, often witty, that summed up an argument, or some aspect of a life or case, with epigrammatic force. De Quincey recognizes this aspect of declamation in noting that rhetoric requires "closeness" and "condensation" as well as the "scintillation of wit" to be true to its essential nature (10:94); "inflation of style" was "radically hostile to the condensation of keen, arrowy, rhetoric" (10:95-96). The product of display should sparkle "with a diamond dust of rhetorical brilliancies" (10:101) or glitter like the "coruscations of the aurora borealis" (10:94). De

Quincey's figures of light point as well to his appreciation of the chromatics or colors of rhetoric—Seneca's *colores*. These refer to the cast or tone of an argument that colors its interpretation or to the particular arguments intended to throw a different light on events and actions. This aspect of rhetorical display is retained in De Quincey's argument that the end of rhetoric is not thoroughgoing persuasion but momentary assent to a given proposition, achieved by giving it "*colourable* support" (emphasis mine), that is, "by giving an impulse to one side, and by withdrawing the mind so steadily from all thoughts and images which support the other as to leave it practically under the possession of a one-sided estimate" (10:91).

The final component of declamation—its *divisio*—refers to the most effective disposition of arguments to achieve both assent and approval. Broadly, arguments were divided into questions of *ius* (law) and *aequitas* (equity). Was an agent legally entitled to act as he did and was he morally justified in doing so? More narrowly and technically, arguments might turn on considerations of the *stasis* of a case, on basic questions concerning whether the issue at hand was one of fact, definition, quality, or procedure. Though such questions organize the presentation of materials of the opium-eater's "case" in his "Preliminary Confessions," they are not applied mechanically, since that would be fatal to the operation of genius, and, as we shall see, De Quincey labored to maintain at all costs the appearance of his genius. The strength of genius was not attentiveness to the "field of daily experience" or the facts of a case or the technicalities of law but the ability to entertain "a vast variety of questions" on "innumerable themes" (10:266) and to embellish discourse "with a wide circuit of historical, or of antiquarian, nay, even speculative discussion" (10:380). This "style of liberal excursus" (10:381) De Quincey found in Edmund Burke, Thomas Browne, and a few others but preeminently in Cicero, who, as moral philosopher, polymath, and rhetorician, offered De Quincey a stimulating precedent for his rhetoric of display.

Though not immediately associated with declamatory practice, Cicero declaimed throughout his life in Greek and Latin. Even though Cicero declaimed *causas,* Bonner notes that Cicero generally preferred *theses* to *causas* as he aged: "In his later years, Cicero seems to have been particularly attracted to declaiming on philosophical themes . . . he refers to his recent private exhibitions among friends at Tusculum as his *senilis declamatio,* and calls the exercises *scholae* ('disquisitions'), 'after the manner of the Greeks,' a word which is interesting as preparing the way for the Senecan *scholastica*" (30-31). The matter of these exercises—on poverty, on the humble life, and on other broad philosophical topics—call to mind the subjects that De Quincey thought well-suited for rhetorical development: "the goodness of human nature and its wickedness; the happiness of human life and its misery; the charms of knowledge and its hollowness" and all such general topics where "the affirmative and negative are both true" (10:91). Yet it is not simply a matter of analogues here; De Quincey was familiar with Cicero's positive valuation of elaborating *theses,* and, in "Style," credits him with distinguishing the *quaestio infinita* (or vague question), which was favorable to the exercise of invention and style, from the *quaestio finita* (or circumstantiated question), which was not (10:226).

De Quincey's knowledge of the *quaestio infinita,* or *thesis,* is evident in his definition of rhetoric as the art of providing "colourable support" for "any given *thesis*" (emphasis mine). The argument that rhetoric entails elaborating a *thesis* refers to the long-standing discursive practice of proposing a general topic or theme as the ground for philosophical inquiry and speculation. The *thesis* often took the form of a question, hence the translation of the term as *quaestio* or *infinita quaestio.* As the word *infinita* suggests, the *thesis* technically investigated a subject without reference to particular persons, places, or times; it was opposed to the *hypothesis* or *quaestio finita*, which considered a subject in the context of specific facts and circumstances. The former was well-suited for training in philosophy, the latter for training in rhetoric, and for some time—in theory, at least—the *thesis* was the exclusive property of philosophy.[4] Yet, beginning with Hermagoras, the *thesis* gradually was incorporated within rhetoric, since it was evident that discussion of particular cases touched on general questions—the nature of virtue, vice, equity, justice, good, evil, piety, and the like—and that the disposition of cases depended, to a great extent, on the nature of the general principle under discussion. In addition, the exfoliation of a *thesis* was thought to give any particular speech variety and elegance; for Cicero and Quintilian, it was an important resource for copiosity.[5]

Cicero's interest in reclaiming the discussion of general principles for rhetoric—an interest he did not possess in his youth—is related to his project of joining rhetoric and philosophy, of wedding wisdom and eloquence. The success of his project depended on the orator's education as a complete individual familiar with all areas of knowledge and schooled in philosophy, the study of which was essential to a full, copious, and impressive exposition of subjects. This ideal lies behind Quintilian's perfect orator as well—the good man speaking well whose eloquence is wisdom. What both Cicero and Quintilian envisioned was a reinvigoration of general culture along Isocratean lines; their models for such a program were, in fact, early Greek philosophers and wise men, among whom they counted the Sophists, who claimed to possess all knowledge and the answers to all questions.[6] These polymaths, who are similar to the polyhistors De Quincey so much admired—Herodotus, Leibniz, Coleridge—in their capacity to compass all knowledge,[7] are prototypes of the philosopher/man of genius whom the opium-eater identifies with and claims to be in the *Confessions of an English Opium-Eater.*

De Quincey's purpose in the *Confessions* is to "display the marvelous agency of opium" (78), to "emblazon" its power for "exalting the colors of dream scenery" and for "strengthening the sense of its fearful 'realities'" with the ultimate end of "displaying the faculty itself" (*Suspiria* 88).[8] The vocabulary—"displaying," "emblazoning," "exalting," and "strengthening"—indicates the epideictic function of the *Confessions* and establishes it as an example of the literature of display that De Quincey alludes to in his essays "On Rhetoric," "Language," and "Style."

In these essays, De Quincey argues that an artist's excellence consists of his ability to view an object under multiple and complex relations. The result is a copious discourse capable of producing an "electric kindling of life between two minds" through "sympathy with the object discussed in its momentary coruscation of shifting phases" (10:268-69). He recognizes, however, that an audience's attitude toward an object of discussion or toward a writer often interferes with its ability to survey that object and so introduces as "ministerial" arts those practices that do "not affect the thing which is to be surveyed, but the eye of him who is to survey" (10:92). Among these are "any arts which conciliate regard to the speaker" and thus "indirectly promote the effect of his arguments" (10:92).

In the context of the *Confessions,* these "ministerial" arts figure importantly because, if the opium-eater is to "emblazon" the power of opium and the dreaming faculty, he must, in his words, "forestall that question and give it satisfactory answer . . . 'How came any reasonable being to subject himself to such a yoke of misery'" (4)—that is, he must answer how he came to develop a debilitating opium addiction. Unless resolved, that question would "interfere with that degree of sympathy which is necessary in any case to an author's purpose" (4); without justifying his actions and clearing his name, the opium-eater stands little chance of creating sympathy for the objects of his attention.

In response, the opium-eater initiates a narrative wherein he portrays himself as a "victim of circumstances—familial, constitutional, social" (Young 57). The language he employs to justify his revisionary account—his insistence that he elaborates the circumstances of his *"case"* (emphasis mine) to correct misrepresentation and erroneous public opinion—throws a rhetorical cast over his "Preliminary Confessions" and suggests, in particular, that he is applying to his situation the colors of rhetoric. This suspicion is confirmed when the opium-eater argues that one's offenses "approach, or recede from, the shades of that dark alliance [with guilt], in proportion to the probable motives and prospects of the offender, and the palliations, known or secret, of the offence" (2). His efforts to place his actions in a positive light are reminiscent of the "sophistry" of declamatory exercises in which speakers often extricated their character from indefensible or impossible situations by elaborating extraordinary motivations and extenuating circumstances. Admitting the facts of his difficult case, the opium-eater provides a rationale to favorably account for them; that is, De Quincey provides a *hypothesis,* which, in one of his accounts of casuistry ("The Story of a Libel"), he properly identifies as concerning matters where "the question is about a cause: certain phenomena are known and given: the object is to place below these phenomena a basis capable of supporting them, and accounting for them" (3:163). As De Quincey was aware, the *hypothesis* was another name for the Roman causa. Both turned on definite questions concerning facts and persons. Though, as we have seen,

De Quincey preferred generalized or slightly circumstantiated questions to those involving the determinate data of real life, he conceded the value of special illustration. He notes that "even Cicero could not pursue his theme through such barren generalizations as to evade all notice of special cases" (8:312). Special cases infused discourse with life and interest, hence the opium-eater's assertion that he provides a narrative of his youthful adventures "to render the confessions more interesting" (4). Special cases also provided matter for speculation; they opened up new areas of inquiry by challenging general principles and laws. The hypothetical test cases of Roman *causas* and *controversiae* were always meant, to some extent, to test the validity and scope of the law and norms of behavior; so too the opium-eater's "judicial" confessions, which he offers to "justify a breach of the general rule" (2).[9]

The opium-eater's special case requires special pleading, and the opium-eater admits that his account may be "open to doubts of casuistry" (2)—a practice related to declamatory exercises to the extent that they evolve from a consideration of the particulars of persons, times, and circumstances. Doubts of casuistry refer not only to concerns about the sometimes dubious practice of that art but also to questions raised about the quality of doubtful actions in relation to general rules. De Quincey's interest in casuistry—what he understood as the study of cases or those "oblique deflexions from the universal rule" (8:313)—lay with its potential as an instrument of speculation, though he recognized that some might pursue their investigations "into unhallowed paths of speculation" (8:311).

In narrating his case, the opium-eater extenuates and excuses his behavior by creating sympathy for his condition. Describing his suffering in London, for example—despite his assertion that he would not harass the feelings of his readers—the opium-eater argues that "extremities such as these, under any circumstances of heaviest misconduct or guilt, cannot be contemplated, even in description, without a rueful pity that is painful to the natural goodness of the human heart" (16). His strategy is weak on several counts: it not only concedes the possibility that the opium-eater may indeed be guilty of wrongdoing but also asks his readers to identify with nature in an abject attitude when, as De Quincey makes clear in "On Knocking at the Gate in Macbeth," they would rather identify with what is great and awe-inspiring in that nature.[10] In defending his actions, then, the opium-eater must fashion and aggrandize an image that will evoke from his readers sympathy grounded in admiration, not pity. The figure that he chooses is the man of genius.

The figure of the man of genius stands behind and organizes much of the material of the "Preliminary Confessions," which presents a partial anatomy and encomium to genius. This section of the *Confessions* clearly engages a Romantic topos and develops thesis material—in this instance, a theme: "On Genius," or "On the Irritability of Men of Genius," or, as De Quincey notes elsewhere in discussing the character of men of genius, "other disagreeable tendencies ending in *ty* or *ness*," such as "idleness and vanity" (11:377). The opium-eater's genius consists in his ability to turn his faults and disagreeable tendencies to good account, to make, in good rhetorical fashion, what seemed to be the worst in his character appear to be the best. For example, the opium-eater's flight from Manchester grammar school, initially recalled as an act of folly and boyhood error, is reevaluated in light of his genius. From the vantage point of custom and the general rule, his flight is an act of disobedience and an instance of prodigality. From the standpoint of his genius and its intuitive grasp of the laws of the human heart, it is an index of romantic sensibility and an assertion of freedom. As the opium-eater recalls in the 1856 edition of the *Confessions,* his resolution to depart issued from "some dark oracular legislation" (3:278), uttering "from hidden recess: 'Let there be freedom'" (3:279).

Other questionable acts are similarly revalued. The opium-eater's commerce with marginal, "polluted" creatures of London, damnable in the eyes of polite society, is justified because it is favorable to the development of his moral and intellectual qualities. His slumming develops "such a constitution of the moral faculties as shall give him [the moral philosopher] an inner eye and power of intuition for the vision and mysteries of our nature" (5). The knowledge so acquired is communicated to his readers as he extends the compass of their sympathy by speaking what is "genial in man, viz. to the human spirit" (4:308). The vanity that some critics (including Coleridge) saw in the publication of the *Confessions* is now interpreted as an act of generosity demonstrated by the opium-eater's willingness to suffer for his readers' sake (though, as noted in the Preface, he hopes the "benefit resulting to others, from the record of an experience purchased at so high price" [2] will extenuate his actions).

In the "Preliminary Confessions," then, the opium-eater rehabilitates his character by appealing to his genius, which introduces a new frame of reference by which to judge his actions. The self-display typically associated with Sophistic rhetoric serves an important function here: it provides the surety that the opium-eater is a "moral philosopher" well qualified to explore the mysteries of human nature.

That surety is provided, in part, by the opium-eater's treatment of *theses* material virtually identical with the themes De Quincey cites in "On Rhetoric" as being the matter for rhetorical display: on the happiness of human life and its misery, the goodness of human nature and its wickedness, the fragility of prosperity to the meditative mind and its security in youthful thought. He also introduces questions that usually are the staple of moral essays: What is the nature of virtue? Is there progress in virtue? What is the relation of riches to virtue, of poverty to virtue?

The open-ended nature of these themes and questions generates possibilities and paradoxes. They involve "a pro and a con, with the chance of right and wrong, true and false, distributed in varying proportions between them" or "no chances at all because the affirmative and negative are both true" (10:91). The rhetorician might with equal justice argue one side of a topic or another, or both, in *utramque partem,* as the opium-eater does in demonstrating the power of opium in the "Main Confessions."

In the "Pleasures of Opium," the opium-eater sets himself the challenge of displaying the positive aspects of what appears to be a totally unpraiseworthy subject. He gives himself two tasks, tasks that De Quincey assigns to the rhetorician in his statements on the rhetoric of display: (1) to give an impulse to one side "by withdrawing the mind so steadily from all thoughts and images which support the other as to leave it practically under the possession of a one sided estimate" (10:91); (2) to aggrandize some aspect of truth "by means of striking and various thoughts" (10:92). The first task engages the opium-eater's polemic method, as it involves him in meeting objections and answering doubts as well as in producing counterarguments. The second task engages his figurative skills and aims at establishing the power and impressiveness of his subject.

The opium-eater begins his praise of opium by dispelling the doubts and darkness surrounding his subject from previous mistreatment. He rejects out-of-hand damaging testimony on the subject: "upon all that has been hitherto written on the subject of opium . . . I have but one emphatic criticism to pronounce—Lies! lies! lies!" (39). He then proceeds to disabuse his audience of several erroneous suppositions concerning opium: the first, that opium is a depressant; the second, that it is an intoxicant; the third, that it produces torpor in the user. He proves this last point "illustratively," not "argumentatively" (to use his words), drawing on two examples from his experience that demonstrate how opium excites and stimulates the system. The first shows how on a Tuesday or Saturday night, after "a debauch of opium," he frequented the opera house and was able "to construct out of the raw material of organic sound an elaborate intellectual pleasure" (45). The second shows how he walked among the London poor and participated in their lives without sadness through the power of his sympathetic imagination. In both cases, what is emphasized is the mind's ability, through the agency of opium, to actively harmonize the raw material of reality and create scenes of order and beauty.

The opium-eater sums up the positive aspects of opium in the concluding passages of the "Pleasures" when he discusses the reveries that are the "crown and consummation of what opium can do for human nature" (48). The phrase "crown and consummation" indicates the progressive nature of the argument in praise of opium as the opium-eater moves his readers from a reductive view of opium as simply a drug "dusky brown in color" to an enlarged view of opium as a divine, ministering agent holding the keys of paradise. Seated at an open window before the sea, apparently as dumb and motionless as the opiated Turks he had decried, the opium-eater nonetheless is shown to be in a state of active intellection. The movement of his mind harmonizes the multiplicity he perceives by reconciling opposites: earth and ocean, calm and agitation, "infinite activities, infinite repose" (49). Presented as an emblem of the mind, the scene is shown to reflect the mind's order, legislation, and harmony under the influence of opium. Rather than producing torpor or intoxication, opium is shown to stimulate intellectual activity and compose the mind that composes the world.

It is inevitable, however, that the one-sided estimate in the "Pleasures" should give way to the contradictory and equally one-sided estimate in the "Pains," because rhetoric, as De Quincey envisions it, is characterized by movement and ultimately has its end in displaying an object in "its momentary coruscation of shifting phases" (10:269). In juxtaposing the "Pleasures" and the "Pains," De Quincey ironizes and qualifies both perspectives, establishing the paradoxical structure of the *Confessions* that critics have long noted.[11]

As a response to the "Pleasures," the "Pains" constitutes a tour de force performance of his rhetoric of display. His job is temporarily to withdraw the reader's mind from arguments of his own making. Using the same topics he employs in the "Pleasures," he provides the counterpoint in the "Pains" by simply reversing the arguments. For example, where he had argued in the "Pleasures" that opium orders the faculties and brings harmony and legislation to one's life, he shows in the "Pains" how opium confused his mental and spiritual capacities and reduced his life to incoherence. Opium had a palsying effect on his intellectual faculties; under its influence, he proceeded by fits and starts and was incapable of formulating any extended project because his mind, like his notes, was "disjointed." When he did conceive a project—his *De Emendatione Humani Intellectus,* for example, or his *Prolegomena to All Future Systems of Political Economy*—he had neither the power nor the will to complete it; he succumbed to "intellectual torpor" produced by the "Circean spells" of opium (66). This reversal of perspective holds for his dream scenery as well. In the "Pleasures," his reverie over the harbor of Liverpool is harmonious and balanced; in the "Pains," his dreams are fragmented and distorted.

To use De Quincey's words, the "Pains" is a "bravura" performance in which a "difficult and intractable subject" is mastered by a skillful "passage of execution" (11:220). The appropriate response to such a performance is admiration for the artist's virtuosity, despite De Quincey's insistence that the "brilliancy" or "adroitness" of the expounder is not the end of rhetorical display but "the absolute interest of the thing expounded" (10:268). In the *Confessions,* these two functions are, in fact, inseparable: display of the object, opium, and by extension the faculty of dreaming, results in the aggrandizement of the subject, the opium-eater, since he is uniquely qualified, by virtue of his genius, "to reveal something of the grandeur which belongs *potentially* to human dreams" (*Suspiria* 87). In emblazoning the world of the imagination, he simultaneously glorifies the man of imagination because, unlike those too dull to "dream magnificently," he is possessed of a "constitutional determination to reverie" (*Suspiria* 87). He possesses, in other words, a rare commodity, which he is not hesitant to market.

In this, the *Confessions* is "a clever man's book" (175), as Marilyn Butler has said, and she notes that De Quincey exhibits "a rhetorician's cunning" by manipulating us to accept and admire the exceptional character of his dreams, since "his credit with us is pinned to their exclusive, distinguishing excellence" (174-75). Her words are carefully chosen, the word *credit* accurately identifying the literary marketplace as a significant context informing the *Confessions*. For we must not forget that the publication of the *Confessions* coincided with De Quincey's emergence as a professional man of letters. His entry upon the scene of writing was understandably accompanied by some anxiety—hence the anonymity of his *Confessions,* or so we might surmise. It is no surprise, then, that questions of worth and economy predominate in the "Preliminary Confessions," which is his introduction to his readers. Like the moneylenders in London and Lord of D——— at Eton, readers are asked to evaluate the character of the opium-eater and underwrite his activities. Is he a person to be credited? Should his story have currency? Is he the original he claims to be or a counterfeiter reproducing his readers' desires and sympathies in a kind of closed circuit? Is reading him worth an expenditure of time and energy, and will it reward their investment?

In light of these questions, the opium-eater's burden—if he is to establish himself as a professional man of letters—is to demonstrate the productive power of his genius and speculations, to disclose to his readers not what they know already but such novelties and rare glimpses of the mysteries of human nature as might stimulate their reflection and speculation. In terms of De Quincey's rhetoric of display, his challenge is to provide "light to *see* the road" and "power to *advance along* it" (10:261). He succeeds on both counts, creating, through copious rhetorical display, "contagious ardour" and "sympathy with the object discussed in its momentary coruscation of shifting phases" (10:269). Such display in *utramque partem,* the mark of inventive genius and the sign of originality that validate his claims to authorship, is also evidence of that particular linguistic genius which characterizes sophistic rhetoric at its speculative best.

## NOTES

1. Quotations from Thomas De Quincey's prose are from *Collected Writings.*
2. See William Covino.
3. Aristotle, *On Rhetoric* 1.2.1., 36.
4. For an overview of *theses,* read S. F. Bonner 2-11. For in-depth discussions of *hypotheses,* particularly in relation to fiction, see Wesley Trimpi, "The Ancient Hypothesis" and "The Quality of Fiction."
5. In *Orator* 14. 45-46, Cicero contends that the outstanding orator removes discussion to a general inquiry in order to expand his topic. He remarks that Aristotle trained young men in developing *theses* "not for the philosophical manner of subtle discussion, but for the fluent style of the rhetorician, so that they might be able to uphold either side of the question in copious and elegant language" (341). Quintilian (10.5.10-12) argued that developing indefinite questions, or *theses,* enabled the student to demonstrate true merit by revealing a power "to expand what is naturally compressed, to amplify what is small, [and] to lend variety to sameness"; see *Institutio Oratoria* 119.

6. On the encyclopedic knowledge of the Sophists and their abilities to address any question, see Cicero, *De Oratore* 3.22.127-30, 99-101. Among those who joined philosophy and rhetoric, Cicero mentions Gorgias, Isocrates, and Thrasymachus; he argues that the separation of the two arts of discourse was the specific responsibility of Socrates (3.16.59-61, 49-50). Quintilian recounts the general outline of the story in *Institutio Oratoria* 1. Pr. 9-13, 11.

7. De Quincey compares Coleridge and Leibniz as "polyhistors," or "catholic students," in "Letters to a Young Man" (10:16-19). His discussion of Herodotus as the father of prose and encyclopedist is found in "Philosophy of Herodotus" (6:96-99).

8. Quotations from *Confessions of an English Opium-Eater* and *Suspiria De Profundis* are from Thomas De Quincey, *Confessions of an English Opium-Eater and Other Writings,* ed. Grevel Lindop.

9. The burden of a great part of Bonner's study of Roman declamation is to demonstrate that many declamations, though sometimes fantastically elaborated, were based on Roman law; see especially 84-132.

10. The difference is based on a distinction De Quincey draws between a "sympathy of pity" and a "sympathy of comprehension" (10:391).

11. See, for example, Roger Ramsay.

# Part II
# Classical Rhetoric

# IV

# ROMANTIC PROSE AND CLASSICAL RHETORIC

*John R. Nabholtz*

> The love of truth conjoined with a keen delight in a strict, skilful, yet impassioned argumentation, is my master-passion....
>
> —Samuel Taylor Coleridge
> (*Miscellaneous Criticism* 315)

Lamb's Elia essays, Hazlitt's familiar essays, and De Quincey's "modes of impassioned prose" have long been recognized as distinctive examples of Romantic prose expression and have received fairly extended analysis of their artistic, formal, or rhetorical properties. Yet these works constitute only a small portion of the literary prose of the period; for that matter, the familiar essay and "modes of impassioned prose" constitute only a small portion of the writings of Hazlitt and De Quincey, respectively. A much larger percentage of Romantic prose is argumentative: whether it be Wordsworth explaining and defending the principles of his poetry in various prefaces, or condemning the action of the British authorities at the Convention of Cintra, or addressing the freeholders of Westmorland on the election of 1818; Coleridge, denouncing the conduct of the war against France in 1795, or urging the upper classes to make the Bible "The Statesman's Manual," or extolling the life and character of Sir Alexander Ball in the concluding essays of *The Friend,* or in various works seeking to inculcate appropriate principles of art, morality, or religion; Shelley, condemning Lord Ellenborough for his sentencing of D. I. Eaton, or calling upon the nation to mourn the death of Princess Charlotte, or setting forth "A Philosophical View of Reform"; or Southey, vindicating his character and political opinions in *A Letter to William Smith, Esq., M. P.* I could, of course, cite many more authors and titles, but certain classes emerge quite distinctly. Some of these prose works, such as Coleridge's *Statesman's Manual* and Shelley's "Philosophical View of Reform," are concerned with recommending action or principles of behavior for the achievement of some future good; others are concerned with assessing guilt or innocence over some past action or decision, such as Wordsworth's *Convention of Cintra* and Southey's *Letter to William Smith;* still others are concerned with the praise or blame of some man or institution, such as Coleridge's tribute to Ball and Shelley's *Address to the People on the Death of the Princess Charlotte.* This threefold distribution of argumentative prose into *deliberative, forensic,* and *epideictic* is derived from classical rhetoric as expounded by Aristotle and elaborated by Cicero and Quintilian, through whom it became the staple of education in England and throughout the Western world until well into the nineteenth century. I am suggesting that our understanding and appreciation of much of the prose written by the English Romantics will be increased by a consideration of their texts in this tradition. It is simply not enough to blanket all their prose as "expressive," "personal," or "imaginative"; we need a method of analysis that will truly suggest what the Romantic writer was about in constructing his prose arguments. The tradition of classical rhetoric is one such method, one in which all the Romantics had been trained from their grammar school days.

Intensive reading of the classical rhetoricians was traditionally the province of the university. Hazlitt attended lectures on Quintilian at the Unitarian New College at Hackney and presumably received practice in constructing the classical oration, for the policy at Hackney was that "at the end of every session there were public proceedings at which students delivered 'Orations' in English and Latin" (McLachlan 252).[1] Hazlitt's absorption of classical rhetoric is clear from the critical notes to his collection *The Eloquence of the British Senate* (1807), in which he quotes and repeatedly applies Quintilian's dictum that "passion makes men eloquent."[2] Aristotle dominated the curriculum at Oxford, and the final examination for which De Quincey had to prepare in 1808 required a "perfect mastery of the minuter details of logic, ethics, and rhetoric . . ." (Hogg 109). At Cambridge, mathematics had to a considerable extent supplanted classical studies, but the orations of Demosthenes were still the subject matter for examination during Wordsworth's days at St. John's.[3] As Christopher Wordsworth notes, Aristotle, Thucydides, and Cicero were also studied, and for a purpose: "The *thesis* which opened every Respondency in the Schools or in College Chapels, gave an opening for exercise therein, and the same purpose was yet better served by the College *Declamations*" (88).[4] Further evidence of the presence of classical rhetoric at Cambridge is found in the topics selected for the annual prize orations and essays; for example, the topic for the Member's Prize in Latin prose in 1789 was "Utrum ad Oratorem fingendum valeat Ars magis, an Natura?" (Wall 369).[5]

The informing influence of classical rhetoric was manifested even earlier, however, in the grammar school training in Latin and English composition. James Penn's *Latin Grammar for the Use of Christ's Hospital* (1761) contains an appendix of figures of speech and rhetoric which were to adorn the essays. And the essays themselves, usually on some moral topic, were constructed by following the precepts formulated in the *Ad Herennium* of Cicero and passed down through various Latin and English composition books: "after having expressed the theme simply, we can subjoin the Reason, and then express the theme in another form, with or without the Reasons: next we can present the Contrary ... then a Comparison and an Example ... and finally the Conclusion ... (*Ad Herennium* IV. xliii.56-58).[6] Seven of Coleridge's essays written at Christ's Hospital have been preserved[7]; they illustrate his mastery of this rhetorical principle of *expolitio*. The first of these, dated June 6, 1788, opens with a statement of the theme: "Temperance is the first step towards making our life happy." Then follows the Reason: "For from Health, which is the natural effect of this Virtue, do we derive the enjoyment of all other advantages." Coleridge then provides an example: "The most exquisite viands become tasteless, and disgusting to one labouring under the gout, or any other painful, but usual effect of excess. Whilst Appetite renders the most simple food a delicacy to the temperate Husbandman." The succeeding two paragraphs present further reasons for the proposition, by citing the bodily and mental results of temperance. The fourth paragraph then presents the Contrary: "But it is impossible, that Reason should dwell in the mind of the Luxurious; over whom the Passions have absolute Command. For how could it preserve it's necessary authority, when the Body is debilitated by Disease, and the unruly Appetites inflamed to Madness by Wine!" The essay concludes with a Similitude: "Thus, like a ship driven by Whirlwinds, the intemperate man drives on from one excess to another, till at last he splits on the Rock of Infamy, or falls a sacrifice to Poverty and Despair. Whilst Temperance, like a skilful Pilot, guides her followers safe from all these Misfortunes to Honour, Peace, and Happiness."

Two of the most widely used grammar school texts of the period provide further testimony to the presence of classical rhetoric in the curriculum. The student probably first encountered the name of Quintilian in Jean Heuzet's *Selectae e Profanis Scriptoribus Historiae,* an anthology of very short selections from the Roman writers used in the third or fourth year of school for translation exercises and as sources of topics for English and Latin themes.[8] Somewhat later in his grammar school training, he would have encountered *Scriptores Romani,* a popular Eton anthology with extended selections from Quintilian and from Cicero's *Orator, De Inventione, De Oratore,* and *De Claris Oratoribus,* among other texts.[9]

All this suggests that the principles of classical rhetoric were still very much a part of the education of the English Romantics. Indeed, Byron spoke for most of his contemporaries when in 1807 he included Demosthenes, Cicero, and Quintilian among those authors he knew so well that he could "quote passages from any mentioned" (*Works* 1:143). It is not surprising, therefore, that when the Romantics came to write works of persuasive prose, the mark of classical rhetoric should be evident in their productions.

By way of illustrating my remarks, I should like to analyze several of Coleridge's prose works. I focus specifically on his social and political writings, because it was for subjects of public discourse and debate that the rhetorical tradition was originally evolved; furthermore, it was on such subjects that the influence of the tradition was most enduring, as the parliamentary speeches of Burke, Pitt, and Fox attest. The most obvious influence is stylistic. One does not have to turn many pages in Coleridge's political journalism *Essays on His Times* (1: 7, 15, 20, 22, 24, 43, 45) before coming across examples of *anadiplosis, anaphora, antimetabole, climax, epiphonema, epistrophe, isocolon,* etc.—many of which were listed among the twenty-seven figures of speech and fifty figures of rhetoric in the *Christ's Hospital Latin Grammar.* However, the influence of classical rhetoric is found in more significant areas than *elocutio;* I refer to the arrangement of an entire discourse *(dispositio)* or the kinds of arguments employed *(inventio).* The texts I have chosen for detailed examination range from Coleridge's earliest publication through the period of his most significant prose composition: *Conciones ad Populum* (1795), originally delivered as public addresses in January and February of that year, and the first of the Lay Sermons, *The Statesman's Manual* (1816). That Coleridge should employ the principles of classical rhetoric in shaping these public discourses is perhaps not surprising; the extent of that employment, however, is noteworthy.

In terms of *dispositio,* the "Introductory Address" of the *Conciones* includes the statement of the proposition—that we need to "[bottom] on fixed Principles" if we are to be effective patriots—within the two opening paragraphs that constitute the *exordium:*

> When the Wind is fair and the Planks of the Vessel sound, we may safely trust every thing to the management of professional Mariners: in a Tempest and on board a crazy Bark, all must contribute their Quota of Exertion. The Stripling is not exempted from it by his Youth, nor the Passenger by his Inexperience. Even so, in the present agitations of the public mind, every one ought to consider his intellectual faculties as in a state of immediate requisition. All may benefit Society in some degree. The exigences of the Times do not permit us to stay for the maturest years, lest the opportunity be lost, while we are waiting for an increase of power.
>
> Companies resembling the present will, from a variety of circumstances, consist *chiefly* of the zealous Advocates for Freedom. It will therefore be our endeavor, not so much to excite the torpid, as to regulate the feelings of the ardent; and above all, to evince the necessity of *bottoming* on fixed Principles, that so we may not be the unstable Patriots of Passion or Accident, nor hurried away by names of which we have not sifted the meaning, and by tenets of which we have not examined the consequences. The Times are trying; and in order to be prepared against their difficulties, we should have acquired a prompt facility of adverting in all our debates to some grand and comprehensive Truth. In a deep and strong Soil must that Tree fix its Roots, the height of which, is to "reach to Heaven, and the Sight of it to the ends of all the Earth." (*Lectures 1795* 33) [10]

Coleridge used a number of devices here to make his audience "well-disposed, attentive, and receptive," thus fulfilling the Ciceronian requirement for an *exordium*. The nautical metaphor in the opening sentence would be an appropriate and appealing one for the citizens of Bristol whom he was addressing. His identification of his audience as "zealous Advocates for Freedom" and the verbal union of himself and his audience would further dispose him in their favor. The sense of urgency conveyed through the tempest reference and such phrases as "the exigences of the Times," "the present agitations of the public mind," and "the Times are trying" would make the audience "attentive" to the speaker's argument. The climactic Biblical quotation would give weight and authority to the speaker's urgings at this point. Having announced his subject, identified himself with his audience, praised their dedication to freedom, and emphasized the immediacy of the danger, Coleridge would have succeeded in making his hearers "receptive" or "ready to be instructed" by the rest of his discourse, which accordingly begins in the third paragraph with the *confirmatio* of the proposition.

According to Aristotle, examples should ordinarily follow the enthymemes in the proof of the proposition; but if they come before, the speaker "must use a good many of them" (*Rhetoric* 2.20).[11] Regarding proof by example, both Aristotle and Quintilian maintain that it is particularly suited to *deliberative* discourses such as the "Introductory Address," because "as a rule history seems to repeat itself and the experience of the past is a valuable support to reason" (Quintilian III.viii.66-67).[12] Accordingly, Coleridge begins his confirmation with examples of various advocates of freedom in France and England and provides "a good many of them."

The patriots of France cited are two apparently diverse and opposite sorts: the mild-mannered Girondists and the more unscrupulous Robespierre. Yet both serve by example to prove one of the principles on which true patriots must "bottom": namely, if a revolution is to be successful, *all* classes of that society, including the lower classes, must be "morally illuminated." The Girondists "were sacrificed by the Mob, with whose prejudices and ferocity their unbending Virtue forbade them to assimilate"; in the case of Robespierre, whatever "lone-whispered denunciations of conscience" might have acted as restraints on his "enthusiastic" yet "gloomy" and "vain" character were overpowered by "those loud-tongued adulators, the mob" (34-35).

Coleridge then turns to the example of English "oppositionists to 'things as they are,'" whom he divides into four classes. The first of these, "unbraced by cooperation of fixed Principles," veer between republican and aristocratic positions depending upon events in France. "Wilder features characterize the second class." These individuals, also "unillumined by Philosophy," engage in violence and thus unwittingly become "the rude materials from which a detestable Minister manufactures conspiracies" (38). Members of the third class demonstrate a lack of fixed principles by being concerned only with removing their own disabilities without extending the same service to those below them in society. Finally, "we turn with pleasure to the contemplation of that small but glorious band, whom we may truly distinguish by the name of thinking and disinterested Patriots" (40).

Since this last group is a subject of praise and emulation, Coleridge engages in various rhetorical tactics to draw his audience toward them, including "vivid representation" (Quintilian VIII.iii.61-72) in picturing the suffering and imprisonment of Joseph Gerrald: "Withering in the sickly and tainted gales of a prison, his healthful soul looks down from the citadel of his integrity on his impotent persecutors. I saw him in the foul and naked room of a jail—his cheek was sallow with confinement—his body was emaciated; yet his eye spoke the invincible purposes of his soul, and he still sounded with rapture the success of Freemen, forgetful of his own lingering martyrdom!" (41). Coleridge also quotes a long poetic tribute by Southey, "To the Exiled Patriots" (Thomas Muir, Thomas Palmer, and Maurice Margarot), thus fulfilling Aristotle's suggestion that emulation "is excited by those whom poets or panegyrists celebrate in praises and encomiums" (*Rhetoric* 2.11).

The proof by example is now complete; Coleridge has established the *necessity* and, as he illustrates in the case of the fourth class, the *possibility* of acting with fixed principles. The next section is concerned with the means of achieving "general illumination" and of thus preparing citizens for freedom. It opens with the rejection of two suggested means: the appeal to the selfish feelings and the recommendation of Godwin for private societies from which truth would descend to the lower classes. Coleridge dismisses the first out-of-hand as unworthy and rejects the second as impractical from the rigidly inflexible structure of British society. In dealing with these suggested means, Coleridge has utilized what Cicero in *De Inventione* saw as the two primary appeals of *deliberative* discourses, to the honorable and the advantageous (II.li.156).[13] His own solution combines both: "He would appear to me to have adopted the best [most advantageous] as well as the most benevolent [honorable] mode of diffusing Truth, who uniting the zeal of the Methodist with the views of the Philosopher, should be *personally* among the poor, and teach them their *Duties* in order that he may render them susceptible of their *Rights*." And religion, with its promise of other-worldly rewards, is the only means of achieving this goal; for "a Blessing, which not ourselves but *posterity* are destined to enjoy, will scarcely influence the actions of *any*—still less of the ignorant, the prejudiced, and the selfish" (43-44).

Coleridge concluded this section with the authoritative voice of Christ, "Go, preach the GOSPEL to the Poor," and emphasized the point with the stylistic device of *anaphora*: "By its Simplicity it will meet their comprehension, by its Benevolence soften their affections, by its Precepts it will direct their conduct, by the vastness of its Motives ensure their obedience." A further principle is then developed, that the conduct of his patriot-audience must be marked by simplicity and love if they hope to convince those they wish to serve of the validity of their purposes (45-47).

In the conclusion of the "Introductory Address," Coleridge appropriately returns to the urgency of the situation, the threat of massacre and "fierce coercion"; and he repeats his advice that "we cannot therefore inculcate on the minds of each other too often or with too great earnestness the necessity of cultivating benevolent affections," and of observing temperance even in the statement of "virtuous indignation." To achieve this, he advises, "a practical faith in the doctrine of philosophical necessity seems the only preparative." Coleridge enlivens his *peroratio* in two ways: with a colorful metaphor ("It is not enough that we have swallowed these Truths—we must feed on them, as insects on a leaf, till the whole heart be coloured by their qualities, and shew its food in every the minutest fibre") and by invoking the authority of Saint Paul for the final words of the discourse: "Watch ye! Stand fast in the principles of which we have been convinced! Quit yourselves like Men! Be strong! Yet let all things be done in the spirit of Love" (48-49). It should be noted that this climactic quotation is in the form of an *asyndeton,* which Aristotle has specifically cited as appropriate at the end of a discourse; indeed, he had ended his *Rhetoric* with an *asyndeton.*[14]

The second of the *Conciones,* the *forensic* address "On the Present War," observes the following *dispositio:* the *exordium,* including the statement of the proposition that the present war is evil (paragraphs 1-3); a refutation of the charge that the war was just and necessary (paragraphs 4-6); a confirmation of the proposition by the *topos* of consequences (paragraphs 7-19); and a final paragraph of recapitulation and peroration.

Coleridge appropriately employs the *exordium* to render his readers "well-disposed, attentive and receptive." To achieve the first of these goals, he draws upon each of the sources of good will described in Cicero's *De Inventione:* "from our own person, from the person of the opponents, from the persons of the jury [the auditors], and from the case itself" (I.xvi.22). "In the disclosal of Opinion," the *Concion* begins, "it is our duty to consider the character of those, to whom we address ourselves, their situations, and probable degree of knowledge. We should be bold in the avowal of *political* Truth among those only whose minds are susceptible of reasoning: and never to the multitude, who ignorant and needy must necessarily act from the impulse of inflamed Passions." In contrast to this prudent and judicious behavior in "[preserving] this distinction," Coleridge refers to the irresponsible behavior of the "Child of Prejudice and the Slave of Corruption," who will "industriously represent it as confounded: whatever may be the sentiments and language of the present Address, the *attempt* to promote Discussion will be regarded as dangerous, and from fools and from bigots I shall be honoured with much complimentary Reviling, and many panegyrical Abuses." To these unjust opponents he replies: "But the Conduct of the speaker is determined chiefly by the nature of his Audience. He therefore, who shall proclaim me *seditious* because I speak 'against wickedness in high places,' must prove the majority of my hearers to be unenlightened, and therefore easily deluded—or Men of desperate fortunes, and therefore eager for the *Scramble* of a Revolution" (51-52). In this first paragraph, Coleridge has combined three of the four sources recommended by Cicero: he has asserted his own prudent and responsible character; he has shown the irresponsibility of his opponents in abusing him; and he has complimented his audience on their "enlightened" character. These appeals are all expanded in the second and third paragraphs. In a final statement of the *exordium,* referring to the importance of the case itself, Coleridge simultaneously consolidates the good will, attentiveness, and receptivity of his readers: "This Duty [of forming and propagating one's opinions about the state of one's country] we should exert at all times, but with peculiar ardor in seasons of public Calamity, when there exists an Evil of such incalculable magnitude as the PRESENT WAR" (53-54).

The subject is then announced: "a comprehensive view" of the "peculiar crimes and distresses" of the war, which is dealt with extensively in paragraphs seven to nineteen. But first Coleridge must refute the notion that the war was "just and necessary"; for "if the War had been just and necessary, it might be thought disputable whether any Calamities could justify our abandonment of it." He initially makes his point that the war was unjust and unnecessary by the following enthymemic reasoning: "The War might probably have been prevented by Negociation: Negociation was never attempted. It cannot therefore be *proved* to have been a *necessary* war, and consequently it is not a just one" (54).

A refutation of the various reasons offered by the British government for not negotiating then follows. I shall deal here only with the final and climactic procedure of refutation; Coleridge makes a comparison between the situations of England versus France and the American colonies versus England, employing the common *topos* of *a fortiori* in this fashion: if the colonists, who suffered hideous atrocities at the hands of the British, did not refuse to negotiate, why should we, who have less provocation, refuse to negotiate with the French? An impassioned description follows of the happy paradise of the American settlers laid waste by scalping and other horrors carried out by Indians under the instigation of the British authorities. Yet, despite these provocations, "these high-minded Republicans did not refuse to negociate with us" (55-59).

Having completed the refutation that the war against France was necessary and just, Coleridge now turns to the confirmation of the evil of the war by a consideration of its consequences. Following an extended instance of *paralipsis* (59), he deals with these consequences at length (60-73) in an order of ascending gravity: (1) the loss of our national character; (2) the devastation of private morals; (3) the threats to liberty produced by the suspension of the habeas corpus and other actions of William Pitt; (4) the economic hardships of the poor of England, leading them to crime and eventually to punishment by banishment or death, this in turn provoking the government to "crimping" and other measures to sustain the military forces; and (5) the very excesses of the French, "their massacres and blasphemies, all their crimes and all their distresses," caused by the British continuation of the war.

The concluding paragraph of the *Concion* illustrates the two aspects of a peroration discussed at length by Quintilian: the recapitulation of the facts or arguments and the emotional appeal. A recapitulation "serves both to refresh the memory of the judge and to place the whole of the case before his eyes, and, even although the facts may have made little impression on him in detail, their cumulative effect is considerable." Quintilian further recommends that the recapitulation be brief, yet "the points selected for enumeration must be treated with weight and dignity, enlivened by apt reflexions and diversified by suitable figures . . ." (VI.i.1-2). Coleridge writes:

> Our national faith has been impaired; our social confidence hath been weakened, or made unsafe; our liberties have suffered a perilous breach, and even now are being (still more perilously) undermined; the Dearth, which would otherwise have been scarcely visible, hath enlarged its terrible features into the threatening face of Famine; and finally, of US will justice require a dreadful account of whatever guilt France has perpetrated, of whatever miseries France has endured. (74)

The last of these, with the upper-case US, starts the second aspect of peroration mentioned by Quintilian, the emotional appeal. According to all classical rhetoricians, such an appeal has its place throughout the oration, but most especially in the conclusion. Here the appeal takes the form of "Arousal,"[15] as Coleridge poses the challenge: "Are we men? Freemen? rational men? And shall we carry on this wild and priestly War against reason, against freedom, against human nature?" The *Concion* ends with the powerful *epiphonema:* "If there be one among you, who departs from me without feeling it his immediate duty to petition or remonstrate against the continuance of it, I envy that man neither his head or his heart!"

Apart from its famous definitions of symbol and allegory in the main body of the text and discussion of understanding and reason in one of the appendices, *The Statesman's Manual* has never received much critical attention or study. Perhaps one reason is the almost universal opinion that the work is an intellectual and structural hodgepodge. At the time of its publication, Hazlitt asserted that it contained "an abundance of 'fancies and good-nights,' odd ends of verse, and sayings of philosophers: with the rickety contents of his commonplace book, piled up and balancing one another in helpless confusion" (Jackson, *Coleridge: The Critical Heritage* 263). More recent opinions have affirmed that its structure is "awkward" (Woodring, *Prose* 147) and that it is "the most miscellaneous of [Coleridge's] works."[16] Yet the Lay Sermon does have an intelligible argumentative design, derived again from classical rhetoric.

In terms of arrangement, *The Statesman's Manual* falls into these traditional divisions: an *exordium* embracing the first seven paragraphs and including a statement of the proposition that the "higher classes of society" should make the Bible their "Guide to Political Skill and Foresight"; a refutation of objections to this proposition embracing paragraphs eight through twenty-five; a digression of four paragraphs; a confirmation of the proposition in paragraphs thirty to thirty-two; and an extended recapitulation and peroration of sixteen paragraphs. In short, though it is clearly disproportionate in some of its parts, *The Statesman's Manual* is far from being "miscellaneous" in its procedure.

The Lay Sermon opens with a series of enthymemes quickly establishing that the Scriptures are intended for "all conditions of men under all circumstances" and therefore should be made readily available and studied. Having established this premise, the *exordium* then seeks to make its audience "well-disposed, attentive and receptive" by a long, closely connected series of comparative and *a fortiori* arguments. Coleridge first compares the ignorance and disregard of the Scriptures in Catholic countries and in England. He asks "whether, and to what extent," it may be a sin for a Catholic to remain in "spiritual slumber" when the Scriptures are deliberately kept from him by a deceitful priesthood; but, he writes, there can be no doubt about the guilt of Englishmen, to whom the Scriptures are freely available: "The circumstances then being so different, if the result should prove similar, we may be quite certain that we shall not be held guiltless. The ignorance, which may be the excuse of others, will be our crime" (6). A second comparative argument appropriately follows, between the obligations of the lower and higher classes of Englishmen to study the Scriptures. If "the humblest" has the obligation of studying them for "all knowledge requisite for a right performance of his duty as a man and a Christian," then how much more is the obligation upon the higher classes to attain "a more extensive study and a wider use of his revealed will and word." A further comparative and *a fortiori* argument is then used, based on the obligation that accompanies the holders of social rank to examine all sources relevant for the guidance and welfare of a nation: "Do you hold it requisite of your rank to shew yourselves inquisitive concerning the expectations and plans of statesmen and state-counsellors? . . . And should you not feel a deeper interest in predictions which are permanent prophecies, because they are at the same time eternal truths?" (7).

Having appealed to their pride in their religious freedom, to their patriotism, to the obligations of their social standing, and to their intellectual integrity, Coleridge then seeks the benevolence of his readers by complimenting them: "I will struggle to believe that of those whom I now suppose myself addressing, there are few who have not so employed their greater leisure and superior advantages as to render these remarks, if not wholly superfluous, yet personally inapplicable." Another comparison is used, and it is one that leads directly to the proposition of the discourse: "you will indeed have directed your *main* attention to the promises and the information conveyed in the records of the evangelists and apostles: promises, that need only a lively trust in them, on our own part, to be the means as well as the pledges of our *eternal* welfare! . . . Yet not the less on this account will you have looked back with a proportionate interest on the *temporal* destinies of men and nations, sorted up for our instruction in the archives of the Old Testament . . ." (8).

In the conclusion of the *exordium*, Coleridge asserts that present-day conditions have given a special urgency to the value of the Scriptures as guides to political action. The "restless craving for the wonders of the day," "the appetite for publicity," the "general discontent" and "political gloom," can only find relief in the "collation of the present with the past." Again employing the *topos* of *a fortiori*, Coleridge argues: "If this be a moral advantage derivable

# Romantic Prose and Classical Rhetoric

from history in general, rendering its study therefore a moral duty for such as possess the opportunities of books, leisure and education, it would be inconsistent even with the *name* of believers not to recur with preeminent interest to events and revolutions, the records of which are as much distinguished from all other history by their especial claims to divine authority, as the facts themselves were from all other facts by especial manifestation of divine interference" (8-9). He concludes the *exordium* with the authoritative words of Saint Paul: "Whatsoever things were written aforetime, were written for our learning; that we through patience and comfort of the Scriptures might have hope."

Coleridge now begins his refutation of objections: (1) because miracles were used to establish the truth of Scripture, and because we no longer live under a miraculous dispensation similar to that recorded in the Bible, some might conclude that "the Bible is less applicable to us . . ." (9-11); (2) the popular belief that "every age has, or imagines it has, its own circumstances which render past experience no longer applicable to the present case . . ." (11-23); (3) "the notion that you are already acquainted with its contents" and therefore do not need to resort to repeated and fresh examination of Scripture (25-28). *Topoi* of precedent, authorities, and *a fortiori* are used extensively in dealing with and disposing of these objections.

Following his section of refutation, Coleridge proceeds to his proof by illustration: "But do you require one or more particular passage from the Bible, that may at once illustrate and exemplify its applicability to the changes and fortunes of empires?" Before providing a specific example, he engages in a digression (28-33) on the superiority of scriptural history to "histories of highest note in the present age" and other fashionable "guides and authorities." (Interestingly, this digression, with its definitions of symbol and allegory, is the only part of *The Statesman's Manual* that is widely known.) Coleridge then offers his illustration, by citing the relevance of a passage in Isaiah to "the causes of the revolution and fearful chastisement of France" (33-35).[17]

With this, the formal case for making the Bible the "Guide to Political Skill and Foresight" is completed. Of the extended recapitulation that follows, I shall deal only with a single passage, partly because it has been cited as proof that Coleridge is at his best when he is most "unmethodical" (Willey 179-80) and partly to suggest the traditional sources of much that is assumed to be archetypically Romantic. "In reviewing the foregoing pages," Coleridge writes, "I am apprehensive that they may be thought to resemble the overflow of an earnest mind rather than an orderly premeditated composition. Yet this imperfection of form will not be altogether uncompensated, if it should be the means of presenting with greater liveliness the feelings and impressions under which they were written" (43). It should be noted that this appeal to earnest, unpremeditated, and sincere composition is itself an ancient rhetorical tactic designed to win a sympathetic response from the audience; it was as old as Quintilian and was reaffirmed as recently as Joseph Priestly's *Course of Lectures on Oratory and Criticism* (1777), which devoted an entire lecture to the "Forms of Address adapted to gain BELIEF; and, first, of those that imply PRESENT THOUGHT, and an UNPREMEDITATED EXPRESSION."[18] Moreover, as my exposition has indicated, the form of *The Statesman's Manual* is not all that imperfect; Coleridge clearly had in mind the structure of the classical oration and followed its traditional divisions consistently, if somewhat untidily. Even if it were an "overflow," it is by a man who "had thought long and deeply" about methods of argumentation. As early as the second number of *The Watchman* (March 9, 1796), Coleridge had expressed explicitly his concern for proper method in argumentation (55-56), and this concern persisted throughout his life. A "spontaneous overflow" from such a carefully trained and self-conscious rhetorician must be considered within the tradition of that training and that self-consciousness.

The procedures employed in my analyses of Coleridge's *Conciones* and *Statesman's Manual* could profitably be applied to many of the texts cited at the start of this essay; as one might expect, classical rhetoric is particularly relevant for those works addressed to the general public on the social and political events of the day. But it must be said that classical rhetoric was not the only mode of argumentative discourse in the prose of the period. Even within the canon of Coleridge's major works, the rhetorical and argumentative structures are as diverse as the subject matters: the essays *On the Principles of Genial Criticism* employ a Euclidian, geometric mode of argumentation, with definitions, postulates, and *scholia; Biographia Literaria* adopts an autobiographical frame; *Aids to Reflection* is a series of extended commentaries on quotations from Archbishop Leighton and other divines; *On the Constitution of the Church and State* is a "large and dilated epistle" (107), as Coleridge described it. Still, classical rhetoric was a persistent resource for Romantic writers, and its presence is felt in the most unexpected places. That arch-Romantic text *The Confessions of an English Opium-Eater* opens with an *exordium* "To the Reader," in which De Quincey seeks to win a sympathetic hearing from a potentially hostile audience by declaring his reluctance to inflict pain or disgust upon his reader through personal revelations and by citing numerous statistics and the testimony of authorities to emphasize the social and medical importance of his topic. In short, he is seeking to make his reader "well-disposed, attentive and receptive," as Cicero, Sidney, Milton, and Burke had done before him. An examination of Romantic prose in this tradition is necessary for a proper understanding of both the art and the argument of this rich and diverse body of writing.

## NOTES

1. See also Hazlitt's letters to his father from Hackney, 1793 (*The Hazlitts: An Account of their Origin and Descent,* ed. W. Carew Hazlitt [1911], 399-403.)

2. See William Hazlitt, *Complete Works* I: 145, 147, 153-54; VII: 297-300, 313-17. The relevant passage from Quintilian (X.vii.15) was of central importance to

Wordsworth as well, and appeared as the motto of the half-title for the 1802 and 1805 editions of *Lyrical Ballads;* it has also been cited as part of the intellectual background for the Preface to *Lyrical Ballads* (*Prose Works* 1: 176). See also De Quincey's quotation and endorsement of this passage from Quintilian in his essay "Conversation" (1847, 1860) (*Collected Writings* X: 273).

3. Wordsworth had purchased a copy of Demosthenes while still at Hawkshead, possibly in preparation for his university studies (Mark L. Reed, *Early Years* 68).

4. Coleridge's letters from Jesus College (1791-94) speak of his preparation of these declamations, of the praise he received for one delivered in early 1792 on the topic "That the desire of Posthumous Fame is unworthy a Wise Man," and of his composing one in 1794 "on the comparative good and Evil of Novels" (*Collected Letters* I: 17, 24, 71). For the text of the declamation on "the desire of Posthumous Fame," see Anthony John Harding 361-67. Interestingly, the major argumentative strategy of his declamation is the *topos* of *a fortiori,* which figures so prominently in the *Conciones ad Populum* and *The Statesman's Manual.*

5. See also the topics for 1781 and 1812.

6. In his somewhat humorous recollection of the process of composition writing at Christ's Hospital, Leigh Hunt (78) affirms the persistence of the tradition: "You wrote out the subject very fairly at top, *Quid non mortalia,* etc., or *Crescit amor nummi.* Then the ingenious thing was to repeat this apophthegm in as many words and roundabout phrases as possible, which took up a good bit of the paper. Then you attempted to give a reason or two, why *amor nummi* was bad; or on what accounts heroes ought to eschew ambition; after which naturally came a few examples, got out of Plutarch or the *Selectae e Profanis;* and the happy moralist concluded with signing his name."

7. In James Boyer's "Liber Aureus" (British Museum, Ashley MS. 3506). Only one of these—the essays of September 1790 and Jan. 19, 1791—have been heretofore published (*Illustrated London News,* April 1, 1893, 398; Lawrence Hanson, *The Life of S. T. Coleridge: The Early Years* [London: Oxford University Press, 1938], 424-25). I wish to express my appreciation to the British Library and to Mrs. Priscilla Coleridge Needham for gracious permission to quote sections from the 1788 essay on Temperance.

8. First published in France in the early eighteenth century, *Selectae e Profanis* saw London editions of 1775, 1780, 1784, 1796, 1801, 1803, 1806, and 1832. Editions were published in Philadelphia in 1787, 1809, and 1819. As Hunt noted in his *Autobiography,* students at Christ's Hospital turned to the *Selectae* for aid in composing their themes. Apparently Coleridge did just that when in November 1788 he wrote a theme on the careful attention to the education of youth. In the third book of *Selectae,* Heuzet had provided a section on the topic "Maxima debetur puero reverentia," which was illustrated with quotations from Juvenal's Fourteenth Satire, Quintilian, and Aulus Gellius. Coleridge's essay opens with the same quotation from Juvenal and subsequently paraphrases the excerpt from Quintilian. Might not this essay of 1788 constitute Coleridge's first literary borrowing or "plagiarism"?

9. I have found references to editions of *Scriptores Romani* of 1766, 1804, 1825, 1836, 1840, 1848, and 1891. The book was in use at Rugby when Landor was a student there (W. H. D. Rouse 137) and at Harrow when Byron was there (Percy M. Thornton 434). The 1804 edition would have been a text for Shelley at Eton.

10. All quotations from *Conciones* are from *Lectures 1795 on Politics and Religion* in *The Collected Works of Samuel Taylor Coleridge* (1971), which will be cited in my text hereafter simply by page number.

11. All references to Aristotle's text are from the translation by Lane Cooper.

12. See also *Rhetoric* 3.17. All references to Quintilian's *Institutio Oratoria* are from the translation by H. E. Butler.

13. All references to *De Inventione* are from the translation by H. M. Hubbell.

14. "I have done: you all have heard; you have the facts; give your judgment" (*Rhetoric* 3.19). For a very different interpretation of the significance of this final quotation and of the rhetorical procedures employed in the "Introductory Address," see David Sanderson.

15. "When not only we ourselves seem to speak under emotion, but we also stir the hearer" (*Ad Herennium* IV.xliii.55).

16. From the dust jacket of Coleridge, *Lay Sermons*, ed. R. J. White, in *Collected Works*. All quotations from *The Statesman's Manual* are from this edition, which will be cited in my text by page number.

17. As more than one reader has observed, this confirmation is quite skimpy and is the weakest part of the argument. See Hazlitt's reviews in *The Examiner* (Dec. 29, 1816) and *Edinburgh Review* (J. R. de J. Jackson, *Coleridge: The Critical Heritage* 256-58, 274-75); John Colmer (134-35); and Sanderson (328-29).

18. See Quintilian (VI.ii.26-29) and Priestly, *Course of Lectures on Oratory and Criticism* (108-15).

# V

# WORDSWORTH'S *CINTRA* TRACT
## POLITICS, THE CLASSICS, AND
## THE DUTY OF THE POET

*Richard W. Clancey*

Wordsworth's *Cintra* pamphlet is an impassioned, rhetorically sophisticated, populist manifesto. One wonders how and why a Romantic poet living in retirement could become so fervidly involved in politics and war. It is hard to imagine a Cumbrian poet concerned about Napoleon in the Iberian Peninsula. Wordsworth's commitment to the French Revolution had long since abated. Now he saw France as an imperialist power. Like many of his ardent contemporaries, he approved the sending of a British expeditionary force to Portugal for its relief against the French in August 1808. Like many in England, Wordsworth was then appalled when the English, having won a striking victory on August 21, agreed to a spineless armistice completed by August 30 (*Prose* 1:196, 373). This agreement, the infamous Convention of Cintra, was the immediate occasion of the *Cintra* tract, one of Wordsworth's most extensive and complex works.

From August 1807 to May 1808, Napoleon had secured largely a political control of Portugal and Spain; sent in armies of occupation; forced the Portuguese Prince Regent to flee to Brazil; forced both the befuddled King Charles IV and his heir, Ferdinand, to surrender their claims to the Spanish throne; and attempted to force his brother Joseph on the Spanish people as king. There had been riots and then organized insurrection, especially in Spain. England set aside its state of war with Spain, declared its sympathy with the insurgents throughout the Iberian Peninsula, and sent an expeditionary force under the leadership of Arthur Wellesley, the future Duke of Wellington. It was he who defeated the French at Vimiero on August 21 (*Prose* 1:193-96, 374, 379; Thomas, *Wordsworth's Dirge* 3-5).

What had roused the English in their support of the insurgents and ultimately provoked such public disgust with the Convention of Cintra was both the timid treatment of the defeated French invaders and the indomitable spirit of the Spanish. They defied the French and their own vacillating king and crown prince. Wordsworth, though worried about their capacity for political freedom, was inspired by their courage (Thomas 3-10). Deirdre Coleman, commenting on Wordsworth's long recollective disquisition at the beginning of his *Cintra* tract, explains that it was not until France had subjugated Switzerland in 1798 that he had begun to accept England's war against France as justified. Thus, when he read of the brave insurrection against the French by Iberian peoples, Wordsworth saw reemerge the idealism and battle for individual liberty that had characterized the French Revolution in its initial stages. For Wordsworth, "The Peninsular cause was the French Revolution *redivivus*" (Coleman 149).

But Wordsworth's vision of Iberia as France, his sense of a new "bliss" and "dawn," does not completely explain the rhetorical vividness of the *Cintra* pamphlet. Gordon Thomas's comprehensive study of Wordsworth's *Cintra* shows how frustrated Wordsworth was when Lord Lonsdale's opposition made a public meeting in Cumbria impossible. Wordsworth and Coleridge were to have spoken, and the meeting was to have resulted in a petition to the king against the Convention of Cintra. The king had already expressed his displeasure to the City of London for its similar petition. He felt such action prejudged the convention before it had received a fair governmental examination. One of Wordsworth's goals, initially reflected in an early version of his title, speaks to the royal annoyance at prejudgment (*Wordsworth's Dirge* 31-45). His final title with its epigraph reflects that concern implicitly.[1]

Wordsworth's passionate rhetoric projects more than a political argument, even one offered to a king. Wordsworth had to release his feelings; he had to speak from his heart. From a British Library manuscript letter of Robert Southey to his brother Tom, November 22, 1808, W. J. B. Owen quotes the following (in *Prose* 1:197) as to Wordsworth's intention in doing his *Cintra* tract: "Our projected county meeting came to nothing. Lord Lonsdale set his face against it . . . we were convinced that it was hopeless. . . . So Wordsworth went home to ease his heart by writing a pamphlett. . . ."

What is so interesting about this pamphlet is that, as Gordon Thomas reminds us, many Wordsworth scholars find it to be a crucial text in the charting of Wordsworth's so-called decline and his possible betrayal of his liberal political creed of the 1790s. Thomas ends his study with the chapter entitled "The *Cintra* Tract: Apostate's Creed?" (151-65). Did Wordsworth change heart politically and begin its expression with this text? Thomas comments, "Those believers in the poet's apostasy . . . agree in finding it particularly in the *Cintra* tract" (154). Thomas contends that Wordsworth saw France as having betrayed its revolutionary ideals; Thomas finds Wordsworth, however, completely loyal and consistent in the maintenance of his ideals. He also generously summarizes the divergent critical opinion on the tract and on Wordsworth, his political consistency or lack thereof (151-58), but Thomas maintains that the *Cintra* tract is not the work of an apostate but "a great monument to the continuity of Wordsworth's principles" (165).

More recently, Michael Friedman, James Chandler, and Deirdre Coleman have widened the critical perspective on Wordsworth's *Cintra* even more and have raised new questions as to Wordsworth's political consistency or possible change.[2]

The vitality of contemporary critical commentary has surely demonstrated that where, as in the case of the *Cintra* tract, there is so much diverging and yet authoritative interpretation of a text, that very diverging critical discourse itself forms a substantial choric penumbra necessarily attendant upon any enlightened reading of the text. The controversy over Wordsworth's political consistency and the tenor of the *Cintra* tract can help us understand its dynamic as a defense of populist political epistemology. Southey recounts that "Wordsworth went home to ease his heart." What resulted is a political tract that vigorously argues that decent human sentiments, the human heart, can constitute an enlightened wellspring for political philosophy and even for the practical resolution of complex political issues.

Stephen Gill, viewing Wordsworth's tract as a major creative impulse, finds that Wordsworth was most concerned that his treatise "make an impact" (275). Building upon some annoyed remarks of Coleridge, Gill explains that Wordsworth had become so "obsessed" (274) with the pamphlet because its writing caused his mind and spirit to be flooded with "ideas, feelings and convictions which" heretofore he had no reason to discuss "in prose." Gill speaks of this flood of ideas as having been caused by Wordsworth's "subjecting political events to the test of general principles," and thus Wordsworth "was, obliquely, writing as if for the *The Recluse*" (276). Gill calls Wordsworth's pamphlet "a Tract for the Times with a distinctly radical orientation" (277); he sees it as "one of the masterworks of English Romantic prose" (276).

Coleridge had assumed that Wordsworth's principles were clear and fixed, and thus in retirement Wordsworth could compose a great philosophical poem, *The Recluse*. Wordsworth reflects this vision of his friend when he speaks of himself in the preface to *The Excursion* as a poet quietly secure in his native clime, intent upon *The Recluse*, "a philosophical poem . . . [whose] principal subject [would be] the sensations and opinions of a poet living in retirement" (*Prose* 3:5). Gill's characterization of the *Cintra* tract as an oblique part of *The Recluse* project is well drawn. But as Gill's comments suggest, Wordsworth hardly seems a poet reposefully speculative. He is vividly engaged in the application of political principles to current events. There seems as much excitement of invention as determined power of judgment. Wordsworth seems to have discovered a whole range of political application unsuspected before, but familiar and cherished in principle since his first days in France.

Gill speaks of the influence of Milton and Burke on Wordsworth (276). I think we should go back further. Milton and Burke are such firm purveyors of their respective doctrines that Wordsworth may have had—at least implicitly—a classical model, a voice not quite so sure as Milton or Burke, one testy and defensive, facing and sensing a skeptical audience. I would suggest

Demosthenes. What comes to mind immediately is his masterpiece *On the Crown*, in which certain parallels with Wordsworth's *Cintra* tract suggest themselves. Though Demosthenes is vitriolic in his references to his opponent Aeschines, he and Wordsworth share a common task of condemning an adversary—Demosthenes, his accuser; Wordsworth, the creators of the Convention of Cintra. More clearly parallel is the way both Demosthenes and Wordsworth argue political liberty as a national tradition always to be served with honor. Both insist that the ordinary person can and should speak out on political issues, and both argue a special epistemological authority, a unique sensibility informed by deep feeling, that makes such political discourse worthy of public esteem.

As John R. Nabholtz has shown, Wordsworth and most major romantic writers were carefully trained in classical rhetoric ("Romantic Prose" 119-20). There are several important classical references and allusions in Wordsworth's *Cintra*. The epigraph is taken from Horace's *Ars Poetica* (lines 312-15). In the body of the text Wordsworth makes the following dramatic claim in speaking of the revolution against Napoleon in the Iberian Peninsula:

> Doubtless, there is not a man in these Islands, who is not convinced that the cause of Spain is the most righteous cause in which, since the opposition of the Greek Republics to the Persian Invader at Thermopylae and Marathon, sword ever was drawn! (*Prose* 1:229-33)[3]

These battles, Marathon in 490 B.C. and Thermopylae in 480 B.C., were two of the most illustrious events in Greek and possibly all of Western European history (Hooper 157-65; Fine 287, 305, 315).

Wordsworth admired the Greeks, and despite negative comments by De Quincey and Jane Worthington,[4] as a grammar school student he was very well trained in Greek. First of all, at Hawkshead School he had excellent, scholarly headmasters: James Peake, educated at Manchester Grammar School (De Quincey's school) and St. John's Cambridge; William Taylor, trained by Peake at Hawkshead and then Emmanuel College, Cambridge, and graduated 2nd Wrangler; Thomas Bowman, Bampton School, Westmorland, and Trinity College, Cambridge, and graduated 6th Wrangler (Thompson 334-47; Venn). It is William Taylor whom Wordsworth speaks of so affectionately in *The Prelude* as his beloved schoolmaster who "loved the Poets" and inspired Wordsworth to become a poet himself (*Fourteen-Book Prelude* 10.552-56). What is important is that each of these schoolmasters was himself a good classical scholar and clearly a dedicated teacher. Peake and Taylor were the beneficiaries of reformed grammar school training in classics and both attended Cambridge colleges where undergraduate classical study was done very seriously. Demosthenes figured prominently in the classical component of Cambridge education, as will be seen shortly.

Through the work of T. W. Thompson and Robert Woof's extensive annotations on Thompson's text and through Duncan Wu's *Wordsworth's Reading 1770-1799*, Wordsworth's Greek texts at Hawkshead can be accounted for rather completely. Thompson shows from Ann Tyson's ledger that Wordsworth was in the highest class in the school by January 1785. He was "'in Greek,'" and Thompson and Woof and Wu show from Wordsworth's uncle's accounts that the following Greek texts were gotten for Wordsworth: a book of Greek exercises, a Demosthenes, a Homer, a Lucian, and a "'Hendricks Lexicon'" (Thompson 90-91; Woof [91] identifies the lexicon as "Benjamin Hederick's *Lexicon Manuale Graecum,* a Greek-Latin/Latin-Greek word book . . . several editions in the eighteenth century"). Wu reminds us of Wordsworth's imitations and translations among his juvenilia of such Greek authors as Anacreon, Callistratus, and Moschus. He also notes the translations from the Greek Wordsworth knew and used (*Wordsworth's Reading* 2, 24, 105; see also Wu's "Chronological Annotated Edition" for commentaries on Wordsworth's translations from the Greek).

We should also note that Thompson, again citing the Ann Tyson ledger, shows that an *Anabasis* of Xenophon was gotten for Wordsworth's classmate Robert Greenwood (91). If Greenwood studied Xenophon, so must have Wordsworth. The *Anabasis* was a standard grammar school text.

Finally, Wordsworth must have taken his Greek seriously, and his uncles must have respected him for it. The Hederick's *Lexicon* cost a pound (Thompson 91). Books were expensive in those days, but such an expenditure for a Greek dictionary for a lad in grammar school reveals serious purpose and scholarship.

One reason for Wordsworth's commitment probably was that he hoped to secure a fellowship when he went up to St. John's College, Cambridge, the fellowship held by his uncle William Cookson (Gill, *A Life* 40). St. John's College during James Peake's last years there had gone through a reform of its curriculum. Christopher Wordsworth, in his study of Cambridge academic life in the eighteenth century, devotes an appendix to an account of this reform (352-57). Dr. William Samuel Powell had been elected master of St. John's College in 1765 and immediately set out to raise academic standards by instituting twice-yearly examinations for all classes of undergraduates, except for graduating seniors, who would be taking their university or senate house degree examinations. Texts in the major areas of study were set for each class for each examination. A classics text was thus set for each examination as well. One can draw up a classical curriculum or canon by compiling the classical texts set for these examinations. St. John's College, Cambridge, was one of the most prestigious institutions in the English-speaking world. Although the classics did not figure in the final university examinations, the classics still remained a key feature of academic life and a means of earning academic distinction (Schneider 24-38, 164-65). The classical canon from St. John's surely influenced James Peake, the curriculum at Hawkshead, and Wordsworth.

The St. John's College Examination Book, a two-volume set, records the performance of the students, many by name, for each examination. It provides a kind of academic log. At the end of the account of the examinations for each term, the classical texts set for the next examinations are listed. It is from this source that one can construct the St. John's classical curriculum. It is amazing how relatively narrow this curriculum proves to be, and it is important to note that Demosthenes comes up frequently in the examinations for one or the other class, about every third or fourth year. In Wordsworth's time at St. John's, October 1787–January 1791, Demosthenes was assigned for third-year students three times. Wordsworth was examined on a selection of his orations in December 1789.

In his six examinations, Wordsworth is recorded in the College Examination Book to have done well in the classical part of two. There is good reason to believe that he also did well in two others. One of them included a Greek tragedy. His performance in Demosthenes, unfortunately not clearly indicated, certainly could be argued to have been adequate.[5] Thus we know that Wordsworth was well grounded in classics and could perform well in Greek. Since he had begun Demosthenes at Hawkshead School, where there is no question as to his serious commitment to study, his ability to handle Demosthenes and his familiarity with his rhetoric can be presumed.

Our next concern is the reflection of Demosthenes' *On the Crown* in Wordsworth's *Cintra* tract. But before examining this possible relationship, we should look at the key arguments of the *Cintra* tract. As Friedman illustrates so well, it is a complex work with much repetition, but a work not without a plan. He sees it as having a ballad structure, its ideas argued not linearly but by accumulation or incremental repetition (248). I would agree but also point out that Wordsworth pursues a firm sequence of topics and theses. His immediate purpose is to demonstrate the moral-political vacuity of the Convention of Cintra and the need to redouble British support for Spain and Portugal. Through such joint military action, the defeat of Napoleon in the Iberian Peninsula could be achieved. Wordsworth's ultimate goal, running through the entire tract, is to demonstrate the absolute need of certain perennial principles of human feeling upon which any decent polity must depend and the correlative need of their being publicly articulated and applied to common issues of state.

Almost the first two-thirds of the *Cintra* tract recounts the events of England's intervention in Portugal in order to stop Napoleon, the initial enthusiasm of the British people because of the idealism presumed present in this endeavor, and then their shame at the betrayal of traditional British ideals of liberty by the flaccid handling of the French surrender. It is in this part of the work that Wordsworth vigorously bespeaks his anger with those responsible for the Convention of Cintra. Wordsworth recalls British history when its troops "had faced hunger and tempests" (1302) and compares that tradition with the bent caution of Dalrymple and other British generals in Portugal (1327-29).

Wordsworth is careful in his accusations: "Let me not be misunderstood" (1330). He does not charge the generals with a lack of "personal courage" (1333) but "an utter want of *intellectual* courage" (1335-36, emphasis his).

Ultimately the generals did not realize the moral purpose to be achieved in the Iberian campaign. They thought it was merely to extricate the French; Wordsworth claims otherwise:

> It was not for the soil, or for the cities and forts, that Portugal was valued, but for the human feeling which was there; for the rights of human nature.... (1580-82)

Wordsworth's personal passion in denouncing the betrayal of the generals is matched by his fervor in lamenting the dishonor done thereby to the English tradition of liberty:

> O sorrow! O misery for England, the land of liberty and courage ... the home of lofty example and benign precept.... (2714-16)

The force of Wordsworth's emotional commitment goes beyond condemning generals and lamenting betrayed ideals. It is in Wordsworth's emphasis on feeling that we find the central theme of his *Cintra* tract, and here too we find Wordsworth himself discovering anew the worth of moral feeling in building a just political order. His purpose is not to share new ideas

> but to recall to the reader his own knowledge, and to re-infuse into that knowledge a breath and life of appropriate feeling; ... it is only in these feelings that the powers of wisdom exist. (1001-5)

It is Wordsworth's passionate and personal concern with the emotive quality of political aspiration, the decency of its reforming energy, not merely its presence, that makes his arguments so powerful. It is because of moral issues that the framers of the Convention of Cintra have caused such scandal and thus "the People were compelled by a necessity involved in the very constitution of man as a moral Being to pass sentence upon them" (1034-36).

The last part of his tract argues two points, the moral obligation of Britain to aid Spain and Portugal and the right and even authority of ordinary folk to pronounce upon national policy, war, and even the conduct of professional soldiers. The second is Wordsworth's most important thesis:

> Nor let it be blamed in any man, though his station be in private life, that upon this occasion he speaks publickly ... [on] those measures, which are more especially military. All have a right to speak.... Men will and ought to speak upon things in which they are so deeply interested; how else are right notions to spread, or is error to be destroyed? (1658-70)

This advocacy of populist authority is reminiscent of the Preface to *Lyrical Ballads*. Friedman points out that there is such "great" "consonance among these areas of his thought," "ethics, epistemology, psychology, and aesthetics," that it is difficult to isolate the merely political in Wordsworth. His thought is "highly integrated" (247). Our passage in *Cintra* recalls the populism found in the Preface, especially its basic epistemology and linguistics, "such men [in rural society] hourly communicate with the best objects from which the best part of language is originally derived . . ." (*Prose* 1:125).

Wordsworth's personal concern with ordinary folk and their capacities is related to the function of the poet, also described in the Preface: "the Poet binds together by passion and knowledge the vast empire of human society . . ." (*Prose* 1:141). Owen reminds us that Wordsworth refused to allow any reference to his authorship of *Lyrical Ballads* or *Poems* of 1807 on the title page and suggests that Wordsworth may have feared such association would be "injudicious" (*Prose* 1:216). But Wordsworth does put his name on the title page of *Cintra* and he does quote Horace. Most important, his text argues a fortiori that if the people can speak out boldly by right, so can a poet. In *Cintra* Wordsworth overtly argues politics, but covertly he argues the "language of men" doctrine and the authority of the poet as universal prophet. Ultimately poetry can speak to the issues of state.

The place of the poet as commentator on public life, even war, is related to Wordsworth's aesthetic populism, but it also has a classical foundation and classically is part of the function of a poet. The epigraph to the *Cintra* tract comes from an important passage in an important critical text, Horace's *Ars Poetica*. Horace speaks of the office and the authority of the poet in the last third of the poem. The particular context from which the *Cintra* epigraph is taken speaks of characterization and asserts that the poet must know the various personalities, functions, even specific tasks of such professions as that of a senator, a judge, a general sent off to war, "quod sit conscripti, quod judicis officium, quae / partes in bellum missi ducis. . . ."[6] Horace speaks of what a poet must know in order to write authentic drama. Wordsworth goes beyond Horace: because the poet must know human nature so *imaginatively,* he can *advise* humans so specifically, even generals engaged in war. The king did not want any public discussion of the Convention of Cintra. Wordsworth has a subtext. It argues the authority of the poet in the face of the will of a king.

It is this subtext, reflected in the emotive commitment of Wordsworth, that reminds me of Demosthenes and suggests him as a possible model for Wordsworth in the *Cintra* tract. Wordsworth very probably knew well five orations of Demosthenes, *Olynthiacs* 1-3, *Philippics* 1, and *On the Crown*.[7] All five of these orations concern Philip of Macedon, the ultimate nemesis of the Athenian republic and empire. Demosthenes was Athens' great orator and Philip's great enemy. There are obvious parallels between Philip and Napoleon and between the democratic structures and naval power of Athens and the parliamentary politics and naval superiority of Britain. Demosthenes was an experienced orator; Wordsworth a poet in retirement. Yet even here the personal involvement of each rhetorically in great public issues is interestingly similar. Both assimilate the self ethically to a major cause, both identify the self with the community, and both assert, as private individual and voice and witness, their right to speak in public affairs. These are the striking parallels between Wordsworth and Demosthenes.

I focus on Demosthenes' masterpiece *On the Crown* because it epitomizes the perfections of the other orations as they possibly influenced Wordsworth. The background of the oration dates from the earliest years of Demosthenes' public life, when Philip of Macedon was beginning his conquest of Greece. Demosthenes consistently opposed Philip. Because of intrigues in fourth-century B.C. Athenian politics, Philip found a friend in Aeschines. In 343 Demosthenes failed in his suit to prove Aeschines guilty of treason. They became implacable enemies (Ochs 48-51).

Philip eventually did dominate Greece and decisively defeated Athens and Thebes at Chaeronea in 338. Now defeated and directly threatened by Philip, Athens rebuilt its fortifications. Demosthenes was chosen by his section of the city to manage its part of the project. He was given public funds and also contributed funds of his own. In 336, in a common act of friendship, Ctesiphon proposed that Demosthenes be honored with a golden crown. Ample precedent existed for such a gesture, but Aeschines, Demosthenes' old enemy, prevented the tribute to Demosthenes by charging Ctesiphon with violating Athenian law for proposing to crown a public official while he was still in office and his accounts were unaudited, for proposing that the proclamation of the honor be done in a place contrary to the law, and finally for being in error in his claim that Demosthenes in his advice and service had always acted wisely and in the best interests of the Athenian people (for the major points, see Aeschines 282-95 and Ochs 51-58). Aeschines was technically correct in certain aspects of his charge, but the essence of his attack was neither technical nor necessarily concerned with the law. Ctesiphon offered as a main reason for honoring Demosthenes that he had always been zealous for the good of Athens. Aeschines denied this. Aeschines' attack on Ctesiphon and thus Demosthenes' speech defending his friend largely focus on the character of Demosthenes (Ochs 48-52). In essence, *On the Crown* is both his *apologia pro vita sua* and his defense of Ctesiphon. It is the legitimacy, the efficacy, and the sincerity of Demosthenes, his ethos, that ultimately constitute the argument of *On the Crown*.

I suggested as an obvious parallel between Wordsworth and Demosthenes that both must attack an opponent. As noted, Demosthenes is rather crude, using such expressions with respect to Aeschines as "hireling" (52),[8] "pettifogger" (121), "fox" (162), "vermin born" (242). As Cecil Wooten has pointed out, Demosthenes had to defend himself because he consistently opposed Philip and that opposition ended in Athens' defeat at Chaeronea. He sees Demosthenes as using a pattern of argumentative parallels, positive references to himself and negative references to Aeschines. Wooten notes that Kenneth Burke describes this as "'qualitative progression'" (323-24).

The similarity between Wordsworth and Demosthenes is not, then, one of tone but of the vigorous presence of first-person reference in formal argumentation. Both use the first person with energetic variety and dramatic skill. In

*On the Crown* Demosthenes has two specific addressees: his jurors, who probably numbered "several hundred" (Ochs 52), and Aeschines, whom he constantly calls out to at key points in his arguments. Wooten recounts that some scholars are offended by the acerbity employed at times by Demosthenes. But he also notes that the confrontational presence of an adversary can even allow a "'romantic'" cast to the work. Wooten quotes Northrop Frye in the use of this term (325). A. R. Dyck claims that Demosthenes' attack on Aeschines includes "palpable lies" (43) but adds that it is rhetorically successful especially through Demosthenes' use of a "wealth of almost Dickensian detail" (46-47). Wordsworth is not so confrontational, but he is hardly delicate in his characterization of those who signed the Convention of Cintra.

There is a more profound similarity between Wordsworth and Demosthenes. Both are patriots who evoke an awe for their respective states as citadels of personal liberty, peoples whose free traditions deserve genuine reverence. The main defense Demosthenes offers for his constant opposition to Philip is the Athenian tradition of personal liberty. Philip had to be stopped. There was hesitation among the Greek city-states, but Athens stood up to him. Demosthenes is proud that "I withstood him, and constantly warned and taught you not to surrender" (72). In the dark days before Chaeronea, Demosthenes persuaded the Athenians to do all they could to help the Thebans save their liberty because to do less would be unworthy of Athens' heritage (178).

In one of the most poignant passages in *On the Crown*, Demosthenes confronts the supposed shame of defeat at Chaeronea directly. He begins with the unusual remark, "I wish to say something perhaps startling" (199). He goes on to state that even if they had had "prophetic knowledge" and had known that Athens would be defeated,

> yet not even then ought the city to have abandoned her purposes, as surely as she had any regard either for her reputation or her ancestors or for time to come. (199)

As Demosthenes then explains, Athens only "failed of success" and that failure "is common to all men, when such is the pleasure of Providence" (200).

Though Demosthenes may seem quite resigned in this context, he frequently bristles when he addresses Aeschines directly. He probably recalls his opponent's shrill words in *Against Ctesiphon*. In his accusatory speech Aeschines had condemned Demosthenes for the defeat of Athens. He had asked how Athens could possibly pay tribute to Demosthenes, "the author of the late expedition, the man who betrayed our citizens to destruction" (346). Demosthenes pointedly explains to Aeschines and to his jury that he did not cause Athens' defeat. He was only an orator, not its general (246-47). He insists that in its defeat, Athens simply shared in "the common fortune of the world" (254). But here too, as he defends himself, Demosthenes observes that even in defeat, Athens "deliberately chose the path of honour" (254). Like Wordsworth, Demosthenes' ethical identification with his nation is complete. In opposing Philip, Athens and he had no choice. So also in failure. That was caused by fate, but even in failure honor was maintained. This is ethical identification of the highest sort.

In his defense Demosthenes shares another Wordsworthian ideal, the right of the citizen to speak out. In refusing to accept blame for Athens' defeat at Chaeronea, Demosthenes offers a compelling characterization of the orator *and* of the citizen as spokesperson on issues of state. He vividly describes the very day when war broke out between Philip and Athens. Philip had entered Greece and had captured the city of Elatea. Panic had seized Athens. In the morning following the receipt of the news, at the meeting of the assembly, the herald cried out according to Athenian law:

> "Who wishes to address the assembly?" But no one came forward. And though the herald put the question again and again, none the more did any one arise, although all the generals and all the public orators were present, and the common voice of our native land demanded some one to speak for her deliverance. (170)

Because Demosthenes could help Athens, because he understood Philip and his schemes, he stepped forward and spoke. He offered Athens a plan of defense, which was followed. He then served Athens as fully as he could (179-80). The point here is Demosthenes' courage in speaking out. Aeschines apparently said nothing (180). Further on, Demosthenes defends his proposals. They were the best that seemingly could have been made under the circumstances. He should not now be condemned because they failed in execution (191-95).

Wordsworth argues that the ordinary citizen has the right to speak out on public issues. Demosthenes argues the necessity of courage and candor in so doing. Both in effect argue the same thing. Both see in the free citizen the repository of social truth; Wordsworth seems more democratic in recognizing a broader range of population as the source of that truth (3365-83).

Finally, like Wordsworth, Demosthenes bases his right to speak, his public oratorical authority, on his emotional-moral sympathy with his Athenian fellow citizens. It is as though Wordsworth's theory of "a far more philosophical language" nurtured by a common rural experience (*Prose* 1:125) to a degree had been anticipated in fourth-century Athens. As he nears his conclusion, Demosthenes upbraids Aeschines for insincerity. Demosthenes then insists that a good orator should prefer the same goals as his fellow citizens "and should hate and love the same persons as his country" (280). Demosthenes is not urging jingoism. He uses a splendid image to express a shared sensibility: "the man who has his soul thus ordered will say everything with loyal intentions; . . . [he will] ride at the same anchor with the multitude . . ." (281).

Further on Demosthenes points out to Aeschines why, despite Aeschines' nomination, he, Demosthenes, was chosen to give the funeral oration for those who died at Chaeronea. The orator for that solemn duty "should sympathise in his soul—and this sympathy they saw in themselves and in me . . ." (287).

A final tribute of recognition for Demosthenes' shared sensibility came when, after the funeral, "the fathers or brothers of the dead" were to choose a site for the funeral banquet. This should take place "in the house of the man who was most closely connected with the dead," and Demosthenes' home was chosen (288).

It is a powerful image Demosthenes gives of himself as tethered affectionately to and buoyed with his fellow Athenians, rising and falling in the succeeding swells of common events and shared emotional response. It is an image that clearly shows the rhythm of unified sensibility and identity. No wonder they called on him to speak for their dead, and no wonder they recognized "in his soul" a sympathy truly their own. Thus he shared, articulated, and eased their grief. As one of the most important figures and orators in Athenian history, his identification with his nation makes him a voice at one with them, and yet a distinctive voice. He speaks as a citizen whose heritage of freedom allows him always freely to speak out.

We have argued similarities between Wordsworth's *Cintra* tract and Demosthenes' *On the Crown*. One final parallel deserves notice: like Demosthenes Wordsworth cherishes his emotional identification with his nation. And like Demosthenes that identification in spirit has compelled him to express his feelings when the honor of his nation has been traduced. Thus Wordsworth argues so elaborately that the Convention of Cintra be condemned and the liberation of Iberia be vigorously sought. But he argues even more insistently that his arguments themselves be cherished. He speaks as one of the people, and when the people speak with one feeling and in one voice, "it is from these oracles that rulers are to learn wisdom" (2770-71).

Demosthenes was called upon to speak the funeral oration over those who fell at Chaeronea because the expression of feeling is as important as the feeling itself. All along Wordsworth has argued both the importance of feeling and the need for free public expression. Wordsworth gives us an illustration of just how crucial this combination of feeling and expression can be. He has argued insistently that Iberia must be freed; the honor of Britain demands that it support this cause. Wordsworth sees an Elizabethan parallel to the present situation. Under Sir Philip Sidney, England fought for the freedom of the Netherlands. Wordsworth sees Sidney as a model for patriotism and for expression, and he quotes Sidney's dedication to his cause.

Because of his identifying so closely with Sidney, Wordsworth claims membership in "a spiritual community binding together the living and the dead" (4811-12). The present campaign in Iberia is seen all the more clearly as just because of the parallel Wordsworth sees between it and the cause Sidney served so completely in the Netherlands:

> [Sidney] is an Englishman who sacrificed his life in devotion to a cause bearing a stronger likeness to this [Iberia] than any recorded in history. (4818-19)

But Wordsworth does more than discover a parallel; he is emotionally overcome in his act of and expression of his discovery: "The pen, which I am guiding, has stopped in my hand; and I have scarcely power to proceed" (4830-31). Wordsworth does have more to say as he ends his *Cintra* tract, but those words constitute the core of his peroration. Emotionally he has been overwhelmed both by his feelings of solidarity with Sidney and his expression of these feelings. The emotional power of this passage recalls another powerful passage in his tract, where he claims kinship with the Spanish because they too so identified feeling and voice in one reality and did so "with that simultaneousness which has led Philosophers upon like occasions to assert, that the voice of the people is the voice of God" (970-72).

I have urged that the most important argument made by Wordsworth is that the people have the right to speak. Demosthenes shares this theme. The poet and orator simply personify that right. Both poetry and oratory must be freely spoken because there are truths that will always remain undiscovered, even truths most deeply felt, until they are poured out in words. In his evocation of Sidney, we have Wordsworth the poet expressing himself as he has through the *Cintra* tract. His text reveals a person "feeling powerfully" and expressing himself in "language . . . daring . . . and figurative" (*Prose* 1:160). Wordsworth "ease[s] his heart" (*Prose* 1:197) and speaks up to his king. Even in prose somehow he attests that "Poetry is the first and last of all knowledge . . ." (*Prose* 1:141).

## NOTES

1. The title of the tract reads as follows (*Prose* 1:221):

Concerning
THE RELATIONS
of
GREAT BRITAIN,
SPAIN, AND PORTUGAL,
TO EACH OTHER, AND TO THE COMMON ENEMY,
AT THIS CRISIS;
AND SPECIFICALLY AS AFFECTED BY
THE

CONVENTION OF CINTRA:

*The whole brought to the test of those Principles, by which alone the Independence and Freedom of Nations can be Preserved or Recovered.*

Qui didicit patriae quid debeat;—
Quod sit conscripti, quod judicis officium; quae
Partes in bellum missi ducis.

BY WILLIAM WORDSWORTH

2. Deirdre Coleman's "Re-living Jacobinism" emphasizes Wordsworth's sense of "betrayal" (145), focusing on "the apparent kaleidoscope of political perspectives" in

the tract, Coleridge's negative reaction, and Wordsworth's integration of his "earlier beliefs" with Burke (146). James Chandler's *Wordsworth's Second Nature* explains Burke's influence on Wordsworth; he comments specifically on the *Cintra* tract on pages 42-45. Michael Freidman offers an extensive and sophisticated close reading with a Marxist, Freudian, nondoctrinaire perspective. He sees *Cintra* as "brilliantly argued" and urging the values of morality and "the moral necessity of the passions" as the foundation for true "community" (292).

3. All references are to the 1974 Oxford edition of the *Prose Works* by line number.

4. De Quincey comments negatively about Wordsworth's classical education at Hawkshead and, referring to Greek studies, says, "As to Greek, that is a language which Wordsworth never had energy enough to cultivate with effect" (*Reminiscences of the Lake Poets* 127). Jane Worthington generally follows De Quincey's assessment of Wordsworth's classical education and regards Wordsworth as hardly proficient in Greek. She notes that most of Wordsworth's volumes of Greek prose were translations (16).

5. For a summary of Wordsworth's performance in examinations at St. John's, see Ben Ross Schneider, Jr. 13-17, 28-30. See Duncan Wu, *Wordsworth's Reading* 166-68, for more information on set texts and examination results.

6. Horace, lines 314-15; for commentary, pp. 394-96.

7. As noted, Wordsworth was examined in Demosthenes in December 1789. The classics set text according to the College Examination Book was a selection of his orations as edited by Mounteney, i.e., Richard Mounteney, *Demosthenous Logoi eklektoi = Demosthenis Selectae Orationes* [Select Orations], first edition, Cambridge, 1731. By 1791 this heavily annotated (in Latin) text had gone through nine editions. These editions contained four orations of Demosthenes: *Olynthiacs* 1-3 and *Philippics* 1. The College Examination Book listed Demosthenes' *On the Crown* as a separate set text when it was assigned (vol. 2, no page numbers, examination results and texts set for following examinations listed chronologically). It came up alternately with the *Select Orations,* e.g., in Wordsworth's time in December 1788 and June 1791. Thus, though Wordsworth would not have had to prepare *On the Crown* for December 1789, he could well have studied it at Hawkshead and at St. John's since it came up so often as an examination text and because of its primacy among the orations of Demosthenes. I am indebted to Jean Rainwater, John Hay Library, Brown University, for information on the first (1731) edition of Mounteney, and to Duncan Wu for information from the Bodleian Library on Mounteney's first and ninth (1791) editions and the 1715 edition of Aeschines-Demosthenes. Especially, I want to thank Malcolm Underwood, Archivist, St. John's College, Cambridge, for his kind permission and generous assistance, which enabled me to study the College Examination Book.

We should recall that a Demosthenes was purchased for Wordsworth when he was at Hawkshead. This may be reflected in volumes contained in Wordsworth's library at Rydal Mount. The Shaver *Catalogue* lists the following version of Demosthenes' *On the Crown:*

> Aeschines. Aischinou ho kata Ktesiphontos kai Demosthenous ho peri stephanou logos [in Greek]. Interpretationem latinam et vocum difficiliorum explicationem adjecerunt P[eter] Foulkes, J[ohn] Friend. Editio secunda. Gr. & Lat. 2 pt. Oxonii, 1715. 8°. (4)

This title is simply a transliteration of the Greek, which when translated is "Aeschines. *The Oration of Aeschines* Against Ctesiphon *and the Oration of Demosthenes* On the Crown." Typically this kind of Greek edition came with notes, etc., in Latin. Might the volume at Rydal have been Wordsworth's Hawkshead text? Also listed in Shaver is the following general edition of Demosthenes:

> All the orations of Demosthenes pronounced to excite the Athenians against

Philip, King of Macedon ... Translated into English (with notes) by Thomas Leland. Third edition, corrected. 3 vol. 1777. 8°. SC.107: '2 vols, 8vo ... 1777.' (75)

Volume three of this edition contains translations of Aeschines' oration against Ctesiphon and Demosthenes' *On the Crown*.

8. Demosthenes, *Oration*. All references are to the standard divisions of *On the Crown* as used in this Fordham edition of 1941.

# VI

## THE ORATORICAL PEDLAR

*Bruce E. Graver*

Near the end of his review of *The Excursion*, Francis Jeffrey testily inquired:

> Why should Mr. Wordsworth have made his hero a superannuated Pedlar? . . . Is there anything in his learned, abstract, and logical harangues, that savours of the calling that is ascribed him? . . . The absurdity in this case . . . is palpable and glaring; [Wordsworth evinces] his amiable partiality for humble life, by assuring us that a wordy rhetorician, who talks about Thebes, and allegorizes all heathen mythology, was once a pedlar—and making him break in upon his magnificent orations with two or three awkward notices of something he had seen when selling winter raiment about the country—or of the changes in the state of society which had almost annihilated his former calling. (Jeffrey 29-30)

In this attack, Jeffrey articulates one of the chief characteristics of the Wanderer and of *The Excursion* as a whole: the poem is deeply concerned with the nature of eloquence—of eloquence conceived as the moving power of the orator in the full classical tradition. In exploring this interest, Wordsworth has unabashedly styled his hero a rustic orator: from his first appearance in the poem, we are told of his "sweet" and "pure discourse,"[1] in book IV his "eloquent harangue" (IV.1275) attempts to rescue the Solitary from despondency, and with the "impassioned majesty" of his "fervent voice" (IX.291-92) he delivers its closing "Discourse." Jeffrey is also right about something else: there is something jarring (at the very least) about the idea of a pedlar who possesses this kind of wisdom and eloquence. How are we to accept a character whose range of knowledge reaches far beyond the few books we are told he had read and whose conclusions about "Abstrusest matter" seem drawn from the pages of Cicero and Seneca and Lucretius, rather than from independent "reasonings of the mind / Turned inward" (I.65-66)? Just what did Wordsworth have in mind?

We can begin to understand his intentions by considering the relationship of *The Excursion* (1814) to the two most important rhetorical treatises of Roman antiquity, Cicero's *De Oratore* and Quintilian's *Institutio Oratoria*. As Jeffrey suggests, *The Excursion* is an overtly oratorical poem. The title

## The Oratorical Pedlar

itself is derived from the Latin term for rhetorical digression, *excursio*, a fact strangely absent from critical discussions of a poem that celebrates "the mind's *excursive* power" (IV.1263). Its language is also rich in the vocabulary of formal rhetoric: words such as "discourse," "panegyric," "harangue," "encomium," "eloquence," "eulogy," and "persuasion" occur with surprising frequency.[2] Although presented as a dialogue, it rejects the analytical give-and-take of Platonic dialectic in favor of the exchange of formal speeches, the kind of dialogue favored by Cicero himself and exemplified in *De Oratore*.[3] Especially important are the parallels between Wordsworth's portrait of the Wanderer and Cicero and Quintilian's ideal orator. Like the ideal orator, the Wanderer derives his eloquence from moral vision, and in a small rural community this power of speech gives him extraordinary authority in ethical matters. Several details of the Wanderer's biography reflect or modify classical discussions of how the orator ought to be educated. And when one also considers the Stoic elements in his philosophical positions, it becomes evident that the ideal orator of Cicero and Quintilian must be one of the primary models for Wordsworth's philosophical pedlar.[4]

In making this argument, however, I do not intend to diminish the force of Jeffrey's complaint. Rather, my aim is to focus more clearly on what his complaint really was. That a pedlar, even an extraordinary pedlar, should possess oratorical skill is more than odd; it is subversive of a system of rhetorical education devised in antiquity and institutionalized again in the Renaissance, whose avowed aim was to mold the sons of privileged families into skilled political leaders. Jeffrey understood this threat, as did Hazlitt and, in a different way, Lord Byron. But classical rhetoric has largely disappeared from our schools today. Consequently, we have difficulty with poems such as *The Excursion*, whose very title contains a pun that few understand.[5] Until we recover the rhetorical vocabulary we have lost—that is, until we historicize the language of criticism itself—we cannot come to terms with the poem by which nineteenth-century readers knew Wordsworth best, the poem which Keats called one of the three things to rejoice at in his age (Keats, *Letters* I:203).

In a passage added to *The Pedlar* in 1804,[6] the narrator of *The Excursion* pauses to recognize that

> many are the Poets that are sown
> By Nature; Men endowed with highest gifts,
> The vision and the faculty divine,
> Yet wanting the accomplishment of Verse. . . .
>     these favored Beings,
> all but a scattered few, live out their time,
> Husbanding that which they possess within,
> And go to the grave, unthought of. (I.77-80, 88-91)

The Wanderer is one of these, a Wordsworthian incarnation of the poetical rustic, a Stephen Duck lucky enough not to have been discovered and brought to town. Yet he is also much more. "Strongest minds," asserts the narrator,

> Are often those of whom the noisy world
> Hears least; else surely this Man had not left
> His graces unrevealed and unproclaimed.... (I.91-94)

And so he hopes to rescue him from oblivion by "record[ing] in verse" "some small portion of his eloquent speech..." (I.98, 102). The phrase "eloquent speech" is crucial. In the eighteenth century, "eloquent speech" was synonymous with oratory, and its use here indicates how closely Wordsworth associated the arts of rhetoric and poetry.[7] This association has been noticed before. In writing of *The Prelude,* Herbert Lindenberger argued that the oratorical nature of Wordsworth's verse is an important "sign of [his] commitment to the public realm" and his "desire to maintain communications with the world of affairs." And thus Lindenberger asks us to

> accept the presence of its [*The Prelude's*] rhetoric and willingly suspend our disbelief in the aesthetic validity of this art, which has suffered so great a decline in prestige during the last 150 years that by our own time it has been relegated to the realm of its probable origin, that of political oratory, and specifically the backwoods variety. (106)

That Wordsworth emphasizes the Wander's eloquence, then, indicates that this pedlar is not just some rural piper, rich in woodland ditties, nor even a latter-day Thresher Poet. He is instead a rustic orator, whose wisdom and mastery of language are used to guide and direct the public and private affairs of his isolated community. It is the narrator's task to turn this eloquence into verse, transforming the Wanderer's speech into the philosophical poetry he never was able to write.

The close association of poet and orator is a Ciceronian idea.[8] In the first book of *De Oratore,* Lucius Licinius Crassus asserts that the poet is "closely linked to the orator," then calls him the orator's "partner and almost equal" (I.xvi.70).[9] In Book III, when discussing the necessity of mastering a variety of styles, Crassus again links the two:

> This can in the first instance be observed in poets, who are next of kin [*proxima cognatio*] to orators; how different from each other are Ennius, Pacuvius, and Accius, and among the Greeks Aeschylus, Sophocles, Euripides, although by all of them almost equal praise is won for their different styles of writing. (III.vii.27)

The passage from *Excursion* I that I have just been discussing may actually be modeled on *De Oratore.* In Book II, as Cicero introduces the second day of the dialogue, he explains to his brother why he has chosen Crassus and Marcus Antonius as his principal speakers:

And so I was readier to commit to writing a conversation they [Crassus and Antonius] once had about this subject, first, that I might remove that opinion, which had always existed, that one of them was not very learned and the other was not learned at all; second, that I might preserve in writing [*custodirem litteris*] those notions about eloquence which I considered to have been marvelously expressed by those great orators, to the extent that I might be successful in capturing their thought; and finally, by heavens, insofar as I could, to rescue from oblivion and silence their reputations, which were already waning. For if they could have been known from their own writings, perhaps I would have considered there to be less need for this work of mine; but since one of them had written little, at least that survived, and had written that while young, and the other had left no writings at all, I thought I owed it to such great minds that, while we still held them in living memory, I would render that memory immortal, if I could. (II.ii.7-8).

Crassus and Antonius, like the Wanderer, are both remarkable for their eloquence; like him, they have left little or nothing in writing and are in danger of being forgotten. And insofar as they are remembered, it is as men who were largely unlearned and hence have become the object of some scorn. So Cicero, like Wordsworth's narrator, is self-consciously attempting to preserve something of their eloquence, along with their views on how it is attained, as a kind of memorial tribute. In addition, the order in which Wordsworth presents his ideas, and in places even his phrasing (for example, "I will here preserve in verse" and "custodirem litteris"), may depend on Cicero. The implication is that Antonius and Crassus, Cicero's models of the good orator, are models for Wordsworth's "eloquent Old Man" (IX.459).

Just as important to *The Excursion* is Quintilian's *Institutio Oratoria,* especially the discussion of pathos in books VI and X. Quintilian stresses, above all, that the orator must himself feel any emotions he wishes to stir in others: "The prime essential for stirring the emotions of others is, in my opinion, that we feel the emotions ourselves" (IV.ii.26).[10] But how, he asks, can that be accomplished?

> There are certain experiences which the Greeks call *phantasiai,* and we call *visiones,* through which images of absent things are so represented to the mind, that we seem to see them before our eyes and actually to have them at hand.... When the mind is at leisure, or filled with empty hopes and daydreams, we are so absorbed by the visions which I speak of that we seem to travel, to sail, to fight, to speak to people, nor do we seem to imagine these things, but to do them.... From such visions comes enargeia, called by Cicero *illustratio* and *evidentia,* by which we seem not to tell but to show, moved just as if we were present at the actual event. (VI.ii.29-32)[11]

Deeply felt emotion, then, is the source of eloquence; without the ability to recreate powerful feelings within himself, the orator cannot hope to succeed. In Book X, Quintilian repeats these ideas and adds the following:

> Pectus est enim, quod disertos facit, et vis mentis. Ideoque imperitis quoque, si modo sint aliquo adfectu concitati, verba non desunt. (For it is feeling and power of mind which makes us well-spoken. For this reason, even the ignorant do not lack words, if only they are excited by some emotion.) (X.vii.15)

Both of these passages were well known to Wordsworth. Book VI is echoed in the 1802 addition to the Preface to *Lyrical Ballads*, and the first sentence of the passage from Book X was quoted as a motto for *Lyrical Ballads* 1802 and 1805.[12] But more germane to my purposes are the ways in which Quintilian's ideas inform Wordsworth's representation of the Wanderer. Early in the Wanderer's biography, we are told:

> While yet a Child . . .
> He had perceived the presence and the power
> Of greatness; and deep feelings had impress'd
> Great objects on his mind, with portraiture
> And colour so distinct, that on his mind
> They lay like substances, and almost seemed
> To haunt the bodily sense. . . . (I.134-39)

>             he thence attained
> An active power to fasten images
> Upon his brain; and on their pictured lines
> Intensely brooded, even till they acquired
> The liveliness of dreams. (I.144-48)

Besides stressing the peculiar power of his memory—which, according to Quintilian, is "the surest sign of genius" (I.iii.1) in young students—these lines demonstrate that the Wanderer possesses exactly the imaginative capability that Quintilian believed necessary for eloquent speech. His *visiones* are the Wanderer's lively dreams. Later in Book I, the narrator confirms this capability when he tells us:

>             He had rehearsed
> Her homely Tale with such familiar power,
> With such an active countenance, an eye
> So busy, that the things of which he spake
> Seemed present. . . . (I.614-18)

Nor is it the narrator only that is moved by his eloquence. After the Wanderer's lengthy discourse in Book IX of the poem, the Pastor's wife remarks:

> I love to hear that eloquent Old Man
> Pour forth his meditations, and descant
> On human life from infancy to age.
> How pure his spirit! in what vivid hues
> His mind gives back the various forms of things,
> Caught in their fairest, happiest attitude!

> While he is speaking I have power to see
> Even as he sees.... (IX.459-66)

Once again, the Wanderer's power to make his audience see what he describes, a power that springs from the vividness of his own imagination, is the distinguishing characteristic of his eloquence. In this respect also, his character seems modeled on the ideas of Roman rhetoricians.

Also important to Wordsworth's conception of the Wanderer is the close association between oratory and philosophy, which is discussed at length in both *De Oratore* and the *Institutio*. Throughout *De Oratore*, Crassus argues for the importance of philosophical study to the orator. In Book I, he asserts that the orator must have philosophical training because only by that means can he gain the knowledge of human nature necessary to his calling. In Book III, he notes that originally the study of eloquence and philosophy were one and the same, and blames Socrates for their separation into two distinct disciplines. This rift has hurt both philosophers and rhetoricians, for the two groups have subsequently looked down on one another, to the detriment of both. For Crassus, and by extension for Cicero himself, the perfect orator must be an accomplished philosopher as well.

Quintilian not only stresses the necessity of philosophical study but argues further that the ideal orator must be morally virtuous. "We teach, then, the perfect orator," he writes in the Proem to Book I, "who cannot exist unless he be a good man; consequently, we require in him not only an exceptional ability in speaking, but a virtuous character as well" (I.Pr.9). This is a position he returns to throughout the treatise, most emphatically in Book XII:

> For I do not only say that it is proper for the orator to be a good man, but that no one can be an orator unless he is a good man.... Therefore, the same person can never be a bad man and a perfect orator. (XII.i.3, 9)

Nor can the orator simply be virtuous by nature; only through the study of philosophy can he acquire the necessary moral discipline:

> Since therefore the orator is a good man and cannot be understood apart from virtue, virtue, even though it derives its impulses from nature, nevertheless must be perfected by education.... (XII.ii.1)

> Authors who teach about virtue must be read thoroughly, so that the life of the orator may be joined with knowledge of matters divine and human. (XII.ii.8)

Quintilian then subdivides philosophy into its three main branches—dialectic, ethics, and natural philosophy—and discusses the relevance of each to the orator's duties. Dialectic is of obvious importance,

> since it is often useful both in definition, and classification, and separating those things which are different, and resolving ambiguity, distinguishing, dividing, enticing, entangling.... (XII.ii.13)

Yet, since his aim is "not only to teach but even to move and delight his audience" (XII.ii.11), the orator must not get bogged down in too much subtlety of argumentation. Ethics also is entirely suited to oratory: forensic and deliberative rhetoric nearly always turn on moral questions, and epideictic, "which is comprised of the duties of praise and blame, often concerns itself with discussion of right and wrong" (XII.ii.16). Natural philosophy, too, needs careful attention—in Quintilian's view, perhaps more than the other two. It is, he says,

> richer than the other branches of philosophy for exercising oratorical skill, in as much as divine subjects require a loftier form of speech than human ones.... Finally, how can eloquence be understood at all by men ignorant of the best things? (XII.ii.20-21)

Throughout this discussion, Quintilian repeatedly makes clear that he is not arguing that orators must be philosophers. Indeed, he believes the solitary life of the philosopher to be radically opposed to the orator's life of public service. Rather, he asserts that the good orator must constantly discourse on philosophical subjects, and without a clear understanding of them, true eloquence can never be attained.

The Wanderer is a rusticated version of Cicero and Quintilian's philosophical orator. He is emphatically a good man, and throughout the poem serves as the voice of moral virtue. His goodness, we are told, has much to do with his upbringing. His stepfather "zealously bestowed" on him

> Needful instruction; not alone in arts
> Which to his humble duties appertained,
> But in the love of right and wrong, the rule
> Of human kindness, in the peaceful ways
> Of honesty, and holiness severe.[13]

And these were lessons not just learned:

> the very Children taught
> Stern self-respect, a reverence for God's word,
> And an habitual piety, maintained
> With strictness scarcely known on English ground. (I.114-17)

So the principles of moral goodness are laid in his mind and maintained with a piety so "austere and grave" that it is as reminiscent of Stoic ethics as of orthodox Christianity.[14] Although the Wanderer has read little in the way of ethical philosophy, Wordsworth asserts that

> He had small need of books; for many a Tale
> Traditionary, round the mountains hung,
> And many a Legend, peopling the dark woods,
> Nourished Imagination in her growth,

> And gave the Mind that apprehensive power
> By which she is made quick to recognize
> The moral properties and scope of things. (I.163-69)

Later in life, this "apprehensive power" is augmented by his wide experience of

> Men,
> Their manners, their enjoyments, and pursuits,
> Their passions and their feelings. . . .
> Hence it came
> That in our best experience he was rich,
> And in the wisdom of our daily life. (I.341-43, 371-73)

Thus he becomes "beloved" (II.56) in his community, offering "the voice of an experienced Friend" (II.64), serving as "a judge" (II.75) in moral issues, and giving "sentence / So grounded, so applied, that it was heard / With softened spirit,—even when it condemned" (II.78-80). He is, in short, the moral guide of an entire rural community.

The Wanderer is accomplished in dialectic and natural philosophy as well as in ethics. His skills in dialectic are evident throughout the poem, especially in those books, such as IV and IX, where he delivers his long argumentative speeches and responds to specific objections and counterarguments, usually voiced by the Solitary. But it is as a natural philosopher that the Wanderer is most interesting. The tenets of his philosophy are summed up in the opening lines of Book IX:

> "To every Form of Being is assigned . . .
> An *active* principle:—howe'er removed
> From sense and observation, it subsists
> In all things, in all natures, in the stars
> Of azure heaven, the unenduring clouds,
> In flower and tree, in every pebbly stone
> That paves the brooks, the stationary rocks,
> The moving waters, and the invisible air.
> What e'er exists hath properties that spread
> Beyond itself, communicating good,
> A simple blessing, or with evil mixed;
> Spirit that knows no insulated spot,
> No chasm, no solitude; from link to link
> It circulates, the Soul of all the Worlds.
> This is the freedom of the Universe;
> Unfolded still the more, more visible,
> The more we know; and yet is reverenced least
> And least respected, in the human Mind,
> Its most apparent home." (IX.1.3-20)

Worthington argued that this passage is derived from Stoic natural philosophy, perhaps directly from Cicero's *De Natura Deorum,* and even contains translations of several key Stoic terms (52-53). Newton Stallknecht (276-81) countered that Wordsworth's primary debts are not to Cicero but to Shaftesbury and Kant, who "contribute toward the formulation of modern Stoicism...." Whatever his source, we are not told that the Wanderer had read such works; rather, his biography implies that his natural philosophy is the product of observation and meditation. Consider, for instance, the following passage from Book I:

> in the after day
> Of Boyhood, many an hour in caves forlorn,
> And 'mid the hollow depths of naked crags
> He sate, and even in their fix'd lineaments,
> Or from the power of a peculiar eye,
> Or by creative feeling overborne
> Or by predominance of thought oppress'd,
> Even in their fix'd and steady lineaments
> He traced an ebbing and a flowing mind,
> Expression ever varying! (I.153-62)

These lines trace his earliest perceptions of the ideas articulated in Book IX: they are presented as conclusions derived from his observation of natural phenomena, not as the products of reading. Later we are told that "before his eighteenth year"

> often, failing at this time to gain
> The peace required, he scanned the laws of light
> Amid the roar of torrents, where they send
> From hollow clefts up to the clearer air
> A cloud of mist, which in the sunshine frames
> A lasting tablet—for the observer's eye
> Varying its rainbow hues. (I.293-98)

This is an unmistakable reference to Newton's *Optics,* and, in a very general way, the Wanderer seems to draw conclusions similar to Newton's.[15] Yet we are not told that he had read the *Optics;* his conclusions, once again, are presented as the products of observation, not reading. Wordsworth seems to imply that given a powerful enough mind, the Wanderer's kind of ideal eloquence can be self-taught, or derived from a combination of experience, habits of meditation, and limited yet carefully chosen reading.

It is on the issue of formal education that *The Excursion* departs most noticeably from the Roman ideal of the orator. Though granting great importance to natural talent, Cicero nevertheless insists that the orator be rigorously educated, not only in his own art but also in all subjects upon which he might be called to speak. The range of those subjects is very broad indeed.

> The power of eloquence is so great that it embraces the origin, force, and developments of all things, of all virtues, duties, and of all nature, which gov-

erns the customs, minds, and life of mankind, and determines the customs, laws, and rights, and controls the state, and expresses everything that concerns whatever topic gracefully and copiously. (III.xx.76)

Quintilian is just as insistent. The average orator, he says, may owe more to nature than to education, but not the perfect one. Indeed, his treatise itself is an attempt to set out systematically the curriculum and methods of a rhetorical education, and that curriculum includes poetry, music, astronomy, philosophy, and geometry as well as law and rhetoric itself.[16] Such an education is extremely expensive and can be meant only for a privileged few, such as the imperial family Quintilian himself served. George Kennedy even suggests that the ideal orator Quintilian described would have had to be an emperor.[17] Given both writers' emphasis on the political importance of the orator—Cicero goes so far as to credit the power of oratory with civilizing mankind (I.viii.33)—it seems clear that this education is one of the most visible means by which a patrician elite exercised and maintained its political power.

In this light, we can begin to see how problematic Wordsworth's Wanderer really is. He is not just an absurd anomaly; his self-taught wisdom and eloquence, comprehensive of even Chaldean astronomy and the practices of Greek rhapsodes, represents a threat to the power of the educated classes. It is this threat that underlies the attacks of Jeffrey, Hazlitt, and Byron: "'Pedlars' and 'boats' and 'wagons'! Oh! ye shades / Of Pope and Dryden, are we come to this?"[18] These attacks are not without foundation; nor were they unforeseen. Wordsworth anticipates them himself within *The Excursion*, through the voice of his skeptical Solitary. Near the beginning of Book VIII, describing with a certain dry humor the function Wordsworth's pedlar has in fact performed in the poem, the Solitary makes an absurd extension of that function to the entire class of pedlars. Not just the Wanderer, he claims, but *all* pedlars are the knights errant of the modern world, wandering about "hill and dale, / Carrying relief for Nature's simple wants" (VIII.47-48). Then, after turning them into the happy husbandmen of Virgil's *Georgics* as well,[19] he defines their noble quest:

> Versed in the characters of men; and bound,
> By tie of daily interest, to maintain
> Conciliatory manners and smooth speech;
> Such have been, and still are in their degree,
> Examples efficacious to refine
> Rude intercourse; apt Instruments to excite,
> By importation of unlooked-for Arts,
> Barbarian torpor, and blind prejudice;
>   Raising, through just gradation, savage life
> To rustic, and the rustic to urbane. . . .
> Could the proud quest of Chivalry do more? (VIII.62-71, 81)

This exaggerated praise turns pedlars, Jeffrey's dealers in "flannel and pocket-handkerchiefs" (Jeffrey 30), into the prime agents for civilizing uncultured rustics. The absurdity is indeed palpable and glaring. It turns the Wanderer into a lower-class Quixote, tilting madly against "Barbarian torpor, and blind prejudice."

The old man either misses or ignores the Solitary's irony. "Happy . . . [t]hey who gain / a panegyric from your generous tongue!" (VIII.82-83) he rejoins, then launches into his invective against the Industrial Revolution, in which he blames modern industrialism for depriving human labor of its dignity and human beings of the "liberty of mind" (VIII.321) that he thinks characteristic of rural life. And so the Solitary is forced to get more explicit. The eyes of "the whistling Plough-boy" (VIII.398), he says, are not bright with intellectual freedom; rather, they are

> Wide, sluggish, blank, and ignorant, and strange;
> Proclaiming boldly that they never drew
> A look or motion of intelligence. . . .
> This torpor is no pitiable work
> Of modern ingenuity. . . .
> —This Boy the Fields produce: his spade and hoe,
> The Carter's whip which on his shoulder rests
> In air high-towering with a boorish pomp,
> The sceptre of his sway; . . .
> In brief, what liberty of mind is here?
> (VIII.410-12, 421-22, 425-29, 433)

This is exactly the position expressed by Hazlitt in his two-part "Observations on Mr. Wordsworth's Poem *The Excursion*." "All country people hate each other," he wrote. "Ignorance is bad enough, but rustic ignorance is intolerable." (*Complete Works* 4:122-23) Nor does the Wanderer object to this crude, Crabbe-like portrait, even in his lengthy response to it in the middle of Book IX. So much for the moral superiority of the country. However much Wordsworth may seem to praise rural life and admire the rustic orator he has invented as its spokesman, he never loses sight of the difficulties such a character presents, and he anticipates our ambivalence by articulating it himself.

I conclude by turning to the Wanderer's response to the Solitary, and in so doing, return to the whole question of education. For that response is a prophetic vision of universal, state-supported education, which would act as an antidote to ignorance and a guarantor of national liberty. With such a system in place, Britain would at last fulfill her imperial destiny:

> Change wide, and deep, and silently performed,
> This Land shall witness; and, as days roll on,
> Earth's universal Frame shall feel the effect
> Even 'till the smallest habitable Rock,
> Beaten by the lonely billows, hear the songs
> Of humanized Society; and bloom
> With civil arts. . . . (IX.384-90)

Thus by "Culture" and "Education,"[20] not by "destruction," Britain shall "Shew to the wretched Nations for what end / the Powers of civil Polity were given!" (IX.413-15) In short, eloquence will be available to all, not just the privileged few, and Britain, like the Rome of Augustan propaganda, shall lead the world to a new and better age.[21] As late twentieth-century readers we smile at such naïveté, or perhaps even shudder. But we do not need the perspective of two centuries to do so; we need only listen to the poem. Shortly after the Wanderer ends his speech, "the gentle Lady" (IX.418) of the Vicarage whispers in the narrator's ear, and with her words I will close:

> I love to hear that eloquent Old Man
> Pour forth his meditations, and descant
> On human life from infancy to age.
> How pure his spirit! In what vivid hues
> His mind gives back the various forms of things,
> Caught in their fairest, happiest attitude!
> While he is speaking I have power to see
> Even as he sees; but when his voice hath ceased,
> Then, with a sigh I sometimes feel, as now,
> That combinations so serene and bright,
> Like those reflected in yon quiet Pool,
> Cannot be lasting in a world like ours,
> To great and small disturbances exposed.[22]

### NOTES

1. Throughout I quote from the Woodstock facsimile of the first edition of *The Excursion*. For ease of reference, I include the corresponding line numbers from *Poetical Works* V. The phrase "sweet discourse" is in the *apparatus criticus* for I.62-63; "pure discourse" is found at I.73.

2. According to Lane Cooper's *Concordance*, "panegyric" and "encomium" can be found in *The Excursion* and nowhere else in Wordsworth's verse; five out of six instances of "persuasion" and "persuasively," nine out of twenty instances of "eloquence" and "eloquent," and fifteen out of thirty instances of "discourse" are also in the poem.

3. George A. Kennedy (*Art of Rhetoric* 209) makes this point about the form of *De Oratore*. Lee M. Johnson (*Wordsworth's Metaphysical Verse* 125ff.) discusses *The Excursion* as "a poetic successor . . . to the philosophical dialogue, in which difficult themes may be developed discursively and at leisure." As obvious as this assertion seems, it is nevertheless the case that even Judson Lyon's study, which is still the most thorough investigation of the poem's sources, mentions no philosophical dialogues except Berkeley's *Alciphron* (29-60). More recently, Alan G. Hill has suggested that the *Octavius* of Minucius Felix, itself a Ciceronian dialogue, is a model for *The Excursion*.

4. Jane Worthington (43-74) has discussed at length the Wanderer's Stoicism. Her study, despite its close attention to Cicero's political and philosophical writings, has almost nothing to say about his rhetorical ones. Quintilian's *Institutio Oratoria* is mentioned in an appendix but not discussed.

5. The only reading of *The Excursion* to use much of the vocabulary of classical

rhetoric is Johnson's (*Wordsworth's Metaphysical Verse* 123-174). Johnson talks of the *narratio, propositio, refutatio,* and *peroratio* of Book IV, and discusses Book IX as a *peroratio*. Kenneth Johnston (273) refers to "the Wanderer's peroration." But the norm is represented by Susan Meisenhelder (70-76, 213-228) who, even when talking about the Wanderer's "rhetorical role" (an entry in her index), never employs the language of classical rhetoric to describe it.

6. The passage first appears in MS. E² of *The Pedlar*. According to James Butler, editor of Wordsworth, *The Ruined Cottage and The Pedlar* (32-33, 378-379), this manuscript "must have been written quite close to" March 6, 1804, when Dorothy Wordsworth began copying MS. M, the copy of *The Pedlar* Coleridge took with him to Malta.

7. See, for example, Hugh Blair's discussion of eloquence in Lecture 25 (1860, 261-73). In both MSS. E² and M of *The Pedlar,* the phrase is "eloquent words" (*The Ruined Cottage and The Pedlar* 391). The revision to "eloquent speech," which occurs in MS. P (*Poetical Works* V:11), suggests that when revising *The Pedlar* for *The Excursion*, Wordsworth wanted to emphasize the Wanderer's role as an orator.

8. I am indebted to Richard W. Clancey for this observation.

9. Citations are to the Loeb Library edition. Translations sometimes depend on the Loeb version, but are usually my own.

10. Citations are to the Loeb Library edition. Translations sometimes depend on the Loeb version, but are usually my own.

11. George Kennedy (*Quintilian* 75) believes that "the rhetorical theory outlined in th[is] passage is apparently chiefly a contribution of Quintilian himself."

12. See *Prose Works* I:176-77, where both passages are cited. The editors cite similar passages in Dennis, James Beattie, and Hugh Blair; Blair himself quotes these passages of the *Institutio*. The relevant passage from the Preface to *Lyrical Ballads* reads:

> To these qualities he has added a disposition to be affected more than other men by absent things as if they were present; an ability of conjuring up in himself passions, which are indeed far from being the same as those produced by real events, yet . . . do more nearly resemble the passions produced by real events, than anything which, from the motions of their own minds merely, other men are accustomed to feel in themselves:—whence, and from practice, he has acquired a greater readiness and power in expressing what he thinks and feels. . . . (*Prose Works* I:138)

13. These lines were removed from *The Excursion* in 1827. They can be found in the *apparatus criticus* to I.111, *Poetical Works* V:11-12.

14. Worthington (59-74) discusses the place of Stoic ethics in Wordsworth's poetry; she asserts that "the ethics of Stoicism is concentrated in the writings . . . published between 1807 and 1815" (59).

15. This passage and its connection to Newton are discussed by W. K. Thomas and Warren Ober (37-38).

16. Kennedy (*Art of Rhetoric* 207) claims that "Quintilian's greatest achievement was his expansion of a review of rhetorical theory into a whole program for the education of the orator." Quintilian's argument for including rigorous geometrical training in his curriculum (I.x.34-49) needs attention in Wordsworthian criticism, especially given Wordsworth's insistence on the importance of geometry in his own development. Lee Johnson's study, for instance, does not mention Quintilian at all.

17. "It is difficult to think that Quintilian's great orator in the fullest sense can be anyone other than some future emperor, especially when we recall the picture in book one where the teacher is compared to Aristotle taking Alexander the Great upon his knee, or the fact that Quintilian had become tutor to Domitian's heirs. As Plato had longed for a philosopher-king, so Quintilian longs for an orator-emperor" (Kennedy, *Art of Rhetoric* 512).

18. *Byron, Don Juan* III.100.1-2 in the Oxford *Byron*.

19. In a general way, this passage is indebted to two famous passages from the Georgics: I.125-46, the so-called Jupiter theodicy, and II.458-74, Virgil's praise of rural life. More specifically, "irksome toil" (VIII.50) is a translation of Virgil's "labor ... improbus" (*Georgics* I.145-46); this phrase was also used by Milton in *Paradise Lost* IX.242. "Kind Nature's various wealth is all their own" (VIII.61) is Wordsworth's free version of "dives opum variarum," (*Georgics* II.468); this line was first composed in 1788, as part of his attempt to translate various passages from *Georgics*. For a fuller discussion, see Graver (141-42).

20. See the *apparatus criticus* to IX.392-93, *Poetical Works* V:298.

21. The Wanderer's speech, as a whole, echoes Jupiter's prophecy in *Aeneid* I.257-96.

22. The 1814 version of these lines is recorded in the *apparatus criticus* to IX.459-73, *Poetical Works* V:301.

# VII

# WORDSWORTH'S *POEMS, IN TWO VOLUMES* (1807) AND THE EPIDEICTIC TRADITION

## *David Ginsberg*

William Wordsworth's *Poems, in Two Volumes* of 1807 has received the harshest criticism of any of his verse collections. Yet it contains many of his best-liked and most anthologized poems—the short lyrics on humble objects, the greater lyrics "Ode to Duty," "Resolution and Independence," and the Immortality Ode. Contemporary critics charged that in this collection Wordsworth had descended from a "system" of simplicity to downright silliness. His apparent attraction to "trivial" or "unworthy" subjects was essentially explained away as the aberration of his poetic powers.[1]

In his review of the 1807 collection, Francis Jeffrey, one of Wordsworth's harshest critics, wrote:

> It is possible enough, we allow, that the sight of a friend's garden spade, or a sparrow's nest, or a man gathering leeches, might really have suggested to such a mind a train of powerful impressions and interesting reflections; but it is certain, that, to most minds, such associations will always appear forced, strained, and unnatural; and that the composition in which it is attempted to exhibit them, will always have the air of parody, or ludicrous and affected singularity. All the world laughs at Elegiac stanzas to a sucking-pig—a Hymn on Washing-day—Sonnets to one's grandmother—or Pindarics on gooseberry-pye; and yet we are afraid, it will not be quite easy to convince Mr. Wordsworth, that the same ridicule must infallibly attach to most of the *pathetic* pieces in these volumes. (Reiman pt. A, 2: 431; emphasis mine)

I place into dialogue with these remarks the following by Wordsworth:

> As the *pathetic* participates of an *animal* sensation, it might seem—that, if the springs of this emotion were genuine, all men, possessed of competent knowledge of the facts and circumstances, would be instantaneously affected. And, doubtless, in the works of every true poet will be found passages of that species

of excellence, which is proved by effects immediate and universal. But there are emotions of the pathetic that are simple and direct, and others—that are complex and revolutionary; some—to which the heart yields with gentleness; others—against which it struggles with pride; these varieties are infinite as the combinations of circumstance and the constitutions of character. ("Essay, Supplementary to the Preface [1815]," in Zall 185; first emphasis mine)

Jeffrey admits the possibility that lowly, common objects—such as flowers, dogs, cats, birds, and garden spades—can incite powerful thoughts and feelings in their observer, but he denies that these effects can become subjects for serious poetry because they are "unnatural." Genuine emotion associated with common objects cannot rise above the level of pathos, cannot become part of the social ethos. The heart "struggles with pride" against such emotions because they are "revolutionary": they do not conform to the "competent knowledge of facts and circumstances" that most men possess. Yet Wordsworth insists that passions arising from contact with common animate and inanimate objects are fit subjects for poetry as long as these objects are "creative," i.e., they incite recognizable human emotions in the beholder who takes notice of them. Any subject is "eminently poetical," says Wordsworth, if as an object in nature there predominate in it "certain affections more or less permanent, more or less capable of salutary renewal in the mind of the being contemplating these objects."[2]

Jared Curtis has written that reviewers of the 1807 lyrics were not irritated by the poet's having "sucked divinity from flowers" but by his "deliberate emphasis upon the movements of his *own* mind and the great significance he assigned to them." In short, says Curtis, Wordsworth was accused of seeing "too much in too little" (*Wordsworth's Experiments* 32). Stuart Curran agrees with Curtis's assessment, writing that "what is most to be prized in this collection, it might be said, is exactly what Jeffrey detested in it: no other poet has ever written the small so very large or been so true to the value of its inner, absolute life" ("*Multum in Parvo*" 251). Furthermore, both critics see the 1807 *Poems* as Wordsworth's continuing experiment in poetry begun with *Lyrical Ballads*. Curtis observes that the lyrics written in the spring of 1802 (and later published in 1807) "contemplate significance in apparent triviality," a "process" whereby Wordsworth was carrying out "experiments" in symbolic form and symbolic language (*Wordsworth's Experiments* 41, 59-79). And Curran remarks that *Poems, in Two Volumes* was a systematic "assault on the received standards of poetry . . . by which Wordsworth hoped to revolutionize not simply the language of poetry, but its subject matter and the way it was read as well" (234).

In describing what many of the 1807 lyrics do, these and other critics have remarked that they praise, or celebrate, their humble subjects. Curtis observes that in the first Celandine poem in *Poems* (1807) the poet promises "songs in praise of what he loves"; and in the second Celandine poem the speaker "scold[s] himself for his ignorance . . . of the literary tradition, 'thy store of other praise'" (52). Moreover, says Curtis, "the first Daisy poem is another hymn of praise," as is the third Daisy poem (53). Curran notices that many of the short lyrics "celebrate" their subjects: "In 'The Orchard Pathway' [the opening section of *Poems*] Wordsworth begins by celebrating the solid and unprepossessing claims of the natural in 'To the Daisy' . . ."; and "The 'Moods of my Own Mind' begins with a poem 'To a Butterfly' and continues with verses celebrating twilight, ending after nine intervening poems with another 'To a Butterfly' and another celebration of twilight (235 and passim). And Carl Woodring notes that "not always fancifully as in the first of four lyrics entitled 'To the Daisy,' all of Wordsworth's poems and lines in praise of humble creatures carry an ethical, social, and political burden" (*Politics* 99). But despite the significant recognition that "the poet supplies his own praise" (*Wordsworth's Experiments* 53) in many of the 1807 lyrics, critics have not pursued this as an indication of Wordsworth's experiments with the epideictic poetic tradition. By reconsidering the *Poems, in Two Volumes* in light of the rhetorical-poetical genres of praise and blame, I shall show that the collection represents Wordsworth's innovation in the epideictic tradition he assimilated through his study of sixteenth- and seventeenth-century formal and metrical practice.[3]

Helen Darbishire and Jared Curtis have pointed out that in composing the poems of the 1807 collection, Wordsworth was experimenting with the forms and metrics of English Renaissance poetry.[4] Between 1802 and 1807 Wordsworth had read much sixteenth- and seventeenth-century English poetry in the volumes of Robert Anderson's *British Poets,* and undoubtedly had familiarized himself not only with the forms and metrics but also with the genres popular in the Renaissance.[5] If, as O. B. Hardison has written, "Renaissance lyric is more obviously influenced by epideictic rhetoric than any other genre" (95), Wordsworth was in effect modeling his own poetry after the Renaissance epideictic tradition.

The importance of epideictic rhetoric in the Renaissance cannot be overestimated.[6] Epideictic theory found its way into Renaissance culture through "classical rhetoric texts and hundreds of new works of rhetoric and literary criticism produced between 1450 and 1700" (Vickers, "Epideictic" 505). In addition to rhetoric books, there were three other ways in which epideictic reached the Renaissance. First, many Renaissance writers assumed that classical epic, such as Virgil's *Aeneid,* was "essentially an epideictic genre" because they interpreted allegorically the presentation of the acts of Aeneas as praise of heroic virtue (506). Another important reason for the influence of epideictic on Renaissance poetry is the paraphrase of Aristotle's *Poetics* by the twelfth-century Arab philosopher Averroes that "every poem and all poetic discourse is blame or praise. And this is evident from examination of the poems themselves, which concern matters of will—the honorable or the base." O. B. Hardison has asserted that this paraphrase "was accepted in Europe at face value" (35, 34). This bald equation of poetry with rhetoric continued to exert influence on Renaissance literary criticism even after the sixteenth-century recovery of the authentic text of Aristotle had disproved it. Some Italian Renaissance critics continued to claim that "all poetic discourse is either praise or blame," or that the poet is "a perfect man skilled in praise and blame" (Vickers, "Epideictic" 506). A third reason for epideictic's reign is the Renaissance emphasis in rhetorical training on "the ability to argue both sides of a question." For instance, praise of something entails dispraise of something else, usually its opposite. This training was put to use by many Renaissance writers in creating paradoxes, which either praise what is unpraiseworthy or blame what is praiseworthy. Examples of this genre in the Renaissance are legion. Its popularity is born of "the prevailing tendency in Renaissance thought . . . to subject all human activities and insights to praise-blame discriminations" (507, 509).

Such discriminations bear out Brian Vickers's assertion that the Renaissance favored an essentially "ethical conception of literature." The prestige of epideictic was, according to Vickers, not so much based on its applicability to a wide range of subjects as on its "exclusive identification with ethical choices and avoidances." One important instance of this way of thinking, continues Vickers, is George Puttenham's sixteenth-century *Arte of English Poesie,* in which the poetic genres are "organized according to the principles of epideictic" (507, 508).

A. Leigh DeNeef cites Puttenham's work as one of several by English Renaissance rhetoricians that form a "movement away from the formulaic methodology of earlier rhetoricians" in rhetoric manuals toward a simpler listing of rhetorical topoi as "an abridged encyclopedia of possibilities" (214, 218). Instead of how-to textbooks, rhetoricians were providing historical reference guides to rhetoric. This "general theoretical shift" from strict prescriptions to broad possibilities of rhetoric is in part responsible for the prevalence of epideictic topoi in Renaissance lyric poetry, especially Pindaric odes, which celebrated a great variety of occasions. Once topology had superseded methodology, epideictic came to include the celebration of "*any* act and *any* subject."[7] The epideictic tradition was broadened to include such poems as Herrick's "Welcome to Sack" in addition to more "classical" poems celebrating royalty, nobility, and other "heroic" acts and objects.

One symbolic potential of epideictic to which DeNeef adverts is the reflexive nature of praise. While epideictic poetry patently reflects the virtue of its subject, it latently points to the speaker-praiser as himself praiseworthy. And as he is worthy of praise, so is his song. This interconnectivity of the elements in the act of praise has also been emphasized by Joel Fineman, who writes that "as early as Aristotle . . . it is recognized that the rhetorical magnification praise accords its object also rebounds back upon itself, drawing attention to itself and to its own rhetorical procedure. . . ." He also refers to the "circular dynamics by means of which the poetry of praise becomes a praise of poetry itself" (5).

The Renaissance lyrics Wordsworth read between 1802 and 1807 were unquestionably influenced by epideictic rhetoric. Critics have noted in particular that his reading of the poetry of Spenser, Daniel, Ben Jonson, and Milton gave the 1807 *Poems* their "color" of diction and "melody" of cadence, their "charm or fineness" (Darbishire xxxix; Curtis, "Wordsworth" 36). If epideictic poetry in the Renaissance was indeed taken to be "the master model of poetry per se" (Fineman 1), Wordsworth surely absorbed the model in preparation for writing his lyrics, so that he could represent himself as saying with confidence: "I will sing, as doth behove, / Hymns in praise of what I love!" (Curtis, *Poems* 81, "To the Small Celandine," lines 63-64) If we accept that the influence of rhetoric did not stop abruptly with the English Romantic poets, we can come to appreciate these poems in light of epideictic rhetoric.

Wordsworth's "trivial" poems on plants, animals, and inanimate objects in *Poems, in Two Volumes* fall within the ancient rhetorical tradition of "adoxography," or the praise of "things without honor."[8] Indeed, the epigraph printed on the title page of *Poems* in 1807—"hereafter shall our Muse speak to thee in deeper tones, when the seasons yield me their fruits in peace"—gestures toward this tradition: it is from the Virgilian poem *Culex,* commonly found on a list of precedent works in praise of trivial subjects which English Renaissance poets used to introduce their own works of this kind.[9] The epigraph has been taken to refer to Wordsworth's "renew[ed] expectations concerning *The Recluse*'s eventual completion," as well as to the 1807 collection's relative insignificance.[10] Notwithstanding, Stuart Curran in his essay "Multum in Parvo" recognizes the significance of the collection, and his remark that the collection represents Wordsworth's having "written the small so very large" tellingly relates itself to "Much in Little," the title of Kitty Scoular's essay on the poetry of "trivialities" of the English Renaissance.

Scoular writes that there were several reasons for the interest of English Renaissance poets in plants and small creatures. For one, commonplace objects were revered for their religious implications and for their value to science. Second, they were admired for the fine craftsmanship thought to have gone into their making. Finally, they were considered proof of nature's wit and ingenuity: when made large through a microscope they were often thought to resemble larger creatures or to "mirror some aspect of divine truth in small space" (84-87).

The Virgilian phrases "the task is slight; its glory nothing small" and "if small things may compare with great" became, according to Scoular, "the *credo* of many poets treating commonplace subjects" (89). The poets justified their poetic magnifications of these subjects as entertainment, as having political significance to society, or as "emblems containing elevated thoughts in a humble body" (89). Regardless of their aims, however, the poems consistently employed the tactics of epideictic rhetoric.

Such tactics can also be found at work in Wordsworth's "trivial" poems on flowers in the 1807 collection. Wordsworth opens his *Poems, in Two Volumes* with a celebratory poem called "To the Daisy." When the poem was published again in his 1815 collection, Wordsworth added the following epigraph from a poem by the Renaissance poet George Wither, speaking of his muse:

> Her divine skill taught me this,
> That from everything I saw
> I could some instruction draw,
> And raise pleasure to the height
> Through the meanest object's sight.
> By the murmur of a spring
> Or the least bough's rustelling;
> By a Daisy whose leaves spread
> Shut when Titan goes to bed;
> Or a shady bush or tree;
> She could more infuse in me
> Than all Nature's beauties can
> In some other wiser man. (*P2V* 65)

Wordsworth's epigraph ends there, but Wither continues a few lines later with the following:

> Therefore, thou best earthly bliss,
> I will cherish thee for this,—
> POESY! thou sweet'st content
> That e'er heaven to mortals lent.
> Though they as a trifle leave thee,
> Whose dull thoughts can not conceive thee;
> Though thou be to them a scorn
> That to nought but earth are born;
> Let my life no longer be
> Than I am in love with thee.
> Though our wise ones call thee madness,
> Let me never taste of gladness
> If I love not thy maddest fits
> More than all their greatest wits.
> And though some too seeming holy
> Do account thy raptures folly,
> Thou dost teach me to contemn
> What makes knaves and fools of them.
> Oh, high power! that oft doth carry
> Men above—— (Ellis, *Specimens* 90)

Wither speaks of his muse as working through the medium of the daisy, as well as through other commonplace objects. If the daisy incites the poet to celebrate it in verse, the poem may easily be misunderstood as "merely" a tribute to a wildflower, instead of one to Poetry, by those readers who "as a trifle leave thee, / Whose dull thoughts can not conceive thee." The daisy is here the "flower of the muses" whose triumph is celebrated. Wordsworth appropriately chose the epigraph to indicate that he saw fit to celebrate the poetry of the commonplace, a type of poetry with a venerable tradition, albeit an oft-misunderstood one.[11]

"To the Daisy" proceeds in the circular manner of epideictic discourse outlined by DeNeef: "it will begin in praise and end in praise; the middle merely amplifies the deed(s) to justify the praise" (221). In the first stanza, the speaker tells of turning from the "pleasure high and turbulent" of his youth to the simpler pleasure he now derives from the likes of the Daisy:

> In youth from rock to rock I went,
> From hill to hill in discontent
> Of pleasure high and turbulent,
>     Most pleas'd when most uneasy;
> But now my own delights I make,
> My thirst at every rill can slake,
> And gladly Nature's love partake
>     Of thee, sweet Daisy! (*P2V* 65:1-8)

The last two lines are an acknowledgement of the daisy's power to conduct "Nature's love" to the speaker. This recognition is followed by eight stanzas that illuminate, or amplify, the "deeds" of Nature's love emanating from the daisy, a common flower which grows in profusion everywhere, in all seasons, under all conditions. In beholding the singular, emblematic acts or motions within such profusion, the speaker is moved to an "overflow" of thoughts that brim over into an amplificatory speech act.

The speaker goes on to amplify the daisy's acts of fellowship in nature: it soothes and delights the seasons and greets the lonely traveler in need of a "pleasant thought" (11.9-24).[12] More important, however, is its value to the poet, now and heretofore, which has brought it some measure of fame. Already at this point the speaker is calling attention to the daisy as an object famed and celebrated by previous poets:

> Thou liv'st with less ambitious aim,
> Yet hast not gone without thy fame;
> Thou art indeed by many a claim
>     The Poet's darling. (*P2V* 67:29-32)

It remains for the speaker to say what the daisy means to him personally as a poet, and thereby to place himself in line with earlier poets who have celebrated the flower in the epideictic tradition. The speaker has invoked that tradition through his presentation of a praiseworthy "pattern" belonging to the daisy.[13] His selection and arrangement of "representative actions" of the flower are designed to help the reader "visualize the complete life of the subject" (DeNeef 221). Whatever is particularly praiseworthy about the daisy to the speaker must be amplified to emblematic proportions. To produce a successful epideictic speech act about the daisy, the speaker must demonstrate, not prove, what is praiseworthy in it (221).

A selection of the daisy's praiseworthy actions or motions in stanzas five through nine portrays it as a kind of lower-order muse to the poet. The daisy scares off the poet's melancholy (stanza 5) by bringing on pleasant, albeit fleeting, thoughts and apprehensions (stanza 6). Its importance lies in being a stimulator of thought, an "influence" (1. 70), or an "instinct" (1. 69) to lyric celebration. The daisy also aids the poet in converting his "stately passions," his pathos, into "an humbler urn" of "lowlier pleasure," an ethos that represents "A wisdom fitted to the needs / Of hearts at leisure" (stanza 7). The poet also derives gaiety and devotion from the flower as he witnesses its physical motions (stanza 8). He is moved to imitate the flower:

> When, smitten by the morning ray,
> I see thee rise alert and gay,
> Then, chearful Flower! my spirits play
>     With kindred motion:
> At dusk, I've seldom mark'd thee press
> The ground, as if in thankfulness,
> Without some feeling, more or less,
>     Of true devotion. (11.57-64)

It is important to recognize here and elsewhere in the poem "the circularity which makes praise a distinctive rhetorical practice" (Fineman 5). The deictic markers of "thou" and "thee" referring to the daisy in the poem are also "oriented to the speaking self who speaks them" (Fineman 8). The poet's address to a praiseworthy "thou" and "thee" is reflexively a praise of "I" and "me." This "correspondence or reciprocity between objective reference and subjective self-reference" (Fineman 6) ideally aims toward the elimination of the divide between subject and object. The closing of this divide began in the previous stanza, where the speaker refers to "The homely sympathy that heeds / The common life, *our nature* breeds" (my emphasis). Once again in stanza nine the poet expresses his admiration of the daisy as a source of "genial influence," what Wordsworth will eventually call the faculty of the Fancy.[14]

The whole existence of the daisy has now been "compacted into and imaged in those acts" that represent it as a significant muse to the poet (DeNeef 220). It remains for the speaker to end, as he began, in praise of the daisy:

> Child of the year! that round dost run
> Thy course, bold lover of the sun,
> And chearful when the day's begun
>     As morning Leveret,
> Thou long the Poet's praise shalt gain;
> Thou wilt be more belov'd by men
> In times to come; thou not in vain
>     Art Nature's favorite. (11.73-80)[15]

Because the speaker has by now demonstrated aspects of the daisy that when drawn together fully describe it as a genuine muse, he is justified in predicting future praise for it: "Thou long the Poet's praise shalt gain." But the poet is not the first to praise the daisy. Regarding this, we should take note of Wordsworth's revision of the line in 1807: "Thy long-lost praise thou shalt regain." This emphasizes the rediscovery of both the daisy and its place in the literary tradition of praise. What Michael G. Cooke has written in another context we can say of "To the Daisy": that "the process of [its] imagery has served as the instrument of rediscovery. The image makes the argument for joy" (205). In his rediscovery of the daisy, the poet has placed himself in the line of English poets reaching back to Chaucer who have celebrated the daisy, as well as other lowly, commonplace objects, in lyric poetry.

Poems on animate and inanimate objects have figured strongly in the rhetorical epideictic tradition of poetry since classical times. Many such poems have been ignored, if not ridiculed, by critics because they seem trivial, mean, inessential. While I do not argue that such poems are among the great, I believe I have demonstrated that they stand the test of affording "profitable pleasure" because they were designed to do so rhetorically in the epideictic tradition. There is much more than commonly thought in their "little." They may be among the "things without honor," but in their long tradition they have never been things without pleasure.

Whatever their theoretical views of epideictic, all the critics so far introduced agree that it is carried out via the tactics of praise and blame. According to Lawrence Rosenfield, however, praising and blaming is not what epideictic does. Rather, it "acknowledges and disparages," recognizes or refuses to recognize, the "intrinsic excellence" of its object (133).[16] The epideictic speech act makes apparent to an audience the "radiance" or "luminosity" of an object that would "otherwise remain unnoticed or invisible" (135). Rosenfield's reading of Aristotle on epideictic leads him to point out that Aristotle makes an important distinction between epideictic and encomium: epideictic illuminates the interiority of an object without appraising any of its exterior accomplishments; encomium praises, or esteems, the "extrinsic criteria of merit" based on achievements. Accustomed as we are to equating praise with valuation, we need to recognize that to the ancient Greeks one could be said to praise an object for qualities not extrinsically earned.[17] While laurel crowns and encomia lauded the outer achievements of excellence, epideictic speech acts celebrated the excellence within, regardless of extrinsic circumstances. Displaying an object as we normally see it is *deixis,* but envisioning it beyond the mundane is *epi-deixis,* an extradimensional act. To accomplish *epideixis* the rhetor and his audience of beholders need to overleap reality, to open themselves passionately to the world and its love generally hidden from view and to admire it with gratitude. Appreciation of this kind requires that we "reach out in delight" to things as they intrinsically are beneath the reductive veils of common sense perception. We sit in wonder, not in judgment, of the objects we perceive. And "when our wonder brims over into a desire to speak, we ratify in appreciation" (Rosenfield 138).

Wordsworth's references to his second and third Daisy poems as "overflowings of the mind" (*Poems, in Two Volumes* 238) and his poetry at large as "the spontaneous overflow of powerful feelings" (in Zall 19) accord with the pre-Socratic Greek account of the epideictic speech act as the "re-creation of aesthetic revelation" experienced by "those who are open to the wonder of what is, in the very fact that it is, . . . [who are] arrested by some particular of everyday life when they detect in it an indication of the ground from which springs all reality" (Rosenfield 138).

Wordsworth himself gives a clear example of such arrest in his explication of "With ships the sea was sprinkled," included in the 1807 *Poems*. There the speaker is represented as looking out indifferently over the sea "sprinkled with ships," until his attention is suddenly fixed on one of them. The result of this is significant:

> This ship to all the rest I did prefer,
>
> making her a sovereign or a regent, and thus giving body and life to all the rest; mingling up this idea with fondness and praise—
>
> where she comes the winds must stir; and concluding the whole with
>
> On went She, and due north her journey took.
> ("Letter to Lady Beaumont" [1807], Zall 82-83)

The poem demonstrates a Romantic innovation in the epideictic tradition. It is a depiction of the onset of epideictic celebration, in that it distinguishes "that casual attention by which our eyes drift aimlessly to the merely sensational from its more profound counterpart, appreciation, in which mind and soul fasten effortlessly in a moment of understanding" (Rosenfield 141). In this instance the bystander is transformed into a beholder. The epideictic speaker wants nothing less than to give testimony to his "wonder-at-invisibles," to charm rather than coldly persuade his audience to see meaning where none apparently resides (140). Moreover, the speaker does not attempt to confer meaning reductively on his subject by way of topic systems, because these linguistically delimit his experience of the world. What appears to him in his "mind's eye" indeed finds expression in an appreciative overflow of words whose import is criticized by those unwilling to look generously at the things of this world.

Those who harshly criticized the 1807 *Poems* upon publication for its "low, silly and uninteresting" subjects were confusing "the mental act of reaching out to welcome reality" (Rosenfield 136) with "mental bombast," thereby dismissing the "radiance" inherent in unassuming things.[18] To comprehend an epideictic act, one must first be open to the possibilities of acknowledgement of such radiance. Wordsworth has written that "with an eye made quiet by the power / Of harmony, and the deep power of joy, / We see into the life of things" ("Tintern Abbey" 11.47-49). This "life" is indeed the "luster visible only to *nous* ('the mind's eye')," which is "the mind's capacity for a serene but concentrated meditation on the imperishable" (Rosenfield 137). We will be better able to see "into the life" of many of the 1807 poems if we recognize that in Wordsworth we have a Romantic champion of epideictic discourse.

## NOTES

1. For the range of animadversion on *Poems, in Two Volumes,* see Donald H. Reiman (pt. A, vols. 1 and 2), a convenient reprinting of contemporary reviews of Wordsworth. Notwithstanding, William Hazlitt defended the 1807 lyrics on commonplace subjects when he wrote that "no one has shown the same imagination in raising trifles into importance: no one has displayed the same pathos in treating of the simplest feelings of the heart" (cited by Jared Curtis, *Wordsworth's Experiments,* 32 n. 5).

2. In his letter to Lady Beaumont (May 21, 1807), Wordsworth, referring to the poems in the "Moods of My Own Mind" section of *Poems, in Two Volumes,* writes:

> There is scarcely a Poem here of above thirty Lines, and very trifling these poems will appear to many; but, omitting to speak of them individually, do they not, taken collectively, fix the attention upon a subject eminently poetical, viz., the interest which objects in nature derive from the predominance of certain affections more or less permanent, more or less capable of salutary renewal in the mind of the being contemplating these objects? This is poetic, and essentially poetic, and why? because it is creative.

3. By comparing the lyrics to elegies, hymns, sonnets, and Pindarics on trivial subjects, even Francis Jeffrey, who had little praise for the 1807 *Poems,* unintentionally alluded to forms of poetic praise widely accepted by medieval and Renaissance critics (see DeNeef 205).

4. See Jared Curtis, "William Wordsworth and English Poetry" (28-29), and Helen Darbishire (xxxix, 353-463, 465-70). Note also A. F. Potts's remark that in the 1807 *Poems* "there is a residuum of pieces effortful, almost pseudoliterary, as if deriving from models he was trying to redeem or remake" (157-58); Stuart Curran's remark that "Wordsworth had no intention of liberating poetry from its tradition. Quite the contrary, his program seems to have been one of liberating poetic tradition from the museum where it had been encased in all its pastness, of breathing new life into what had been assumed to be dead. . . . [This] principle can be discerned in every form Wordsworth adapts to his use" ("Wordsworth and the Forms of Poetry" 126); and Alan Grob's observation of "the appearance in 1802 of an important new Wordsworthian genre, the lyric apostrophe to nature's more familiar and common objects" (205).

5. See Curtis, "William Wordsworth and English Poetry" (28-29), Potts (67-150), and William Heath (23, 24, 124-27).

6. My survey of the epideictic tradition is indebted to several studies: T. C. Burgess, "Epideictic Literature"; O. B. Hardison, Jr., *The Enduring Monument: A Study of the Idea of Praise in Renaissance Literary Theory and Practice;* Ernst R. Curtius, *European Literature and the Latin Middle Ages,* chaps. 4, 8, 9; George A. Kennedy, *The Art of Persuasion in Greece* and *Classical Rhetoric and Its Christian and Secular Tradition from Ancient to Modern Times;* A. L. DeNeef, "Epideictic Rhetoric and the Renaissance Lyric"; Brian Vickers, "Epideictic and Epic in the Renaissance"; Barbara K. Lewalski, *Donne's "Anniversaries" and the Poetry of Praise;* D. A. Russell and N. G.

Wilson, eds., *Menander Rhetor;* Lawrence W. Rosenfield, "The Practical Celebration of Epideictic"; and Joel Fineman, *Shakespeare's Perjured Eye,* introduction.

7. Cf. A. S. Pease, "Things Without Honor": "Almost all subjects, . . . living, inanimate, or abstract, were material for the [Greek and Roman] panegyrist" (27). This broadening of the possibilities of epideictic in the Renaissance was also facilitated by late Roman rhetoricians who increasingly recognized that "the distinction between a poem and an epideictic oration . . . was often only metrical" (Hardison 32). Perhaps Wordsworth refers to this distinction between two types of epideictic literature when he says that

> it would be a most easy task to prove to [the Reader], that not only the language of a large portion of every good poem, even of the most elevated character, must necessarily, except with reference to metre, in no respect differ from that of good prose, but likewise that some of the most interesting parts of the best poems will be found to be strictly the language of prose, when prose is well written. (Preface to *Lyrical Ballads* [1802], Zall 45-46)

8. See Pease. "Adoxography" was a type of laudation recognized by the third-century rhetorician Menander in his *Peri epideiktikon.*

9. See William Wordsworth, *Poems, in Two Volumes* (49), for a facsimile of the title page containing the Latin epigraph. This Cornell edition, edited by Jared Curtis, will be cited hereafter for all quotations of the poetry and its Advertisement, and referred to parenthetically as *P2V,* with page and line numbers together given thus: page(s):line(s). I cite Curtis's English translation of the epigraph from p. 26 of his introduction to this edition. See also Kitty W. Scoular (94) regarding the use of Virgil's *Culex* to introduce works praising trivialities.

10. Alun R. Jones (xv). Both Jones and Curtis cite in their respective editions Spenser's English translation of the Latin epigraph from his poem *Virgil's Gnat,* lines 9-11.

11. Another example of Renaissance poetry about daisies is Robert Herrick's "To Daisies, not to shut so soone":

> 1. Shut not so soon; the dull-ey'd night
>    Ha's not as yet begunne
>    To make a seisure on the light,
>    Or to seale up the Sun.
>
> 2. No Marigolds yet closed are;
>    No shadowes great appeare;
>    Nor doth the early Shepheards Starre
>    Shine like a spangle here.
>
> 3. Stay but till my *Julia* close
>    Her life-begetting eye;
>    And let the whole world then dispose
>    It selfe to live or dye. (Patrick 221)

This poem uses the daisy figure to express the poet's desire to challenge the mortality of his love. The short-lived flower (the "day's eye") can hold off death, "the dull-ey'd night," only as long as it is opened up in tribute to the sun. It is celebrated, or praised, as long as it celebrates or praises. The identification of the daisy with Julia, eye-to-eye, as "life-begetting" emphasizes the universal harmony among the suns of this world—the Sun, the daisy, and Julia. This hyperbolic comparison is an example of Renaissance paradoxical praise, placing the small on par with the great. With regard to the possible influence of Robert Herrick's poetry on Wordsworth's in *P2V,* the Cornell photocopy of Dove Cottage Papers, MS Verse 81B, contains thirteen lyrics by

Robert Herrick, seven of them flower poems: "To Daisies," "To Primroses," "The Primrose," "To Blossoms," "To Daffodils," "The Sacred Rites of the Rose," and "Go, happy Rose." The manuscript came to my attention by way of notes 15 and 18 of Jared Curtis's article "William Wordsworth and English Poetry of the Sixteenth and Seventeenth Centuries"; he cites the manuscript—which besides Herrick's poems also includes the titles of lyrics by several other prominent Elizabethan and Jacobean poets—as evidence of Wordsworth's strong interest in English Renaissance poetry. Subsequently, my inspection of the MS revealed that half of Herrick's poems in it were flower poems. Also worth noting is Geoffrey Hartman's remark in *Wordsworth's Poetry 1787-1814* that "Herrick's poems are influenced by . . . *The Greek Anthology*" and it may be that the latter is a common source for both Herrick and Wordsworth (380). (Hartman [260] devotes a chapter to the "major lyrics" written 1801-7 and included in *Poems, in Two Volumes,* but he does not discuss "Wordsworth's most familiar pieces" found in it. He implies that the 1807 poems are not "consciously innovative.") According to Kitty Scoular, "For the growth of interest in the writing of short poems on insect, animal, or plant, 1494, the year of the first printing of the *Greek Anthology*," is an important date.

12. The lines praising the daisy as a flower for all seasons are:

> When soothed a while by milder airs,
> Thee Winter in the garland wears
> That thinly shades his few grey hairs;
>     Spring cannot shun thee;
> Whole summer fields are thine by right;
> And Autumn, melancholy Wight!
> Doth in thy crimson head delight
>     When rains are on thee. (11.9-16)

Here we have an adaptation of "the commonplace epideictic topic *laus quattuor temporum*" (Hardison 86) to praiseful comparison of a lowly flower, the daisy, with the four seasons. Such a comparison is tantamount to a kind of poetic conceit, an epideictic paradox, since it reduces high things (the seasons) by praising a low one (the daisy). It may be observed here also that of the three daisy poems in *Poems, in Two Volumes,* the first one describes the daisy as an agent of the muses (or even a small muse itself), while the second and third are examples of the poet under the influence of the daisy-muse.

13. Reference to epideictic "pattern" is made by DeNeef, that "one of the primary functions of the epideictic is to crystalize the life of an individual into a memorable pattern" (228), and by Vickers, citing Hardison, that "the theory was that epideictic praised nobility and made morality attractive, creating 'a pattern of virtue'" (510).

14. James Heffernan observes that "a good example of [the operation of the faculty of Fancy] is 'To the Same Flower' [titled 'To the Daisy' in Curtis's *P2V* 238-39]." This poem and the one following it were to Wordsworth "overflowings of the mind in composing the one [which comes first in *P2V*]" (238). In this poem the poet's Fancy works thus: "And many a fond and idle name / I give to thee, for praise or blame" (*P2V* 238: 13-14).

15. Regarding the tradition of celebrating flowers in poetry, Wordsworth commented on the last four lines of this stanza in an 1815 note: "See, in Chaucer and the elder poets, the honours formerly paid to this flower" (*P2V* 403). In *Legend of Good Women,* Chaucer praises the little red-and-white English daisy, which was "much employed in fourteenth-century poetry for allegorical reasons." The speaker in the poem tells of how the daisy "upryseth erly by the morwe [morning]" and spreads itself "ayein the sonne," and how it closes again at dusk (Gardner 269).

16. Compare Rosenfield's use of the term *acknowledgement* here to Wordsworth's in the following statement:

> Nor let this necessity of producing immediate pleasure be considered as a degradation of the Poet's art. It is far otherwise. It is an acknowledgement of the beauty of the universe, an acknowledgment the more sincere, because it is not formal, but indirect; it is a task light and easy to him who looks at the world in the spirit of love: further, it is a homage paid to the native and naked dignity of man, to the grand elementary principle of pleasure, by which he knows, and feels, and lives, and moves. (Preface to *Lyrical Ballads* [1802], Zall 51)

In support of his own view of epideictic as "the acknowledgement of radiance," Rosenfield quotes Hannah Arendt: "Pleasure, which is fundamentally the intensified awareness of reality, springs from a passionate openness to the world and love of it" (136). Moreover, later in his essay Rosenfield writes that "our acknowledgement of the epideictic speaker's ethos is a joining with him, as he has already joined with what is, in order that we too may go to an encounter with Being, to behold that which is excellent in a spirit of loving attention" (146). This encounter with Being, suggests Thomas McFarland, is a Heideggerian sighting of "pure presence" in the visible ("The Longer Romantic Lyric" 240).

17. In this regard, see not only Rosenfield but also Charles Paul Segal.

18. In the introduction to *Poems, in Two Volumes,* Curtis writes that "in his review Jeffrey praised the sonnets but scorned the poet's 'low, silly, and uninteresting subjects.' Wordsworth began to contend almost immediately with the common charge of triviality and with the more subtle criticism, by Coleridge, of his 'mental bombast.'" To Rosenfield the term *epideictic* is part of the "vocabulary" of "radiance." His view is that "still smarting from the excesses of German idealism, we label all felt experiences 'subjective' and consequently confuse the mental act of reaching out to welcome reality with those counterfeit emotions comprising sentiment. We thus find ourselves dismissing as 'maudlin' the very acknowledgement of radiance that is necessary to comprehend epideictic."

# VIII

## THE CASE FOR WILLIAM WORDSWORTH
### ROMANTIC INVENTION VERSUS ROMANTIC GENIUS

*Theresa M. Kelley*

> The predecessors of an original Genius of a high order will have smoothed the way for all that he has in common with them;—and much he will have in common; but, for what is peculiarly his own, he will be called upon to clear and often to shape his own road:— he will be in the condition of Hannibal among the Alps.
>
> William Wordsworth (*Prose* 3: 80)

> It is easy to find hidden things if their places are pointed out and marked, and, in like fashion, if we wish to track down an argument we should know places.
>
> Richard McKeon[1]

Writing in 1815 to chastise readers and critics unable to discern his original genius, Wordsworth deploys the figure of Hannibal making his own way through the Alps to dramatize the heroic, self-authorized productivity that distinguishes ordinary road builders and poets from the genius of a Hannibal or a Wordsworth. For readers ever since, Wordsworth's self-representation has helped to shape critical understanding of romanticism, together with a larger set of cultural assumptions about originality that have in turn grounded theories of writing and creativity for most of the twentieth century.

And yet Wordsworth's notice of Hannibal in the Alps is shot through with signs of its rhetoricity, signs that cut across the declared figural logic of poetic self-origination. For if Hannibal is not a poet-precursor, he is nonetheless a precursor, the very type and pretext of heroic and imperial inventiveness, recognized as such by Wordsworth's contemporaries and, most notably, by Napoleon. Before and after his successful Alpine passage in 1800, travelers and classicists repeatedly guessed or declared which pass Hannibal had used to cross the Alps. In Jacques-Louis David's 1802 painting of Napoleon at the St. Bernard Pass, commissioned and closely supervised by Napoleon himself, two names—Hannibal and Charlemagne—were inscribed in the rock below the general (by 1802 first consul and soon to become emperor) astride his charging mount (Nicholson 97-102; Woodring, "Road Building" 23-29).[2] For Wordsworth writing in 1815, the figure of Hannibal had already become a Romantic commonplace for the self-made hero and strategist. And, like ancient rhetorical commonplaces, this one invokes a string of precursors.

I am interested here in the implications of Wordsworth's double figural itinerary for our understanding of the kind of Romantic invention he is said to have authorized. In his absorbing study of modes of invention in the Western tradition, Gerald Bruns calls its Romantic expression "that power of original conception" to which he opposes versions of the classical rhetorical model that are his subject. As Bruns makes clear, this account of Romantic "invention" has two poetic consequences: a desire to "authorize or lay claim to an original moment of discourse" and a preference for the "closed or systematically self-contained text" whose "characteristic unity" New Criticism investigated (102). A similar claim impels Terry Eagleton's analysis of the emergence of imaginative literature as a separate category during the Romantic era, when "the literary work itself comes to be seen as a mysterious organic unity" whose counterpart is "the intuitive, transcendental scope of the poetic mind" (18). The post-Romantic residual of this view of Romanticism is suggested by the claim that modernist poetics require or display "act[s] of mind" that seek the unity of their supreme fictions (2-7).

Poststructuralist skepticism about the version of Romanticism created and sustained in the name of original genius and organic unity has done little to dislodge this critical consensus. As compositional theory begins to defend the role of rhetorical invention (LeFevre 33-47), Romanticism is still cast as the anti-inventional "other" in the history of rhetoric. In their anthology of key texts in the rhetorical tradition, Patricia Bizzell and Bruce Herzberg present Romantic values such as "solitude, spontaneity, expression of feeling and imagination" as a collective marker for the "antirhetorical" character of the period (665). John Bender and David Wellbery argue that the distinctive rhetoricality of post-Renaissance culture is shaped by Romantic poets' disavowal of rhetoric as the ground of their poetic theory. In this fashion, Bender and Wellbery claim, Romanticism extends the legacy of Descartes to assert that "poetic talent and imagination dwell solely within the inwardness of the subject" (11). But for other recent critics, the Romantic (and post-Romantic) cult of antirhetorical originality and organic unity has become something of a liability. As Jerome McGann's successive polemics against a self-authorizing "romantic ideology" make clear, the figure of Wordsworth as an heroic "original genius" can be used to critique the very aesthetics of sublime genius that readers have until lately preferred to celebrate (81-92).

Against this tide of praise and blame, I want to array a different argument, one initially indebted to critics who have been attentive to historical and generic pressures on claims to originality, Romantic or otherwise (Bloom, *Anxiety of Influence* 57; McFarland, *Originality* 85; Hollander 42-45; Weinsheimer 49-92).[3] My understanding of Wordsworth's rhetoricity extends the logic of Donald Wesling's contention that rhetoric still operates as "a written or unwritten manual of poetics" for Romantic poets who cannot "escape" but who may "wrench" or twist traditional rhetorical and poetic practices in the direction of their own poetic interest (2-3).[4] But whereas Wesling believes that the Romantic age marks the end of rhetoric "as a collective and prescriptive mode" (3), I contend that Wordsworth's poetic practice, said to be exemplary (for good or ill) of Romantic poetics, is complexly bound to the exigencies of traditional rhetoric even as it wrenches away from specific tropes or devices. For beneath the brilliantly arrayed display of the most patently self-absorbed Romantic speakers, including Wordsworth's, there exists a pattern of citation that is cumulative, historical, and social.[5] This poetic invention is, moreover, less original or sublimely "Romantic" than it is classical and rhetorical. For although it displays little poetic interest in the ordinary, conventional account of the commonplaces as clichés or set pieces that speakers use to indicate a shift in topic or point of view (Lanham 110-11), Wordsworth's invention is a thoroughly Romantic disposition of the rhetorical and imaginative value classical rhetoricians claimed for commonplaces, reimagined as places in landscape and in texts that writers devise in order to consult them, to discover what they can say by invoking what has already been said.

In fundamental ways, pertinent for modern critical theory beyond the immediate reach of Romanticism, this description of Wordsworth's invention queries a telling poverty in Romantic and post-Romantic polemics about the opposition (to put it in its least oppositional form) between individual talent and tradition, or between the two poles offered by social and epistemological theory since the Enlightenment: individual agency and received structures. The social and citational nature of Wordsworth's inventional practice argues for a subtler duality within poetic structures and for our critical recognition of how agency and improvisation interpolate or honeycomb a received tradition of figures and poetic techniques. What I have in mind is a version of Pierre Bourdieu's understanding of improvisation as the working out of available cultural practices, as modified by Anthony Gidden's theory of structuration, which argues for the possibility of innovation from within or against a form or structure. Indeed, Giddens contends that this is how innovation must occur, that it cannot make its way except by way of existing structures, which I understand to include aesthetic forms of all kinds, as these are handed on by traditional rhetoric and poetics (Bourdieu 78; Giddens, "Structuration Theory" 204-5).[6]

As the citational paths created within this essay are intended to make clear, its argument is inventional on a classical hook, which is to say that its claims are widely indebted to texts and critics indicated throughout. An account of the general shape of my debt to poststructuralist critics, beginning with Paul de Man, will help to specify the turns of agreement and disagreement that occur within the loose rubric authorized by classical inventional strategies. As de Man and other critics have recognized, however indifferent Romantic writers appear to be to the classical and neoclassical prescriptions they identified with the rhetorical tradition, their poetics is subtly and pervasively rhetorical.[7] By investigating the citational or intertextual character of Romantic poems, critics have tacitly articulated the kind of textual study that informs my consideration of what W. J. T. Mitchell has called (after Harold Bloom) those "secret paths" among poems, authors, and periods (Bloom, quoted in Mitchell, "Influence" 643), paths that collectively define the kind of invention Romantic poets require. The relative silence in poststructuralist criticism about this feature of Romantic rhetoric—a silence that is surprising given the metacritical reflexivity of this criticism—may register a lingering, neo-Romantic suspicion of a mode of discovery that is deeply social as well as textual and, as such, wholly unlike the kind of invention we expect of sublime original genius, with or without Hannibal and elephants.

My consideration of the role of classical invention in Wordsworth's poetics begins with the sense of place authorized by his remarks about Hannibal in the 1815 "Essay, Supplementary to the Preface." The figures that animate Wordsworth's discussion of how earlier poets have "smoothed the way" for an original genius like himself specify a preoccupation with topography and place that is at least as much rhetorical as it is literal. Here Richard McKeon's advice about knowing places suggests how we might read Wordsworth's self-comparison to Hannibal among the Alps. As the figure who had authorized Napoleon's self-invention as a brilliant military strategist on his way to conquer northern Italy, "Hannibal" specifies the mix of obviousness and indirection that distinguishes his invention, on and off a classical hook. I am interested in the "hidden places" Wordsworth often invokes in *The Prelude* as the sources or basis of his poetic "power." These places, I argue, are rhetorical places, at once well known and hidden in the folds of poetic figures and landscapes.

Two classical traditions inform this reading of Wordsworth's inventional practice. The first is the ancient use of the *topoi* or "commonplaces" to find or discover what can be said to advance an argument (Quintilian 4: 211-14). Like his contemporaries, Wordsworth seems to have largely ignored the lists of topics that the ensuing rhetorical tradition used to codify advice offered by classical rhetoricians about the topics of invention and argument—advice that eighteenth-century writers of rhetoric tended to cast aside (Howell, *Eighteenth-Century* 98-101; Blair [1784] 296-97).[8] Instead, Wordsworth characteristically manages topics or commonplaces as Cicero had hinted they ought to be managed, not so much as lists but as sources hidden except to those willing to look for them:

> I have sketched these topics as shortly as possible. For if I wished to reveal to somebody gold that was hidden here and there in the earth, it should be enough for me to point out to him some marks and indications of its positions, with which knowledge he could do his own digging, and find [*inveniret*] what he wanted. (*De Oratore* 1: 322-23)

Whether he had Cicero's specific advice in mind or not, Wordsworth deploys inventional strategies in *The Prelude* in ways that suggest a speaker and a poet quite ready to do his own digging, to find (invent) what he needs from what he uncovers.

A second tradition in classical rhetoric, the use of mnemonics to help speakers remember what they plan to say, reappears in Wordsworth's poetics under the pressure of fears about the loss of memory or of the capacity to recall, fears the speaker of *Lines Composed a Few Miles above Tintern Abbey* finally subdues by imagining that Dorothy Wordsworth's "mind / Shall be a mansion for all lovely forms, / Thy memory be as a dwelling-place" (*Poetical Works* 2: 263). Behind these strong echoes of the 108th Psalm lies a long, evocative tradition in the history of rhetoric that includes Augustine's comparison (203-5) of his mind to a mansion of remembrance and retrospective accounts of how the art of memory began. Cicero explains that the poet Simonides was called out of a banquet hall by divine visitors, leaving other guests still seated. During his absence the ceiling of the hall collapsed, killing the host and the guests and disfiguring the bodies so badly that relatives could not identify the dead. But Simonides, who remembered where everyone had been sitting, could (*De Oratore* 2: 351-54). The art of memory required that speakers mentally deposit key images or turning points in an argument in various architectural features, called simply "*loci*," or places, of a large building or an otherwise well-defined space. By returning to this place in memory or in fact, speakers could recall (literally as well as figuratively) key images from their assigned places. As Frances Yates has suggested, what speakers deposited were likely to have been *topoi*, insofar as the commonplaces articulated turning points in the inventional stages of argument (1-3, 31). Especially among early classical rhetoricians, then, the term *topoi* may have meant "place" in two overlapping registers—the architectural place where a rhetorical figure or image would be put and the figure itself. Cicero recognizes this cooperation between etymology and rhetorical practice when he considers "the several sources or commonplaces [*argumentorum sedes ac loci*]" (1: 166).

Wordsworth's return to the kinds of images and turning points in arguments that classical rhetoricians called *topoi* dramatizes the radical, in the sense of etymologically authorized, twinness of *topoi* as literal or topographical places and as rhetorical figures or places of argument. If there is confusion here, it seems oddly deliberate, as if Wordsworth had chosen to dig up a doubling of place and figure long submerged in discussions of rhetorical commonplaces.

The inventional work of the 1805 *Prelude* begins in the opening lines of the poem and continues as the speaker inventories topics he may or may not take up. For Bruns, Geoffrey Hartman's account of this beginning shows how "the failure of invention doubles as a kind of self-inauguration" (Bruns 103).[9] My understanding of this strategic "failure" is that it doubles as invention. Having said he cannot go on, that his harp is "defrauded," the speaker goes on to list, then examine, several possible arguments, ending with "some philosophic song / Of truth that cherishes our daily life" (*The Prelude* [1805], Book 1, lines 230-31, p. 40 of the Norton edition). True, this theme is itself soon cast aside ("still I find / Some imperfection in the chosen theme"), yet this failure is a further spur to invention, an effect that the poem may mark with the verb *find,* the usual English translation for *invenio.* Even the notorious question with which Wordsworth had begun the two-part *Prelude* of 1798-99 ("Was it for this?") and which in later versions succeeds the speaker's seemingly failed inventory of possible topics, is modeled on a kind of questioning whose origins John Hodgson has traced back to Virgil (Hodgson, "Virgilian Questionings" 125-36).

Thus even when his capacity for invention seems to fail, Wordsworth's speaker makes considerable use of classical protocols for invention as the art of discovering what can be said. Whereas Don Bialostosky reads these protocols as one sign that the book is structured like a classical argument, I argue that Wordsworth's use of classical inventional tools is less positivist than it is crucially ambivalent about the figural *topoi* his poetic argument lets loose, as though he had recognized that figures tend to swamp rhetorical tropes insofar as the latter refer, as Bialostosky notes, to marked, and thoroughly controlled, turning points in arguments (*Wordsworth* 219-23). Wordsworth's figures articulate turning points, but their argumentative path is less secure, more like a hidden repository of inventional paths than the directed plot of one of Cicero's orations.

Precisely because the speaker of the expanded *Prelude* of 1805-6 is unable to command a single topic or line of argument in later books, he requires the wide-ranging sources that inventional strategies make available. Gone from this version of the poem is the tentative admission of 1799:

> I perceive
> That much is overlooked, and we should ill
> Attain our object if, from delicate fears
> Of breaking in upon the unity
> Of this my argument, I should omit
> To speak of such effects as cannot here
> Be regularly classed, yet tend no less
> To the same point, the growth of mental power
> And love of Nature's works.
> (*The Prelude* [1799], Book 1, lines 250-58, p. 7)

The punning ambivalence of this excised declaration, which asserts that the speaker looks over the supposed unity of his argument even as he misses or overlooks a great deal else,[10] resurfaces in a different lexical form in Book 5 of the 1805 *Prelude,* where the strain of trying to keep a single argument in view is dramatically conveyed.

Midway into the book, its speaker admits that "my drift hath scarcely / I fear been obvious" (lines 290-91, p. 166). The admission is even more explicit in the 1832 (once called the 1850) version, which records a tense variant also found in MS. M, the fair copy of Books 1 through 5 which Mary Wordsworth probably completed in early 1804 (Reed, *Middle Years* 636-37). In 1832, Wordsworth writes "my drift I fear / *Is* scarcely obvious" (my emphasis, lines 292-93, p. 167). Whereas the present perfect "hath been" indicates a drifting action begun in the past which may (or may not) be continuous, "is" firmly declares present continuation and makes no promises for the shape of the narrative to follow. The speaker merely says he is drifting without making any claim to reform. Wordsworth's substitution of the simple present is made more emphatic by the placement of "Is" at the beginning of the line, separated from its subject, "drift," in the preceding line by the parenthetical "I fear."

Thus if the 1805 text can be understood to say that the speaker's drift will be more apparent and thus more controlled in the rest of the book, the 1832 version and its early manuscript source suggest that all of Book 5 is adrift. For readers who assume that a good Romantic poem displays or seeks organic unity, this is not simply an awkward line. It is an embarrassing moment in the text. Perplexed by this evidence of a poet not up to the task of revision, the editors of the first parallel text edition of *The Prelude* comment: "it is strange that though the poem underwent such continued revision, Wordsworth did not improve this prosaic and unnecessary statement" *Prelude,* ed. de Selincourt and Darbishire, 544n.).

Wordsworth's stubborn play on the meanings of *drift* rehearses both sides of the modern critical debate about the coherence of this book and the expanded *Prelude.* New Critical readers looked for a unified, organic structure in its preoccupation with death, loss, and immortality (Shakir 156-67; Morkan 246-54; Weiner 209-20; Barth 69-75; Havens 2: 375-76). Other readers have objected that however hauntingly it returns to these themes, Book 5 remains an odd assortment of narratives unwillingly yoked together by a speaker whose awkward transitions betray his uneasiness (Jaye 32-50; Chase 13-31; Manning 87-114; Wolfson, "Illusion" 917-35; MacGillvray 99-115; J. Wordsworth and Gill 503-25). In brief, where some readers have found a drift or line of argument that, if not obvious, is enough to keep the poem afloat, others have found a poetic argument that is only adrift, listing badly as Wordsworth's speaker avoids or explains away deluge and drowning, mentions few books by name, calls natural objects "books," and comments rather episodically about the role of books in the mind's education. Yet Book 5 is, as almost every reader sees, a very "bookish" book just under its aggregate surface. Its allusions and citations indicate an array of sources or books that, while not

## The Case for William Wordsworth

overtly named, are intrinsic to the figural texture of its argument: books about deluge, about geometry, about saving treasure, among others.[11]

So considered, Wordsworth's "drift" declares an inventional strategy that has little in common with what we ordinarily think of as Romantic invention but much in common with the *topoi* and *loci* of classical rhetoric. Here Wordsworth shapes and clears his own path by reimagining commonplaces as those his speaker finds because he must in order to continue, not because he writes by rhetorical prescriptives. At the risk of remythologizing this distinction, I suggest that what makes Wordsworth's adaptation of rhetorical invention "Romantic" is its circumvention of the lists of *topoi* so much in disrepute by the middle of the eighteenth century and, even more singularly, its radical, in the sense of fundamental, return to the ground of pathos that animates so many classical accounts of the value of topics. When the speaker of *The Prelude* begins Book 5 with an extended lament about the loss of books and their accumulated knowledge to deluge or cataclysm, the figures of deluge and submersion let loose what is barely contained in Cicero's advice to the novice orator:

> I will hurry him off to that source where no sequestered pool is landlocked, but from it bursts forth a general flood; to that teacher, who will point out to him the very homes of all proofs [*qui illi sedes et quasi domicilia omnium argumentorum commonstret*], so to speak, illustrating these briefly and defining them in terms. For in what respect could a speaker be at a loss, who has contemplated everything to be employed in a speech? (*De Oratore* 1: 162-63)

At the beginning of Book 5 of *The Prelude,* when the poem loses the narrative momentum of earlier books, the speaker openly engages a Wordsworthian anxiety about loss that paradoxically sustains the disparate narrative energies of this book by invoking a "general flood" of sources or pretexts to surround its opening query.[12] What the poem gains from this invocation is no "landlocked pool," no tightly constructed poetic unity, but the flood of figures needed if the speaker is to go on to meet the stories and losses derived from Wordsworth's adult experiences in revolutionary France and back at home. In *The Prelude,* especially in Book 5, the topics of invention are those half-hidden commonplaces whose contents the speaker begins to search out and half-disclose when he asks how to save the products of human intellect, which are "frail" and thus vulnerable as nature's products are not:

> it grieves me for thy state, O man,
> Thou paramount creature, and thy race, while ye
> Shall sojourn on this planet, . . .
> for those palms atchieved
> Through length of time, by study and hard thought,
> The honour of thy high endowments.
> (*The Prelude* [1805], Book 5, lines 3-9, p. 152)

Citing Shakespeare's Sonnet 64, the speaker declares that man "might almost 'weep to have' what he may lose" (line 25, p. 152), the "garments" of knowledge endangered by cataclysm. If the term *garments* echoes a figure used by ancients and moderns to characterize rhetoric, the Shakespearean lines from which Wordsworth quotes ("This thought is as a death which cannot choose / But weep to have that which it fears to lose") also involve Wordsworth in a less overt allusion to *Paradise Lost*.

As Neil Hertz has argued, the speaker of Wordsworth's poem, who will soon learn in a dream that a deluge is "at hand," recalls Milton's Adam, who will weep "another Floud," the Archangel Michael tells him, to see the effects of the Deluge that is yet to come in the time of Michael's narrative (Shakespeare 72 and Milton 383, quoted in Hertz 15-33). If this Miltonic allusion is indirect, proceeding as it does by way of Shakespeare's sonnet, this citational path is salient in a poem whose speaker begins by echoing (and revising) lines near the end of Milton's epic, saying "the earth is all before me" (Book 1, line 15, p. 28; see Milton 412). The speaker reiterates his filiation with Milton's Adam in Book 5 by using the present tense of the verb *grieve*, the same verb Michael uses in a proleptic past tense to forecast Adam's response to the Deluge:

> How didst thou grieve then, *Adam*, to behold
> The end of all thy offspring, end so sad,
> Depopulation; thee another Floud,
> Of tears and sorrow a Floud thee also drownd.
> (Book 11, lines 754-57, p. 383)

The mixture of indirection and citation that marks Wordsworth's allusion to Milton indicates an uneasy truce between the kind of invention that has been called "Romantic"—invention authored by an original genius working independently to shape and clear his own road—and the classical invention I have identified with Wordsworth's speaker. Oddly enough, the very hiddenness of the textual places this speaker invokes to talk about the devastation of books and all such places lends rhetorical support to the claim that this speaker, like Wordsworth himself, proceeds as an original genius ought—on his own. Yet this sleight-of-hand is only a disguise, and a half-hearted one at that, for an inventional strategy that multiplies its effects as the book proceeds.

Thus the inverted chronological relation between Michael's prophecy of deluge and the tense he uses to convey Adam's future response to the event ("how *didst* thou grieve") is temporarily reversed and refigured in Wordsworth's poem as the speaker first laments a cataclysm that has not yet occurred, then dreams of it—or someone else dreams of it[13]—as if it were the Deluge, the first cataclysm in the human record, yet still "imminent" in the narrative chronology of the poem. The speaker's lament for man as "the child of earth" who might "'weep to have' what he may lose" echoes Genesis and Milton's Adam as he grieves for the lost "children" of his race. Within Wordsworth's Book 5, these echoes are themselves re-echoed in the Arab–Don

Quixote's prophecy of a deluge that will bring "destruction" to "the children of the earth" (line 98, p. 156) and in the satiric account of how "the children of the land" (line 228, p. 162) are miseducated in ways differently destructive of imaginative knowledge.

As topics or commonplaces, these pre-texts provide the speaker with a flood of figures with which to meet the deluge as the historically salient image of the destruction of knowledge by cataclysm, refigured in later books as the threat imposed by the French Revolution and the Reign of Terror on the future of humankind and its collective intellectual achievement. If the digressive "drift" of Book 5 in part expresses the speaker's wish to back away from this history (and narrative future), it also displays his effort to confront the flood of history which these pre-texts bring. Like Cicero, then, the speaker hurries to and through his topics because they are "that source" where words are not a landlocked pool but a "general flood" strong enough to counter the figures of deluge that threaten to engulf the narrative.

And yet, as the Arab dream and subsequent episodes reveal, this speaker does not know whether he prefers the inventional strategy recommended by Cicero, with its cumulative, versional, and digressive energies, or a more closed invention and resulting form. As natural objects and "books," the treasures offered in the dream by the Arab specify both options. The speaker can create (and so far has) a text whose expansiveness the spiral form of the shell reiterates, or he may create a closed text like that formally indicated by the stone. Readers have usually argued that the stone and the shell are respectively geometry and poetry (Havens 2: 410-11; Stallknecht 1-20; Smyser 269-75; Hartman, *Wordsworth's Poetry* 228 and 231; Miller 140 and 144; Ragussis, "Language" 148-65; Bahti, "Figures" 617; Jacobus, "Language" 642; Hodgson, "'Was It for This . . .?'" 145–47). Certainly the identity of the stone is fixed, doubly impaled by a name and a long tradition. It is, as the Arab explains, "Euclid's *Elements*" (line 88, p. 156), the static, immutable mathematical truths handed down from ancient sources (Kelley, "Spirit" 565). But the form of the shell is both geometric and open (even as the form of the stone is geometric and closed). Recalling both Euclid's analysis of conic sections and eighteenth-century interest in the perfect logarithmic spiral of the great conch shell (s.v. "Shells," *Encyclopaedia Britannica*, 1797), Wordsworth's shell is a geometric spiral that produces a prophetic "ode."

Here the "language of the dream" revises earlier oppositions in the book between "poetry and geometric truth," "the works of bard and sage," or even the Arab's implied contrast between durable and fragile "books" like stones and shells. Collectively these adjustments revise the speaker's earlier query: why must the mind "lodge [its] powers in shrines so frail?" (lines 44-48, p. 154). Although it is clearly as frail a shrine as there could be, this point does not occur to the dreamer or Arab. Instead, both celebrate the ode whose "loud prophetic blast of harmony" (lines 96-99, p. 156) is also a prophecy of deluge. This slight reorientation in the speaker's fears about the frailty of books is the consequence of the inventional argument of Wordsworth's book

"On Books." For as its speaker uses the dream narrative to think about saving books and knowledge, the "language of the dream" revises the problem by invoking other texts whose topic is kinds of knowledge or deluge or both. These include Descartes's dreams about the value of poetry and mathematics and various Deluge narratives (Smyser 269-75; Ragussis, "Language" 148-65), including one given in Josephus's *History of the Jews*—the only version to speak, as Wordsworth's Arab does, of burying knowledge to save it from the Deluge and the only one to link a deluge narrative explicitly to the problem of saving knowledge.

According to Josephus, Sesostris of Egypt commanded that the astronomical "inventions" of the ancients be inscribed on two pillars, one stone and one brick, then buried to preserve them from a "twofold destruction" by fire and flood, which Adam was said to have predicted. In the eighteenth century, this story is often used to illustrate the history of mathematics. As such, it appears under this heading in the 1797 *Encyclopaedia Britannica* and in the introduction to William Whiston's edition of Euclid, used by Cambridge undergraduates until the mid–eighteenth century and still widely available to Wordsworth's generation. Wordsworth owned two of these sources and adapted the term *twofold* from the third, Whiston's edition of Euclid (Whiston also translated Josephus's *History*), to describe his Arab's stone and shell as a "twofold treasure."[14]

Among its other textual effects, Wordsworth's use of the Deluge as a commonplace, a source with a "flood" of precedents, makes it only semirelevant to talk about texts versus pre-texts or about a text versus its "sources," as an earlier generation of readers would have described them. For whether Wordsworth works "inside" or "outside" the boundaries of Book 5 of *The Prelude*, the inventional strategy is similarly directed to adapt or revise its sources. From this perspective, there is no ur-Wordsworthian invention or original genius but rather a genius for revision and citation, a capacity for recognizing those texts that will ensure that this poem doesn't become a "land-locked pool."

In the episodes that follow the dream narrative in Book 5, the speaker continues to explore the opposition I have sketched between the claim that a book or poem is or is only a single, self-contained object and the counterclaim implied by the inventional energies of this book—that books are versions of what has been said and, as such, at once fragile and durable and unexpectedly social. The episodes themselves enact the special demands of each kind of "book." Some, notably the satiric account of the infant prodigy and, to a lesser extent, the episode that describes a mother educating her "brood" better than sages do, achieve their declared narrative purpose: to demonstrate what is wrong or right about competing modes of education. As such, they are logically closed, self-contained. Other episodes, including the Boy of Winander and the Drowned Man passages as well as the speaker's recollection of having wished to buy *The Arabian Nights*, subvert the reasons given for telling them.

These episodes are more open-ended, directed less by a declared intention or assertion than by the inventional turns in argument that key figures enact.

Even this distinction requires further modulation insofar as the satirical portrait of the child prodigy introduces figures whose reiteration elsewhere is not always in the service of a sharply defined assertion. The "sages" who "would controul / All accidents" (lines 380-81, p. 172) and thus all innovation reiterate an earlier, more neutral presentation of the "twinned hopes" of "bard and sage" and Wordsworth's 1799 presentation of the story of the Drowned Man as one of many literal "accidents in flood and field." Let loose, in other words, from the controlled purpose of Wordsworth's satire, "sages" and "accidents" engage in a larger set of filiations that specify the inventional and figural registers that converge for Wordsworth when the topic is a flood.

Even when the topic is not a flood, the drift of figures in Book 5 tends to present narratives that are not self-contained, but at once inside and outside Wordsworth's poem. Among the most prominent of those figures concerns Arabs and storytelling. Their presence in Wordsworth's text is very nearly a guarantee that an episode will not convey what it initially or apparently intends to convey. Thus the speaker's recollection of having once wanted to buy *The Arabian Nights* gradually torpedoes his rationale for telling this story: to illustrate his early love of books, especially fairy tales and romances (lines 474-82, p. 176). Whether the speaker wishes or no, this story harbors figures that drift back into Book 5 toward the Arab's two treasures. Here intermediate pressures make a strained affiliation impossible to ignore: Cervante's *Don Quixote,* the book the speaker-dreamer had been reading before he fell asleep and the Arab of the dream, who also reminds the dreamer of Don Quixote ("Of these was neither, and was both at once," line 126, p. 158). Like *The Arabian Nights,* Cervantes's novel is a framed tale told by a liar. The principal narrator is the Arab Cid Hamete Benegeli, described as a liar by the "outside" narrator, Cervantes. Similarly, the narrator of *The Arabian Nights,* Scheherazade, tells lies or "tall tales" to stay alive. Two topics are suggested by the intersections among these episodes. The first concerns the futility of trying to save treasures and books, while the second concerns spinning tales as if they were true or, in the case of Scheherazade, because the teller's life depends on her capacity to keep telling tales.[15]

Both works and their speakers seem to be included in the praise Wordsworth's speaker gives to "forgers of lawless tales," who transform "wish," "power," and "thought" into "deed," "empire," and "possession" (lines 546-55, p. 180). The key term here is *forgers,* inasmuch as it involves both invention and lies. What sages cannot do is left to "forgers of lawless tales" like *Don Quixote* and *The Arabian Nights* to do differently. Here too, whether these works are "inside" or "outside" Wordsworth's poem is at least a half-moot point: lawlessness may require ignoring or putting aside such distinctions. Thus what readers know about Cervantes's novel or Scheherazade's storytelling necessarily extends the reach of readers of Wordsworth's book on "Books." Consider the kinds of narration offered by these two works. Because

Cervantes as narrator questions the reliability of the Arab narrator, we may doubt or modify the view of Don Quixote he presents—the mad, hence deluded, old man. He might be instead, as Wordsworth's dreamer puts it, someone in whose "blind and awful lair / Of madness reason did lie couched" (lines 152-53, p. 158). Scheherazade's narration offers another, more peculiar, lesson by transforming the threat of imminent death into the promise of a long union with her would-be executioner, who had promised to execute her if she didn't tell and keep telling (to each her own). In short, by telling and retelling tales, these speakers differently transform fixed categories by unfixing them. They let go, as sages cannot.

The accidents, deaths, and wishes of Book 5 are not, finally, events its speaker can fully control, any more than the dreamer can expect to save knowledge from the deluge by burying it. Even so, he is haunted by the loss of knowledge as the "garments" of intellect and by death and drowning as the loss of human "garments."[16] In one sense, "garments" are in both instances mere ephemera. The drowned man can and may be brought back to the surface without them, and the voices of the Arab's shell and of tellers of tales suggest that their garments cannot be buried or possessed but must be reinvented. And because the speaker presents but does not interpret the filiations between and among the topics of this book, readers have been invited to do so as they follow the cues provided by explicit citations to other, allied pre-texts and subtexts, which are also, rhetorically speaking, garments—woven into the figural texture of Wordsworth's poem much as textiles gain their distinctive textures by weaving different strands.

The 1805 and subsequent revisions in the Drowned Man episode specify the extent to which this recovery of meaning is collective. In all versions of the passage, the speaker declares that the dead man "bolt upright / Rose" to the surface of the lake (1805, lines 470-72, p. 176). The syntax makes the dead man, rather impossibly, the agent of his own recovery. But the preceding lines, added in 1805 and elaborated in 1835, imply that a "company" who comes to sound the depths of the lake with "grappling irons" is the collective agent of recovery. Much as the text is not absolutely unequivocal about who or what is responsible for this return to the surface, so is it difficult to separate the text of the book on "Books" from its pre-texts or from readings that pursue the figural logic of its invention.

Read together, the 1805 and the 1832 *Prelude* refigure romantic authorship as a collective enterprise, insofar as we might construe collectivity as the textual effect of multiple versions, each written by Wordsworth at different times, under the pressure of different contemporary scenes, readers, and self-presentations (Stillinger 69-78). Thus, for example, the inventional argument of Book 5 probably replays the history of its composition in 1804. Using passages he had written several years earlier and others he probably recorded in notebooks earlier that year, Wordsworth assembled them under the rubric of Book 5 after he abandoned a four- or five-book version of the poem on his life (J. Wordsworth 1-25; Reed, *Middle Years* 628-53). Two features of this manuscript history are instructive. First, it suggests that Book 5 is a versional retelling of passages that existed before March 1804, some of which appear in the 1799 *Prelude,* where they serve a different poetic occasion and argument. Second, two extant manuscripts for the new book, W and WW, give striking evidence of Wordsworth's "drift" from one line of argument and figuration to another (Reed, *The Middle Years* 644). Lacunae in the manuscripts further indicate that they were neither the first nor the last of his efforts to discover his poetic argument at this critical turning point in the composition of the expanded poem.

Thus if the declared theme of Book 5 is "Books," its covert argument is the one implied by its manuscript history—the need to write a more extensive and demanding personal history, one as difficult to secure as the "strange freight" (line 84, p. 156) the Arab hopes to save by burying it. Despite the speaker's attempts to write a poem of "single and determined bounds," the poem tends to drift, frequently in several directions at once. The topics of deluge and drowning return in the books on the French Revolution, and the Drowned Man episode in Book 5 reworks extended similes in Books 4 and 8 that concern seeing or reading what lies submerged beneath the surface of a lake or stream. As fruitful critical attention to all these filiations has made clear, by March 1804 *The Prelude* was on its way to becoming anything but a "land-locked pool."

By way of Wordsworth's "drift" in Book 5, then, the inventional strategies of the expanded *Prelude* transgress the poem's boundary to fold in history by means of figures. From this perspective, the deconstructionist claim that, in Derrida's terms, "il n'y a pas de hors texte"—that referents are "folded in" to texts in ways that continually subvert inside/outside distinctions (Culler, *On Deconstruction* 192-95)—is accurate, though perhaps not in the sense that some critics have been willing to grant. A more telling problematic concerns the extent to which any text can be said to "fold in" material or empirical signs of history. If the "inside" and "outside" of texts and referential claims about them are fused in ways that challenge poststructuralist as well as New Critical assumptions about the boundaries of texts, as I believe they are, what is needed here is a semiotics that is willing to negotiate between figures or signs in texts and the referential or inferential path readers and poets take as they make signs refer.[17] Whether readers will be governed by Wordsworth's insistence that his argument is "of single and determined bounds" (Book 1, line 669, p. 64) is the risk implied or activated by the figural "drift" of his compositional practice. From the perspective of a semiotics that depends on such inferences,[18] Wordsworth's *Prelude* shows how different times, histories, and readers work at what Romantic poems mean and how they mean.

Wordsworth's radical, unanticipated return to classical invention recreates the commonplaces of classical rhetoric which speakers once consulted to discover what it is they can say. In Wordsworth's poetry, the outcome is a textual sociability we have only lately begun to recognize. Even when Romantic poems are not the product of multiple authorship, they frequently register a consultative, social pattern of citation, of poetic discovery, of indebtedness freely undertaken or required to friends and others acting as editors and publishers (Stillinger 9-24). The Romantic and post-Romantic polemic against imitation and for "originality" has been effectively captured by its own Blakean negation. Critics bent on repeating this negation are in turn captured by the "same dull round" and thus interminably bound to the wheel that grinds out debates about, among other topics, Coleridge and plagiarism.

One way (there is always more than one) to turn from this impasse is to theorize the inventional practices of Wordsworth's poetics. Because these practices articulate a sustained relation between individual (here poetic) agency and culture, they undermine critical efforts to construct that relation as monolithically oppositional. In one sense, this is so because all agents are culturally embedded. This, in brief, is the claim illustrated by Bourdieu's analysis of the cultural "habitus" as a set of norms and cultural practices within and to which individuals offer "regulated improvisations" (Bourdieu 78), and by Giddens's more expansive sense of the engagement between agency and culture. Against the constriction that Bourdieu's account imposes on improvisation, Giddens argues ("Structuration Theory") that because agents work *on* culture as habitus and structure, they are not or need not be passively determined by culture. As Giddens and others describe it, this "duality of structure" (i.e., as form worked on from without and from within) makes a space for the contortions of tradition and figure which "forgers of lawless tales" like Wordsworth produce in the habitus of received figures and commonplaces.[19] Working against the law of tales and their transmission and a cultural preference for facts over fictions, poet-forgers craft and (re)fabricate tradition. Guided by this doubly bound sense of culture and poetic agency, readers may find in Wordsworth an inventional strategy not unlike their own.

### NOTES

I am indebted to Susan Wolfson for her close reading of this essay in earlier versions and to Frederick C. Hoerner for conversations about the work of Anthony Giddens and Pierre Bourdieu.

1. Against the grain of McKeon's advice, his remark is quoted without bibliographic citation in Harold Bloom, *Wallace Stevens* (375).

2. As Carl Woodring observes ("Road Building" 29), Wordsworth's figure of Hannibal as a road builder reiterates ancient and modern interest in this aspect of his military strategy, which J. M. W. Turner and almost certainly Wordsworth identified with Napoleon as well.

3. The cult of original genius has origins in the eighteenth century and before. See Joel Weinsheimer (62-89) and Thomas McFarland (*Originality* 1-30). Weinsheimer observes that the value Edward Young assigns to originality depends in fact on imitation (71).

4. For an analysis of metrical indebtedness and innovation in Romantic poetry, see Susan J. Wolfson, "Romanticism."

*The Case for William Wordsworth* 137

5. Marshall Brown, in a *PMLA* Forum letter of 1984 (997), describes this kind of invention as "a correction to the received notion of organic form as self-containment."

6. Since the early 1970s, Anthony Giddens has argued that this opposition does not adequately identify, even on the level of structural theory, the multiple adjustments that agents make on received structures or ideologies. For a recent overview of what Giddens prefers to call structuration, the process by which agents modify structures and are modified by them, see Giddens, "Structuration Theory" (207-21). Other contributors to this volume critique or elaborate the role of structuration theory in Giddens's work. Richard Poirier (57-58) has described invention in American literature much as I argue it occurs in English Romantic poems.

7. See, for example, Paul de Man's "Autobiography as De-Facement," in *The Rhetoric of Romanticism* (67-82); see also Cynthia Chase, *Decomposing Figures,* and Mary Jacobus, *Romanticism.*

8. Wordsworth's inventory of topics at the beginning of *The Prelude* (Book 1, lines 175-230, pp. 38-40) both relies on and toys with readers' expectations that this catalogue of topics will ultimately yield the speaker's chosen subject. Wordsworth's speaker does conclude the list by settling on a version of his "philosophic song of daily life," but this subject has little evidently in common with the list of possible topics offered in the preceding 150 lines.

9. Bruns refers to Hartman's *Wordsworth's Poetry* (33-69).

10. My thanks to Susan Wolfson for calling my attention to this 1799 passage as well as the De Selincourt–Darbishire remark about the survival of Wordsworth's pun on "drift" in later versions of *The Prelude.*

11. This texture is the implied occasion for Mary Jacobus's account of the "language" of Wordsworth's dream ("Apostrophe" 618-44).

12. By contrast, see Bloom's other Romantic and post-Romantic reading of the pressure of sources and pre-texts on successive poets as an engulfing flood that threatens death by drowning (Bloom 154, quoted in McFarland, *Originality* 11).

13. In the 1805 text of the expanded poem, the dream is presented as a friend's (Book 5, lines 49-60, p. 154); in the version now called the 1832 text (called 1850 in the Norton edition cited here), the speaker offers the dream as his own (lines 56-70, p. 155).

14. Euclid and eighteenth-century mathematics are more extensively discussed in Theresa M. Kelley, "Spirit" (566-69) and *Revisionary Aesthetics* (91-100). For the present analysis, it is important to note that eighteenth-century editors of Euclid, like Wordsworth after them, play off and through each other's versions. For example, in his edition of Euclid, Henry Hill (1724) uses the phrase "pillar of mathematics" to describe Euclid's *Elements,* an echo of Whiston's 1710 edition of Euclid, which summarizes Josephus's story of Sesostris burying pillars with the knowledge of the heavens (i.e., geometry) inscribed on them. See Whiston (Preface), Henry Hill (Dedication), Josephus (1: 15-16), and the entry under "Mathematics," *Encyclopaedia Britannica,* 1797.

15. Wordsworth's interest in Cervantes's novel and *The Arabian Nights* is suggested by Shaver's catalogue of the various lists collectively identified with Wordsworth's library. Shaver indicates three different editions, in several languages, for each work (10, 50). This kind of research tool is not simply a catalogue of "sources"; it is circumstantial evidence of dense points, or nodes, in the putative map of Wordsworth's invention.

16. For more extensive analysis of the figural work of Wordsworth's "garments," see Timothy Bahti, "Figures of Interpretation," and Andrzej Warminski, "Facing Language" (43-45).

17. For an analysis of this congruity between formalism and recent poststructuralist criticism, see Alan Liu.

18. The underlying philosophical argument I have compressed here is presented in

Jeffrey Barnouw's defense of Charles Peirce's empiricist semiotics against Derrida's claim that empiricism is unphilosophical. Barnouw notes (78) that for Peirce empirical signs such as those traditionally identified with perception require an inferential shuttle between signs and what they signify. This shuttle is not for Barnouw a Derridean free play of signifiers but a sustained movement of mind between text and world.

19. My argument here is adapted from Mary Robertson's analysis of the value of "deconstructive 'contortion'" for feminist theory and critical practice (712-17).

# IX

# THE INVENTION/DISPOSITION OF *THE PRELUDE*, BOOK I

## *Don H. Bialostosky*

The first book of *The Prelude* has regularly confounded the generic expectations of readers and baffled their attempts to describe or account for its parts. Geoffrey Hartman nicely declares the difficulty from the point of view of readers with narrative expectations of the epic sort when he states that "no poem of epic length or ambition ever started like" *The Prelude* (*Wordsworth's Poetry* 38). Lyric expectations aroused by the first fifty-four lines of present-tense celebration and self-questioning also founder on the subsequent passage that places these lines in quotation marks as the beginning of a past-tense narration. David P. Haney offers autobiography as a genre "midway between" lyric discourse and epic narrative (34), but the term applies only with dialectical distortions to the two main parts of the book, even as it illuminates the function of the question—"Was it for this . . . ?"—that links them. John F. McCarthy attempts to read everything after that question as a "continuous narrative unit," yet he must acknowledge that "the significant link between the episodes of the first section is not chronological but typological" (370, 375, 373). The thematic paragraphs that at first seem to punctuate the narrative later seem to govern it. Timothy Bahti, too, divides the book at the question, "Was it for this?" For him it is preceded by a "negative situation . . . of a poem beginning without either an ontologically stable speaker or an unvexed scene of its own creation" and followed after some "two hundred odd lines" by "the actual beginning of the poem's autobiographical narrative," which is itself characterized by "inarticulateness or blockage of narrative representation" ("Rhetorical Theft" 91, 110). Michael G. Cooke comes closest to recognizing the rhetorical form of the poem, but he finally declares that "it is not a thing of argument, with a systematic assemblage of topics disposed in keeping with proper rhetorical principles. . . . Rather it incorporates argument in its own lyrical-epical system" (204).

Though Romantic and deconstructive readers have found their highest expectations—that the poem would somehow defy conventional expectations—

satisfied in these accounts, all the anomalies their generic hypotheses have produced can be accounted for with the seven-part variant of the classical model of the oration.[1] All the divisions noticed by previous critics and a couple of crucial divisions they have failed to notice take their place in conformity with this paradigm, and only one part is missing, replaced by an authorized optional part. Every schoolboy, including Wordsworth, used to know that the standard oration begins with a proemium, proceeds to a narration and sometimes an exposition, states a proposition, offers a confirmation of it, presents a refutation of other views, and concludes with the necessary conclusion.[2] *The Prelude* Book I lacks a refutation but replaces it with a digression, which sometimes appears before the conclusion (Lanham 112). Wordsworth realizes this pattern in a discourse so rich in figures of thought that it does not immediately impress its argumentative pattern upon us, but I shall show how those figures generally function in relation to the aims of the parts in which they appear.[3] There is more to this book of *The Prelude* than its conformity to this pattern, but our recognition of the pattern can avoid unnecessary bafflements and free our attention for other more appropriate and fruitful inquiries. I regret that I cannot enter the whole first book of the 1805 *Prelude* here into my text or quote the whole of each section I shall analyze, but the analysis follows the order of the book's unfolding and introduces line numbers so that readers may, if they wish, keep track of it in their own texts.[4]

Following Wordsworth himself, we have learned to call the opening section of *The Prelude* I (lines 1-54) the "glad preamble" (VII, 4), but we do not commonly ask what functions a rhetorical preamble serves, what forms it can take, what topics it touches on, or what decorum it observes. The terms "preamble," "proemium," and, indeed, "prelude" all name the opening or introductory move of a discourse. Quintilian links the term "proemium" with the Greek tradition of lyric poetry, in which it named the musical preludes composed by lyre-players to precede their sung poems and win the good will and attention of their listeners (Cousin 211-12). Wordsworth himself describes his preamble as having been sung "aloud in dithyrambic fervour" (VII, 5), and Hartman names it with a phrase from Book V as "'an Ode, in passion utter'd'" (*Unremarkable* 99). Tradition advises speakers in their proems to express hope, prayer, anxiety, and lack of self-assurance to conciliate their hearers' good will, and it recommends presenting extraordinary or important matters to arouse their attention (Cousin 220, 224). It allows the speaker to speak about himself, especially in those cases where ties of friendship exist between him and his subject or his auditor (Carrino). It permits both apostrophe and prosopopeia as appropriate figures of thought, but it warns that the appearance of spontaneity must be especially observed in an opening when the judge's impression of the speaker is on the line (Cousin 224-25).

Wordsworth's "glad preamble" takes the form of an extended prosopopeia or self-impersonation, which is revealed as such only at the end when he declares that he has been recording his own previous spontaneous utterance. His opening paean turns quickly to an apostrophe of welcome to the gentle breeze, to whom he narrates his situation as a recent escapee from the city, declares his problem of choosing a habitation, and asks where he should go.[5] Rather than answering, he turns to elaborate his freedom, celebrate it ("I breathe again"—the very figure of simulation, Kneale notes, that Quintilian points to as an example of the type [37-38]), and return to asking—this time not where he ultimately should go but just where he should turn next. Again avoiding a direct answer, he declares the sufficiency of his freedom even without a chosen destination and then corrects his initial account of his situation by finding in it not merely the joy of freedom but a "gift that consecrates [his] joy" (I, 40); Curtius lists the "topos of dedication," which the Romans commonly called "consecrations," as one of the topics of exordium (86-87). His expressions of uncertainty and hope display the required lack of self-assurance, even as his final self-correction reveals that what is at stake here is more important than the speaker's own freedom and joy—there is promise too of serious contribution to an honorable field of endeavor. The preamble is itself a partial mini-oration with its own proem, narration, proposition, and conclusion; every move in it has a Latin or Greek name in the list of rhetorical figures of thought and forms of argument; its lyric mode recalls the traditional lyric associations of the proem; and even its pose of recorded spontaneity (which from compositional evidence we know to be a pose) satisfies the demands of art. This spontaneous overflow of powerful feeling has been carefully poured into a traditional mold.

Critics have called the preamble by its proper rhetorical name, but they have not known what to call the second part of *The Prelude* I (lines 55-271). John F. McCarthy thus calls it a "post-preamble" (371). David P. Haney recognizes that "we enter the world of narrative" (38-39) at this point in *The Prelude* I, but he sees the shift as part of an elaborate dialectical "series of discursive and narrative divisions which follows the preamble" (40). The dialectical epicycles of his deconstructive analysis can be simplified by the recognition that we here enter the second part of the formal oration, the *narratio*, or narration. This part, as Lanham says, "tells how the problem at hand had come up . . . [and] gives the audience, as it were, the history of the problem" (68). Adopting the classically recommended manner of laying out the events leading up to the problem in chronological order without digressions, this section places the utterance of the preamble as the first event in a chronological series of hopes, disappointments, and self-absolutions that leads to the speaker's present impasse. There is no mystery about shifts of tense from past to past perfect to present in such a narration (see Haney 42-43).

The narrative section is also marked by repeated addresses to the speaker's friend that bring him into the position from which he can learn what has happened to the speaker, by a single self-impersonation of the speaker's past words, and by figures of complaint, wish, and confession that declare the speaker's present difficulty. The narration concludes with another partial mini-oration that declares the proposition that the speaker has many of the requisites for undertaking a "glorious work" (I, 158) but cannot single out "time, place, and manners ... with steady choice" (I, 169-71). His review of the alternative times, places, and manners confirms their plenitude, but the figure of aporia in which he enumerates them enacts his doubt. This subordinate argument concludes not with a choice but with a confession of inability to choose and a wish to escape the issue altogether. The narration ends by confessing that the problem it has traced persists.

Readers of *The Prelude* recognize that Book I takes its most important turn at this point with the question "Was it for this ...?" Wordsworthians and users of a now out-of-date edition of the *Norton Anthology* know that the poem began in its two-book form with this question and that the parts I have so far examined were later added to it. Some rhetoricians might recognize that this question begins the exposition (lines 272-304), the part that introduces the issue to be proved.[6] The question opens an inquiry, or *quaestio,* that asks whether the problem the narration has presented (the antecedent of "this") is the appropriate and necessary outcome of a previously unmentioned cause—the River Derwent's (and, more broadly, Nature's) nurturance of the speaker in his childhood (the as yet undeveloped "it"). The question also opens a vein of recollection that does not directly answer it but does begin to amplify the "it" of the question in a way that leads to a claim about it.

That claim appears in the next and briefest verse paragraph of Book I (lines 305-9), the formal proposition to which all the rest of the argument pertains. Again following its classical role as a brief, formal declaration and division of what is to be proved, the proposition succinctly declares a two-part claim: "Fair seed-time had my soul, and I grew up / Fostered alike by beauty and by fear." This claim is not a yes-or-no answer to the question posed in the exposition by the question "Was it for this ...?" Rather it is a claim about the part of that question that has not yet been examined—the "it" whose bearing on "this" is still uncertain. Nature has fostered him, he claims, both through beauty and through fear.

The vivid accounts of hunting woodcocks, stealing from the raven's nest, stealing a boat, and skating that follow are all introduced to confirm this proposition (lines 309-570)—particularly the part that claims that the speaker was nurtured by fear. And the passages that John F. McCarthy identifies as "three separate paragraphs of reflection and self-congratulation" (373) that "punctuate" those vivid accounts in fact connect those accounts to the proposition that McCarthy does not notice. The elaborately described scenes have occasioned much commentary, but each of the three paragraphs that attempt to subordinate them to the function of confirming the proposition deserves scrutiny as well. The first, following the descriptions of hunting woodcocks and robbing the raven's nest, briefly widens the claim from what fosters the speaker to what fosters the mind of man, but it quickly returns its focus to the speaker and reformulates Nature's framing the mind of man as Nature's framing the speaker as "a favored being" (I, 364-65). Nature fostered him, he suggests, for a special purpose, not, he implies for "this."[7] The second connecting paragraph is the familiar apostrophe to the "Wisdom and spirit

The Prelude, *Book I* 143

of the universe" (I, 427) that follows the boat-stealing passage. It draws the first direct consequence of the confirming evidence not just for the proposition it confirms but also for the question "Was it for this . . .?" You did not just foster me, you fostered me "not in vain" (I, 431), the speaker declares. And not stingily either, he adds. The third connecting paragraph follows the skating scene. It directs a rhetorical question to the "presences of Nature" to confirm again not just *that* the presences of Nature fostered him but that they did so with more than "a vulgar hope," that they ministered to him for something more than "this" (I, 490-93). The proposition formally governs each of these confirmatory summations but the question "Was it for this . . .?" haunts them all as well.

The next two verse paragraphs (lines 501-70) turn to confirm the other half of the proposition, the claim that the speaker was fostered by beauty (or, as he reformulates it in his conclusion, by "pleasure and repeated happiness" [I, 632]). They enumerate some of the changes "of exercise and play to which the year / Did summon us in its delightful rounds" (I, 503-4) both outdoors and within the "lowly cottages in which we dwelt" (I, 526), though they turn at the very last to end the confirmation of the proposition with one more reminder of its fearful side.

The two parts of that proposition, however, have not exhausted all that the speaker has found to say about how Nature fostered him in his childhood, and he adds in the next two paragraphs a formal digression from the proposition that nevertheless serves the larger purpose of showing how well he has been fostered. "Other pleasures" (I, 575) besides those connected with either beauty or fear have been his, he declares, and he goes on to recall occasions of those pleasures and to call on natural forms to bear witness and confirm his experience of them.

At this point the speaker begins his conclusion (lines 609-74). First he concludes the digression by bringing it, too, to bear on the question "Was it for this . . .?" and asserting that the pleasures it points to were "not vain / Nor profitless" (I, 619-20). Next he opens the conclusion of the whole argument by summarizing point by point, as the canons of conclusion require, not only the two parts of the proposition but also the digression he has confirmed.

> And thus
> By the impressive discipline of fear,
> By pleasure and repeated happiness—
> So frequently repeated—and by force
> Of obscure feelings representative
> Of joys that were forgotten, these same scenes,
> So beauteous and majestic in themselves,
> Though yet the day was distant, did at length
> Become habitually dear, and all
> Their hues and forms were by invisible links
> Allied to the affections. (I, 630-40)

He turns then to confess his weakness and to appeal to his friend for sympathetic indulgence—another hallowed topos of rhetorical conclusion. He then oddly transforms the other common concluding topos of showing indignation toward one's opponent by declaring that he has hoped to invigorate and reproach *himself* with his own argument.

This turn makes the absence of the expected refutation understandable, for the speaker here clarifies that he has made his argument in opposition to himself; the whole argument from "Was it for this . . .?" to the conclusion has been an indignant self-refutation. His proposition has been confirmed and expanded to outweigh the problem his narration has presented, to convince him that *it* is sufficiently powerful and good *not* to have been for *this*. But the qualification that follows this passage still allows the possibility that his hopes might be vain and appeals once more—this time with a rhetorical question—for the sympathy and indulgence of his friend.

The speaker declares at the beginning of the next-to-last paragraph that "I began / My story early" (I, 641-42), but we have seen that, except for the narration section itself and perhaps the boat-stealing passage as well, there has been no story here but rather an argument. Even the other vivid descriptions were not presented as episodes or single events but as accounts of repeated kinds of experience, and the overall arrangement of the first book was governed not by a chronological sequence of events but by a formal rhetorical model. Nevertheless, the speaker's sense of having begun a story leads him to declare in the final paragraph his decision to continue telling one and to "bring down / Through later years the story of my life" (I, 666-67). He determines here the issue that he had left in suspense in the aporia of his narration and chooses to make the times, places, and manners of his own life his subject. Though he has not yet fully convinced himself that it was not for this, he has discovered a purpose and the beginnings of a story in the act of trying to persuade himself. The end of his oration marks the formal beginning of his tale, but we should not forget that the end of his oration also marks the end of his oration, and that the narrative expectation projected retrospectively onto Book I cannot account for its argument.

Neither will it do to read backwards from the conscious beginning of the narrative at the end of Book I to take the preceding Book, even in its 1799 version, as a "lyric retrogression" finally transformed into a "narrative progression" (Sheats 477). Book I of the 1799 *Prelude* already contains the outlines of the oration I have just presented. Though it lacks the opening proemium and narration and the formal proposition, all the other parts are in place. Despite the absence of the divided proposition, the two parts of the confirmation already show how Nature impressed the speaker's mind with "beautiful or grand" (line 378) forms, and the digression already adds the impact of "other pleasures . . . / Of subtler origin" (lines 380-81). The vivid descriptions and their thematizing paragraphs are already in place, though some of their figures differ from those of the later version. The conclusion offers the same summary and the same gestures, lacking only the declaration to "bring down / Through later years the story of my life" (1805, I, 666-67).

The crucial difference in Book I of the 1799 text is its insertion of three famous anecdotes, all of which are moved to other places in the later expanded poem—the anecdotes of the drowned man, and the two "spots of time" of coming upon the hanged man's grave and waiting for the horses before Christmas vacation. Wordsworth placed these anecdotes at the end of his enumeration of the changes "of exercise and sport to which the year / Did summon us in its delightful round" (lines 200-201), that is, after the confirmation and before the digression. The passage that introduces them makes clear that they, too, are a digression.[8] He writes:

> All these [changes of exercise and sport], and more, with rival claims demand
> Grateful acknowledgment. It were a song
> Venial, and such as—if I rightly judge—
> I might protract unblamed, but I perceive
> That much is overlooked, and we should ill
> Attain our object if, from delicate fears
> Of breaking in upon the unity
> Of this my argument, I should omit
> To speak of such effects as cannot here
> Be regularly classed, yet tend no less
> To the same point, the growth of mental power
> And love of Nature's works. (247-58)

Wordsworth implies here that the effects he has treated thus far have been "regularly classed"—the effects, I have argued, of fear and of pleasure and repeated happiness (or beauty). It appears, however, that the three anecdotes make a more intrusive digression than the digression that follows on "other pleasures . . . / Of subtler origin," for it not only violates this regular classification but also gets no acknowledgment in the summary of topics offered by the opening of the digression that follows or in the summary offered in the book's conclusion, even though that final summary does include the topic treated in the second digression.

The very intrusiveness of this digression does provoke Wordsworth to declare, however, that he sees himself as constructing a unified argument.[9] Despite his closing (and conventional) apologies for self-indulgence in remembrance of things past, he has been purposefully pursuing an argument in answer to his opening question. Though he has not yet made a "resolute commitment to narrative progression," he is already writing a formally disciplined discourse that pursues an "'appointed task'" and knows when it digresses from that task (Sheats 478). His ultimate removal of the three digressive anecdotes and of this passage of apology for them, as well as his formal completion of the classical oration in Book I of the 1805 text, fulfills the formal intention already evident and self-conscious in 1799, a rhetorical generic intention reducible to neither "narrative progression" nor "lyric retrogression" (Sheats 477).

Sheats's (and Haney's) dialectical opposition between narrative and lyric in *The Prelude* I derives its plausibility from the presence in the text of parts that relate actions and parts that enact figures. Mary Jacobus, too, finds "a division . . . between discursive time and narrative time—a radical discontinuity which ruptures the illusion of sequentiality and insists, embarrassingly, on self-presence and voice . . . [an] incompatibility between the lyric voice of *The Prelude* and its much-desired, 'distracting' epic progress" ("Apostrophe" 172). We have already seen, however, that the narrative parts function in a generic whole not definable as a narrative. The *narratio* tells a story to set up the question "Was it for this . . . ?" and the boat-stealing passage tells an anecdote to confirm the proposition that the speaker was fostered by fear, but *The Prelude* I does not tell a story, though it does discover the beginning of one and the intent to tell it. In a similar way, the early apostrophe to the gentle breeze provokes lyric expectations in those who identify lyric with apostrophe,[10] and the succeeding apostrophes to the river Derwent, the Wisdom and spirit of the Universe, and the presences of Nature revive those expectations in the midst of other sorts of discourse. But the book as a whole does not develop as a lyric or sustain the elevated tones of its apostrophic passages, and the somewhat arbitrary association between apostrophe and lyric diverts attention from the many other figures that constitute the discourse and the many other genres and parts of genres in which apostrophes function. Like the vivid spots of time, the elevated apostrophes attract our attention at the expense of the other figures that environ them and distort our apprehension of the functions all those figures serve and of the genres they work in.

Our rhetorical tradition, as Gérard Genette has shown, is so drastically reduced "within the figurative domain itself" that we do not recognize the range of figures or kinds of figures that the tradition once identified, nor do we recall the canons of decorum that once regulated the use of different sorts of figures in different genres of composition (107).[11] Culler's identification of apostrophe with lyric exemplifies the collapse of the distinctions between figures and tropes, between figures of thought and figures of speech, and among apostrophe, invocation, and anacoenosis (communication or taking counsel with), and it ignores the role apostrophes play in the several parts of other than lyric kinds of discourse, e.g., in the proemium, narration, and conclusion of the classical oration. Culler's version of the dialectical opposition between lyric and narrative works only so long as these reductions go unquestioned and the distinctions we have recovered in this section go unremembered. There is little to be gained beyond a dramatic conclusion in collapsing the "entire poem," as Jacobus does in the end, into "an apostrophe or 'prelude'" (181), if we have workable notions of apostrophes, preludes, and their correlative figures and counterparts. The vertigo produced by such collapsing distinctions in some recent rhetorical criticism may come from its falls into the gaps, even the abysses, in its knowledge of rhetoric.

## NOTES

1. Lee M. Johnson has discovered a version of the pattern operating in Wordsworth's adaptation of the Miltonic sonnet (*Wordsworth* 42-44), and Richard E. Matlak has argued that another version shapes the discourse of both Coleridge's "Eolian Harp" and Wordsworth's "Tintern Abbey."

2. See John R. Nabholtz, "Romantic Prose." See also Nabholtz, *"My Reader My Fellow-Labourer,"* for suggestive connections between Romantic prose and classical rhetoric. Jane Worthington notes one reference to Quintilian in Wordsworth's letter to Charles James Fox of Jan. 14, 1801, and two copies of Quintilian in his personal library (76-77).

3. Ernst R. Curtius places under invention the commonplace division of parts of the classical judicial oration that most historians of rhetoric place under disposition. This division of the "disposition" into "1. introduction (*exordium* or *prooemium*); 2. 'narrative' (*narratio*), that is, exposition of the facts in the matter; 3. evidence (*argumentatio* or *probatio*); 4. refutation of opposing opinions (*refutatio*); 5. close (*peroratio* or *epilogus*)," Curtius claims, "was already anticipated in the five parts or sections of an oration, which for their part provided the clue to 'invention'" (70-71). Curtius goes on in a subsequent chapter to enumerate "topics of the exordium" and "topics of the conclusion" (85-91) that would provide the writer or speaker with matter appropriate to these parts of the oration, justifying his sense that the matter is not generated separately and subsequently distributed to the parts but rather generated to fit the functions each part prescribes.

4. I will be following the text of the 1805 *Prelude* except where otherwise noted. The divisions I am discussing remain in the 1850 text, except that the section I call the proposition no longer stands apart as a separate verse paragraph.

5. Alistair Fowler, who recognizes that the opening of *The Prelude* meets "proemial conventions ... in a deeply implicit form," assimilates the apostrophe to the gentle breeze to an epic invocation of the muse, but the oratorical proemium is a more capacious genre that allows a greater variety of figures than the epic opening and need not be reduced to it. See Fowler (102-3).

6. Lanham identifies this third part of the oration and its function, though it is not as widely recognized by the rhetorical tradition as the two that precede and the three that follow it.

7. Bahti, who reads everything following "Was it for this?" as an autobiographical narrative rather than as an exposition, proposition, and confirmation, diminishes this passage as "twenty lines of reassuring teleology: talk of 'harmony' and the 'reconciling' of 'discordant elements,' summed up in the exclamation 'Praise to the end!'" with no sense of its argumentative function. He thinks its purpose is to "account for the parenthetic 'surely I was led by her [nature],' which introduces the scene of Wordsworth's stealing the boat. This opening line thereby qualifies this theft, too, as an engagement of the persona with nature, even though the specific object of the theft is a boat, rather than birds or eggs" ("Wordsworth's Rhetorical Theft" 112). Bahti ignores the apostrophe to the "Wisdom and spirit of the Universe" that follows the boat-stealing passage, and his theme of "theft" permits him to ignore the skating scene and the passage that follows it as well.

8. Claims for the superiority of the "imaginative writing" of the 1799 text hinge upon these anecdotes, and claims for the centrality of what I am calling here a digression depend upon the thematic remarks about "spots of time" that come between the Drowned Man anecdote and the other two anecdotes in the passage as a whole. The arguments Jonathan Wordsworth and Stephen Gill have made for the 1799 text as a separate and superior poem do not show how this passage integrates into the argument

of the rest of the poem but rather how it stands out from the rest of an argument that, in their view, revolves around it. Wordsworth would appear to have preferred, in the end, to preserve the unity of his argument from the disorienting and distracting power of this passage. See J. Wordsworth and Gill, "The Two-Part *Prelude* of 1798-99" 503-25, and J. Wordsworth, "The Two-Part *Prelude* of 1799" (567-85).

9. The editors of the Norton *Prelude* gloss the word "argument" in this passage as "theme, as in *Paradise Lost,* I, 24: 'the highth of this great argument,'" but I think the better gloss is "connected series of statements or reasons intended to establish a position" (*OED,* sense 4). The digression violates the *form* of the argument Wordsworth has otherwise established but in fact treats the same theme or subject matter, or as he says, "the same point, the growth of mental power / And love of Nature's works" (257-58).

10. See Jonathan Culler, *The Pursuit of Signs* (137, 149), whose account Jacobus follows.

11. For another valuable account of the collapse of rhetorical categories—focused on Hayden White's four-trope Viconian system—see Wallace Martin, "Floating an Issue of Tropes."

# X

# ROMANTIC AVERSIONS
## APOSTROPHE RECONSIDERED

## J. Douglas Kneale

> This is a figure which less than any other would bear abuse.
> —Wordsworth, May 5, 1814

> Yet whence this strange aversion?
> —Wordsworth, *The Borderers*

According to certain recent publications, the figure of apostrophe, or *aversio*, has become something of an embarrassment. Jonathan Culler, who first alleged the embarrassment, has reiterated the assertion: "Apostrophes are embarrassing, and criticism of the lyric has systematically avoided both the topic of apostrophe and actual apostrophes" ("Reading Lyric" 99).[1] The reason Culler gives for such regular or systematic avoidance is that apostrophe represents something "which critical discourse cannot comfortably assimilate"—that is, he suggests, "some innate hostility to voice" (*Pursuit* 137, 136).[2]

Perhaps it comes as a surprise nowadays to be told that discourse has an "innate hostility to voice." Voice, as Jacques Derrida has shown, has always been privileged in Western culture as a guarantor of truth, consciousness, and being—while writing has been repressed as secondary and derivative (*Of Grammatology* 3–26). To resolve this confusion we need to rehabilitate our historical understanding of apostrophe by demonstrating that far from being "systematically" or "regularly" avoided by critics, the figure has a distinguished tradition of commentary, beginning with the classical writers Cicero and Quintilian[3] and moving through the Renaissance and eighteenth-century rhetoricians. Sherry, Peacham, Fenner, Fraunce, Puttenham, Day, Hoskins, Blount, Smith, and Blair—to name more than a few—all regularly and systematically discuss apostrophe. In addition, we need to reconsider apostrophe in relation to the figures of prosopopoeia and ecphonesis in order to view its particular function within a larger oratorical structure of address. What we discover when we pursue this sort of aversion therapy is that apostrophe does indeed represent something which discourse cannot comfortably assimilate: not voice as such, however, but what I shall call the passing of voice, its want or lack, even its sudden removal.

My position may be stated briefly. The current problem with apostrophe stems from associating it with voice rather than with a movement of voice, and the reason for this error, I think, lies in a misunderstanding of rhetoric. Classical rhetoric is fundamentally a vocative form of discourse, always explicitly or implicitly involving a second-person "thou" or "ye"—what Roman Jakobson calls the "conative" function of language (67–68). Thus classical rhetoric has no trope or scheme of address as such because, being derived from forensic oratory, it is intrinsically vocative. It does not, therefore, see its own essence as a trope or deviation. Erich Auerbach, writing on apostrophe and address, puts it this way:

> The theorists have never described or listed the address to the reader as a special figure of speech. That is quite understandable. Since the ancient orator always addresses a definite public—either a political body or the judges in a trial—the problem arises only in certain special cases, if, with an extraordinary rhetorical movement, he should address someone else, *a persona iudicis auersus,* as Quintilian says. ("Dante's Addresses" 270)[4]

Rhetoric does, however, distinguish types and conditions of address—such as, in the Tudor rhetoricians' terminology, the "outcrie" or the "exclamation" and the "turne tale" or the "aversion." I shall attempt to distinguish this latter figure, apostrophe, or *aversio,* from its related forms of address, including exclamation, or ecphonesis, and then demonstrate its operation through a close reading of Wordsworth's "There Was a Boy." By doing so, I hope to show that the central problem with Culler's argument lies in his failure to distinguish, on either historical or theoretical grounds, between apostrophe and address. To put that claim a different way, I mean to show that what Culler's influential essay is really about is not apostrophe but prosopopoeia.

Quintilian discusses the figure of apostrophe at some length in Book 4 (1.63–70) and again in Book 9 (2.38–40, 3.26–28) of the *Institutio Oratoria.* In the first of these instances he argues against certain "cautious and pedantic teachers of rhetoric" (4.1.70) who forbid the use of apostrophe in the *exordium,* or introduction, to an oration, not "because they regard [apostrophe] as illicit, but because they think it useless" (4.1.65). Quintilian's counterargument pragmatically seeks to demonstrate the utility of the figure through a series of examples from Cicero and Demosthenes. But what interests the reader more is Quintilian's first definition of apostrophe: "The figure which the Greeks call *apostrophe,* by which is meant the diversion of our words to address some person other than the judge, is entirely banned by some rhetoricians as far as the *exordium* is concerned" (4.1.63). Two aspects of this definition require comment, since they reappear in nearly all discussions of apostrophe down to the nineteenth century. The first is the notion of apostrophe as a "diversion" of speech *(sermonem a persona iudicis aversum)*. The second point, necessarily related to the first, is that this diversion redirects the speech to someone other than the original hearer—in this case, since Quintilian is dealing with forensic oratory, someone other than the judge. The positing of what later rhetoricians would call the "proper" or intended hearer, and the oratorical diversion from that person to another person, constitute the two chief characteristics of the figure.

In Book 9 Quintilian offers a more elaborate definition, still within a forensic context: "*Apostrophe* also, which consists in the diversion of our address from the judge, is wonderfully stirring, whether we attack our adversary . . . or turn to make some invocation . . . or to entreaty that will bring odium on our opponents" (9.2.38). Quintilian reminds us of the pragmatic, as distinct from ornamental, function of apostrophe in judicial rhetoric: like all figures, its effect is supposed to persuade. Once again the two key points of a proper listener and a diversion from that listener are present.

That is not the case, however, in the pseudo-Ciceronian *Rhetorica ad Herennium,* where the following definition of apostrophe appears in Caplan's translation: "Apostrophe is the figure which expresses grief or indignation by means of an address to some man or city or place or object" (4.15.22). While this definition intimates the close relation between apostrophe and prosopopoeia—by addressing "man or city or place or object" the orator implicitly or explicitly invests the addressee with the animate faculty of hearing—there is a confusion of terminology, because in the original Latin text the word translated by Caplan as "apostrophe" is actually *exclamatio*.[5] As future rhetoricians would insist, exclamation is not the same as apostrophe, though they are indeed similar, both being motivated by passion and having the potential to address people or objects either present or absent, alive or dead.[6] The difference between these two figures, however, is that exclamation does not necessarily contain a turn or diversion from the original hearer; a text may be a consistent exclamation to a reader and yet still not an apostrophe. By contrast, apostrophe always depends on a pre-text.

Apostrophe is literally a turning away, an aversion, as both Richard Sherry and Henry Peacham call it. It is, Peacham says, "a forme of speech by which the Orator turneth suddenly from the former frame of his speech to another . . . which is no other thing than a sudden removing from the third person to the second" (116). "The most usual forme of this figure," he continues, "is in turning our speech from the third person to the second." (116). But Sherry locates the turning elsewhere. "*Aversio,* aversion," he says, "[is] when we turne our speche from them to whom we dyd speake to another personne, eyther present or absent" (60). It is for Sherry thus a turning from one second person to another second person, in an intersubjective or intertextual movement between vocatives. Of the three traditional divisions of rhetoric—

forensic, epideictic, and deliberative—forensic rhetoric illustrates this intersubjective movement most clearly, as when the orator turns aside occasionally, as Hoskins put it in 1599, "to some new person, as, to the people when your speech before was to the judge, to the def[endan]t, to the adversary, to the witnesses" (48). At first glance, Peacham does not seem to agree with Sherry's intervocative definition, as he suggests that the shift of address is from third- to second-person discourse, from "it" to "you." This is not really a disagreement, however, for what Peacham assumes but does not make explicit here is the *intrinsic* second-person form of address in rhetoric, always involving a "proper" listener from whom the speaker can turn to confront an invoked listener.[7]

Other Renaissance rhetoricians concur in these definitions. In *The Artes of Logike and Rhetorike* (1584), Dudley Fenner writes: "Apostrophe or turning to the person, is when the speach is turned to another person, then the speach appointed did intend or require. And this Apostrophe or turning is diversely seene, according to the diversitie of persons. Sometimes it turneth to a mans person....Sometimes from a man to God.... Sometimes to unreasonable creatures without sense" (chapter 8).[8] Angel Day, in the list of tropes, figures, and schemes added to the 1592 and later editions of his *English Secretary*, has the following entry:

> Apostrophe, or Aversio, when wee turne our speeches from one person or thing to another, as if having spoken much of the vanitie of the worlde shoulde thereupon turne and saie unto the world, O world, how sweete and pleasant are the shewes of those things which thou producest: but in taste, how full of too much bitternes? Or in speaking of the certaintie of death, and the little respect thereof had, to turn a mans speach to death it selfe and saie, O death, how bitter is thy remembrance to a man having peace and plenty on his riches, &c. (90)[9]

Eighteenth- and nineteenth-century rhetorical treatises are similarly consistent in their definitions of apostrophe. Thomas Gibbons, in *Rhetoric; Or a View of Its Principal Tropes and Figures* (1767), writes: "Apostrophe is a Figure in which we interrupt the current of our discourse, and turn to another person, or to some other object, different from that to which our address was first directed" (213). Citing Quintilian, Gibbons claims that "this Figure is of admirable service to diversify our discourses, as we direct ourselves to different objects from those we first addressed" (221). Other rhetorical handbooks and treatises follow suit—for example, John Holmes's *Art of Rhetoric Made Easy* (1766), Hugh Blair's *Lectures of Rhetoric and Belles Lettres* (1783), and John Walker's *Rhetorical Grammar* (1822), partly cribbed from Gibbons's *Rhetoric*.

A number of twentieth-century critics and theorists have discussed apostrophe—for example, Sister Miriam Joseph in her exhaustive catalogue of tropes and schemes in Shakespeare (246–47, 390), Paul Fry in his splendid study of the English ode (11), Annabel Patterson (64, 107, 126–28) in her work on

Hermogenes and Renaissance style, Paul de Man on Michael Riffaterre (*Resistance* 27–53), and Riffaterre on de Man (107–23).[10] Here, however, is Jacques Derrida in *The Post Card*, offering a thoroughly historical and conventional definition of apostrophe. Derrida writes:

> The word—apostrophizes—speaks of the words addressed to the singular one, a live interpellation (the man of discourse or writing interrupts the continuous development of the sequence, abruptly turns toward someone, that is, something, addresses himself to you), but the word also speaks of the address to be detoured. (4)

Taken together, these texts from the sixteenth to the twentieth century represent a tradition of definition, example, and commentary on the figure of apostrophe, or *aversio*. A similar tradition could be mapped out here for the figure of exclamation—or *exclamatio*, or ecphonesis, the outcry, as it is variously called. Significantly, the rhetoricians do not include a diversion of speech as part of their understanding of the figure. Peachem once again offers a useful, representative definition:

> Ecphonesis of the Latines called *Exclamatio*, is a forme of speech by which the Orator through some vehement affection, as either of love, hatred, gladnesse, sorrow, anger, marvelling, admiration, feare, or such like, bursteth forth into an exclamation or out-crie, signifying thereby the vehement affection or passion of his mind. (62)[11]

The motive for exclamation must always be passion—it is "not lawful but in extremity of motion," Hoskins says (33)—though this passion must be "simulated and artfully designed," else the outcry is not a figure, as Quintilian stipulates (9.2.27). One of the most common rhetorical signposts for exclamation is the word "O." Thomas Wilson, in his *Arte of Rhetorique* (1560), gives the following instances: "Oh Lord, O God, O worlde, O life, O maners of men? O Death, where is thy sting? O Hell, where is thy victorie?" (205). In *The Mysterie of Rhetorique unvail'd* (1657) John Smith says that exclamation "is expresst or understood by an Adverb of crying out, as Oh, alas, behold; which are the signs of this figure" (140).

It is important to cite these definitions of apostrophe and exclamation more to distinguish their rhetorical differences than to demonstrate their syntactical affinities. We no longer can say, for example, that Wordsworth's line "O there is blessing in this gentle breeze" (*Prelude* 1.1) is an apostrophe *automatically* because of the telltale "O." Only if it were a "turne tale" O, one depending on a rhetorical pre-text or prior discourse, would we be correct in making such a statement. But I wish to turn back to Jonathan Culler's text before going on to Wordsworth's, to develop some of the larger implications of my brief survey.

What is at stake in such a reconsideration of apostrophe? One concern is obviously historical: we discover, as Paul de Man once said of allegory, "a historical scheme that differs entirely from the customary picture" (*Blindness* 208). But another interest is theoretical. By describing apostrophe as a turning from an original (implicit or explicit) addressee to a different addressee, from the proper or intended hearer to another, we emphasize the figure as a *movement* of voice, a translation or carrying over of address. This understanding is crucial if we are to distinguish simple direct address from the turning aside of address, from the rhetorical and temporal movement of apostrophe. In Culler's essay "Apostrophe," however, this distinction is missing; curiously, no definition of apostrophe is given there, despite Culler's admission that a study of apostrophe should require it:

> [I]f we would know something of the poetics of the lyric we should study apostrophe, its forms and meanings. Such a project would confront at the outset complex problems of definition and delimitation, which I here leave aside in order to focus on cases which will be apostrophic by any definition.... (*Pursuit* 137)

"Which I here leave aside": yet whence this strange aversion? Culler seems to assume the straightforwardness of apostrophe, but in fact his choice of texts "apostrophic by any definition" is problematic: "O Rose, thou art sick!"; "O wild West Wind, thou breath of Autumn's being!"; "Thou still unravished bride of quietness..."; and *"Sois sage, ô ma douleur!"* (*Pursuit* 137). While doubtless many teachers, myself included, have called these examples apostrophes, not one of them, by definition, qualifies because there is no vocal turn involved, no "sudden removing," in Peacham's phrase (116): they are all direct exclamations, or ecphoneses, occurring in the *first line* of their respective poems, with no preceding speech, no pre-textual basis from which to turn, no discourse to "interrupt," as Gibbons (213) and Derrida (4) put it.[12] Blake's lyric is addressed to the rose, Shelley's to the west wind, Keats's to a Grecian urn, and Baudelaire's to the single addressee Sorrow. Yet it might be argued that if language is originally figurative, always already tropological, these examples do contain a turn, a trope that animates each of the nonhuman subjects addressed—a rose, a wind, an urn, sorrow. But such a figure is not apostrophe, of course, but prosopopoeia, which does not depend on a rhetorical aversion. My interest, however is in the turn of voice, not the turn or deviation of another figure within voice.

Simply put, the problem is a confusion of apostrophe and address. In his analysis of de Man's essay on Riffaterre's poetics, Culler repeats his error. He misses the turn. Renewing his argument about the systematic exclusion of apostrophe in criticism, Culler attempts to bring de Man on-side by noting that he "takes a considerable interest in apostrophe and some interest in other critics' inclination to avoid and ignore it" ("Reading Lyric" 99). This seems to me to be a crucial misreading of de Man, for what Riffaterre avoids and de Man takes an interest in is not in fact apostrophe. Indeed, the passage from de Man that Culler cites to substantiate his point about apostrophe is actually

# Romantic Aversions

about something else. Culler quotes: "'Now it is certainly beyond question,' de Man writes . . . 'that the figure of address is recurrent in lyric poetry, to the point of constituting the generic definition of, at the very least, the ode (which can, in its turn, be seen as paradigmatic for poetry in general)'" ("Reading Lyric" 100). The "figure of address," not of apostrophe, is de Man's concern here. And de Man is surely right to claim that this rhetorical structure defines a paradigm for poetry. Yet why does he single out the ode with respect to the structure of address? Assuredly because of all poems, the ode is the type that frequently is explicitly addressed *to* someone: Psyche, Autumn, a skylark, the Confederate dead.[13] Of course, other genres do this too, addressing Penshurst, a coy mistress, Peele Castle, or intellectual beauty.[14] But we need to emphasize that this structure of address, this explicit directing of voice, is crucially different from the movement of apostrophe, the redirecting of voice.

This distinction should help to dispel Culler's perplexity in *The Pursuit of Signs* over the lack of discussion of apostrophe in many critics, especially in George N. Shuster's *English Ode from Milton to Keats,* one work Culler singles out to prove his allegation of a systematic scholarly neglect of apostrophe. "The problem of apostrophe ought to lie right at the heart of this book," Culler writes, "but from the outset Shuster engages in instructive maneuvers to exclude apostrophe from his domain" (*Pursuit* 136). Yet the theoretical and definitional error exhibited in his analysis of de Man is present here: the passage Culler goes on to quote is not about apostrophe. Here is Shuster's "maneuver," as quoted by Culler:

> *"The element of address,"* [Shuster] notes in the introduction, "is of no especial significance, being merely a reflection of the classical influence. All the verse of antiquity was *addressed* to somebody, primarily because it was either sung or read and the traditions of song and recitation required that there be a recipient." (*Pursuit* 136; my emphasis)

"Thus," concludes Culler, "*apostrophe* is insignificant because conventional" (*Pursuit* 136; my emphasis).[15] Apostrophe? Could the confusion of terminology, the commentary at cross-purposes, be any plainer? No wonder, then, that Culler says "that one can read vast amounts of criticism without learning that poetry uses apostrophe repeatedly and intensely" (*Pursuit* 136)—especially when what a reader thinks is apostrophe is not apostrophe, when the standard "element of address" is mistaken for the tropological diversion of address. Shuster's argument, perhaps a maneuver nonetheless, is that since classical verse—his focus, like de Man's, is the ode, the text "to" someone—is intrinsically vocative, its essence need not be taken as a deviation, the fundamental taken as "especial."

What really is de Man's interest in his reading of Riffaterre? Plainly, not apostrophe as such, but prosopopoeia, "the master trope of poetic discourse" (*Resistance* 48). And when Riffaterre answers de Man's charges concerning his poetics of reading, he entitles his response simply "Prosopopeia." Apostrophe is related to prosopopoeia, as ecphonesis is, but it is not a necessary relation: one can apostrophize someone (e.g., a defendant in a courtroom) without using prosopopoeia; and conversely one can, as Riffaterre points out, conceive of a text in which, for example, a "besieged city speaks its mournful dirge without having been apostrophized" ("Prosopopeia" 108). Prosopopoeia, Riffaterre writes, "merely lends a voice to a voiceless... entity" ("Prosopopeia" 108). Or even less: sometimes it merely lends an ear, in the way that Wordsworth lends an ear to nature in Book 1 of *The Prelude*:[16] "to the open fields I told / A prophecy" (50–51)—a passage that anticipates in Book 5 those other "open fields, which, shaped like ears, / Make green peninsulas on Esthwaite's Lake" (5.433–34).[17]

> Apostrophe is not a figure, that like Janus, carries two faces with a good grace.
> 
> —Wordsworth, May 5, 1814

What are the consequences of such a theory of apostrophe for reading Wordsworth? By understanding the figure as a "trope," as an arche-trope that literally repeats the "turn" of all figural language, we open up the concept of voice to the force of its differential structure and therefore to its deconstruction.[18] We also begin to perceive the relation between rhetoric and form in a poem such as "Tintern Abbey," which Wordsworth regarded as affiliated with the ode through what he called its "transitions," or turns or strophes, which turn out to be apo-strophes, or *aversios*, invoking first the "sylvan Wye" (56) and then the "dear, dear Sister" (121).[19] Milton's "Lycidas," as pastoral elegy rather than ode, organizes its three-part structure around a similar series of aversions that foreground the movement of voice: "Return, *Alpheus*, the dread voice is past" (124). And Coleridge typically structures his conversation poems and "Effusions" using apostrophes to create the present-past-future, or "out-in-out," transitions that M. H. Abrams has identified as a feature of the "greater Romantic lyric." Some Wordsworthian texts, such as the "Poem... Addressed to S. T. Coleridge," posit a larger structure of rhetorical address and its aversions. *The Prelude* has been called Wordsworth's best conversation poem, but at what point does apostrophe become conversation? Where does trope shade into genre? Or to put the question more directly: how many aversions does it take to make a conversation poem? Let me consider some of these issues in a brief close reading.

The case of Wordsworth is exemplary. As "a man speaking to men" (*Prose* 1: 138), the Wordsworthian poet by definition finds himself in situations of rhetorical address that are potentially apostrophic. I take as the *locus classicus* the text "There Was a Boy," in which the interruptive pause after the opening statement suggests a turning away:[20]

> There was a Boy: ye knew him well, ye cliffs
> And islands of Winander! (*Prelude* 5.364–65)[21]

# Romantic Aversions

As an example of forensic rhetoric, Wordsworth's text illustrates the "sudden removing" of voice, as both relocation and deletion. Indeed, there may have been a boy, but the speaker is *non habeas corpus,* and so must turn from his initial auditor to invoke the corroboration of witnesses: "Ye knew him well, ye cliffs / And islands of Winander!" The vocative itself does not signal apostrophe so much as does the movement from the third-person formula "There was" to the second-person pronoun "ye." This turn or trope, at once apostrophic and prosopopoeic, swerves passionately from an epitaphic statement about the Boy's death to an immediate address to a personified Nature. In doing so it anticipates the subsequent rhetorical and thematic reversals in the episode and implies intertextual questions: who would not testify for the Boy of Winander? who would not sing for him?

Seeking Nature's corroboration is not unusual for Wordsworth. In Book 1 of *The Prelude* a similar moment occurs, with the important difference that no apostrophe is used:

> The sands of Westmoreland, the creeks and bays
> Of Cumbria's rocky limits, they can tell
> How, when the Sea threw off his evening shade,
> And to the shepherd's hut on distant hills
> Sent welcome notice of the rising moon,
> How I have stood, to fancies such as these
> A stranger.... (1.567–73)[22]

No aversion here, not even in the appositional construction, but the powerful prosopopoeia still obtains. The assurance that the sands and creeks and bays "can tell" implies that the poet could turn to invoke their testimony, to call on these natural objects that they might answer him.[23] Their statements as witnesses would be to corroborate the poet's description of his response ("How I have stood ...") to the action of Nature ("when the Sea threw off his evening shade ..."). There is a dialogue between addresser and addressee, between nature and humanity, carried in the "welcome notice" sent by the sea to the "shepherd's hut." "The earth / And common face of Nature," Wordsworth writes following this incident, "spake to me / Rememberable things" (1.586–88). In such a collaborative speech act the poet seeks for no trophies, not even apos-trophes. Though he does not use *aversio* here, Wordsworth achieves a rhetorical effect remarkably similar to that in the first passage: here Nature is personified by being charged with a voice that "can tell"; in the Boy of Winander text, Nature is attributed with consciousness, or knowledge: "Ye knew him well!" But it is, Wordsworth fears, a knowledge purchased by the loss of power, which is to say, by the loss of voice: a power is gone, which nothing can restore. The apostrophic turning to Nature evokes "rememberable things," but also a guilty consciousness: Nature's response implies responsibility. For one can anticipate Wordsworth asking here the accusing question: "Where were ye, nymphs ... ?"—even as he had done some thirteen years earlier in another poem:

> Where were ye, nymphs, when the remorseless deep
> Clos'd o'er your little favourite's hapless head?
> For neither did ye mark with solemn dream
> In Derwent's rocky woods the white Moonbeam
> Pace like a Druid o'er the haunted steep;
> Nor in Winander's stream. ("The Dog—An Idyllium")[24]

The conventional elegiac topos of the invocation to nature is described also by the Wanderer in Book 1 of *The Excursion* (475–81):

> —The Poets, in their elegies and songs
> Lamenting the departed, call the groves,
> They call upon the hills and streams to mourn,
> And senseless rocks; nor idly; for they speak,
> In these their invocations, with a voice
> Obedient to the strong creative power
> Of human passion. (*Poetical Works* 5:24)

"Nor idly": this is no mere pathetic fallacy.[25] The voice that speaks or calls to Nature obeys the "spontaneous overflow of powerful feelings" (*Prose* 1: 127, 149), resulting in apostrophe or exclamation, the voice by "human passion" moved.

The sudden removing of voice is related to a silencing of voice, an overdetermined muteness that is "redoubled and redoubled" (5.378) in "There Was A Boy." First there are the "silent owls" (5.373), then the "pauses of deep silence" (1805: 5.405) that baffle the child, and finally the poet's "mute" address to the grave (5.397). Alternating with these silences is a succession of voices, sometimes choric, sometimes univocal, but always "responsive" (5.376) in their own answerable style. The text follows a sequence of aversions that thematize the adversarial aspect of forensic rhetoric: here, the boy is stationed vis-à-vis nature in a way that resembles a subject-object dialectic, the mind versus the world. But the colloquy in the text troubles this opposition by textualizing it, making "The Boy of Winander" into a type of conversation poem, intersubjective rather than dialectical.

Intersubjective dialogue or familiar colloquy is implied also in the naturalized apostrophe near the origin of *The Prelude*. The sudden beginning in MS. JJ shows a rhetorical aversion from a third-person form of address to an immediate "thou":

> Was it for this
> That one, the fairest of all rivers, loved
> To blend his murmurs with my nurse's song . . . ?
>        . . . For this didst thou,
> O Derwent . . . ? (Norton *Prelude* 1)

Recall Angel Day's example of *aversio,* "as if having spoken much of the vanitie of the worlde [one] shoulde thereupon turne and saie unto the world, O world" (90)—or, in this case, as if having spoken much *of* the River Derwent, Wordsworth should turn and speak *to* it. The 1798 passage continues the apostrophe, with additional notices of "thy silent pools" and "thy streams" (Norton *Prelude* 1), and then just as naturally returns to the original discourse.[26]

The opening of the 1805 *Prelude* uses apostrophe in a similar way, turning from a "there is" clause—"O there is blessing in this gentle breeze" (1.1)— to a series of apostrophes to Nature: "O welcome messenger! O welcome friend! / A captive greets thee . . ." (1.5–6). In the 1850 edition not only are these apostrophes deleted, but the personal pronouns "he" and "his," referring to the breeze, are replaced by "it" and "its," as if to localize the differential movement of voice, or to curb its animating power. But voice in Wordsworth cannot be contained so easily, or halted in one place for long; it is always on the move, even when engraved, like an epitaph, in rocks and stones and trees.[27]

I suggest that the Boy of Winander is a poet "sown / By Nature" and therefore lacking "the accomplishment of verse" (*Excursion* 1.77–78, 80). Yet he engages Nature in what De Quincey was the first to see as a "contest" or challenge to nature (160), in the tradition, as Geoffrey Hartman has suggested, of the singing contest of classical pastoral (*Fate* 183, 290).[28] Challenge, tumult, and battle lead to bafflement, silence, and death, and show us just how high the stakes in this singing contest really are.[29] Francis Jeffrey missed the pastoral conventions of the text when, in his review of Crabbe's *Poems* in 1808, he took Wordsworth's topos to be the "untimely death of promising youth" rather than of a promising poet (135). The linguistic or "poetic" aspect, however, is difficult to avoid, for the opening apostrophe advertises its own intertextuality. The Boy stands with his hands pressed "palm to palm" (5.371) over his mouth in an attitude of devotion or nature-worship, but also in imitation of Juliet's "holy palmers' kiss." Or does he not rather play the swan and die in music? Mouth and voice seem linked to hands and writing by their very contiguity. The intervocative exchange begins, significantly, with the Boy:

> he, as through an instrument,
> Blew mimic hootings to the silent owls,
> That they might answer him; and they would shout
> Across the watery vale, and shout again,
> Responsive to his call, with quivering peals,
> And long halloos and screams, and echoes loud,
> Redoubled and redoubled, concourse wild
> Of jocund din. . . . (5.372–79)

There is a turn here so large as to be a complete reversal. We often think of Wordsworth as borrowing a voice from Nature to inform his poetry, to "naturalize" it as a language of things rather than of words. "Oh! that I had a music and a voice / Harmonious as your own," he says to the breezes and groves in Book 12 (29–30). In this scene as well, the Boy's "mimic hootings" seem borrowed from nature: their mimesis, we naturally assume, is imitative of the owls' song. But the rhetorical structure of the passage creates interference with this reading, because here the direction is reversed: the Boy seems to confer the power of utterance on the owls; he gives away his voice to nature, and is silenced.[30] The sudden removing of voice comes as a "surprise," a "shock of mild surprise" that insinuates a deeper, usurping voice: "the voice / Of mountain torrents" (5.382, 383–84). The text establishes a series of acoustical oppositions between the Boy and Nature—sound/silence, source/echo, stimulus/response—in which the Boy appears to have the priority implied in the first term of each of these pairings. The owls "echo" the Boy: they "answer" him; they are "responsive" to his prior vocal stimulus. But is not this stimulus also a response? The word "mimic" carries not only a temporal reference, alluding to recurrent, pre-textual encounters between the Boy and the owls ("many a time / At evening ... would he stand ..." [5.365–66, 368]), but also a proleptic force, anticipating the present and future exchanges. The Boy of Winander is a Boy Wonder: he is a source that is already an echo, a repetition of recurrence in a finer tone. As examples of what Robert Frost calls "original response," the Boy of Winander's calls foreground their textual self-reflexiveness, their difference from themselves.[31] Whether we read the Boy's hootings as the call of the wild or "the call of the supplement," we are faced with a text redoubled with traces of other voices, other faces.[32]

The earliest version of the text, MS. JJ, with its wavering balance between first-person autobiography and third-person narration, contains a similar mimetic repetition in its description of the "pauses of deep silence" that "mocked" the Boy's skill (Norton *Prelude* 492; 1805 *Prelude* 5.405). "Mocked" becomes "baffled" by 1850, suggesting ridicule and usurpation, but "mocked" also repeats "mimic": silence imitates the Boy's song. To "answer" is not to mimic, unless the answer is echolalic, compulsively or automatically repetitive. The Boy's hootings, as onomatopoeic mimicry, are motivated. But they are also motivating: they stimulate both sound and silence. If we give linguistic and temporal priority to the Boy, however, we construct a hierarchy that is quickly undone by Nature; his voice is removed, suddenly deleted or overpowered by the silence of the grave. But even silence can be repeated: near his grave, Wordsworth writes, "A long half hour together I have stood / Mute ..." (5.396–97). The image of Wordsworth silently confronting a grave recurs throughout his poetry (for example, in both "spots of time," in the drowned man episode, even in the blind Beggar passage),[33] and tells us what is different about this elegiac moment. Why is the poet mute? Is he "struck dumb," as Paul de Man would say, because the poet is "frozen in [his] own death" (*Rhetoric* 78) as a result of being apostrophized by the Boy? Yet how would this explain the animating power of the trope? The Boy experiences the ultimate aversion, being "rolled round in earth's diurnal course" (*Poetical Works* 2: 216), while the poet completes the circuit of address through his "mute dialogue" (2.268) with the grave. Instead of reading the Boy's epitaph, as we might expect him to do, he appears as if he were *listening* to it, quietly awaiting the Boy's call, like the silent owls earlier. The Boy's death is not the death of voice, but only a sleep and a forgetting of it: the personified church near which he "slumbers" is described as "forgetful" (5.402):

> Of all her silent neighbourhood of graves,
> And listening only to the gladsome sounds
> That, from the rural school ascending, play
> Beneath her and about her. (5.403–06)

"Listening only to the gladsome sounds": that is, not listening to the Boy, who nevertheless yet speaks? The "sounds" that "play," like music, about the "silent neighbourhood of graves" repeat the "jocund din" of the Boy's earlier colloquy. Death is not the end of voice for Wordsworth, but only another turning of voice—into stone or "speaking monument" (*Prelude* 8.172), or the epitaphic "speaking face of earth" (*Prelude* 5.13).

The conferring of speech on nature, anticipated in the personifying apostrophe to the cliffs and islands, implies that the poet calls on these natural objects to have them testify, to make them "responsive to his call" or invocation. Reiterating this movement, the Boy plays Narcissus to the owls' Echo, giving them a voice but half their own. The poet, through his poem, mutely "answers" the Boy, whose hootings are now "the ghostly language of the ancient earth" (*Prelude* 2.309), *de profundis*. Gray's "Elegy," with another mute inglorious poet in another country churchyard, reverberates in the mind: "Ev'n from the tomb the voice of Nature cries" (41).

The turning aside of address, even to the point of its turning around, carries us far into the interplay of voice in Wordsworth. In these "turnings intricate of verse" (*Prelude* 5.603), directional shifts from cause to effect, or from expostulation to reply, become redoubled when we discover that the source is already an echo, self-mimicking in its repetition. Like the "dear Sister" in Book 14 of *The Prelude* (265) or, even more, like Eve in another of Frost's poems, the Boy of Winander teaches the birds to sing: "Never again would birds' song be the same. / And to do that to birds was why [he] came."[34]

## NOTES

1. In an essay entitled "Apostrophe," Jonathan Culler claims that whatever else apostrophes may be, "above all they are embarrassing: embarrassing to me and to you" (*Pursuit* 135). Many critics have referred to this essay. E.g., Mary Jacobus, explicitly echoing Culler, writes: "Apostrophe, as Jonathan Culler has observed, is an embarrassment" ("Apostrophe" 171). Barbara Johnson also cites Culler's argument: "Jonathan Culler indeed sees apostrophe as an embarrassingly explicit emblem of procedures inherent, but usually better hidden, in lyric poetry as such" (185). And Patricia Parker also turns to Culler on this point: "The vocative, or apostrophe, remarks Jonathan Culler in the course of a well-known essay on the subject . . . is also

frequently a subject of embarrassment" (30). Because it is allegedly so embarrassing, the figure, Culler asserts, has been "systematically repressed or excluded by critics" (*Pursuit* 137); more specifically, Jacobus argues, it has been "regularly ignored by writers on the ode" ("Apostrophe" 171). In another essay Culler repeats his thesis: "[A]postrophes are awkward and embarrassing. . . .Critics either ignore them or transform apostrophe into description" ("Changes" 39, 50).

2. For additional examples of critics who have referred to Culler on apostrophe, see Cynthia Chase (68), who reiterates Culler's argument approvingly, and L. M. Findlay (336–40), who challenges Culler on his analysis of temporality in apostrophe.

3. James A. Arieti and John M. Crossett point out that the earliest use of the word *apostrophe* is in Philodemus, first century B.C.; it was not until much later that the word became used in its technical rhetorical sense (101).

4. I am indebted for this reference to Paul H. Fry's citation of Auerbach in *Poet's Calling* 298 n.6.

5. This inaccurate translation has caused other commentators to fail to distinguish the two terms. See, e.g., Annabel M. Patterson (128 n.10), where, in her discussion of the *Rhetorica ad Herennium,* she follows Caplan in equating apostrophe and exclamation.

6. Since Longinus, the prerequisite for a sublime apostrophe or prosopopoeia has been passion or elevated emotion in the speaker or writer. Without this rhetorical sine qua non, both figures are in danger of falling from the sublime to the ridiculous. "How ridiculous," Coleridge is reported as saying, "would it seem in a state of comparative insensibility to employ a figure used only by a person under the highest emotion, such as the impersonation of an abstract being, and an apostrophe to it" (*Shakespearean Criticism* 2: 103). Wordsworth, who is frequently thought of as dismissing prosopopoeia altogether in his Preface to *Lyrical Ballads,* makes an important yet traditional qualification: personifications, he writes, "are, indeed, a figure of speech occasionally prompted by passion, and I have made use of them as such" (*Prose* 1: 131). Hence it goes without saying that Culler's deliberately corny apostrophe in "Apostrophe" (*Pursuit* 135) fails precisely because it lacks this one prerequisite. The point is that no figure is inherently embarrassing; only bad figures are so.

7. Fry writes: "[A]postrophe, the blanket form of *invocatio,* is defined in all the Rhetorics as a turning aside to address some absent hearer. . . .The poet speaks these asides to a pro tem audience and then re-turns to the audience that is understood to be listening, as it were, under contract" (11). My only amendment to this definition is that the hearer does not need to be absent, as my examples from Quintilian, Sherry, and Hoskins make clear.

8. Cf. Abraham Fraunce, in *The Arcadian Rhetoric* (1588): "*Apostrophe* turning away, is when the speech is turned to some such person to whom it was not first prepared, sometimes the turning is to men . . . sometimes from men, to Gods . . . sometimes to a dumb and senseless creature" (cap. 30). Puttenham, in his *Arte of English Poesie* (1589), has an entry on "Apostrophe, or the turne tale," in which we "either speake or exclaime at some other person or thing" (198–99). "The Greekes," he says, "call such figure (as we do) the turnway or turnetale" (199).

9. Other examples could be added, though some later rhetoricians simply repeat without acknowledgment these basic definitions. Thomas Blount, for example, in *The Academy of Eloquence* (1654), takes his definition from John Hoskins's *Directions for Speech and Style* (1599), as does John Smith in *The Mysterie of Rhetorique unvail'd* (1657).

10. Numerous contemporary handbooks also define apostrophe. Both the *Princeton Encyclopedia of Poetry and Poetics* and Holman's *Handbook to Literature,* to take only two well-known examples, give essentially correct definitions of the figure (though they both err in their choice of texts meant to illustrate apostrophe, on grounds that I shall demonstrate later).

11. Cf. Puttenham, who gives the following definition of "Ecphonesis or the Outcry":

> The figure of exclamation, I call him [the outcrie] because it utters our minde by all such words as do shew any extreme passion, whether it be by way of exclamation or crying out, admiration or wondering, imprecation or cursing, obtestation or taking God and the world to witnes, or any such like as declare an impotent affection. (177)

12. This is the point where the *Princeton Encyclopedia* and Holman's *Handbook* err. They both offer as an example of apostrophe the first line of Wordsworth's sonnet "London, 1802": "Milton! thou shouldst be living at this hour...."

13. See Paul de Man's note explaining how all "poem[s] of address" (*Resistance* 48) could be entitled *Prosopopoeia*—"As they in fact often are, though preferably by the more euphonic and noble term 'ode' or 'Ode to X'" (*Resistance* 53 n.22). It should be added that for de Man, X here refers to an inanimate object.

14. There exists a genre or mode of "address" as such: Wordsworth's "Address to My Infant Daughter Dora," "Address to Kilchurn Castle," and "Address from the Spirit of Cockermouth Castle" are examples. Similarly, Wordsworth's more than three dozen poems entitled "To X" (e.g., "To a Butterfly," "To Joanna," "To the Daisy," "To a Skylark," "To H. C.") all announce themselves as instances of this mode. One could add the genres of the verse epistle, conversation poem, hymn, sonnet dedicatory, etc., to this category. Hence I differ with Fry's terminology in his discussion of "the apostrophe called 'To H. C.'" (157). By definition, no poem called "To X" can be an apostrophe; apostrophe is a figure, not a genre.

15. Cf. Chase, who closely paraphrases Culler here: "Critics as various as George Shuster (in *The English Ode from Milton to Keats*) and Michael Riffaterre (in *La Production du texte*) have tended to dismiss apostrophe as being insignificant because it is simply conventional" (68).

16. But in Wordsworth, it should be added, the ear usually implies a voice to follow, often in alien, surprising, or usurping ways, as the Boy of Winander episode demonstrates.

17. How are we to account for the persistence of this error in Culler and those who follow him? Here we can only speculate. It may not be enough to say that the problem begins with Culler's incorrect definition of apostrophe and that therefore everything that stems from this misunderstanding is wrong, for what Culler has to say about the temporality of apostrophe is useful. Nor is Culler the first person to make the mistake, as a glance at any of a number of handbooks will show. A better way might be to begin with the effect and work back to the cause—that is, to begin with the notion of embarrassment and then attempt to figure out why apostrophe, of all figures, might be the source of such ticklishness or discomfiture. But here too we reach a dead end, for nowhere does Culler explain exactly why apostrophes are necessarily embarrassing; as I suggest, some are, and some aren't. I suspect the real motive for misreading has to do with a larger misunderstanding of Romanticism—perhaps the unexamined tendency to see it in terms of Mill's opposition between rhetoric or eloquence as public discourse ("heard") and poetry as private and subjective ("overheard") soliloquy (12). If, as Shelley said, the poet "is a nightingale, who sits in darkness and sings to cheer its own solitude with sweet sounds," then it is possible that a reader might misunderstand this to imply that the poet-nightingale has no need of rhetoric, no artfulness in its unpremeditated song. What could be sillier than a diversion of address when you're just talking to yourself? But this surely by now outdated view of Romantic lyricism neglects what Shelley goes on to say in the same sentence: the poet may be a nightingale, but "his auditors are as men entranced by the melody of an unseen musician, who feel that they are moved and softened, yet know not whence or why" (486). As Shelley

well knew, a word like *entranced,* from Longinus on, has clear associations with rhetoric and the power of persuasion: this bird is convincing. Or to turn the tables, in anticipation of my reading of Wordsworth's "There Was a Boy," the poet is an owl, whose auditors are moved and then "removed," as Peacham would say, through an aversion of voice. Much work, obviously, still needs to be done to dispel lingering fallacies about Romantic or lyric voice; we need, I think, to revise our understanding of Romanticism from the perspective of the history of rhetoric. Quite apart from social history or politics, the unwritten history of Romanticism lies in the history of its words. The present essay is one chapter in this unwritten history.

18. As I have described it, apostrophe may be thought of as a movement of language analogous to the Saussurean notion of "difference"—that is, the play or shuttling of terms within a closed language system. Every signifier evokes or recalls every other signifier in the system, so that the linguistic sign is constituted as an effect or function of this periphrasis. For Derrida, language attempts to cover up this effect of difference through a vocabulary of presence (*Writing and Difference* 279–80); linguistic identity thus is seen not as a function of movement, a turning or troping of signs, but as a stable self-presence. The concept may be applied to our case. If the question of apostrophe is not one of voice as such but of the movement or translation of voice from one addressee to another, then it is possible to see why apostrophe, as the very figure of difference—intersubjective, intertextual, intervocative—might be mistaken for address, the shuttling mistaken for presence. Apostrophe, however, is a carrier of voice, not voice itself. Regarding the concept of voice in Wordsworth, see Geoffrey H. Hartman's essays "Words, Wish, Worth" and "Timely Utterance" for the connection of voice and divine fiat (*Unremarkable* 90–119 and 152–62), "Blessing the Torrent" for the relation of voice to the domestication of the sublime (*Unremarkable* 75–89), and "The Use and Abuse of Structural Analysis" for voice in a ghostly or intermediary mode (*Unremarkable* 129–51).

19. In 1800 Wordsworth added the following note to "Tintern Abbey" in *Lyrical Ballads:* "I have not ventured to call this Poem an Ode; but it was written with a hope that in the transitions, and the impassioned music of the versification, would be found the principal requisites of that species of composition" (R. L. Brett and A. R. Jones 296). I am suggesting rhetorical grounds for considering this poem as an ode. Fry interprets Wordsworth's statement in a contrary, but persuasive, way: "'Tintern Abbey,' Wordsworth's greatest lyric," he writes, "is nothing like an ode" (179). Fry's echo of Shakespeare's sonnet ("My mistress' eyes are nothing like the sun") confirms the logic of what he goes on to say: "It is most probable that Wordsworth thought 'Tintern Abbey' too good to be called an ode" (179). However, cf. Lee M. Johnson, who argues that "Tintern Abbey" is "a blank verse Pindaric ode designed as a double golden section" (*Wordsworth's Metaphysical Verse* 19).

20. See Hartman's comments on what he sees as the eloquent "break" after the statement "There was a Boy" (*Fate* 183, 289, 341 n.10).

21. The bibliography of modern commentary on the Boy of Winander is long and varied. Here are some selected sources. For the definitive reading of the episode in relation to the theme of self-consciousness, see Hartman, *Wordsworth's Poetry* (19–22); see also his discussions in *Criticism in the Wilderness* (222–25) and *Fate* (182–83, 286–92). Other valuable studies include Heather Glen (264–71) and Morris Dickstein (379–82) for parallels with Coleridge's "The Nightingale"; Robert Rehder (81–89), A. H. Gomme (509–12), and Frank McConnell 166 on syntax; Leslie Brisman, *Poetry of Choice* (262–65) and *Romantic Origins* (337–61, 373), on "voice"; D. G. Gillham (82–83), William Shullenberger (115–17), A. W. Phinney (67–70), and Mary Jacobus, "Managing Books" (215–18), on language; Helen Regueiro (54–57, 88, 107), on incompleteness of self; Stephen J. Spector (86–88, 103–04) on mirror imagery; Thomas R. Frosch (1: 185–86, 192), Lionel Morton (23, 29–32), Richard J. Onorato (193–97), and Susan J. Wolfson (923–25), for a psychoanalytic approach; Tilottama Rajan,

"Death of Lyric" (198–200), on intertextualization; William H. Galperin (624–25), Karl R. Johnson (197–204), Joel Morkan (253), Kenneth R. Johnston (141–43), on education; Frances Ferguson (77, 167–70, 242–49), on episode as "reading"; Andrzej Warminski, "Missed Crossing," (991–96), Jonathan Arac (63–64), and Cynthia Chase (13–31) on interpretation. See also Michael Ragussis, *Subterfuge* (30); David Ferry (87–89); Ernest Bernhardt-Kabisch (490); J. Robert Barth (71–72); F. W. Bateson (21, 25, 28–30); Steven Lukits (156–60); Evelyn Shakir (163); C. C. Clarke (6–8); John F. Danby (111–14); Roger N. Murray (107–9); Aldous Huxley (57–58, 155–56); David Ellis (114–20); Herbert Lindenberger (41–43); John Jones (91–93); J. R. Watson (147–49).

22. Cf. David P. Haney, who cites this passage to trace the development of Nature in Book 1 of *The Prelude* "from a *ministering* force . . . to a *witnessing* agent" (59) and ultimately to a narrator who recounts "what the poet cannot" (60).

23. The turning to Nature in "There Was a Boy" could stand as a textbook example of Quintilian's fourth class of metaphor, in which animate things are substituted for inanimate things (*Institutio* 8.6.9–11). But this metaphorical substitution, one immediately recognizes, is also a prosopopoeia. Quintilian elaborates: "[A]bove all, effects of extraordinary sublimity are produced when the theme is exalted by a bold and almost hazardous metaphor and inanimate objects are given life and action" (8.6.11). His example demonstrates how metaphor, apostrophe, and prosopopoeia at times (especially in sublime writing occasioned by passion) may be interimplicated.

24. *Poetical Works* (1: 264). This text is more than pseudo-Miltonic pastiche, for it shows the sixteen-year-old Wordsworth experimenting with several poetic conventions at once: the tradition of pastoral elegy, the translation of Wales into the Lake District, and the invocation of Druid lore. Even the simple trimeter of "Nor in Winander's stream" seems unarguably derived from the style of "Lycidas."

25. There is a strong creative power in the ambiguity of the antecedent of "they speak." Who speaks? "They" obviously can be read as referring to "The Poets" three lines earlier, but following so closely upon the catalogue of hills and streams and rocks, the simple clause "they speak" can also be read as personifying these "senseless" objects, thus validating Wordsworth's claim that the poetic invocation is not "idly" done.

26. A related shift of pronouns is also found in the Boy of Winander fragment in MS. JJ: the turn from the third-person "he" and "his," referring to the Boy, to the speaking "I" and "my" at line 12 and thereafter complicates the issue of original authorial intent, since by the time the poem appears in *Lyrical Ballads* (1800) the pronouns have been changed back to third person. It is not, as is often claimed, simply a question of Wordsworth's switching from first- to third-person discourse: the text *originally* (i.e., in MS. JJ) is divided over the identity of the Boy. See Norton *Prelude* (492).

27. For the intersection of voice and the master trope of epitaph in Wordsworth, see my *Monumental Writing*, esp. 72–99.

28. In his *Recollections*, De Quincey recounts how Wordsworth once described his imaginative processes, using as illustration his own text "There Was a Boy"—"that exquisite poem in which he describes a mountain boy planting himself at twilight on the margin of some solitary bay of Windermere, and provoking the owls to a contest with himself" (160). "Provoking" is just the word; as syllepsis it conflates literal voicing and figural confrontation.

29. I have not forgotten that Wordsworth originally describes the vocal interchange as "a wild scene / Of mirth and jocund din" (Norton *Prelude* 492). But this "play" has its serious side, in the way that the skating episode in *The Prelude* Book 1 has its own "alien sound / Of melancholy" (1.443–44) that cuts across the "rapture" (1.430) of the child. One might pursue further parallels between the Boy of Winander episode and the skating scene in terms of the interplay of voice and echo.

30. There is a prosopopoeia within prosopopoeia here, in the conferring of "voice" on Nature. Wordsworth turns to apostrophize/personify the cliffs and islands and then recounts the story of the Boy of Winander. Within that story the animating power of voice again is used to personify Nature through the "mimic hootings." Though no apostrophe is explicit with the Boy, there is nevertheless a strange "diversion" of discourse when the owls stop answering and "the voice / Of mountain torrents" responds instead. The effect is as if the speaker had turned from his "proper" listener to an invoked listener "unawares" (5.385). As such, the narrative *in* the Boy of Winander passage may be read as a repetition-with-a-difference of the narrative *of* the Boy of Winander episode.

31. See Frost's poem "The Most Of It" for an intertextual gloss on the Boy's sound effects:

> He thought he kept the universe alone;
> For all the voice in answer he could wake
> Was but the mocking echo of his own
> From some tree-hidden cliff across the lake.
> Some morning from the boulder broken beach
> He would cry out on life, that what it wants
> Is not its own love back in copy speech,
> But counter-love, original response. (368)

32. See Derrida, *Writing* (211), for "the call of the supplement." Any approach to a deconstruction of the Boy of Winander's "speech act" must be chastened by Derrida's reminder that "it is not enough to recall that one always writes for someone; and the oppositions sender-receiver, code-message, etc., remain extremely coarse instruments. We would search the 'public' in vain for the first reader: i.e., the first author of a work" (*Writing* 227). What it means to be the "first" sender or "first" receiver is precisely what the Boy of Winander episode puts in question.

33. See my *Monumental Writing* (91–99) for a reading of the blind Beggar as "living epitaph."

34. See the extended apostrophe to the sister (*Prelude* 14.232–75), in which she is praised for "teach[ing] the little birds to build their nests / And warble in [the] chambers" of the poet's rocklike soul (14.255–56). Compare the "daylong voice" of the Eve-figure in Frost's poem "Never Again Would Birds' Song Be The Same" (369):

> Admittedly an eloquence so soft
> Could only have had an influence on birds
> When call or laughter carried it aloft.
> Be that as may be, she was in their song.
> Moreover her voice upon their voices crossed
> Had now persisted in the woods so long
> That probably it never would be lost.
> Never again would birds' song be the same.
> And to do that to birds was why she came.

# XI

# SHELLEY AND THE CICERONIAN ORATOR

*Stephen C. Behrendt*

Percy Bysshe Shelley's view of rhetoric is intimately related to his practical understanding of the complex mediated relations that exist among the individual author and his or her various audiences. Shelley maintained perhaps the strongest sense among the Romantic authors—even including Coleridge—of the nature and function of oratory as Cicero conceived it, as the eloquent public discourse of an exemplary mind committed to the public welfare. Throughout his writings, and particularly in *De Oratore,* Cicero links the orator (whose ideal form he refers to as "the perfect orator")[1] with the public good of the state and its citizens alike: "I consider, that by the judgment and wisdom of the perfect orator, not only his own honor, but that of many other individuals, and the welfare of the whole state, are principally upheld" (*DO* 14).

This view accords perfectly with that which Shelley seems to have held—and which he sought both privately and publicly to convey about himself—virtually from the start of his career as scholar, intellectual, author, philosopher, and patriot. Given that the prototypical Ciceronian orator's discourse unites "intellectual depth" with "civic usefulness" (Kennedy, *Classical Rhetoric* 89), it is surely no coincidence that Shelley singles out Cicero for particular praise in *A Defence of Poetry,* not just for style but also for substance: "his language has a sweet and majestic rhythm, which satisfies the sense, no less than the almost superhuman wisdom of his philosophy satisfies the intellect; it is a strain which distends, and then bursts the circumference of the hearer's mind, and pours itself forth together with it into the universal element with which it has perpetual sympathy."[2] Characteristically, Shelley allows the "it" following the semicolon to govern both preceding nouns, language and wisdom, vehicle and substance. Nor is it mere coincidence either that the *Defence* proceeds immediately from its author's remarks on the brilliance of Cicero's language to the sort of statement that at once succinctly reveals both Shelley's train of thought and the company with which he chose throughout his life to associate himself: *"All the authors of revolutions in opinion* are necessarily poets as they are inventors" (*PP* 485; my emphases).

As early as 1812 Shelley cast himself both physically and rhetorically in the role of public speaker in his abortive in situ attempt to play a role in Irish emancipation. His *Address to the Irish People* (1812) is only the first among a series of occasional essays whose titles—some of which employ the specific word *address*—reflect Shelley's consistent concern with the efficacy of oratory and its centrality to contemporary discourse. Indeed, in a noteworthy passage in the Preface to *Prometheus Unbound* (1819) Shelley later listed those public figures who are "in one sense, the creators, and, in another, the creations of their age." While his final list includes poets, philosophers, painters, sculptors, and musicians, Shelley originally included orators in this list as well.[3] His decision to delete orators from his final list may reflect his appreciation of the particular temporality of the orator's art, which, like the actor's, transpires in time and space in a fashion that was irrecoverable before the age of modern technology. Or perhaps it reflects a growing suspicion on his part about the more purely pragmatic, worldly, and ultimately less idealistic stance of the opportunistic orator as Cicero represented him in the character of Antonius. For the discussion that ensues in *De Oratore* between Crassus and Antonius raises the thorny issue of the relation in oratory between surface attractiveness of form and inhering honesty of content, and with it slippery matters of ethics. Crassus is never entirely without his Antonius, Shelley may finally have reasoned; nor is the principled use of rhetoric by the committed orator ever entirely free from all taint of calculated misrepresentation, no matter how lofty the heights to which it invites us to lift our eyes. Whatever motivated it, Shelley's deletion of orators from his list in 1819—the year of the Peterloo Massacre, which responded to a particularly volatile exercise in public oratory in Manchester—is worth noting.

That he refers in letters and formal works alike specifically to Cicero, in whose works he read widely, and that he originally included orators in his pantheon of notables, hints at the extent of Shelley's preoccupation with rhetoric and oratory. Moreover, that Shelley linked the rhetorical strategies of the antinomian political agitator Jesus Christ (whom he respected and admired in his specifically political role) with those of "the successful orator" (as we see in his *Essay on Christianity*) suggests further that Shelley saw in the political activist a figure who fused one strain of the classical rhetorical tradition with another strain—one particularly congenial to the melioristic Shelley—that emerges in the New Testament in the figure of Jesus Christ: orator, statesman, and martyr. Shelley numbered among the models he most respected two radical dialogic speakers who died for their causes: Socrates and Jesus. Given the nature of Cicero's life and death (his hands and head—the emblems of his oratorical powers—were cut off and nailed up in Rome) in relation to his political and intellectual activism, he too figured easily and naturally for Shelley as a martyr.

Like all three of these precursors, Shelley regularly employed in his works both overt dialogic form (as in his dramas, or in the prose of *A Refutation of Deism*) and covert or embedded (as in *Julian and Maddalo*).[4] Shelley had from the start associated with political activism and its consequences several figures with whom he repeatedly aligned himself in his writing and in his life experience. He invoked the precedents of Socrates and, later, Jesus at moments of personal crisis from which he was attempting either to extricate himself or to manufacture rhetorical capital. Shelley was not unique in such self-positioning, though, as we discover in the Preface to Cantos 6 through 8 of *Don Juan*, where Byron invokes the memories of Socrates and Jesus for precisely the same purpose: "Socrates and Jesus Christ were put to death publicly as *Blasphemers*, and so have been and may be many who dare to oppose the most notorious abuses of the name of God and the mind of man. But Persecution is not refutation, nor even triumph: the 'wretched Infidel,' as he is called, is probably happier in his prison than the proudest of his Assailants" (*Byron* 590).

His practice suggests that in his deliberate self-fashioning as orator and prophet Shelley was attempting to entwine and update the classical and Christian strains of rhetorical tradition in a new, heterogeneous rhetoric more directly suited to the volatile times of Regency England and to the vexing diversity of audiences—of "listeners"—that had evolved with the expansion of literacy, a development that was itself assisted by the rapid growth of the print medium and of the public spokespersons who embraced, adopted, and manipulated that medium. There is also some historical precedent for Shelley's project in the frequently overlooked tradition of eighteenth-century pulpit oratory whose physical monument, the enormous body of sermons published in that century, nevertheless probably accounts for only a fraction of the sermons actually preached. One view attributes this explosion of published homiletic literature to the formal sermon's particularly close relationship to public affairs during the eighteenth century. That is, while in earlier ages and again later, sermons typically exhibited a more strictly religious character suited to the demands of public worship, in the eighteenth century the sermon possessed "firm and conscious ties with secular society," so that matters as diverse as politics, education, philosophy, and literature both made demands upon sermons and created demands for them (Downey 10). This aspect of civic engagement within the public homiletic tradition was not lost upon Shelley, whose professions of atheism may overshadow but cannot erase his acquaintance with this tradition.

It has been proposed that Jesus and the evangelists who recorded his history in the Gospels "created a new speech" grounded in an unprecedented immediacy of language and imagery and in which "the form in which Jesus and his followers spoke and wrote could not be separated from what they communicated" (Kennedy, *Classical Rhetoric* 128). Shelley's task, in his prose no less than in his poetry, was to formulate a comparable new speech, one whose ultimate capacity to empower lay in the communal relationship it strove to establish with its audience and which was therefore able to "engage the reader in the play of interpretation" without unilaterally binding its audience "in the iron grip of manipulative machinery" (Tetreault 16). Shelley's writings in all genres exhibit repeated attempts rhetorically to reach out to the reader, to draw the reader into community with the author, to engage the reader not just at the intellectual and rhetorical levels but also at the emotional and experiential. These attempts are always undertaken ostensibly in a spirit of intellectual inquiry and sociopolitical benevolence, with an implied promise that the reader retains the liberty characteristic of free and open discourse. At the same time, Shelley reserved to himself the right, especially in the prose works, to manipulate his reader into intellectual and emotional roles and positions that would predispose that reader to a fair hearing—even to acceptance—of arguments that Shelley would advance. After all, while Shelley may invite dialogue, what he publishes is a text, an artifact that by its physical nature is necessarily an elaborate monologue by the author, regardless of the seeming dialogical forms it may embody. The act of writing for public consumption is by nature one based to a significant extent both on a rhetorically generated illusion of community and dialogue and, as we shall see, on intellectual seduction carried on through the vehicle of eloquence.

Shelley had made Cicero's acquaintance early on in his time at Eton, where he delivered one of Cicero's speeches on July 30, 1810. He probably reread him during his brief stay at Oxford, where the curriculum for fifth- and sixth-form boys included among the works which the boys were supposed to read "Dr. Middleton's Cicero," the "standard" edition by Conyers Middleton, 1741 (White, *Shelley* 1: 35).[5] Advising Thomas Jefferson Hogg in 1813 that he had been studying "many of Cicero's philosophical works," Shelley dubbed Cicero "one of the most admirable characters the world ever produced."[6] Earlier in the same year Shelley had in *Queen Mab* numbered Cicero with Socrates and Marcus Aurelius Antoninus as preeminent among the virtuous spirits of the ancient world (*Queen Mab* II.176–79). The influence of Cicero's *De Natura Deorum* is apparent in that poem and its notes, as it is also in *A Refutation of Deism* (1814) and, later, in *Prometheus Unbound* II.v.23–28, in the myths of Aphrodite/Venus that Shelley refashions in his figure of Asia.

Shelley's familiarity with Cicero grew further still as a consequence of his reading program during the summer of 1815, when he was especially struck with "some passages of wonderful power" in the (probably first) Oration against Verres, a work in which Cicero employs a tactic that Shelley adopts frequently in his political prose, the prefaces to his poems, and even his personal letters: the rhetorical ploy of offering the audience (for Cicero, the judges; for Shelley, his real or invented readers) an opportunity to distinguish themselves by following his presumably sage and constructive advice. In his rhetorical stance in the prosecution of Verres, in fact, Cicero modeled for Shelley the posture of civic-minded self-sacrifice which the young Romantic often adopted in his own self-characterizations: Cicero observes that while the trial stands to bring the judges "great popularity" (or great discredit), "to me it will bring much toil and anxiety" (*Selected Works* 56). In a subsequently canceled passage of his preface to *Adonais* (1821), Shelley lamented that although his efforts as author stemmed from "the ardent & unbounded love I cherished for my kind," they had earned him "public calumny," "censure," and "unsocial contempt" out of all proportion with the intentions or the consequences of his publications.[7] Intent upon benefiting his audience, Shelley observes here and elsewhere, the author or orator risks misunderstanding, rejection, even persecution as the reward for his civic-minded sacrifices.

Shelley wrote to Hogg that on the whole he regarded Cicero's Orations as inferior in effect and interest to his metaphysical essays; nevertheless, the Oration for Archias disappointed him only by its brevity.[8] It is probably no coincidence that the subject of this oration is a poet, for throughout his career Shelley regularly associated himself with—and read his own experiences in terms of—poets and philosophers of preceding ages. That scheme of associations is in fact one of the distinctive features of Shelley's self-inscribed affiliation with the philosophers—and particularly with the orators and rhetoricians—in whose lives and experience he saw his own experience and his own consuming passions prefigured. Shelley's career discloses a consistent pattern of self-mythologization that turns on the figure of the committed public figure of whom the poet/philosopher/orator is the epitome. Cicero had held that the "great man" is master alike of philosophy and rhetoric, each of which is useless without the other. More important, Cicero appreciated the centrality of the orator and philosopher to the body politic, articulating in his writings and in his life alike an awareness of the extent to which such a figure is unavoidably political. For Cicero, the ideal environment for this public figure—at once philosopher and patriot—is a totally free society: "a constitutional republic in which persuasion rather than violence is the instrument of political power" (DeLacy 114). In a passage from the Preface of *Hellas* which his publisher suppressed, Shelley implicitly numbered himself among that "new race" who labored for a similar environment in contemporary England despite the oppressions practiced against them and their country by "the privileged gangs of murderers and swindlers, called Sovereigns" (*PP* 410).

Shelley involved himself early on with issues of freedom of expression and freedom of the press, launching a public career that would include works in prose and poetry alike that were deemed rhetorically inflammatory, morally and politically subversive, and spiritually heretical. Rising to the defense of Daniel Isaac Eaton, the radical publisher who had been prosecuted by the government for republishing the third part of Paine's *Age of Reason,* Shelley drafted an energetic if not consistently effective response in the form of his *Letter to Lord Ellenborough* (1812). Writing to William Godwin, Shelley tellingly shifts topics (without even beginning a new paragraph) from a discussion of his growing distrust of Christianity and his preference for "the virtues & genius of Greece & Rome" to a disarmingly direct query about the Eaton affair:

> What do you think of *Eaton's* trial & sentence. I mean not to insinuate that this poor bookseller has any characteristics in common with Socrates or Jesus Christ, still the spirit which pillories & imprisons him, is the same which brought them to an untimely end. Still, even in this enlightened age, the moralist & reformer may expect coercion analogous to that used with the humble yet zealous imitator of their endeavours. I have thought of addressing the public on the subject, & indeed have begun an outline of the address.[9]

Notice that Shelley specifies that he has begun an address on the subject, an indication that his model was more oratorical than strictly literary in nature. This oratorical bent is entirely consistent with his angry question in the same letter, only a few lines before the passage just quoted: "Shall Socrates & Cicero perish whilst the meanest hind of modern England inherits eternal life?"[10] My point is not so much to link Socrates and Jesus with Cicero as predecessors of equal stature in Shelley's mind as to indicate that already in 1812 the young reformer brought to his envisioned project in public consciousness-raising a Ciceronian perspective.

Nor did Cicero disappear from the constellation of significant persons, sociopolitical circumstances, and rhetoric in later years. In *A Defence of Poetry*, for instance, Plato and Cicero reappear in company with Bacon as exemplars of prose writers whose works exhibit the "measured language" traditionally regarded as virtually the exclusive domain of poetry.[11] Shelley's remarks here elaborate upon Wordsworth's assertion in his Preface to the *Lyrical Ballads* that there is no essential difference in the language appropriate to either genre. "The distinction between poets and prose writers is a vulgar error," Shelley writes (*PP* 484–85).[12] Indeed, Cicero makes the same point about "poets, who have the nearest affinity to orators," "being somewhat more restricted in numbers, but less restrained in the choice of words, yet in many kinds of embellishment his rival and almost equal; in one respect, assuredly, nearly the same, that he circumscribes or bounds his jurisdiction by no limits, but reserves to himself full right to range wherever he pleases with the same ease and liberty" (*DO* 199, 24).

Nor would Shelley have resisted seconding Cicero's contention that the greatest orator must be a comprehensive scholar and humanist:

> In my opinion, indeed, no man can be an orator possessed of every praiseworthy accomplishment, unless he has attained the knowledge of every thing important, and of all liberal arts, for his language must be ornate and copious from knowledge, since, unless there be beneath the surface matter understood and felt by the speaker, oratory becomes an empty and almost puerile flow of words. (*DO* 11)

> [N]o one is to be numbered among orators who is not thoroughly accomplished in all branches of knowledge requisite for a man of good breeding. (*DO* 24)

Cicero's point is not far from Milton's observation in the *Apology for Smectymnuus* that "he who would not be frustrate of his hope to write well hereafter in laudable things, ought himself to be a true poem, that is, a composition and pattern of the best and honorablest things" (Milton 694), a remark that itself fashions the exemplary individual in rhetorical terms.

More congenial still to Shelley must have been Cicero's conviction that the orator must also be a skilled writer:

> But the chief point of all is that which (to say the truth) we hardly ever practice (for it requires great labor, which most of us avoid); I mean, to write as much as possible. *Writing is said to be the best and most excellent modeler and teacher of oratory;* and not without reason; . . . all the thoughts and words, which are the most expressive of their kind, must of necessity come under and submit to the keenness of our judgment while writing; and a fair arrangement and collocation of words is effected by writing, in a certain rhythm and measure, not poetical, but oratorical. Such are the qualities which bring applause and admiration to good orators; nor will any man ever attain them unless after long and great practice in writing. . . . (*DO* 42–43; Cicero's emphases)

A passage like this one could not fail to strengthen Shelley's conviction about the rectitude of the public course he was charting for himself, nor to validate it through a demonstrably significant historical precedent.

In one of the most detailed examinations of Shelley's philosophical skepticism since the pioneering work of C. S. Pulos, Terence Allan Hoagwood observes that Sir William Drummond's *Academical Questions* "was evidently Shelley's favorite work of modern philosophy" (Hoagwood 2).[13] Hoagwood notes that Drummond's title itself derives from Cicero's *Academica,* which was published in 1553 under the title *Academicarum quaestionum,* a title that was translated as *Academic Questions* in later nineteenth-century editions (Hoagwood 2, 213n.). Over and over in his work Shelley constructs variations on the skeptical debate: overtly in *A Refutation of Deism* (1813), for instance, and more covertly in works like *Alastor* (1816) and *Julian and Maddalo* (1819). But the rhetorical framework and assumptions of skepticism are everywhere apparent. Perhaps skepticism's chief attraction for Shelley lay in its utter lack of intellectual closure: a thoroughly dialectical system, skeptical philosophy is inherently incapable of absolute resolution or equilibrium, but must be always pressing forward to question every proposition, every seeming "answer." This is precisely why the skeptical tradition figures with particular prominence in Shelley's political writings and why those writings must have seemed to the conservative sociopolitical establishment of his time to be especially dangerous. For without absolute values—closed answers—which an authoritarian thinker or society could invoke to impose closure and limit inquiry, not just the skilled rhetorician but potentially every thinking being held the potential for complete liberty, complete personal freedom, of expression as of thought. Such is the utopian philosophical anarchism that informed the writings of Tom Paine, William Godwin, and others whom Shelley admired (Scrivener, Royle and Walvin, Stafford).

Indeed, it is in his oppositional role that the Ciceronian orator is of greatest interest to the antinomian Shelley. Perhaps the key passage in *De Oratore* is that which paints the orator as political activist, a passage worth quoting in full:

> We are not contemplating, in this discourse, the character of an every-day pleader, bawler, or barrator, but that of a man who, in the first place, may be, as it were, the high-priest of this profession, for which, though nature herself has given rich endowments to man, yet it was thought to be a god that gave it, so that the very thing which is the distinguishing property of man might not seem to have been acquired by ourselves, but bestowed upon us by some divinity; who, in the next place, can move with safety even amid the weapons of his adversaries, distinguished not so much by a herald's caduceus as by his title of orator; who, likewise, is able, by means of his eloquence, to expose guilt and deceit to the hatred of his countrymen, and to restrain them by penalties; who can also, with the shield of his genius, protect innocence from punishment; who can rouse a spiritless and desponding people to glory, or reclaim them from infatuation, or inflame their rage against the guilty, or mitigate it, if incited against the virtuous; who, finally, whatever feeling in the minds of men his object and cause require, can either excite or calm it by his eloquence. (*DO* 60–61)

So neatly does this passage seem to gloss a host of Shelley's works in prose and poetry alike that it is tempting simply to interpolate their titles among Cicero's stipulations: "to expose guilt and deceit" (*Letter to Lord Ellenborough, Address to the Irish People, Address to the People on the Death of the Princess Charlotte*), "to restrain them" (*A Proposal for Putting Reform to the Vote throughout the Kingdom, The Cenci*), "to protect innocence from punishment" (*Letter to Lord Ellenborough,* the efforts on behalf of Richard Carlile), "rouse a spiritless and desponding people" (*The Mask of Anarchy* and the shorter political poems of 1819 like "Song to the Men of England"), "reclaim them from infatuation" ("England in 1819," *The Masque, Hellas* [especially the canceled sections of the preface]), "inflame their rage against the guilty" (*The Masque,* the Princess Charlotte pamphlet), "or mitigate it" when it is incorrectly turned against the virtuous (the efforts on behalf of Eaton, Carlile, and the "Derbyshire rebels").

Cicero offered Shelley a particularly congenial model for his own view of the contemporary activist, radical, prophet, and patriot epitomized in the eloquent public figure of the orator, the individual gifted alike in mind and in language. Taken in light of Cicero's model, Shelley's characterization of the poet as "the unacknowledged legislator of the world" suggests that one reason why the poet's legislative function (at least in Shelley's Regency England) is not acknowledged is that the modern world has already begun to regard artistic and political activity as essentially separate and even mutually exclusive.[14] Shelley, of course, rejects this separation entirely in the *Defence,* where genius (philosophical as well as aesthetic) involves "the connexion of poetry and social good" (*PP* 492). Indeed, the more closely one reads the *Defence* as a work either about politics or about poetry (and poetics), the more inescapable becomes the fact of their inextricable linkage: they are in fact alternative aspects of one another dependent for their nature and identity merely upon the external circumstances governing each activity and its consequences. This is why in his discussion Shelley continually juxtaposes poetry and society, the poet and the state.

The majority of the individuals Shelley cites in the *Defence* have been involved, by definition, primarily in public discourse. The epic poet, especially in the classical period, was first a public performer and only secondarily and ex post facto a writer (or transcriber) of verses originally sung to a physically present audience. Likewise, the majority of the philosophers (including the specifically political) Shelley mentions are characterized by their fondness for dialogic forms of public discourse. That both the writing activity and the reading activity have become private, isolated—and isolating—acts in which the earlier speaker-listener relationship is superseded by a writer-reader one, is a distinctly modern phenomenon. In his *Proposal for Putting Reform to the Vote throughout the Kingdom* (1817), Shelley calls for meetings and assemblies at which public discussion might take place. Twenty years earlier, in *Political Justice,* William Godwin had likewise reminded his readers of the need for public discussion as a means of promoting both personal and sociopolitical improvement.[15] That such open discussion had been a fixture of English public-house and coffee-house life (to cite only two locales) is of course a commonplace. But that a political activist like Shelley feels called upon in 1817 to remind his readers of this traditional forum suggests the extent to which that activity was in fact diminishing in proportion to the spread of literacy and the growing privatization of the reading act.

Rhetoric, Renato Barilli has written, is "a comprehensive, total way of using discourse" in which "the physical aspects of speech are not sacrificed to the intellectual dimension" (Barilli vii). It is a system of discourse that is at once presentational and intellectual, involving as it does both conditions and techniques of delivery and matters of intellectual content. When the public speaker—the orator of Cicero's model—is compelled by circumstances to become the public writer—the posture represented in Shelley's public discourse, particularly but not exclusively in the prose—the physical aspects of that presentational manner must be transferred to and embodied in the written text. In the dialogue that transpires in *De Oratore* between Crassus (Cicero's chief representative) and Antonius, the matter of presentation figures large when it comes to the orator's effectiveness at persuasion. Antonius in fact echoes Crassus's requirement that the orator be an exemplary individual when in Book II he speaks at length about how "the morals, principles, conduct, and lives" of the orators should be meritorious so that they will predispose the audience toward them and their causes, and against their adversaries, whose traits "should be such as to deserve censure" (*DO* 132–33). While some of the favorable characteristics—like softness of voice, expressiveness of countenance, and mildness of speech—belong primarily to the presentational aspect of the orator's role, Antonius lists others that are properly and effectively embodied as well in the orator's written text: good-naturedness, liberality, gentleness, piety, "grateful feelings," freedom from selfishness and avarice, and "every thing that characterizes men of probity and humility." The fuller the presence of these characteristics in the orator, he contends, the more they will generate benevolence in the audience and alienate the affections from those persons in whom they are perceived to be absent: "the contrary qualities to these, therefore, are to be imputed to your opponents" (*DO* 132–33). Shelley follows this prescription to the letter in case after case, both in his letters—where he is always at pains to appear generous, unassuming, charitable, nonjudgmental, and eager for advice or even correction—and in public statements intended for publication and hence for public consumption—where he portrays himself in similar fashion as an advocate for benevolence and the common good eager to risk misunderstanding and rejection alike at the hands of an uncharitable and impercipient majority as a necessary consequence of his commitment to the national (indeed the universal) welfare of the human community.

This is not to say that Shelley ignored, any more than Cicero had, the fact that the sway over the audience's judgment purchased by the orator's eloquence is an advantage much to be sought. Crassus associates eloquence, not surprisingly, with virtue generally and in particular with that power which gives voice to the mind in such a way "that it can impel the audience whithersoever it inclines its force." Given this awesome power, which necessarily carries with it a significant ethical and intellectual obligation, it is "the more necessary that it should be united with probity and eminent judgment; for if we bestow the faculty of eloquence upon persons destitute of these virtues, we shall not make them orators, but give arms to madmen" (*DO* 255). Crassus's remark presumes a productive and responsible link between the orator's skill and the inherent rectitude of the "man of good breeding" who recurs throughout Cicero's work. In Book II Antonius counterposes the example of the (at least potentially) unprincipled application of eloquence by the irresponsible orator whose goal is not truth but power, not understanding but mere assent: "our mode of speaking is to be adapted to the ear of the multitude, to fascinate and excite their minds, and to prove matters that are not weighed in the scales of the goldsmith, but in the balance, as it were, of popular opinion.... For there is nothing ... of more importance in speaking than that the hearer should be favorable to the speaker, and be himself so strongly moved that he may be influenced more by impulse and excitement of mind than by judgment or reflection" (*DO* 127, 131). And yet Antonius does no more here than expand upon Crassus's very early observation that he knows of nothing more noble than "to be able to fix the attention of assemblies of men by speaking, to fascinate their minds, to direct their passions *to whatever the orator pleases, and to dissuade them from whatsoever he desires*" (*DO* 13; my emphases).

The line separating the responsible uses of eloquence from the irresponsible is a fine one, in other words, and whether or not one crosses it (or is perceived to have done so) depends upon both the orator and the audience, for as Shelley wrote in 1811, "great responsibility is the consequence of high powers."[16] Now this is precisely the issue to which Shelley addressed himself repeatedly in his poetry and prose. Shelley began early on to distinguish among what he envisioned as a variety of distinct and frequently nonoverlapping audiences, and to address each in a form of discourse he deemed appropriate to it. In his poetry he distinguished among "esoteric" works, addressed like *Prometheus Unbound* to "the highly refined imagination of the more select classes of poetical readers" (*PP* 135), and "exoteric" works like *The Masque of Anarchy,* "Song to the Men of England," "Similes for Two Political Characters" ("To Sidmouth and Castlereagh"), and "A New National Anthem," intended instead for a mass readership that included the minimally literate of lower- and middle-class English society. He likewise identified various readerships somewhere in the middle, as we recognize in his comment to Leigh Hunt that *Julian and Maddalo* employs "a certain familiar style of language to express the actual way in which people talk with each other whom education and a certain refinement have placed above the use of vulgar idioms."[17]

Shelley's remark, which echoes Wordsworth's pronouncements in the Preface to *Lyrical Ballads* about the "language really used by men" (Wordsworth, *The Poems* 1: 869), points to the larger subject of the language, style, and rhetoric appropriate both to multiple audiences and to diverse literary productions. Practical and applied rhetorical theory in eighteenth-century England as it was represented in works like George Campbell's *Philosophy of Rhetoric* (1776), Hugh Blair's *Lectures* (1780), and Lindley Murray's *English Grammar* (1795) had made it easy to dismiss from serious consideration any discourse attributed to a "vulgar" source and had rendered increasingly difficult the formulation of a variety of discourse appropriate for any but the most elite class of audience. Indeed, by the end of the eighteenth century there seems to have been general agreement that when it came to public discourse "there were two types of language which were intrinsically related both to class distinction and to qualities of mind" (Olivia Smith 29). Shelley suggests as much in the same letter to Leigh Hunt when he admits the inappropriateness even of "the familiar style" to "the treatment of a subject wholly ideal." Needless to say, the general feeling was that the "vulgar" idiom—or anything smacking of it—was fit neither for employment nor for consumption. It was the radical journalists—the Paines, Eatons, Woollers, Hones, Cobbetts, and Carliles—who would eventually batter down this door by means of a mushrooming print medium whose force and scope grew to irresistible proportions. It is not insignificant that Shelley read these authors, defended them, and adopted their rhetoric in his own works. It was less to enfranchise the specifically "vulgar" than to expand the parameters of the "polite" that Wordsworth and—more insistently and systematically—Shelley undertook rhetorical projects that paralleled those of the radical journalists.

The rhetorical features of Shelley's compositions (or "performances"—perhaps the more strictly accurate term) varied in direct proportion to the nature and characteristics of the several audiences Shelley half perceived and half created.[18] Shelley possessed a shrewd sense of what today would be termed "marketing strategies"; he knew how to package his works and how to publicize them, although his precarious personal circumstances ultimately prevented his personally manipulating the means of carrying through most of his schemes and placed him in the shaky hands of less committed (or less reckless) associates whose continued residence in England (and whose natural desire to avoid prosecution and imprisonment) made caution a watchword. Nevertheless, his early plans to "plant" comments and reviews in the periodical press (as he did in connection with *Zastrozzi* and *Queen Mab*)[19] reveal a sensitivity to diverse means of gaining access to readerships by stimulating natural human curiosity. Likewise, his plan early in 1813 for publishing a collection of "Biblical Extracts" in an impressive, expensive format similar to Godwin's *Essay on Sepulchres* (1809) reveals an awareness of how to gain through apparent association.

At the same time, however, Shelley concurred with Cicero in holding the supremacy of substance over presentation, of content over form. Nevertheless, he appreciated as well as Cicero did the advantage for the former of careful manipulation of the latter, and he understood that preparing an audience for receptivity required assessing it in advance and approaching it at least in part on its own terms. Cicero claimed that success in persuasion rests upon three things: "that we prove what we maintain to be true; that we conciliate those who hear; that we produce in their minds whatever feeling our cause may require" (*DO* 114). In fact, the latter two objectives facilitate the first. Discussing the career of Jesus in his *Essay on Christianity*, Shelley virtually describes and justifies his own procedure when he analyzes the rhetorical subterfuge Jesus practiced with particular effectiveness:

> Jesus Christ did what every other reformer who has produced any considerable effect on the world has done. He accommodated his doctrines to the prepossessions of those whom he addressed. He used a language for this view sufficiently familiar to our comprehensions.... Let not this practice be considered an unworthy artifice.... All reformers have been compelled to practice this misrepresentation of their own true feelings and opinions.... In fact, truth cannot be communicated until it is perceived. The interests therefore of truth required that an orator should so far as possible produce in his hearers that state of mind in which alone his exhortations could fairly be contemplated and examined. Having produced this favorable disposition of mind Jesus Christ proceeds to qualify and finally to abrogate the system of the Jewish law. (*CW* 6:242–43)

Shelley forthrightly acknowledges in this passage the orator's particular advantage (which Antonius pinpoints in *De Oratore*, as we have seen) for manipulating the emotions as well as the intellect of the audience. Having secured with the audience a favorable reception through speech, bearing, and prior reputation for mildness and good will, Shelley proceeds, Jesus was able the more effectively to attack and to subvert the audience's own system without producing immediate and instinctive resistance.

But there is more, for Shelley also observes of Jesus that "like a skilful orator (see Cicero de Oratore [sic]), he secures the prejudices of his auditors, and induces them by his professions of sympathy with their feelings to enter with a willing mind into the exposition of his own" (CW 6:242). What is perhaps most remarkable about this passage is not what Shelley wrote but what he deleted. For in his manuscript draft his verb was not *induces* but rather the far more telling *seduces*.[20] One can understand why Shelley altered his word in an essay he contemplated publishing, but one can equally well appreciate that Shelley's original word captures exactly the spirit of that variety of oppositional rhetoric which operates not by aggressive confrontation but rather by subtle persuasion, by gentle manipulation, by seduction. Overcoming unreasoning (and therefore unreasonable) opposition is the dissenting rhetorician's first task, and it is therefore imperative to manufacture sympathy, the surest sign of one's acceptance into a community of discourse. One is inevitably reminded in all of this of Plato's *Phaedrus*, to which *De Oratore* functions diversely as imitation, continuation, and commentary (even the initial setting under the plane tree is carried over). In that dialogue Socrates explicitly links rhetoric with human good, and the orator with the good of the community. "Since the function of rhetoric is in fact to influence men's souls," he tells Phaedrus, the effective orator must know and understand the varieties of souls that exist, and must address his or her discourse accordingly and with care: "to the types of soul thus discriminated there corresponds a determinate number of types of discourse" (*Phaedrus* 517). Only by "knowing" the souls of his or her hearers by entering deliberately and in advance into a bond of full sympathy with them (or by engineering such a bond) does the orator acquire the power to move the audience, "addressing a variegated soul in a variegated style that ranges over the whole gamut of tones, and a simple soul in a simple style" (*Phaedrus* 523).

David Hume, another of Shelley's favorite skeptical philosophers, had written that "the chief source of moral distinctions" is sympathy, a power located not in the rational intellect but rather in the matrix of human feelings (Hume, *Treatise of Human Nature* 618). This principle receives its finest articulation in Shelley's call in the *Defence* for that love which is "a going out of our own nature, and an identification of ourselves with the beautiful which exists in thought, action, or person, not our own" (PP 487), an action of moral unselfishness whose most powerful motivation lies in the shared imaginative acts of writing and reading—or in speaking and listening, as Cicero might have put it. As Shelley remarks in *An Address to the Irish People* (1812), "you cannot alter a man's opinion by beating or burning, but by persuading him that what you think is right, and this can only be done by fair words and reason" (CW 5:221). This generous approach to his audiences invites—even demands—reciprocal generosity on the audience's part. It is an approach firmly grounded in the principles of Ciceronian rhetoric and one that is an integral part of the image of the public prophet and patriot—the committed orator—that Shelley sought throughout his life to fashion for himself.

## NOTES

1. "Since I have to speak of the orator, I must of necessity speak of the perfect orator; for unless the powers and nature of a thing be set before the eyes in their utmost perfection, its character and magnitude can not be understood " (Cicero, *De Oratore* 216). All quotations from *De Oratore* follow the 1970 Southern Illinois University Press edition and are noted parenthetically in the text as *DO*.

2. *Shelley's Poetry and Prose* 485. References to the *Defence* and several other of Shelley's works follow this Norton edition, designated hereafter as *PP*.

3. See Bodleian library MS. Shelley e. 2, fol. 35 recto. Sculptors were added to the original list, perhaps when orators were deleted.

4. It is worth recalling that Shelley was fond of sending off copies of his works in prose and poetry alike to engage their recipients in dialogic correspondence; *The Necessity of Atheism,* which Shelley seems to have sent out widely under a variety of pseudonymous disguises, offers a particularly striking early instance.

5. When Mary Shelley read Cicero in 1820, this was the edition she used; see her *Journals* 1: 326–27.

6. To Thomas Jefferson Hogg, Nov. 26, 1813, *Letters* 1: 380.

7. See the Bodleian Library MS. Shelley adds. e. 20, fol. 11 recto.

8. To Thomas Jefferson Hogg, late August 1815, Sept. 22, 1815, *Letters* 1: 429, 432.

9. To William Godwin, June 11, 1812, *Letters* 1: 307–8.

10. To Godwin, *Letters* 1: 307.

11. In the *Essay on Christianity,* in which Shelley refers explicity to Cicero's *De Oratore,* he likewise cites Bacon's *Novum Organum* within the context of his discussion of Jesus's rhetoric. See *Complete Works* 6: 242–43. This edition (the "Julian edition") is still the standard for many of the prose works and is the source used here for those works for which better scholarly editions are not available; citations are identified parenthetically in the text as *CW*.

12. See also William Keach (20–21).

13. Pulos's landmark study, *The Deep Truth,* was followed by Lloyd Abbey's *Destroyer and Preserver,* which dealt primarily, as its full title suggests, with the poetry. Hoagwood's is the only sustained study of the skeptical context specifically and exclusively of Shelley's prose.

14. When Eugene McCarthy sought the Democratic nomination for President of the United States in 1968, for instance, much was made of the fact that McCarthy was a poet as well as a politician, the former being portrayed by politicians and journalists alike as somehow precluding his ability to be the latter.

15. See, for instance, Godwin's remarks on the social and political function of conversation in his *Enquiry* (Godwin 1: 285–300).

16. To Elizabeth Hitchener, Nov. 26, 1811, *Letters* 1: 196.

17. To Leigh Hunt, Aug. 15, 1819, *Letters* 2: 108.

18. Walter J. Ong has written especially pertinently about this general phenomenon of the author's formulation of her or his audience, and perhaps nowhere so succinctly as in one of his titles: "The Writer's Audience Is Always a Fiction." Shelley's efforts to direct his works to particular "targeted" audiences has been the subject of several extended studies, including Webb, Scrivener, and Behrendt.

19. Shelley wrote to Edward Fergus Graham in April 1810, instructing him to buy favorable reviews of *Zastrozzi* (*Letters* 1: 5–6); in an attempt to publicize the suppressed *Queen Mab,* he seems to have authored several long extract-reviews of it in the *Theological Inquirer* in 1815.

20. See the Bodleian Library MS. Shelley e. 4, fol. 23 recto.

*Part III*

*Biblical Rhetoric*

# XII

## PROPHETIC FORM
### THE "STILL BETTER ORDER" OF BLAKE'S RHETORIC

*Leslie Tannenbaum*

If, as Blake insists, the Bible is the great code of art, then we must turn to the Bible for the concept and rationale of Biblical form that underlies his prophetic books. But first we must look at Blake's ideas about form, as articulated in his prose writings. In a late illuminated work, "On Homer's Poetry," Blake protests against the concept of an externally imposed unity in a work of art:

> Every Poem must necessarily be a perfect Unity, but why Homers is peculiarly so, I cannot tell: he has told the story of Bellerophon & omitted the Judgment of Paris which is not only a part, but a principal part of Homers subject
> But when a Work has Unity it is as much in a Part as in the Whole, the Torso is so much a Unity as the Laocoon. (*Complete Poetry and Prose* 269)

In "On Virgil," which is etched on the same plate as Blake's comments on Homer, the form produced by the Aristotelian concept of unity is called "Mathematic Form," as opposed to Gothic, which is "Living Form." Blake's preference for organic form is reiterated, this time with reference to pictorial composition in his *Vision of the Last Judgment,* where he says that "All Art is founded" not upon the "General Masses" of a composition, but upon the minute discrimination of the manners, intentions, and characters of individual parts (550). The subordination of the general to the particular, with a reliance upon internal coherence among the parts rather than upon an externally imposed order, was precisely the principle that Blake, like many of his contemporaries, found to be operating in the Bible.[1] In Biblical poetry, as Murray Roston has pointed out, form is subordinated to significance, with the basic unit of Hebrew verse being the self-contained distich of parallel lines that embody a concrete and "vividly concise picture," thus leading to particularization and creating form by simple juxtaposition (22–24). In the prophetic books of the Bible, the same principle works on a larger scale: particular units are

185

combined to form whole books that are connected through the internal coherence of their parts.

In fact, this principle of internal coherence that informs the prophetic books of the Old Testament, as opposed to the principles of unity, chronology, and symmetry, eluded many of the classically trained eighteenth-century literary critics and Biblical exegetes. Even Bishop Lowth, who was the unquestioned authority on Biblical poetics and who had produced a highly acclaimed translation of Isaiah, failed to find such a principle operating in the prophetic books of the Old Testament. Lowth, of course, was the discoverer of the principle of parallelism in Hebrew poetry, and thus he established that prophetic poetry consisted of the accumulation of individual distichs (*Sacred Poetry of the Hebrews* 2:24–59). He restricted his definition of prophetic poetry to those verse passages that predict future rewards or punishments (64–65). Such poetry, Lowth maintains, does not often display any regularity of form: "In respect to the order, disposition, and symmetry of a perfect poem of the prophetic kind, I do not know of any certain definition which will admit of general application. Naturally free, and of too ardent a spirit to be confined by rule, it is usually guided by the nature of the subject only, and the impulse of divine inspiration" (69). Some of the prophetic poems do display regularity of form, however, and it is only from these that Lowth selects examples, in deference to the neoclassical prejudices of his audience, to show that in the prophetic books of the Bible there are many instances of poems "which may with propriety be classed the most perfect and regular specimens of poetry" (69).[2] Thus Lowth, acceding to the age's preference for external form,[3] hints at but does not pursue a principle of internal form.

When Lowth looks at the total form of the prophetic books, he again shows his limitations. He observes that the writings of the prophets often contain genres other than prophetic poetry: historical narratives, prose orations, sacred odes, and elegies (*Sacred Poetry of the Hebrews* 2:60–61, 64). But he does not attempt to explain how all of these various forms cohere within a given prophetic book; nor can he find coherence among seemingly disconnected prophecies that are juxtaposed in the writings of the prophets.

When faced with these difficulties, Lowth falls back upon the opinion of previous commentators, resolving that any incoherence in the writings of the prophets must be attributed to either the irrational nature of the divine afflatus that completely overwhelms the prophet or to the possibility that the prophetic book in question was a collection of individual prophecies that were imperfectly collected by redactors (86).[4]

Since Lowth had begun to argue for the presence of art or design in the writings of the Old Testament prophets, he should have gone forward to vindicate the inspiration of the Biblical prophets on the basis of their aesthetic integrity and coherence. This, at least, was implied by Thomas Howes, who in "Doubts Concerning the Translation and Notes of the Bishop of London to Isaiah, vindicating Ezekiel, Isaiah, and other Jewish Prophets from Disorder in Arrangement" (1783), castigates Lowth for falling back upon received assumptions and claims to extend the work begun by Lowth. Howes, it should be noted, announced that he was not concerned with proving the inspiration of the Hebrew prophecies; his main purpose was to establish the authenticity and the aesthetic integrity of those works. If, as the deists claimed, some of the prophecies were written after their accomplishment rather than before, Howes is not disturbed. He is content to prove that at least those prophecies were composed shortly after their fulfillment had taken place, while those events were fresh in the writer's memory and were uncorrupted by tradition. By establishing the authenticity of scriptural facts and dates and thus getting freethinkers to acknowledge the authenticity and antiquity of the contents of the prophetic writings, Howes leaves the freethinkers' "denial of the reality of the prophecies" with "no other effect than to substitute good human testimony for the events in question instead of that which is divine" (116).

While Howes thus claims that his arguments provide reasonings that will be available to all, leaving readers to draw whatever inferences that they can, "consistently with a good conscience at the bar of Reason and Judgment" (117), he reveals throughout his arguments a concern for freeing believing Christians from the spurious arguments of previous Biblical commentators, for removing from the prophetic books the attribution of "a disorder [that] seemed to many to render the arrangement unworthy of being ascribed to divine agency," and for making the arguments for the inspiration of the prophets plausible again (211, 213, 215, 227–28, 259–63, 269). By asserting that "the best human works approach the nearest to divine" and by showing that the art of the Old Testament prophets is compatible with divine inspiration (269), Howes brings Biblical criticism in line with contemporary literary theories of inspiration, natural genius, and poetic grace—thus making the Bible the *locus classicus* of the issue of inspiration vs. mechanical composition, artlessness vs. art.[5] Going beyond Lowth, Howes reconciles these conflicting theories of composition and satisfies the need to believe that inspiration is not inconsistent with art and intelligible form.

Although Howes focuses on Lowth's notes and introduction to his translation of Isaiah, he sees Lowth's error as symptomatic of a larger problem that had existed in Biblical tradition from the time of Saint Jerome until the eighteenth century—the assumption that the writings of the Hebrew prophets were in a state of disorder, that they were "an irregular jumble of history, poetry and prophecy, as has disgusted some candid christians, and distressed all" (227). Looking back to Biblical tradition for an explanation of a possible alternative method of arrangement, Howes concludes:

> Now, excepting Jerome, not one of the interpreters, down to the translator [Lowth], seems to have had the least idea of the possibility of any better and more reasonable order of arrangement, than that of the *chronologic* order in which the prophecies were *delivered;* but this is by no means true, for there are at least two other kinds of order, and both preferable, viz. that of *historic order* in which the prophecies were accomplished, and also that *oratorical*

*order* which might be thought best suited to the purpose of *persuasion and argumentation.* (138–39)

Here Howes extends Jerome's suggestion that there might be a more useful order than chronological order and goes on to maintain that whenever a prophet departs from chronological order of delivery, he does so to "substitute a better order of arrangement, namely, either the order of *historic accomplishment,* or the still better order of oratorical and persuasive *argumentation"* (139).

This "still better order" Howes also calls "poetic arrangement" (293).[6] Howes claims that this poetic or oratorical order is better than the historical order of accomplishment for a number of reasons. First, his arguments for the historical order are based upon facts of Biblical chronology that he has yet to prove, and he himself admits that we cannot always be certain of some of these facts (332–33). Second, whenever the prophet claims that a prophecy has been fulfilled by a specific event, he becomes a fallible interpreter of previous prophecies rather than the communicator of inspired truths (146–47). Finally, the whole purpose of the historical order, in which a prophet cites the fulfillment of an earlier prophecy made by a previous prophet or by himself, is to establish the credibility of any predictions that the prophet may make about the future (178–79); and Howes seems to be anxious to de-emphasize the predictive nature of prophecy in order to establish its credibility on the basis of its rhetorical or visionary function.

The rhetorical function of prophecy as Howes conceives it is derived from his concept of the character of the prophet:

> Upon the whole then we find, that the Jewish prophets were members, if I may be allowed the expression, of the *opposition,* which subsisted in those days, and they figured among the leading patriots of their country; who took very free, yet necessary liberties in criticizing and condemning the measures of their kings, nobles, priests and people, both in their private and public capacities; and how unwelcome soever any facts they might foretell, yet they employed sufficient *indicia divinae potentiae* to convince all parties who did not obstinately resist conviction, that the events they foretold would certainly arrive: these temporary and occasional harangues delivered at different times, yet all tending to the same purport, as "Did I not tell you this before? and did I not tell you true?" were afterwards combined by their respective authors into one continued metrical oration of admonition; and entered as *protests,* to be preserved for the instruction of succeeding ages, concerning the obstinacy of kings and the infatuation of the people, notwithstanding the signs of the times. (214–15)

In order to advance their arguments concerning political and religious policy, the prophets eschewed the "beaten track and vulgar round" of chronological order (140) and adopted either the historian's privilege of placing events immediately after those earlier events and attitudes that caused them, or the poet or orator's method of interrupting the chronological or historical order of events to juxtapose two or more distant events that support a general assertion or theme (149). This oratorical order could also include the citation of the fulfillment of a previous prophecy by an earlier prophet or by the prophet himself in order to establish the veracity of a new prophecy that he was about to make; the juxtaposition of events that show the opposite fates accompanying belief or disbelief, obedience or disobedience; or the gathering of prophecies "concerning similar subjects, or concerning neighboring nations, or similar nations, such as Heathens in distinction from Jews, or concerning similar ranks of persons in the same nation: accordingly they will be found sometimes actually thus to arrange together their prophetic exhortations to the Jewish kings; and in like manner those relative to the priests and prophets, and also those relative to the people at large" (150). These and other methods were employed by the prophets "in order to connect together their several *argumentations,* to avoid confusion, and to render their transition from one subject to another more natural and obvious" (150–51).

The writings of the prophets, then, are always coherent, using at alternate times either the chronological, historical, or oratorical method of arrangement to create "one continued exhortatory oration or prophetic poem out of the several parts" (152). Moreover, since these prophetic writings are poetic, as has long been allowed by all, there is no reason for readers to be perplexed by the abrupt and bold transitions, which we also find in the lyric poetry of the classical age. Although the Greeks and Romans exhibit greater art and skill in oratory, the writings of the prophets are "venerable specimens of the rude efforts of reason as well as genius in those early ages of composition" (263), exhibiting a degree of perfection that was suitable to the character of the speaker and the audience of those rude times (212). Furthermore, older than the classics, the prophetic books of the Bible contain rhetorical modes that were later adopted by Athens and Rome. According to Howes, the writings of the prophets contain a fusion of genres that were later separated and perfected by the Greeks.

There is no direct evidence that Blake read Howes's treatise, which was published in Howes's *Critical Observations on Books, Antient and Modern* (1776–1813), but it is highly probable that Blake heard of Howes's ideas. Joseph Johnson, for whom Blake had been engraving since 1780 and with whose circle Blake was familiar, published in 1785 William Newcome's translation of Ezekiel, which stated Howes's thesis in the preface and excerpted portions of Howes's treatise in the notes.[7] Howes's *Critical Observations* would also be known to Johnson's circle, of which Priestley was a part, since they contained an attack on Priestley.[8] But even if Blake had no knowledge of Howes, direct or indirect, he would have been aware of many of the principles of prophetic form that were delineated by Howes, for although Howes, as he himself claims, was the only writer to carefully explain the principles of unity underlying the Old Testament prophecies, similar ideas about the structure of prophecy were available in contemporary works on rhetoric and literary criticism, commentaries on the Old Testament prophets, and, most importantly, commentaries on the Book of Revelation, which was universally acknowledged to be the summation and the most perfect embodiment of all Biblical prophecy.[9]

Howes was not the only writer to deemphasize the predictive nature of prophecy and insist upon its rhetorical function. Charles Daubuz, in his commentary on Revelation, maintained that prophecies are written "not to satisfy men's curiosity, but to serve as good Argument," to increase the faith, hope, and patience of Christians; prediction is secondary and serves only to further this end (103). John Gill observed that the commission of the Old Testament prophets "lay very much in shewing the people, to whom they were sent, their sins and transgressions; to convince them of them; to reprove them for them; to call them to repentence and reformation; or otherwise tell them they would issue in their ruin" (v, iii).[10] Similarly, Fénelon, in his well-known and highly influential *Dialogues on Eloquence in General,* describes the Biblical prophets as orators who use bold figures and actions to rouse the audience's passions and direct them toward truth and right action (96–98). Fénelon's "true orator," who must necessarily be a poet in order to "imprint things on the hearer's mind" and thus raise his audience to a perception of the truth through the imagination, is echoed by Howes's interchangeable use of the words poetry and oratory.[11] This concept of the prophet as poet and orator is part of the Augustinian tradition, of which Fénelon is the eighteenth-century embodiment, and which finds its expression in the concept of the orator in Milton's prose works.[12] Blake's explicit acknowledgment of this aspect of the prophetic tradition is revealed in *Jerusalem,* where in the introductory "To the Public," prophet, poet, and orator are one.[13]

This emphasis on the prophet's role as orator led other critics and commentators besides Howes to note and explain the basic fact of prophetic structure, which had been originally pointed out by Jerome—that prophecy did not employ chronological order. As Howes himself was probably aware, Vitringa, in his frequently reprinted rules for interpreting prophecy, stated that the Biblical prophets broke chronological order to serve specific oratorical ends. The same point is developed in Samuel White's commentary on Isaiah (xxviii–xxxvi).

But more frequently than the commentaries on the Old Testament prophecies, the commentaries on Revelation dwelt upon the rhetorical function of nonchronological order. Joseph Mede, whose *Key of the Revelation* (1627) was constantly alluded to, summarized, and quoted in eighteenth-century commentaries, was the first to point out that Revelation abandons chronological order in favor of synchronic order that permits the prophet to expand upon and clarify particular issues.[14] Charles Daubuz, like Howes, finds this method analogous to that of the best historians, "who endeavor to give a full Account of every Matter as they take it in hand, to make a compleat system of the whole, interposing Digressions; and then returning to the principal Matters, by giving such Hints and Transitions as suffice to let us understand to what they belong, and how, as to Point of Time, they come in or end with the rest" (19–20). Johannes Albrecht Bengel, whose commentary on Revelation in his famous *Gnomon of the New Testament* (1734) was reprinted in abridged form in John Wesley's *Explanatory Notes Upon the New Testament*, observes:

> Indeed the whole structure of it breathes the art of God, comprizing in the most finished compendium, things to come, many, various; near, intermediate, remote; the greatest, the least; terrible, comfortable; old, new; long, short; and these interwoven together, opposite, composite; relative to each other at a small, at a great distance; and therefore sometimes as it were disappearing, broken off, suspended, and afterwards unexpectedly and most seasonably appearing again. In all its parts it has an admirable variety, with the most exact harmony, beautifully illustrated by those digressions which seem to interrupt it. In this manner does it display the manifold wisdom of God shining in the economy of the church through so many ages. (2:313)

This godlike creation of unity in diversity was also embodied in the prophet's combining many genres into one work. Howes, of course, was not pointing to this conclusion when he claimed that Old Testament prophecy contained all genres. But his claim, intended for an audience whose taste was essentially neoclassical, was a sophisticated reworking of the traditional belief that the Bible's divine origin was also manifested in the fact that it contained all wisdom.

Within the multiform and nonlinear structure of prophecy, the poet-orator was free to provide multiple perspectives on the same theme or the same event. Eichhorn observed this quality in Ezekiel, opening with a statement that is strikingly similar to Blake's concern with the "minute particulars" of form: "A generally acknowledged character of Ezekiel is, that he minutely distinguishes every thing in its smallest parts. What the more ancient prophets brought together under one single picture, and to which they only hinted, and what they explained with the utmost brevity or shewed only from one side, that he explains and unfolds formally, and represents from all possible sides."[15] In Revelation, given its synchronic pattern that Mede discovered, this multiplicity of points of view is more apparent and was noted by such commentators as Henry Hammond, Philip Doddridge, Richard Hurd, Charles Daubuz, and David Pareus.[16]

Thus the principles of prophetic structure explained by Howes—the emphasis on the rhetorical function of prophecy, the subordination of chronological order to thematic order, the juxtaposition of episodes without proper transitions, the use of digressions, the combining of various genres, and the use of multiple perspectives—were available in the scattered observations of seventeenth- and eighteenth-century critics and commentators, particularly those who dealt with Revelation. But there were other principles either hinted at or ignored by Howes that were educed by other writers, particularly ideas about the dramatic and visual nature of prophecy.

Almost all of the commentators on Biblical poetry in general and prophetic poetry in particular remark upon the boldness of transitions in scriptural writing. Many commentators extend this observation to draw analogies between prophecy and drama. Samuel Horsley, in describing Isaiah's visionary style, had recourse to a theatrical metaphor: "In prophecy, the curtain (if the expression may be allowed) is often suddenly dropped upon the action that is going on, before it is finished; and the subject is continued in a shifted scene, as it were, of vision. This I take to be a natural consequence of the manner in which futurity was represented, in emblematic pictures, to the imagination of the prophet" (73–75).[17] Moreover, Mede, like Horsley, insists upon the pictorial nature of prophecy; but Mede goes on to assert that Revelation is literally a work of composite art, combining pictures and language, since "those visions concerning the Seales were not written by Characters in letters, but being painted by certain shapes, lay hid under some covers of the Seales; which being opened, each of them in its order, appeared not to be read, but to be beheld and viewed."[18]

Although the multimedia form of Revelation, as Mede perceives it, is an obvious prototype of Blake's visionary forms dramatic, it must also be remembered that Revelation and the books of the Old Testament prophets contain emblematic actions performed by the prophets themselves, actions that communicate pictorially the prophet's divine message. In Revelation, Saint John is a participant in his own vision, performing a significative action by eating the small book (10:9–10). Blake explicitly states his awareness of this aspect of Biblical prophecy when, in the second Memorable Fancy of *The Marriage of Heaven and Hell,* Ezekiel explains that the cause of his eating dung and lying alternately on his right and left sides was "the desire of raising other men to a perception of the infinite" (*MHH*, pl. 13). Fénelon, among others, understood such "figurative actions" to be the effect of divine inspiration (96). The prophet thus makes his own body the form of his message. Blake's essentially figurative art, which illustrates his prophecies, using the human body to express spiritual states, can be seen as an extension into the plastic arts of the prophet's dramatic use of the human form to shape and reinforce his verbal message.

Blake's use of the principles of prophetic form, as they were understood by his contemporaries, is markedly present in his early prophecies. His episodic narration and his use of abrupt transitions and rapidly shifting scenes are immediately apparent in *America,* for instance, where the scenes constantly shift back, forth, above, and even below the Atlantic; where Orc's speech on plate 8 is followed without any preparation by the war song of Albion's Angel on plate 9, followed by an equally sudden shift to the hills of Atlantis on plate 10. In *Europe,* the song of the sons of Urizen is abruptly followed by Enitharmon's song, without any indication of a change in speaker (4:9–10). The most extreme example of this trait is to be found in *Africa,* where often each line marks a new location in time and space, as Blake traces the transmission of Urizen's law and religion:

> Adam shudderd! Noah faded! black grew the sunny
>    African
> When Rintrah gave Abstract Philosophy to Brama in the
>    East:
> (Night spoke to the Cloud!
> Lo these Human form'd spirits in smiling hipocrisy War
> Against one another; so let them War on; slaves to the
>    eternal Elements)
> Noah shrunk, beneath the waters;
> Abram fled in fires from Chaldea;
> Moses beheld upon mount Sinai forms of dark delusion.
> (3:10–17)

Blake also resembles the Biblical prophets in his practice of disrupting the chronological sequence of events in his early prophecies. One important method of creating this disruption is, as several critics have pointed out, Blake's use of illustrations to arrest narrative movement. Karl Kroeber notes, for instance, that the illustrations to Urizen militate against any temporal order that may exist in the narrative because of the distinct integrity of each individual plate, which creates a tableau effect, and because many of the illustrations do not illustrate the text in any conventional sense and are not arranged sequentially (9–11).[19] Similarly, Jean Hagstrum points out that Blake's works are made up of tableaux in which "the proper movement is . . . both literally and metaphorically, from plate to plate. There is no onward rush of temporal movement" (84).

Hagstrum and W. J. T. Mitchell attribute this effect not only to Blake's use of illustrations but also to his poetic practice, since Blake's poetry, even without the illustrations, disrupts the reader's sense of chronological movement.[20] One verbal technique that Blake uses to achieve this effect is borrowed from Ezekiel and Revelation: the practice of first giving a vision in brief and then elaborating on it in detail.[21] Thus the events depicted in the preludia to *America* and *Europe* and in Eno's prefatory song in *The Book of Los* are contracted versions of the same events that the ensuing prophecies elaborate upon. In *Europe* there are not one but two treatments of the same events that are simultaneous with the action of the Preludium.[22] And Urizen's speech in Chapter II of *The Book of Urizen* narrates events that are simultaneous with the events of Chapter I. Furthermore, as Mitchell maintains, the first eight chapters of *The Book of Urizen* are really "alternative performances of the same event" (Poetic and Pictorial Imagination" 353). This principle of simultaneity, as we have seen, is most apparent in the book of Revelation and was publicized by Mede and the numerous commentators who followed him.

Besides simultaneity, Blake, like the Biblical prophets, uses digressions to disrupt chronological sequence. In *America* Blake temporarily halts the escalating conflict between England and America with a brief description of the history of Atlantis (10:5–10), and in *Europe* a longer digression describes the building of Verulam (10:1–23). In *Africa,* after summarizing the transmission of law and religion in ancient times and before continuing his chronicle into the eighteenth century, Blake offers a flashback that tells the story of Har and Heva's reaction to the effects of that transmission (4:5–12). In *The Book of Ahania* Blake uses digression more fully than in any of the other early prophetic works, with each chapter interrupting the narrative with a digression. Each of the first four chapters stops the action to elaborate upon the creation of a particular element that plays an important part in the narrative present.

Blake also follows the prophets in offering within a single work multiple perspectives on a given event or issue. In *America*, for instance, he offers several interpretations of the coming of Orc. In fact, the whole poem is a clash of viewpoints, as the debate between Orc and Albion's Angel in plates 6 to 9 makes evident. Orc, of course, perceives his energies to be joyful and renovative, whereas Albion's Angel perceives them to be destructive and fearsome. On plates 10 to 11, a third point of view is offered by the thirteen angels on their magic seats in the Atlantean hills. *Europe* offers three different visions of the eighteen hundred years of European history: the introduction presents the fairy's perspective, the preludium is the nameless shadowy female's, and the prophecy itself is divided between the English people's and Enitharmon's.[23] Susan Fox maintains that *Europe* is the only prophetic work before *Milton* to present "a layered organization of multiple perspectives," that is, a variety of points of view on the same event, superimposed upon each other. The other prophecies offer different perspectives, but these "perspectives are ordered consecutively and responsively, even when they are perspectives on the same event" (12). *Africa* offers a variety of reactions to Urizen's law, and *Asia* presents three points of view concerning the revolution in Europe: those of the Kings of Asia, Urizen, and Orc. In *The Book of Urizen*, the perspective shifts between the Eternals, Urizen, and Los. Similarly, Ahania's lament at the end of *The Book of Ahania* offers an alternate view of the action of the poem, as does Eno's song at the beginning of *The Book of Los*.

These various perspectives are not only presented by shifts in scene and point of view in Blake's narrative but are also represented by Blake's illustrations, which can contradict each other, contradict perspectives offered in the text, even offer perspectives that are totally different from any given in the text.[24] All of these possibilities can be seen in *America*, whose fourteen plates that comprise the Prophecy present a "dynamic 'single' visualizable picture— of shifting multiple perspectives" (Erdman 103).

Blake's use of verse and illustration to create multiple perspectives in *America* and in his other prophecies, as Erdman suggests, makes his prophecies windows into or promptbooks for a "mental theater" in which the reader achieves imaginative vision (93). In this perception and in his calling *America* "an acting version of a mural Apocalypse" (95), Erdman approaches what we now understand to be an important inheritance from the prophetic tradition: the dramatic use of multiple perspectives within the prophetic or apocalyptic theater, which is originally located in the mind of the prophet and which, through the communication of his prophecy, is relocated in the mind of the reader. The Apocalypse and the Old Testament prophecies were understood to be dramas in which different perspectives, rather than different characters, contended with each other (Wittreich, *Angel of the Apocalypse* 181; "Opening the Seals" 42–43). This understanding of the dramatic nature of prophecy was elucidated in Pareus's commentary on Revelation, which "was absorbed into eighteenth-century commentaries on Revelation and treatises on prophecy" ("Opening the Seals" 36). Other critics besides Erdman have understood that Blake's "Visionary Forms Dramatic" involve contending perspectives rather than characters, especially since Blake's "characters" represent different points of view rather than fully rounded individuals,[25] but few have understood that this important principle of prophetic structure comes from Biblical tradition.

Blake, in his handling of multiple perspectives, also follows prophetic structure within a given prophetic book by using multiple styles and genres that contain these different perspectives and hold them in dynamic tension.[26] The dramatic effect of Biblical prophecy is particularly heightened by the prophet's adoption of the dramatist's technique of using "choric devices both to lead an audience toward, and to jostle it into adopting, new perspectives" (Wittreich, "'Poet Amongst Poets'" 106). This dynamic interaction between lyric and other modes in Blake's prophecies is noted by Swinburne, who regards Blake as a poet whose "lyrical faculty had gained and kept a preponderance over all others visible in every scrap of his work" and who states that Blake's "endless myth of oppression and redemption, of revelation and revolt, runs through many forms and spills itself by strange straits and byways among the sands and shallops of prophetic speech" (188, 194). Swinburne observes that in Blake's prophetic books this diversity of styles and forms included "gigantic allegory," epic narrative (in which the poet "passes from the prophetic tripod to the seat of a common singer"), and many examples of Blake's "grand lyrical gift," some of those lyrical passages being "not always unworthy of an Aeschylean chorus . . . each inclusive of some fierce apocalypse or suggestive of some obscure evangel" (195). George Saintsbury, commenting on the variety of rhythms in Blake's verse, notes, "it has been said that more or less regular lyrics occur" in some of the prophetic books (3: 127), a statement reminiscent of Lowth's commentary on the poetry of the Hebrew prophets. And more recently, Alicia Ostriker perceives in Blake's prophecies "a limited number of distinguishable styles," which include that of "narrative, oratory, lyric, incipient naturalism and the Job-like piling up of rhetorical questions" (123–24, 158–70). Ostriker further observes that Blake's works adopt from the Bible "the rhetoric of lamentation, song of praise, pastoral, aphorism, invective" (127).[27]

Thus the mixture of history, oratory, lyric, and other modes that Howes, Lowth, and others perceived in the prophetic books of the Bible is an important structural principle operating in Blake's prophetic books. In *America* we see a number of distinct genres: the song of Orc on plate 6, "The morning comes, the night decays, the watchmen leave their stations" (6:1), is an almost universally recognized set piece,[28] which echoes the watchman's songs in Ezekiel 7:1–15 and Isaiah 21:12; plate 8 contains a prophetic speech by Orc that echoes Esdras, Daniel, and Revelation; plate 9 contains the response of Albion's Angel, which takes the form of a war chant with the repeated refrain, "Sound! sound! my loud war-trumpets & alarm my Thirteen Angels!" There are a number of other rhetorical set pieces, including two recognition speeches, one by the shadowy daughter of Urthona (2:7–17) and the other by Albion's Angel (7:3–7), and the rhetorical questions modeled on the Book of Job that are spoken by Boston's Angel (11:4–15). *Europe,* which has been called a "collage of techniques" and a "series of set pieces loosely linked together" (Ostriker 168–69), exhibits a variety of poetic forms and styles: a fairy's song (iii: 1–6) couched in what Ostriker calls Blake's "middle, expository style" (168), a lament sung by the nameless shadowy female (1:4–2:16), a bacchic choric song by the sons of Urizen and Enitharmon (4:3–14), Enitharmon's triumphal song (6:1–8:12), a parodic version of an Ovidian metamorphosis (12:15–20), and an aubade sung by Enitharmon (13:9–14:31). *Africa* is a combination of annal and Ovidian fable, the latter being the tale of Har and Heva, whereas *Asia* contains a lament by the Kings of Asia and a prophetic vision that echoes Ezekiel's vision in the vale of dry bones (*Song of Los* 7:31–40). Needless to say, *Africa* and *Asia,* two divergent works that contain divergent forms, constitute a single work, *The Song of Los,* which juxtaposes them and holds them in tension.

This multiplicity of styles and forms is also present in the illustrations to Blake's prophetic books. In his combining of different pictorial and poetic genres, as well as in his adoption of the other properties of prophetic form that Biblical critics and commentators were also aware of, Blake makes the "still better order" of Biblical prophecy the structural model upon which his visionary forms dramatic are built. He found in the Bible a concept of art that is visual, dramatic, and rhetorical, that combines spectacle and confrontation, that acts upon the reader and enjoins the reader to act in response to it.

**NOTES**

1. See M. H. Abrams, *The Mirror and the Lamp* (184–95).
2. Lowth chooses for his examples Isaiah 34 and 35 because of the symmetrical relationship of these two prophecies (2:70–80).
3. See Abrams, *Mirror and Lamp* (201).
4. Robert Lowth, *Isaiah: A New Translation* (5). The first edition of Lowth's *Isaiah* was published in London, 1778. Lowth, of course, was correct in perceiving Isaiah to be a collection of scattered prophecies collected by redactors, but the age demanded—or, rather, the deists and defensive Christians demanded—that the Bible have intelligible form.
5. For a discussion of these theories, see Abrams, *Mirror and Lamp* (184–225).
6. See also Thomas Howes (296, 333).

The *"Still Better Order"* of Blake's Rhetoric                               197

7. See William Newcome (lxv, 114, 118, 122, 123, 125, 129, 133).

8. In Volume 3 of *Critical Observations on Books,* Thomas Howes printed "A Discourse on the Abuse of the Talent of Disputation in Religion, Particularly as practiced by Dr. Priestley, Mr. Gibbon, and others of the modern Sect of Philosophic Christians" (1–36). Priestley responded to this in an appendix to his *Letters to Dr. Horsley,* and Howes answered Priestley's reply in his preface to the fourth volume of *Critical Observations on Books.*

9. Of course there are important differences between Revelation and Old Testament prophecy, the most obvious being the recognizably coherent and schematized structure of Revelation (see Richard Hurd 324). Furthermore, the apocalyptic mode differs from the prophetic mode in some very fundamental ways. But since Revelation grew out of Old Testament prophecy, reshaping its elements and making new additions (see Hurd 317–23; Newcome xxvi), there are important structural elements that both modes share.

10. The first edition of this work was published in London, 1748–63.

11. See Fénelon (82–83); see also Wilbur Samuel Howell, *Eighteenth-Century British Logic and Rhetoric* (511).

12. For Fénelon's relationship to Augustine and the Augustinian rhetorical tradition, see Howell, *Eighteenth-Century British Logic and Rhetoric* (505), and Ruth Wallerstein (15–17, 54–55). For Milton's relationship to Augustinian rhetoric, see Joseph Anthony Wittreich, Jr., "'The Crown of Eloquence.'"

13. Blake's concept of the "true Orator," who varies his verse to suit his subject (*Jerusalem,* pl. 3), appears to be a direct echo of Fénelon's true orator, who uses a variety of styles in each discourse, adjusting his style to his subject (*Dialogues* 136–37). Fénelon, in turn, probably derives this idea from Augustine's *Confessions,* in which Augustine says, "I indited verses in which I might not place every foot everywhere, but differently in different metres; nor even in any one metre the self-same foot in all places. Yet the art itself by which I indited, had not different principles in these different cases, but comprised all in one" (quoted in Wallerstein 36). Blake, of course, could have read Augustine (see Richard Downing 662 and John B. Beer), but it is also likely that he knew Fénelon's *Dialogues,* since William Stevenson's translation was reprinted several times (Howell, *Eighteenth-Century British Logic and Rhetoric* 518) and since Blake admired Fénelon enough to identify him as a "Son of Eden" in *Jerusalem* (72:48–50). Whether the source of Blake's concept of the prophet as poet and orator was direct or indirect, the concept is part of the tradition of Augustinian rhetoric, which is ultimately rooted in the Bible (see Erich Auerbach, *Literary Language and Its Public* 50–52).

14. For summaries of Mede's explanation of the synchronic form of Revelation, see Hurd (332–43) and Daubuz (19–20).

15. Johann Gottfried Eichhorn, *Introduction to the Old Testament,* quoted in Newcome (xxiii).

16. See Henry Hammond (883); Philip Doddridge (6: 362); Hurd (340–42); and Daubuz (47–48). For Pareus's ideas about perspectivism in Revelation, see Wittreich, *Angel of Apocalypse* (181).

17. Compare Horsley's statement with Northrop Frye's idea of the "Bard's Song" in Blake's *Milton* as a series of "lifting backdrops" (332).

18. Unpaginated translator's note in Joseph Mede. Actually, the statement is taken from a letter by a certain Mr. Haydock that the translator quotes.

19. See also W. J. T. Mitchell, "Poetic and Pictorial Imagination" (356) and "Blake's Composite Art" (58–59).

20. See Jean Hagstrum (87) and Mitchell, "Blake's Composite Art" (69–70, 72–73) and "Poetic and Pictorial Imagination" (354).

21. See Eichhorn in Newcome (xxii) and Thomas Newton (467–68). See also Wittreich, "Opening the Seals" (43).

22. See Susan Fox (10–12).
23. Ibid.
24. See Mitchell, "Blake's Composite Art" (67); Karl Kroeber (10–12); and Anne Kostelanetz Mellor (134).
25. See, for instance, Kroeber (11–12); Mitchell, "Blake's Composite Art" (68); and Alicia Ostriker (111–12, 149–50).
26. See Wittreich, "'Poet Amongst Poets'" (106).
27. Minimizing the effect of the Bible on Blake's concept of structure, Ostriker misses the point that all of those modes that Blake adopts were incorporated into the structure of Biblical prophecy.
28. See, for instance, Alicia Ostriker (158); David V. Erdman (97); and Harold Bloom, *Blake's Apocalypse* (127–28).

# XIII

# ROBERT LOWTH'S *SACRED HEBREW POETRY* AND THE ORAL DIMENSION OF ROMANTIC RHETORIC

*Scott Harshbarger*

> Since then it is the purpose of sacred Poetry to form the human mind to the constant habit of true virtue and piety, and to excite the more ardent affections of the soul, in order to direct them to their proper end; whoever has a clear insight into the instruments, the machinerey as it were, by which this end is effected, will certainly contribute not a little to the improvement of the critical art. Now although it be scarcely possible to penetrate to the fountains of this celestial Nile, yet it may surely be allowed us to pursue the meanders of the stream to mark the flux and reflux of its waters, and even to conduct a few rivulets into the adjacent plains.
>
> Robert Lowth, *Lectures on the Sacred Poetry of the Hebrews*

It is something of a paradox that during an age which saw a virtual explosion of literate learning in European society there arose among intellectuals of the eighteenth century an intense interest in non- or semiliterate cultures. Such interest has often been characterized as a delusive primitivism, M. H. Abrams, for example, calling it "a curious aberration of sociological speculation," saved, however, by the role played by eighteenth-century investigators of "Primitive Language and Primitive Poetry" in the development of Romantic expressivism (*Mirror and Lamp* 83). More recent scholarship has taken a different tack. Alan Bewell sees in such typical Enlightenment concerns the early stirrings of anthropology, "the study of the origins and development of mankind in its widest sense" (17). Citing Don Bialostosky, Bewell suggests how the rhetorical concerns of Romanticism are tied to the anthropological investigations of the eighteenth century: the "idea that Wordsworth is concerned with demonstrating how the thoughts of particular individuals are embodied in the distinctive ways they speak can be usefully placed in the anthropological framework" (24).

One of the most influential framers of such rhetorical anthropology was Robert Lowth, whose lectures on Old Testament poetry demonstrate how the classical rhetorical tradition provided crucial conceptual tools for the inquiry into forms of communication a full account of which has yet to be developed.[1] What made Homer, Hebrew verse, and the folk balladeers of Scotland and England significant to the Romantics was not, as Abrams would have it, their indifference to audience (83) but their rootedness in oral models of communication. Exemplified by Lowth's lectures and epitomized by Hugh Blair's *Lectures on Rhetoric and Belles Lettres,* the eighteenth-century inquiry into oral literature helped to create within the dominantly literate intellectual culture of the late eighteenth and early nineteenth centuries an oral rhetorical countercurrent which, seeing no incompatibility between "expressive" and "pragmatic" discourse, would give Romanticism much of its rhetorical appeal, social relevance, and revisionary force.

The contending rhetorical currents of the eighteenth century are very evident in the education of Robert Lowth, whose own rhetorical work would reflect a telling combination of the classical and the native, the old and the new. Hailing from a region of England which, as Brian Hepworth points out, produced many of the primary instigators of that movement commonly called pre-Romantic,[2] Lowth benefitted from the seminary at Winchester, which, founded by William Wykeham in the fourteenth century, provided Lowth with "a direct link with the Middle Ages in England, precisely at the time when Classical influences were waning in the imagination of English writers" (19). Like Winchester, Oxford's New College (also founded by Wykeham) trained Lowth in both the traditional, classical curriculum and the new, protoscientific approach to knowledge, which tackled such traditional concerns as the origin of man by focusing on material circumstances. Fueled by numerous travel narratives describing exotic and "primitive" peoples and guided by an empirical approach that may have had as much to do with the Epicureanism of neoclassicism as the protoscientific method promulgated by the Royal Society, this movement sought to uncover ultimate principles of numerous institutions by analyzing the conditions that gave them birth.[3] Though perhaps ultimately motivated by a quasi-theological myth of origins, this search would prove extremely profitable for rhetorical anthropology, insofar as it caused scholars to consider how communication, and in particular poetic communication, was influenced by the available media. It is in this province of the primitive that Lowth would make his greatest contribution.

*De sacra poesi Hebraeorum* has generally been regarded as pivotal in the development of a set of critical principles and values that found fruition in Romantic poetry. The lectures were, in the words of Stephen Prickett, "to transform Biblical studies in England and Germany alike" and "do more than any other single work to make the Biblical tradition, rather than the neoclassical one, the central poetic tradition of the Romantics" (105).[4] Delivered between 1741 and 1750, published in 1753, and translated into English as *Lectures on the Sacred Poetry of the Hebrews* in 1787, the lectures demonstrate that Lowth himself was a virtuoso rhetorician, although not of the trope-mongering kind he regularly derides during the course of his lectures. For while Lowth's critical apparatus derives mainly from classical rhetoric, his nondogmatic and flexible use of these instruments enables him to uncover a rhetoric significantly different from that developed in the Greco-Roman tradition.[5] Extremely sensitive to the historical contingency of all rhetorical forms, Lowth reveals a rhetoric appropriate to the historical conditions that, he insists, give the Hebrew poetry its unique rhetorical power.

That classical rhetoric provided Lowth with the conceptual tools to begin his analysis of Old Testament poetry, however, attests to the importance of that tradition in helping to bring forth Romantic rhetoric. Lowth's most obvious and important debt to that tradition is his view that all discourse, including poetry, serves a purpose.[6] "Poetry is commonly understood to have two objects in view," comments Lowth, "namely, advantage and pleasure, or rather an union of both. I wish those who have furnished us with this definition, had rather proposed utility as its ultimate object, and pleasure as the means by which that end may be effectually accomplished" (I, 6–7). With such a utilitarian conception in mind, Lowth argues that "the writings of the Poet are more useful than those of the Philosopher, inasmuch as they are more agreeable" (I, 8). More specifically, "by the harmony of numbers, by the taste and variety of imagery," poetry can "captivate the affections of the reader, and imperceptibly, or perhaps reluctantly, impel him to the pursuit of virtue" (I, 11).

Lowth's indebtedness to the classical tradition is also suggested by his constant reference to its major authors. Homer, Pindar, Solon, Aeschylus, Plato, Alcaeus, Lucretius, Virgil, and Horace provide examples of the essential role poetry has played in creating, sustaining, and defending civilization. It is from the vantage point of the most ancient Greek writers that Lowth is able to glimpse some of the oral features common to both ancient Greek and Hebrew poetry,[7] in particular their common paedeutic and legislative function. Instancing "Solon, the most venerable character of antiquity, the wisest of legislators, and withal a poet of no mean reputation," Lowth notes that "when any thing difficult or perplexing occurred in the administration of public affairs, we are informed that he had recourse to Poetry" (I, 27). Like the classical pagan poets, the Greek and Roman rhetoricians serve as stepping stones to the promontory from which Lowth discerns the promised land of the ancient Hebrew rhetoric. Aristotle, Cicero, and Quintilian make regular appearances, sometimes as adversaries but often as sources of ideas or terminology.

Whereas Lowth deplores "all those forms of tropes and figures, which the teachers of rhetoric have pompously (not to say uselessly) heaped together" (I, 75–76), he regularly employs such rhetorical terms as "invention," "arrangement," "style," and "exordium."

Lowth's use of the classical term *topic* for the commonplaces of sacred Hebrew history illustrates how the critic uses a familiar rhetorical term to chart unfamiliar terrain. "The Chaos and the Creation," "the universal deluge," "the emigration of the Israelites from Egypt," "the descent of Jehovah at the delivery of the Law"—all are "sacred topics," i.e., "allusions to the actions of former times, such as possess a conspicuous place in [Hebrew] history" used to "illuminate with colours, foreign, indeed, but similar, the future by the past, the recent by the antique, facts less known by others more generally understood" (I, 187). Although Lowth contrasts the deployment of such topics with their use in classical literature, such commonplaces are, in fact, comparable to the proverbial formulae of classical literature which Eric Havelock sees as essential components of oral tradition, and from which, as Frank D'Angelo has argued, the analytic topoi eventually evolved (50–68). Thus, beginning with a classical rhetorical concept, Lowth uncovers an example of Hebraic formulae—an "established mode of expression"—whose origins predate the development of both literacy and the classical rhetorical tradition.[8]

As Lowth reminds us, however, "our present concern is not to explain the sentiments of the Greek but of the Hebrew writers" (I, 106). And it is finally his emphasis on ultimate rhetorical purpose which leads Lowth away from the model of discourse provided by classical rhetoric and toward a rhetoric more appropriate to sacred Hebrew poetry. For Lowth, the overriding purpose of Hebrew poetry is to shape and reshape within the minds of the community the values, customs, and events that constitute the culture.[9] Citing this as "the principal end and aim of poetry," Lowth gives as "illustrious proof" Moses' final address to Israel, "which he composed by the especial command of God to be learned by the Israelites, and committed to memory: 'That this song may be,' says God himself, 'for a witness against the people of Israel, when they shall depart from me; this shall be a testimony in their mouths; for it shall not be forgotten, nor shall it depart out of the mouths of their posterity for ever" (Deut. 31: 19, 21; quoted in Lowth, II, 19).

This rhetorical imperative, as Lowth makes clear, is due to the particular historical condition of non- or semiliteracy prevalent in the ancient Middle East during the formation of ancient Hebrew poetry, a condition that put a high value on memorable communication: "the only mode of instruction, indeed, adapted to human nature in an uncivilized state, when the knowledge of letters was very little, if at all diffused, must be that which is calculated to captivate the ear and the passions, which assists the memory, which is not to be delivered into the hand, but infused into the mind and heart" (I, 88).[10] Such an approach had been pioneered by the Scottish classicist Thomas Blackwell, whose astoundingly influential *Enquiry into the Life and Times of Ho-*

*mer* (1837)[11] argued that Homer's rhetorical power was a result of the bard's creating his poetry on the cusp of civilization, when, according to Blackwell, "Letters were . . . but little known" (82). Because of a general "Want of Records," "they had in those days no other Method of knowing the Transactions of former Ages, than by Tradition and Converse with the Guardians of Knowledge" (187). Basing his interpretation, at least in part, on the thesis that poetry existed to conserve crucial cultural knowledge, Blackwell notes that the poets "are quoted as the Fountains of History, the Judges of Politicks, and Parents of Philosophy" (108). In contrast to learning history from books, Homer "would hear their Statute-Songs and legal Hymns, handed down for thousands of Years, and containing the Principles of their primitive Theology" (169).

As Rolf Lessenich has remarked, "Robert Lowth was to Old Hebrew poetry what Thomas Blackwell was to Homer" (150). And like Blackwell, Lowth is well aware of the crucial role played by poetry in transmitting culture in the absence of a developed writing system: "In each of these departments Poetry was of singular utility, since before any characters expressive of sounds were invented, at least before they were commonly received, and applied to general use, it seems to have afforded the only means of preserving the rude science of the early times; and in this respect, to have rendered the want of letters more tolerable" (I, 82). In this regard, early Hebrew culture was like that of Greece, which "for several successive ages was possessed of no records but the poetic. . . . The laws themselves were metrical, and adapted to certain musical notes . . . delivered . . . to the ingenuous youth to be learned by rote, with accompaniments of musical melody, in order that by enchantment of harmony, the sentiments might be more forcibly impressed upon their memories" (I, 83–84). Like later readers of Lowth's work, his commentator sees in the common cultural practices of preliterate people and the rhetoric developed out of such practices a key to a common humanity: "These instances of a practice so agreeable to that of the Hebrews existing among a people so remote, serve to prove the great similarity in the human mind throughout all the countries of the globe, and shows that the most natural and early mode of preserving facts, has been by verses committed to memory, rather than by written documents" (I, 85, n.10).

With this historical condition in mind, Lowth performs a stylistic analysis of Old Testament verse, looking for those features "capable of interesting and affecting the senses and passions, of captivating the ear, of directing the perception of the minutest circumstances and of assisting the memory in the retention of them" (I, 80). And as we have seen, while Lowth is at great pains to underscore his departure from classical rhetoric, he also makes use of that body of writing for authority and terminology, here to formulate his most important contribution to the stylistic study of Hebrew verse. Having remarked on "the accurate recurrence of the clauses" in Hebrew poetry, a characteristic which, "in any other language would appear a superfluous and tiresome repetition," Lowth quotes from Cicero's *Orator:* "in certain forms of expression there exists such a degree of conciseness, that a sort of metrical arrangement follows of course. For when words or sentences directly correspond, or when contraries are opposed exactly to each other, or even when words of a similar sound run parallel, the composition will in general have a metrical cadence" (I, 101–2).

What is for Cicero a way of describing "certain forms of expression" becomes the basis for Lowth's all-encompassing principle of parallelism: "The Hebrew poets frequently express a sentiment with the utmost brevity and simplicity, illustrated by no circumstance, adorned with no epithets (which in truth they seldom use); they afterward call in the aid of ornament; they reappear, they vary, they amplify the same sentiment; and adding one or more sentences which run parallel to each other, they express the same or a similar, and often a contrary sentiment in nearly the same form of words" (I, 100). Such a poetic takes as its principal structural unit "sense," which is then varied, amplified, or counterpointed by parallel passages: "In the Hebrew poetry ... there may be observed a certain conformation of the sentences, the nature of which is, that a complete sense is almost equally infused into every component part, and that every member constitutes an entire verse" (I, 68).[12]

In attributing the "proximate cause" of the parallelism characteristic of Hebrew poetry to the ancient connection between poetry and music, in particular "the custom of singing in alternate chorus," Lowth shows how the verse form grew out of a particular oral tradition. Here he quotes from Exodus, in which "we learn that Moses with the Israelites chanted the ode at the Red-sea; for 'Miriam the prophetess took a timbrel in her hand, and all the women followed her with timbrels, and with dances; and Miriam answered them,' that is, she and the women sung the response to the chorus of men" (Exod. 15: 20, 21; II, 25–26). In this tradition, we see the profoundly communal function of oral poetry: not only the prophetess but her "audience" participates in the creation of the poetic act, the reciprocal nature of which is figured in the parallel structure of Hebraic verse, a feature that would persist long after the preliterate practice that gave it birth had passed into oblivion.

The union of form and content typical of oral tradition, which is given full rein in the poetic principle of parallelism, became a means, as Murray Roston has argued, for healing the breach between thought and expression endemic to a moribund strand of neoclassicism (23). Albert Lord noted that the poetic formula in oral poetry "is the offspring of the marriage of thought and sung verse" (31). This is fully exemplified by Hebraic parallelism, since, as Roston points out, "in Hebrew verse, artistic form is subordinated to subject-matter, and it is the sense of the passage itself which creates the rhythm, ... the self generating emotional force of parallelism, which pulsates in rhythmic unison with the sense" (23). In such composition, there is no clear-cut distinction between "form" and "content": sense itself is memorable only insofar as it is part of a larger poetic pattern. In the oral tradition, poetry truly is the incarnation rather than the robe of thought.

By treating formal characteristics as expressions of a particular form of thought shaped by oral tradition, Lowth pointed the way toward a less formalist, more psychologically oriented understanding of poetry. Indeed, as Lowth makes clear, he is describing not only a kind of poetry but a particular form of thought: "the manner of living, of speaking, of thinking, which prevailed in those times, will be found altogether different from our customs and habits" (I, 113). Reflected in and shaped by the reciprocity of oral communication, this habit of thought puts less emphasis on subordination and classification and more on coordination, analogy, and association. With the open-ended notion of "likeness" as its ordering principle, parallelism itself takes a number of forms. Writes Stephen Prickett, "Lowth himself distinguished no less than eight different kinds of parallelism. From the simplest forms of repetition or echo that we find in synonymous parallelism, it could provide endless variation, comparison, contrast . . . through to antithesis and even dialectic" (110). Rather than see the essence of poetry as residing in formal meter, the Romantics would link poetry and prose to corresponding mental states, the poetic representing forms of thought less readily available to literal-minded persons.

In addition to helping Lowth recognize and account for Hebrew verse's most striking formal characteristic, the oral-rhetorical framework established by the critic makes him keenly sensitive to other features that contribute to memorability. The oral underpinnings of Hebraic imagery help to account for Lowth's most distinctive contribution to the ongoing eighteenth-century discussion of the sublime, which, because of the high value placed on "heightened" expression within the oral linguistic economy, is a pervasive feature of Hebrew poetry. If most elements of the classical tradition quickly recede as Lowth uses them to uncover new and ancient forms, this element of that tradition is brought front and center. Lowth offers a particularly striking example of the way in which the Hebrew poet expresses God's threatened destruction of Jerusalem:

> And I will wipe Jerusalem
> As a man wipeth a dish;
> He wipeth it, and turneth it upside down.
> (2 Kings xxi, 13; I, 155)

In this passage, the parallelism, the repetition, the familiar image, and the bold comparison all serve the requirements of a communal memory unaided by writing. In a later lecture on the sublime, Lowth gives a comparable example:

> And the Lord awaked, as out of sleep,
> Like a strong man shouting because of wine.
> (Psalm lxxviii; I, 363)

"From ideas, which in themselves appear coarse, unsuitable, and totally unworthy of so great an object," writes Lowth, "the mind naturally recedes and passes suddenly to the contemplation of the object itself, and of its inherent magnitude and importance" (I, 364). It is no accident that oral tradition is filled with the sensational or that the sublime is proverbially linked with the ridiculous. When the entrenched associations of the familiar are themselves associated with the shock of the strange, the memorability of the product is greater than the sum of its parts.

Lowth also points to the conditions of ancient Hebrew life and the character of oral expression that give rise to figures of the highest sublimity, expressions "which no person in a tranquil state of mind, and quite master of himself, would venture to employ" (I, 319). From this is derived "that vivid and ardent style, which is so well calculated to display the emotions and passions of the mind" (I, 321). Such a style fulfills the true nature of poetry, which Lowth importantly conceives in terms of what the Greeks, according to Eric Havelock, called *"mousike,"* the intense form of "personal commitment, of total engagement and of emotional identification" characteristic of the oral tradition (160). Writes Lowth, "Poetry itself is indebted for its origin, complexion, emphasis, and application, to the effects which are produced upon the mind and body, upon imagination, the senses, the voice, and respiration by agitation of passion" (I, 366).

It is at this point that Lowth comes nearest the "expressive" pole which Abrams took as the defining feature of Romantic rhetoric. In his *Lectures* Lowth writes,

> The original and first use of poetical language are undoubtedly to be traced into the vehement affections of the mind.... Every impulse of the mind, however, has not only a peculiar style and expression, but a certain tone of voice, and a certain gesture of the body adapted to it: some, indeed, not satisfied with that expression which language affords, have added to it dancing and song; and as we know there existed in the first ages a very strict connexion between these arts and that of poetry, we may possibly be indebted to them for the accurately admeasured verses and feet, to the end that the modulation of the language might accord with the music of the voice, and the motion of the body. (I, 79–80)

Although Lowth suggests a possible distinction between private poetic inspiration and its social expression, his grounding in the historical circumstance of oral poetic creation allows him to socially link the two. Lowth draws on eighteenth-century rhetorical anthropology to argue a direct connection between the "vehement affections of the mind" and poetic expression, a connection made by speech, insofar as "every impulse of the mind" has "a certain tone of voice, and a certain gesture of the body adapted to it." Without the addition of memorable patterns, the great affections of the mind would lack lasting social force; recollected in dancing and song, such language is powerfully suited to convey and sustain a culture's deepest beliefs and values. Writes Lowth:

Poetry, in this rude origin and commencement, being derived from nature, was in time improved by art, and applied to the purposes of utility and delight. For as it owed its birth to the affections of the mind, and had availed itself of the assistance of harmony, it was found, on account of the exact and vivid delineation of the objects which it described, to be excellently adapted to the exciting of every internal emotion, and making a more forcible impression upon the mind than abstract reasoning could possibly effect; it was found capable of interesting and affecting the senses and passions, of captivating the ear, of directing the perception of the minutest circumstances and of assisting the memory in the retention of them. Whatever therefore deserved to be generally known and accurately remembered, was (by those men, who on this very account were denominated wise) adorned with a jocund and captivating style, illuminated with the varied and splendid colouring of language, and moulded into sentences comprehensive, pointed, and harmonious. (I, 80–82)

Still, there is no doubt that the powerful forms of oral rhetoric uncovered by Lowth and others in the eighteenth century came to be used for purposes other than those for which they had evolved. In literate culture, oral rhetoric becomes less a means of preserving information than a way of uniting author and audience in a way pursued only fitfully by a rhetorical tradition formed by Plato's attack on such sympathetic bonding.[13] What once served as the primary psychological mechanism for indelibly imprinting the cultural tradition in the psyches of the participants of the poetic performance becomes a means of engaging an audience through a maximum of conscious and unconscious appeals. Since, as a variety of eighteenth-century philosophers were recognizing, the deepest beliefs and values resided not in conscious rationality but unconscious sentiment, poetry, which in lieu of letters had to learn the language of sense and sentiment for the sake of cultural survival, was still an indispensable resource. For Lowth, then, the most effective instruction is that which aims at shaping the emotions: "Because the Poet teaches not by maxims and precepts, and in the dull sententious form; but by the harmony of verse, by the beauty of imagery, by the ingenuity of the fable, by the exactness of imitation, he allures and interests the mind of reader, he fashions it to habits of virtue, and in a manner informs it with the spirit of integrity itself" (I, 13).

For this reason, Lowth believes that the poetry most closely associated with song is best suited to encourage "that generous elevation of sentiment, on which the very existence of public virtue seems to depend" (I, 20). Having quoted an ancient ballad, Lowth writes, "If after the memorable Ides of March, any one of the Tyrannicides had delivered to the populace such a poem as this, had introduced it to the Suburra, to the assemblies of the Forum, or had put it into the mouths of the common people, the dominion of the Caesars and its adherents would have been totally extinguished: and I am firmly persuaded, that one stanza of this simple ballad of Harmodius would have been more effectual than all the Philippics of Cicero" (I, 26). In posing a "simple ballad" against "all the Philippics of Cicero" Lowth brings head to head the two competing rhetorics deeply embedded in the history of Western discourse, leaving little doubt as to which, in the long run, is more socially powerful.

The work which perhaps best serves to demonstrate and enact Lowth's lasting influence on both Romantic literature and the culture as a whole is Hugh Blair's *Lectures on Rhetoric and Belles Lettres*. Published in 1783 and going through more than a hundred editions, Blair's lectures have been extremely influential in consolidating and propagating the rhetorical investigation of the eighteenth century.[14] By recapitulating many of the features of Lowth's analysis of Hebrew poetry, Blair's lectures reveal the impact of the rhetorical anthropology underlying the oral dimension of Romantic rhetoric; also, by harboring within its covers more traditionally literate concerns, the *Lectures on Rhetoric and Belles Lettres* forces a recognition of the dynamic conflict inherent in the "new rhetoric" and the oral and literate cultures which produced it.

Lowth's most obvious influence on Blair's lectures can be seen in his chapter on *The Poetry of the Hebrews*. Here Blair makes clear that his chapter is, in fact, a cursory summary of Lowth's work and that "'De Sacra Poesi Hebraeorum,' ought to be perused by all who desire to become thoroughly acquainted with this subject" (II, 386). Arguing that the Old Testament does contain poetry—a fact which, like Lowth, he uses to provide a defense of the poetic art—Blair notes that poetry is allied to music and that the major formal feature of Hebrew verse is parallelism, a feature derived from the practice of alternate singing. Following Lowth, Blair attributes the special power of Hebrew sublimity to its perspicuity, derived from a "conciseness" of expression. "Writers who attempt the Sublime," he remarks, "might profit much, by imitating, in this respect, the Style of the Old Testament" (II, 392).

But it is in the lecture on the origin and progress of poetry that Lowth's anthropological approach is most apparent. "In order to explore the rise of Poetry, we must have recourse to the deserts and the wilds; we must go back to the age of hunters and of shepherds; to the highest antiquity, and the simplest form of manners among mankind" (II, 314). Like Lowth, Blair finds in such passionate expression "the first beginnings of Poetic Composition." And also like Lowth, Blair ascribes the form such sentiments take to music and ultimately to the memorial function that music serves: "before Writing was invented, Songs only could last, and be remembered. The ear gave assistance to the memory, by the help of Numbers; fathers repeated and sung them to their children; and by this oral tradition of national Ballads, was conveyed all the historical knowledge, and all the instruction, of the first ages" (II, 317). Thus, "as we have reason to look for Poems and Songs among the antiquities of all countries, so we may expect, that in the strain of these there will be a remarkable resemblance, during the primitive periods of every country" (II, 318).

There are, however, telling differences between Lowth's and Blair's work, differences that flow from their respective rhetorical aims. As we have seen, in his lectures Lowth takes great pains to distinguish sacred Hebrew poetry from the literature and rhetoric of the classical tradition, even as he uses that tradition to analyze the poetry of the Old Testament. However, by discovering the principles of Hebrew poetry in the conditions of pre- or semiliterate culture, Lowth suggested an even deeper bond between pagan and sacred literature. Because Blair's lectures are concerned with establishing a general rhetoric rather than analyzing the culture's primary sacred book, he is freer to pursue the commonality between the poetry of the Old Testament and other ancient literature: "That strong hyperbolical manner which we may have been long accustomed to call the Oriental manner of poetry (because some of the earliest poetical productions came to us from the East), is in truth no more Oriental than Occidental; it is characteristical of an age rather than of a country; and belongs, in some measure, to all nations at that period which first gives rise to Music and Song" (II, 318).

This commonality is crucial to Blair, since it provides the basis for a universal rhetoric based on the common communicative expressions of humanity, a commonality best represented, for Blair, by oral communication. Why this should be so, and why so many of the great eighteenth-century critics and philosophers interested in non- or semiliterate culture should hail from Scotland, we need to consider not only Blair's rhetorical purpose but also his social context. In *The Ballad and the Folk,* David Buchan comments on

> a general dichotomy so pronounced in eighteenth-century Scotland as to be dubbed a "national schizophrenia." . . . By the eighteenth century, Scots who wanted to get on in the world had to learn "to speak properly," as the revealing phrase has it, that is, to speak English. Literate Scots became accustomed to carrying two languages in their heads: English for writing, Scots for speaking, English for "proper" occasions, Scots for "real" life. The upshot was a peculiarly Scottish dissociation of sensibility whereby, as Edwin Muir put it, Scotsmen felt in Scot and thought in English. This psychic cleavage helps explain why Scotland retained such a rich stock of folk literature up to the present century. Because their language was the language of feeling and their ethos exemplified the native outlook on life, the Scottish ballads provided—as work in English could not—aesthetic correlatives organically suited to the Scottish spirit and emotional constitution, and thereby fulfilled an important need in the national psychology; they helped maintain a sense of native identity against the pervasive threat of alien anglicization. (69)

Like Lowth's Winchester, Blair's Scotland was very much of two worlds, with the anthropological interest (and social anxiety) of the new fueling investigation into the old. A glance at the table of contents of Blair's work, in which we find chapters on Hebrew poetry, Homer, and the origin of poetry bound with chapters on perspicuity, precision, and in-depth analysis of the prose style of Joseph Addison, suggests that Scotland's "national schizophrenia" is well represented in the *Lectures on Rhetoric and Belles Lettres.* Indeed, Blair's popularity outside Scotland and England may be due to the fact that the schizophrenic culture which produced it was, to a large extent, Anglo-American culture writ large. That is, the cultural situation in Scotland, in which "writing" assumed an authority often at odds with ways of living, feeling, and thinking associated with oral communication, threw into relief tendencies that were rapidly overtaking a culture that, for the first time, was becoming predominantly oriented toward the letter.[15]

Blair comments explicitly on the differences between writing and speech in a way that confirms Buchan's thesis and serves to point out the strong oral bias of the New Rhetoric. Having given writing its due for its role in the

> instruction of mankind; yet we must not forget to observe, that spoken Language has a great superiority over written Language, in point of energy or force. The voice of the living Speaker, makes an impression on the mind, much stronger than can be made by the perusal of any Writing. The tones of voice, the looks and gesture, which accompany discourse, and which no Writing can convey, render discourse, when it is well managed, infinitely more clear, and more expressive than the most accurate Writing. For tones, looks, and gestures, are natural interpreters of the sentiments of the mind. They remove ambiguities; they enforce impressions; they operate on us by means of sympathy, which is one of the most powerful instruments of persuasion. Our sympathy is always awakened more, by hearing the Speaker, than by reading his works in our closet. Hence, though Writing may answer the purposes of mere instruction, yet all the great and high efforts of eloquence must be made, by means of spoken, not of written, Language. (II, 136)

With this affirmation of the superiority of the spoken, Blair concludes his chapter "Rise and Progress of Writing." While the writer of cool and precise Addisonian prose holds the stage in Blair's lectures, an ancient Hebrew bard waits in the wings.

Springing from the rhetorically divided nature of eighteenth-century society, oral-rhetorical anthropology provided resources for poets, critics, and philosophers attempting to cope with the challenges of the new rhetorical world created by a burgeoning print culture. Along with providing a rhetoric that recognized and exploited the full range of psychological persuasion, oral-rhetorical anthropology revitalized the concept of the "Bard," thereby enabling the poet to imagine himself as central to the culture, forging the subtle emotional links binding society together on a level far removed from the superficial "revolutionary" changes wrought by print technology. As James Chandler has argued, such a rhetoric, grounded in the conservative function of oral transmission, could form the basis of a politically conservative ideology, linking Edmund Burke and William Wordsworth via an "ethos of speech."

However, while one aspect of the orality seems ideally suited to sustain cultural continuity by linking generations via a full range of psychological appeals, another aspect could also make it a powerful tool of change. The very nature of the oral situation, in which, as Blair put it, "tones, looks, and gestures ... operate on us by means of sympathy, which is one of the most powerful instruments of persuasion," could make it a more authoritative expression than writing. For this reason, oral traditions have often served as regulators and correctives of sacred writings—from constitutions to Bibles—that are inherently incapable of changing with changing times. This aspect of the oral is no more dramatically demonstrated than in Paul's address to the Corinthians, in which, attempting to reinterpret the law of the Old Testament without completely undermining its authority, Paul posits an expression of God greater than that in which the old law was embodied. Proclaims Paul:

> Ye are our epistle written in our hearts, known and read of all men: / Forasmuch as ye are manifestly declared to be the epistle of Christ ministered by us, written not with ink, but with the Spirit of the living God; not in tables of stone, but in fleshly tables of the heart. / And such trust have we through Christ to God-ward: / Not that we are sufficient of ourselves to think any thing as of ourselves; but our sufficiency is of God; / Who also hath made us able ministers of the new testament; not of the letter, but of the spirit: for the letter killeth, but the spirit giveth life. (2 Cor. 3: 2–6)

Through this revisionary strategy Christianity would replace the cold, jealous abstraction embodied in the letter with the spoken presence of the living gospel.

Paul's sense that the spoken word can be a more spiritual expression of God than the letter is not mistaken. For as a number of scholars have recently pointed out, there is a deep connection between religion, orality, and revision. Writes William A. Graham in *Beyond the Written World: Oral Aspects of Scripture in the History of Religion:* "The oral dimension is ... the one most intimately bound up with the major personal and communal roles of scripture in religious life, especially those that move not only in the intellectual or ideational realm, but also in that of the sense" (155).[16] Moreover, Graham finds "a correlation between highly oral use of scripture and religious reform movements" (161). Such a correlation sheds new light on the oft remarked upon religious character of Romantic poetry, as well as its "protestant" or revisionary stance.[17] The Romantics' general oral emphasis,[18] as well as their challenge of oppressive features of "the letter," suggests that Romanticism and reformist religious movements share this revisionary strategy. It appears that at certain points in the history of religion, or perhaps any book-based tradition, the very thing that makes "the Book" an object of reverence—the authoritative fixity of the written word—is perceived by some as oppressive, necessitating a depriviledging of the literal as such in order to recapture the persuasive sense of spontaneity and personal involvement available in oral contexts. Romantic revisionism, then, perhaps isn't so much a *"misprision"* of texts (Bloom, *Anxiety* 19–45) as a liberating of the lively word imprisoned by an epistemology which has granted greater authority to the letter than to what Wordsworth called the living voice.

While, as a number of historians have pointed out, the great changes and challenges of the eighteenth century were in large measure unleashed by the new communicative possibilities of a burgeoning print culture,[19] many of the critics, philosophers, and poets of the period would attempt to understand and meet those challenges by participating in and drawing on nearly a century of oral-rhetorical anthropology: a loosely concerted attempt to discover the rhetorical, psychological, and sociological principles inherent in forms of communication which had to make their way without the help of the technology of writing but which, because of their psychological appeals, social aims, and revisionary potential, seemed more relevant than ever. Emerging in conjunction with the new literacy of the modern world, then, the New Rhetoric may be viewed as the attempt to reconstitute rhetoric, literature, and thought itself in accordance with qualities suggested by speech: spontaneity, individuality, sympathetic responsiveness to a living audience, and, perhaps most important, the construction within literate culture of a living tradition as much dependent on the revisionary spirit of dialogue as on the fixed presence of the letter.

Indeed, the Romantics would recognize and cultivate the tension between print and speech, letter and spirit, allowing it to influence and, in important respects, create the themes and cruxes of their work. The joyfully weeping child of Blake's Introduction to the Songs ambivalently presides over a communications revolution in which pure piping to a living audience is turned into confinable forms that can easily become the "Thou Shalt Nots" of Urizen's Book of Brass. While one of Wordsworth's speakers in one of his most famous poems declares books "a dull and endless strife" ("The Tables Turned"), Emerson observes that "Books are the best of things, well used; abused, among the worst . . . as love of the hero corrupts into worship of his statue. Instantly, the book becomes noxious. The guide is a tyrant" ("The American Scholar"). More often than not, Romantics portray themselves or their characters as victims of the "letter": Manfred, who dwells with "books and solitude"; Bartleby the Scrivener, whose life becomes a dead letter; Hester Prynne, for whom the letter serves the same purpose as the mark of Cain.

Nonetheless, it neither can nor should be overlooked that the leading figures of the Romantic movement in England and America were themselves highly literate, and so, in large measure, owed their craft and sensibility to lettered culture. Thus, while their conscious loyalty is often to oral values and sensibilities, there is often present within these authors a strong undertow dragging them in the direction of what are typically literate preoccupations and frames of mind. Coleridge, his "abstruse researches" persistently at odds with his "natural man," is perhaps the best example of this dual allegiance, while Shelley's Godwinian rationalism makes him a close second. Keats counsels pity for those who "have not / Trac'd upon vellum or wild Indian leaf / The shadows of melodious utterance" (*Fall of Hyperion* 4–6, 361), while Byron muses, "'Tis strange, the shortest letter which man uses / Instead of speech, may form a lasting link of Ages" (*Don Juan* III: 88, 684). Of equal importance are the external forces which, empowered by the printing press and its attendant institutions, impinge directly on the Romantics' oral projects. Furthermore, there is no reason why the oral and the literate should be conceived only as contradictory rather than as contrary states, which, as in the self-printed poetry of William Blake, make for a creative tension bordering on the apocalyptic. Much of the Romantics' appeal, I would argue, is owing to their dramatization of a rhetorical-cultural rift that, brought to light by the eighteenth-century inquiry into oral culture, shaped the work of authors we now call Romantic.

## NOTES

1. For an account of the state of scholarship in oral poetry, see Paul Zumthor.
2. William Collins, Edward Young, and Joseph Spence, as well as the three Wartons, all came from Winchester (Brian Hepworth 19).
3. See Hepworth (47–62). For an account of the influence of the Epicurean Revival on the new materialist philosophy of the Restoration and beyond, see Richard Kroll (85–179).
4. See also Murray Roston as well as Vincent Freimarck's Introduction to Lowth's *Lectures*. I here cite the 1969 reprint of the 1787 edition of Lowth's text.
5. See Freimarck (v) as well as James L. Kugel (274).
6. For a discussion of the purposive character of classical rhetoric, see George A. Kennedy, *Classical Rhetoric* (4).
7. In this respect, Lowth is one among many eighteenth-century critics and poets who saw an uncanny resemblance between the formal features of the oldest Greek and Hebrew poetry. See Donald M. Foerster (21).
8. For an illuminating discussion of the relationship among orality, literacy, and classical rhetoric, see Robert Connors.
9. Here I must enter two notes, one a qualification, one a defense. First, the difference between this rhetorical imperative and those of the classical rhetorical tradition is one more of emphasis than absolute difference. To measure the difference in emphasis, however, we need only consider the role that "memory" plays in the classical rhetorical tradition, where it is the art that helps the orator remember his speech; little attention is paid to the speech's impact on communal memory. Second, this interpretation of Lowth's interpretation is precisely counter to that of Brian Hepworth, who claims that in Hebrew poetry "Mnemosyne, the ancient Greek goddess of memory, is no longer the mother of the Muses" (90). Hepworth bases this claim on Lowth's assertion that the power of the sublime is distinct from the poetry of reason, in which "the understanding slowly perceives the accuracy of the description in all other subjects ... being obliged to compare them by the aid and through the uncertain medium, as it were, of the memory" (Lowth, quoted in Hepworth 90). I believe Hepworth is confusing memory as a way of creating effects through reason with memory as effect attained primarily through nonrational methods. It is the latter that makes Mnemosyne the mother muse of all ancient oral literature.
10. For a modern discussion of this topic see Eduard Nielsen.
11. See Rolf Lessenich (138).
12. The importance of parallelism for defining Hebraic verse has been a topic of contention in recent years. For James L. Kugel, the parallelism in Old Testament poetry is so complex and various as to render the concept next to useless. On the other hand, Robert Alter still finds it to be the key to understanding the semantic dynamics of Hebrew verse, accusing Kugel of throwing the baby out with the bathwater (4). Neither

Kugel nor Alter, it should be noted, follows Lowth in considering the role played by oral transmission in influencing the formal complexity and communal dynamics of parallelism.

13. See Havelock and Connors.

14. Jonathan Wordsworth reports that Coleridge checked out a copy of Blair's rhetoric from the Bristol Library in January-February 1798 (*The Music of Humanity* 263n.).

15. For elaboration of this admittedly gross generalization see Harvey Graff; Walter Ong, *Orality and Literacy;* Karl Kaestle; Elizabeth Eisenstein; and Robert Altick. Some put the tip toward dominant literacy at the turn of the eighteenth century, while others fix it as late as the mid–nineteenth century. These two estimations suggestively encompass that period of literature we now call Romantic.

16. See also Harold Coward.

17. See, for example, Harold Bloom: Romantic poetry "is a kind of religious poetry, and the religion is in the Protestant line, though Calvin or Luther would have been horrified to contemplate it" (*Visionary Company* 140).

18. In a 1990 MLA paper, "How the Romantics Recited Their Poetry," David Perkins remarked that "for the Romantics poetry was a strongly 'temporal' and oral art—an art realized in time by the voice." Perkins's paper is a concise proof that, generally speaking, the Romantics regarded the text more as a repository of voice than a system of signs.

19. See, for example, Eisenstein.

# Part IV
# Enlightenment Rhetoric

# XIV

# THE NEW RHETORIC AND ROMANTIC POETICS

*James Engell*

From 1750 through the 1780s a group of professors and divines completely renovated the study of rhetoric and applied it to contemporary English literature. These critics, who might be called the New Rhetoricians to distinguish them from their more classical formalist counterparts in the Renaissance and earlier eighteenth century, altered the course of British letters and provided a basis for the Romantic veneration of the expressive and emotional power of figurative, "natural" language. The New Rhetoricians, properly considered a unified movement, are, prior to the twentieth century, the most important and cohesive group of critics in English. The appeal of their lectures and volumes, often used as texts on both sides of the Atlantic, lasted into Queen Victoria's reign.

Depending on how large a net is cast, the New Rhetoricians encompass anywhere from a half-dozen to scores of lecturers, ministers, and educators—anyone who wrote an essay on syntax or a how-to book on style and elocution. But the important names are few, though some transcend the group through other activities: Adam Smith, George Campbell, Joseph Priestley, Hugh Blair, James Beattie, and, if we stretch a bit, Thomas Gibbons, Lord Kames, Thomas Sheridan, and Robert Lowth.[1] It was a great day for Scotland. Not until the mid–twentieth century would a group of English-speaking critics study, in so thorough and systematic a fashion, the psychological, semiotic, and linguistic foundations of literature.

Considering language as a series of signs and significations, time-honored terms they used with frequency and care, the New Rhetoricians became the first British critics to mount a collective effort to explain literature and literary form in the light of semiotics and the structure of language. Specifically championing the idea of "theory," they developed, to borrow the title of George Campbell's important work of 1776, a "philosophy of rhetoric." (I. A. Richards would consciously revive this phrase for the title of his 1936 volume, part of a larger attempt to resurrect principles of the New Rhetoric as a basis for modern critical study.) The last major rhetorics of the old stock appeared in the late 1750s: John Lawson's *Lectures Concerning Oratory* (1758) and John Ward's *System of Oratory* (1759).[2]

The New Rhetoricians deserve their epithet, if only because their books are no longer handbooks, and they consistently refute Samuel Butler's charge of jargon and mere classification (*Hudibras* I.i.89–90):

> For all a rhetorician's rules
> Teach nothing but to name his tools.

And although they draw on classical rhetoricians, they subordinate formal divisions, long lists of terms, and rote strategies in favor of a robust psychological approach, natural style, and a firm linguistic and grammatological foundation. Adam Smith, in his *Lectures on Rhetoric and Belles Lettres* (1762–63, but delivered as early as 1748), sets the fresh tone when he asserts that it was from "Figures, and divisions and sub-divisions of them, that so many systems of rhetoric, both ancient and modern, have been formed. They are generally a very silly set of books and not at all instructive." The new rhetorics—beginning with Smith's own *Lectures* and including principally George Campbell's *Philosophy of Rhetoric* (1776), Hugh Blair's *Lectures on Rhetoric and Belles Lettres* (1783), Joseph Priestley's *Lectures on Oratory and Criticism* (1777, but delivered first in 1762), James Beattie's *Essays on Poetry and Music As They Affect the Mind* (1776), and, to a lesser degree, Lowth's *Poesi Sacra Hebraeorum* (1753), Kames's *Elements of Criticism* (1762), Thomas Sheridan's *Elocution* (1762), and Thomas Gibbons's *Rhetoric* (1767)—remain useful explorations in the theory and practice of literature. Echoing their emphases, Jonathan Culler has said that the labels of rhetoric are "a sterile and ancillary activity.... But a semiological or structuralist theory of reading enables us simply to reverse the perspective and to think of training as a way of providing the student with a set of formal models which he can use in interpreting literary works."[3] Insofar as a single statement could suffice, this virtually summarizes the New Rhetoricians' program.

In its wider sense rhetoric means the power of language, and the art of rhetoric analyzes the means by which that power may be obtained. But the New Rhetoric was intended as both a complete system of criticism and a guide to improving style and taste. Blair, in his *Lectures on Rhetoric and Belles Lettres,* claims that criticism, taste, and rhetoric are nearly synonymous (I: 8–9). The New Rhetoricians invoke Aristotle, Dionysius of Halicarnassus, Longinus, Cicero, and Quintilian, but they wish primarily to establish the "radical principles" of language and literature (Campbell, *Philosophy of Rhetoric* I: 95). And the literature they examined was by and large not ancient but emphatically contemporary. Rhetoric, they decided, derives from rigorous close reading, observation, and the study of the actual practice of writers. It goes beyond analysis and interpretation; it shows the structure of language in interplay with the process of composition, as well as how effective writing may be reinforced and faults avoided. The goal is improved understanding and improved praxis. Rhetoric begins with practice, proceeds through theory, and returns to the original acts of speaking and writing. Its procedure shifts between the descriptive and prescriptive.

Even while pursuing elaborate systems and theory, the New Rhetoricians profess an empirical bias. Their theories derive from wide reading and return to specific, formative examples. At the outset of his *Lectures on Rhetoric and Belles Lettres,* Blair expresses the group spirit: "The rules of Criticism are not formed by any induction, *a priori* . . . that is, they are not formed by a train of abstract reasoning, independent of facts and observations. Criticism is an art founded wholly on experience." Hume, in "Of the Standard of Taste" (1757), likewise remarked that the basis for "rules" of art "is the same with that of all the practical sciences, experience."

The general claim is that any critic who understands both a text and responses to it must possess two kinds of knowledge: a command of interpretation and the possible significance of a text; and, in order to gauge the purpose and success of that text in rousing its audience and communicating with it, a psychological acuity—the critic must know the mind and the passions, intellect and emotion, as expressed not just in literature but in experience at large.

The New Rhetoricians are among the most perceptive psychologists of their time. If close reading was one leg of the stiff twin compass they used to measure literature, then the other leg was nothing less than knowledge of human nature—not as some steady and unchanging construct, but through personal observation, reflection, and study. The critic becomes a psychologist in order to help the student of rhetoric become one too. In this sense at least, the rhetorician is a humanist and a moralist—not a preceptor of moral rules, but one who studies mores. Quintilian made this connection centuries ago (II: IV, ii, 8–9). Its fundamental truth resurfaces in the university titles of several New Rhetoricians: they are professors of moral philosophy. To emulate great poetry requires an open approach to mores—to "life and manners," that key phrase informing so many pieces of criticism from Dryden through Hazlitt, and repeated by Johnson in his *Preface to Shakespeare.* This openness to experience is part of the reason Johnson readily forgives Shakespeare's mingled drama as "a practice contrary to the rules of criticism," for "there is always an appeal open from criticism to nature." We approach nearer "to the appearance of life." This is not so much a hot pursuit of some vaguely defined eighteenth-century image of permanent human nature as it is an attempt to bond together thinking about language and thinking about behavior. Priestley, who confirms that a person must be "in some sense, a *logician* before he be an orator," qualifies this statement immediately: "More especially is it of consequence . . . to be well acquainted with *human nature,*" with the "passions, prejudices, interests and views" of the audience—in short, with "principles of human actions" (*Oratory and Criticism* 3–4).

As schoolboys, most New Rhetoricians were whipped into mastering difficult Greek and Latin texts. They took careful reading as a matter of course.

What they add is an insistence on the means by which passions, emotions, and human motives are portrayed through the use of language, especially figures. Riding the crest of the Scottish Common Sense School and the associationists' approach, Lord Kames begins *Elements of Criticism* with a rough introduction to psychology. Campbell's *Philosophy of Rhetoric*, first delivered to "a private literary society" in 1757, commences with "a tolerable sketch of the human mind," for only with this in hand, he says, can we "ascertain, with greater precision, the radical principles of that art, whose object it is, by the use of language, to operate on the soul of the hearer." The origin of poetry and of those imitative arts aimed at "internal tastes," and the "springs" by which these arts "can be regulated, must be sought for in the nature of the human mind, and more especially in the principles of the imagination" (I, vii, 12).[4] This is a profound connection, a critical view that, perhaps more than any other single one, has shaped European and American literature of the last two hundred years: the principles of criticism become nothing less than the principles of imagination itself. As Coleridge would say in the *Biographia*, "The *rules* of the IMAGINATION are themselves the very powers of growth and production" (II: 84).

Although we now recognize this as the main critical stance developing in the middle and late century, Campbell goes further and claims that not only is criticism based on psychology, particularly on the imagination, but the converse: psychology may best be understood through criticism. "In this view," rhetoric "is perhaps the surest and the shortest, as well as the pleasantest way of arriving at the science of the human mind" (I: 16).[5] Hans Aarsleff explains Condillac's importance for linguistics in a similar vein. Condillac realizes that "with the use of artificial signs, language puts thought in control of itself" (*Language in England* 23).[6] Grasped and followed to its source, the taxonomy of rhetoric does more than name or reflect; it also analyzes states of consciousness and psychological phenomena. Linguistic tools belong to the workshop of the mind. The link between states of mind and figures of speech, between psychology and stylistics, was hinted at in English as early as John Hoskins's *Directions for Speech and Style* (composed 1599–1600), in which Hoskins admits that, "though all metaphors go beyond the signification of things, yet they are requisite to match the compassing sweetness of men's minds, that are not content to fix themselves upon one thing but they must wander" (8). The mind will be delighted with its own activity, and will direct it, through the exercise of metaphor and invention.

Emphasis on psychology, rudimentary at first, matured rapidly. Above all, it meant, as Thomas Gibbons phrased it, that "Rhetoric is by no means restrained to the truth and precision of Logic" (*Rhetoric* 448). It is not strictly logical because we are not. The passions are involved, and they are essential. No wonder language deconstructs itself. "So far therefore it is from being an unfair method of persuasion to move the passions," says Campbell, "that there is not persuasion without moving them" (I: 200).[7] Hazlitt, who studied under Priestley, imbibed this principle, and John Mahoney has called Hazlitt's criticism *The Logic of Passion*. Its godparents are the New Rhetoricians. Unless wild and genuinely out of control—today we would say verging on the psychotic—passion strengthens all acts of the psyche, and its language. "When in such a degree as to rouse and kindle the mind, without throwing it out of the possession of itself," Blair claims, passion "is universally found to exalt all the human powers. It renders the mind infinitely more enlightened, more penetrating, more vigorous and masterly, than it is in its calm moments" (*Lectures* II: 6). The idea of passion as the enemy of reason had been generally debunked by this time. Campbell desires the orator to engage "all . . . powers of the mind, the imagination, the memory, and the passions. These are not the supplanters of reason, or even rivals in her sway; they are her handmaids" (I: 187). From here it is a short step to Wordsworth's concept of imagination as "Reason in her most exalted mood."

Every trope or figure may be grasped as the specific "sign" or "vehicle" of a feeling or emotion. Wordplay is mind play—or a play of passions—and at its best associates all our sensibilities. A particular trope or figure does not always represent the same feeling, but certain passions may be more closely linked with certain figures. A simple metaphor may show love or hate; asyndeton may express the excitement of anger or joy. What is crucial is that the mind is thrown into emotional activity and, guided by the meanings of individual words, interprets the figure in a way that heightens all feeling and perception. Blair sees the key to metaphor as abridged resemblance that creates a self-aware intuition: "The mind . . . is exercised without being fatigued; and is gratified with the consciousness of its own ingenuity." All figures are "prompted either by the imagination or by the passions" (*Lectures* I: 296, 275).

This attitude emerged into a science of psychology, and critics such as Thomas Sheridan, father of the playwright and politician, decried the wide difference in "principles" and "definition or descriptions" contained in the "variety of treatises which have lately been published on the passions" (*Course* xii). But Sheridan and others saw that inasmuch as rhetorical language was based on passion rather than "pure logic," it was foolish to expect it to communicate precisely, or to transmit exactly what an author intended. It is a "common delusion," Sheridan says, "that by the help of words alone" we can "communicate all that passes" in our minds. We need to recall that "the passion and the fancy have a language of their own, utterly independent of words, by which only their *exertions* can be manifested and communicated" (xii, emphasis added).[8]

With the new psychological interest, perceptions of both nature and what it meant to imitate nature through the medium of language changed. "Truth to nature" became something of a complicated, if not stale, injunction. Nature may be external, but once we perceive it, and especially when we express it in words, it is twined with the psyche.[9] We give it human reference—we humanize it. Nature is an endless text read with all our senses. Art ceases to imitate or describe nature and begins instead to imitate our experience of nature. Nature is unemotional; we bring to it our passion and express our feelings to others; we imitate states of consciousness not only by the meditative language of reflection but also through the text of nature as we inscribe nature in a psychologically attuned language. The New Rhetoricians establish a critical theory that becomes the spine of Romantic poetics and criticism.[10] In many ways the New Rhetoricians have more in common with Hazlitt, Coleridge, and Wordsworth than with Johnson, Goldsmith, and Reynolds—though the changing emphasis of Reynolds's *Discourses* (1769–1791) derives in part from his acquaintance with the new rhetorics.

The stance of the New Rhetoricians produced immediate repercussions. As rhetorical language is used by the poet to animate nature—to express the peculiar interaction of Psyche and Pan—we find ourselves "humanizing nature," a gift Coleridge claimed for Shakespeare. The New Rhetoricians also anticipate Hazlitt's concept of "gusto," and what Keats called the "greeting of the spirit." In poetic language, the ideal of sympathy or sympathetic identification of poet with subject depends on similitudes, on figures of speech, if only simple metaphors. As Beattie tersely put it, "The philosophy of Sympathy ought always to form a part of the science of Criticism."[11] Character criticism, such as Maurice Morgann's *Essay on Falstaff* (1777), grew in interest and acuity.

In conjunction with the psychological approach to rhetoric and nature, at least three other ideas emerged. First, personification or prosopopeia was analyzed so that it hinged on the verb rather than on an adjective or noun. The more a human motive or feeling is attributed to a natural form or, more intensely, to an action of that form, the more effective. Blair marks three levels of personification. The "obscure degree" comes buried in common adjectives: "a raging storm, a deceitful disease." A higher level tends to personify substantive nouns (Johnson's Wolsey with "Law in his Voice and Fortune in his Hand") or natural objects as they act in sympathy with us. Blair cites Homer, Shakespeare, and Milton for this excellence, as when Eve,

> So saying, her rash hand in evil hour
> Forth reaching to the fruit, she pluck'd, she eat;
> Earth felt the wound; and nature, from her seat
> Sighing through all her works gave signs of woe,
> That all was lost. (*Paradise Lost* IX, 780–84)

But in the highest personification, objective nature and subjective humankind act as one. The forms of nature "are introduced, not only as feeling and acting, but as speaking to us, or hearing and listening when we address ourselves to them." This boldest use, so many instances of which are found in Wordsworth, is, according to Blair, "the style of strong passion only." So Eve, on quitting Eden, says:

> Must I thus leave thee, Paradise? thus leave
> Thee, native soil, these happy walks, and shades,

> Fit haunt of Gods? where I had hope to spend
> Quiet, though sad, the respite of that day,
> Which must be mortal to us both. O flowers!
> That never will in other climate grow ... (XI, 269–274)

In sum, personification works effectively when it avoids abstractions, substantives, stasis, and mere description; it succeeds when it involves the actions and passions of nature and psyche together, breaking down the barrier between them until nature becomes a human cosmos (Blair, *Lectures* I: 327, 330, 332–34, 335). Thomas Gibbons gives a similar example, the "case when Milton tells us, that *nature sighed,* and *the sky wept some sad drops* upon our first parents eating the forbidden fruit" (Gibbons, *Rhetoric* 394).[12]

Second, the New Rhetoricians reexamined the relation of poetry and truth (or "reality") under the headings of Kames's "ideal presence" or "waking dream," Blair's "pleasing illusion," Trapp's "wide difference between falsehood and fiction," and Campbell's "fiction of the mind" or "of the imagination."[13] All these, however interpreted, look ahead to Coleridge's "willing suspension of disbelief" or "negative faith," or even further ahead to Oscar Wilde's "lying" and further back to Sidney's "feigning," where the poet neither lies nor tells the truth.

What is the upshot of this concept of illusion or presence, this fiction or dream, and is anything added to its presentation by Dryden, Johnson, and Hume? (The topic is often slanted toward stage illusion.) Carried to its extreme, the position of the New Rhetoricians yields a remarkable conclusion: the pleasure or delight caused by the arousal and chemical-like mixing of our passions is produced by style, by a mysterious power or impression *(stylus)* of words as they cohere and create; all truth in literature is symbolic in nature because words are themselves purely relational and symbolic. Language can make contradictions to experience consistent, "disagreeables" can "evaporate," for a new mode of experience—an imitation of mind experiencing nature, not a copy of nature—is created.

Third, the New Rhetoricians became aestheticians by defining aesthetic values in terms of emotionally charged figures of speech that imitate perceived nature and percipient mind in interplay. The pathetic, the marvelous, the sublime, and especially the beautiful are to a large degree constructs of words as symbols as well as objects in and of themselves. Metaphoric language brings the sensuous within the bounds of intellectual communication. Without such language, without rhetoric, the aesthetic sense would be mute, even undeveloped. The dream of Kames or Keats awakes in "the fine spell of words," in poetry which "alone can save / Imagination from the sable charm / And dumb enchantment." Aesthetics and rhetoric are intimate allies, actually interdependent, a point stressed by Beattie's *Essays on Poetry and Music As They Affect the Mind.*

Although I am not dealing primarily with aesthetic theory, we should note that the Rhetoricians looked with acuity at the verbal definitions and embodiments of aesthetic values. There were great obstacles to overcome: "no word in the language is used in a more vague signification than Beauty," remarks Blair (*Lectures* I: 81, 75). The word was never adequately defined and, by the late nineteenth century, began to lose currency as a critical term with any theoretical weight. Moreover, nature or experience as much as language may be the source of aesthetic feelings, but language is the only possible means of naming and analyzing those feelings and, as such, *any* science of aesthetics becomes bound up in significations of words.[14]

As long as rhetoric flourished, the beneficial effects of what we call the New Criticism flourished also. The New Critic is a species of rhetorician. Leo Damrosch has noted that Ned Softly, the character in Addison's *Tatler* 163, is actually "A New Critic striving to be born" ("Significance" 430).[15] It is dangerous to equate "close reading" (in whatever context) with the New Criticism, but the two overlap. Critical examples and passages given by the New Rhetoricians are often exercises in close reading. Blair's last five lectures (XX–XXIV) examine, paper by paper—even sentence by sentence—several *Spectators* (nos. 411–14) on the pleasures of the imagination, and Swift's letter to the Earl of Oxford. Blair's close reading, often done with real literary imagination, can also gauge rhetoric and stylistics with a micrometric vengeance. In one section he devotes almost a full page to the fact that Addison does not repeat the article *the* when he writes, "Our sight is the most perfect, and most delightful of all our senses" (*Lectures* I: 410).

Many examples given by the New Rhetoricians are found later in the practical criticism and commentary of Romantic poets. Wordsworth, in his note to *The Thorn,* cites the song of Deborah to show that "repetition and apparent tautology are frequently beauties of the highest kind" (*Poetical Works* II: 513). Coleridge, at the end of chapter 17 of the *Biographia,* cites Wordsworth, to show that "Such repetitions I admit to be a beauty of the highest kind" (*Biographia* II: 57). When Thomas Gibbons analyzes the passionate repetition of a word or phrase as *epanaphora,* from the Greek meaning "I repeat," he quotes as one example Deborah's "triumphal ode, where she describes the death of Sisera by Jael, *Judg.* v. 27. 'At her feet he bowed, he fell, he lay down; at her feet he bowed, he fell: where he bowed, there he fell down dead'" (*Rhetoric* 207–8, 210).[16] These are the very words Coleridge uses to close his chapter. And when Wordsworth, in his 1815 Preface, commends Milton for describing Satan in flight as "*hanging in the clouds* like a fleet far off at sea," he echoes Beattie's praise that "Satan flying among the stars is said by Milton to '*Sail* between worlds and worlds': which has an elegance and force far superior to the proper word *Fly*" (*Essays* 263).

Beattie makes it clear that rhetoric should bend language—especially the language of poetry—toward the *less* artificial, but also away from the merely commonplace. This principle informs his claim that "the utility of figurative expression" lies "in making language more *pleasing* and more *natural*"; or, "that by tropes and figures language may be made more natural and pleasing, than it could be without them. It follows that tropes and figures are more necessary to poetry, than to any other mode of writing" (285). The poet, in quest of "sympathies he would communicate to others" (285–86), speaks a natural language and "addresses himself to the passions and sympathies of mankind" (287).[17] Wordsworth's 1800 Preface—in which the poet is a man prompted by the spontaneous overflow of powerful feelings, speaking the real language of men to men—is a short distance away. Almost forty—perhaps as much as fifty—years earlier, Adam Smith told his students that "the perfection of style consists in express[ing] in the most concise, proper, and precise manner the thought of the author, and that in the manner which best conveys the sentiment, passion, or affection with which it affects—or he pretends it does affect—him, and which he designs to communicate to his reader" (*Lectures* 51). Smith was not specifically discussing poetry, but that is also to the point, for, like Wordsworth, he saw no essential difference between the language of prose and poetry. Smith is already supporting a natural rhetoric based on sympathy and affect: "When the sentiment of the speaker is expressed in a neat, clear, plain, and clever manner, and the passion or affection he is possessed of and intends, *by sympathy,* to communicate to his hearer, is plainly and cleverly hit off, then and then only the expression has all the force and beauty that language can give it. It matters not the least whether the figures of speech are introduced or not." They of course can be, and are particularly effective, "as they happen to be the just and natural forms of expressing that sentiment" (22–23).

The New Rhetoricians examine the fundamental nature of literature as symbolic communication. This rich and problematic study grasps the relations between words, ideas, and things. Locke is the seminal figure here in the English considerations. As Horne Tooke would note, it may be a mistake to call Locke's major work an essay on the Understanding; it is actually on grammar, language, and words. Hans Aarsleff asserts a pivotal role for Locke in a great shift in linguistic studies: "Locke stood on the line between past and future" (*From Locke to Saussure* 24).[18] The disclosure adopted by the New Rhetoricians—who were the "future"—sounds familiar to us and refers specifically to ideas, signs, signification, thing signified, and language as a vehicle. There is no *naturalité du signe* for the New Rhetoricians. Unanimously they reject it and, except for onomatopoetic words, declare our correspondence between sound and meaning to be "arbitrary." Campbell best sums up the position: "Language is purely a species of fashion ... in which, by the general, but tacit consent of the people of a particular state or country, certain sounds come to be appropriated to certain things, as their signs, and certain ways of inflecting and combining those sounds come to be established, as denoting the relations which subsist among the things signified." In other words, "every smatterer in philosophy will tell us, that there can be no natural connexion between the sounds of any language, and the things signified" (*Philosophy of Rhetoric* I: 340).[19]

Combining the theoretical and practical, the New Rhetoricians conclude that communication by words must be imperfect. Words and things enjoy no intrinsic relation, as Byron laments in *Childe Harold* (3.114):

> I do believe
> Though I have found them not, that there may be
> Words which are things, hopes which will not deceive . . .
>
> I would also deem
> O'er others' griefs that some sincerely grieve;
> That two, or one, are almost what they seem,
> That goodness is no name, and happiness no dream.

So, although the New Rhetoricians agree that "in matters of criticism, as in the abstract sciences, it is of the utmost consequence to ascertain, with precision, the meanings of words, and . . . to make them correspond to the boundaries assigned by Nature to the things signified," they also realize that words signify not things imperfectly, but only imperfectly signify the ideas *of* things. They read Locke carefully. This is what Wordsworth refers to as the "sad incompetence of human speech,"[20] and perhaps what Shelley means when he has Demogorgon say, "the deep truth is imageless." Each phrase or sentence, even each definition of a word—let alone a long text—becomes a complex interplay of variously imperfect signs, a free play of differing signifiers (Campbell, *Philosophy of Rhetoric* I: 38–39). All language thus proceeds by a kind of relational metalepsis. But however faulty, linguistic communication does operate within a range of conventions and saves itself from collapsing into "nonsense," where every interpretation is equally valid and itself equally interpretable into yet more interpretations. Metalepsis may be all we have, but it is clearer than obfuscation or total distrust of language. Perfect clarity or "true" communication is a mirage, a collective delusion, but at least one that keeps us walking.

Shelley briefly expresses the social and self-referential nature of language at the outset of the *Defence*. If our "social sympathies" develop and we use language to communicate what we see each do as "a social being," then "even in the infancy of society" we will "observe a certain order in . . . [our] words and actions, distinct from that of the objects and the impressions represented by them, all expression being subject to the laws of that from which it proceeds."

Metalepsis abridges the self-referential nature of language and provides a model by which words, as arbitrary signifiers, relate to each other in order to salvage sense from chaos. In metalepsis, as John Ward's *Oratory* defines it,

> two or more Tropes, and those of a different kind are contained under one word, so that gradations or intervening senses come between the word that is expressed, and the thing designed by it. The contests . . . between Sylla and Marius proved very fatal to the *Roman* state. Julius Caesar was then a young man. But Sylla, observing his aspiring genius, said of him, In one Caesar there

are many Mariuses. . . . Now in this expression there is a *Metalepsis,* for the word *Marius,* by a Synecdoche or Antonomasia, is put for any ambitious or turbulent person; and this again by a Metonymy of the cause for the ill effects of such a temper to the Public. So that Sylla's meaning, divested of these Tropes, was, that Caesar would prove the most dangerous person to the *Roman* state that ever was bred in it; which afterwards proved true in the event.[21]

Inasmuch as each word in a figure, sentence, or text, side by side or in proximity with other words, not only signifies one thing or rather one idea of a thing or an action, but also may signify part of the confluence of many other words or tropes, we might extend Ward's analysis and say that all language and all texts (from *teks,* meaning, among other things, to weave) proceed by a kind of metalepsis. All language is arbitrary; meaning inheres and coheres in the differences but also in the transitive identities of the signifiers. We must communicate with imperfect, self-referring signifiers or else, like Gulliver's dumb philosophers, hand each other objects. Naturally enough, many important acts in life still use ritualistic objects as well as words: water, bread, wine, rings, dust, ashes, candles, and eggs.

The New Rhetoricians see that the process of thought and understanding proceed only by means of language of some sort, only by semiosis, and in language by the relational or generally metaleptic processes of signs and figures. We cannot think other than by signs. The mind not only communicates by images and signs; it cannot even think without them. Campbell asks pointedly, "what hath given rise to the distinction between ratiocination and imagery?" (*Philosophy of Rhetoric* I: 192).[22] Coleridge later proposed an essay on the impossibility of thinking without images! Rhetoric, which creates and employs language, not only is a vehicle; it may be viewed as part of thought itself. Words used habitually become icons of such power that they are "greater" than the nature and the ideas they signify. Campbell admits that the connection "between words and things is, in its origin, arbitrary." Yet, he goes on, "the difference in the effect is not so considerable as one would be apt to imagine. In neither case is it the matter . . . but the power of the sign that is regarded by the mind" (*Philosophy of Rhetoric* II: 112–13).[23] As for words that in essence become things, Childe Harold "found them not," yet later Byron in *Don Juan* (3.88) protests

> But words are things, and a small drop of ink
> Falling like dew, upon a thought, produces
> That which makes thousands, perhaps millions, think. . . .

Language is the vehicle of thought, and without it thought remains inert, not only incommunicable but perhaps unthinkable. Language as a "vehicle" is a premise of the new rhetoric. Emerson, brought up on the New Rhetoricians, remarks in "The Poet" that "all language is vehicular and transitive, and is good, as ferries and horses are, for conveyance, not as farms and houses are, for homestead" (*Collected Works* III: 20).[24] Though Locke and Johnson use "tenor," I have not found it in the New Rhetoricians. However, "vehicle" appears abundantly in them. I. A. Richards was reading them when, discussing Kames, he introduced tenor and vehicle in his own *Philosophy of Rhetoric* (1936).

Much of the new rhetoric depends on a realization that words are imperfect and slippery signifiers. This helps to explain the neoclassical and eighteenth-century obsession with clarity—not that writers and critics trusted words, but that they distrusted them and their possible abuses so much. Priestley urges, "A regard to *perspicuity* would direct us (if we would be understood) to explain distinctly the meaning of every word we use, that is of the least doubtful signification" (*Lectures* 47).[25] Language is a cutting edge blunted by use; it must be sharpened constantly. But the dialect of the tribe must be kept up, and for us there is only the trying. Campbell puts it succinctly: we try "to convey our sentiments into the minds of others. . . . Language is the only vehicle by which this conveyance can be made."

The New Rhetoricians glean fresh perspective on style from the general imperfection of language. This lack of ultimate precision and accuracy of language permits and encourages individual style. With perfect communication, style would be impossible. (Only "correctness" would attain—and this is the poetic value most prized when clarity of expression is at stake.) Priestley, in his *Lectures on the Theory of Language, and Universal Grammar,* shows that by substituting and employing "other words of similar signification" in different orders and degrees of precision we arrive at a particular emphasis, rhythm, and sense. It is in the awareness and command of the elusive qualities of signifiers and significations, grammar, sound, and syntax that "the accuracy and excellency of style doth greatly consist" (163, 164).

The New Rhetoricians establish a psychological basis for a figurative, natural language expressing the action of the mind in a state of excitement or strong emotion. More than any other group or critic, they also link our classical heritage of rhetoric, from Aristotle through the Renaissance, with modern semiology and linguistics. (Campbell's work especially demands more attention.) Yet the New Rhetoric presents no single synthesis. Ironically its insights prove inimical to systematic logic, for these critics realize that literature, conceived as rhetoric, derives its greatest power from affective expression. As Blair states, the poetry or eloquence "which gains the admiration of mankind . . . is never found without warmth, or passion. Passion, when in such a degree as to rouse and kindle the mind, without throwing it out of the possession of itself, is universally found to exalt all the human powers. It renders the mind infinitely more enlightened, more penetrating, more vigorous and masterly, than it is in its calm moments" (*Lectures* II: 6).[26]

Some of the dullest books are those purporting to explain the methods and mysteries of great literature. The New Rhetoricians are dull at times, but they are rarely opaque. They avoid what Arnold later calls the "jargon of modern criticism." Many of them were academics, but they address the generally educated public. They assert that the *telos* of critical study is the persuasive use of language, not only as it scrutinizes our critical faculties and systems, but as it incites us to think, feel, and act. They realize that literature qua literature, as a separate discipline, is an ornament of society. But it can be thought of as a vital necessity if it furthers or is associated with other goals, cultural values, or larger concerns of human conduct.

As with all literary or critical movements that perceive literary values and styles not simply as ends in themselves but having at least the possibility of affecting human ends and needs at large, the New Rhetoricians neither subvert nor support prevailing literary taste. They prove both conservative and liberal, even radical and reactionary. They are at once scientific—that is, loosely systematic and empirical—yet their intuition rejects rigid positivism. They trust the perceptions of a developed, catholic taste and a trained ear.[27] Their major aim is to improve the practice of education and religion in general; they hardly set out to form a school of criticism, at least not self-consciously. Any one of them would first consider himself a theologian, economist, educator, moral philosopher, or public servant. One remarkable feature of their criticism taken in the gross is that we rarely encounter an explicit distinction between fiction and exposition such as essays, sermons, and speeches. (This is apparent as early as Smith's *Lectures* of 1748–51.)[28] Literature, at least conceived from the standpoint of rhetoric, is for them one body. Many New Rhetoricians are divines who want their students to write and deliver good sermons and to read and appreciate not only the doctrine of the Bible but its beauty and poetry as well. We can say without exaggeration that one impetus for the new criticism of the later eighteenth century was religion, but certainly not with a doctrinal or moralizing streak. As Alexander Carlyle said in speaking to the General Assembly of Scotland in 1793, "There are few branches of literature in which the ministers of this church have not excelled. There are few subjects of fine writing in which they do not stand foremost in the rank of authors."

One example of this reasoned, felt use of rhetoric for the purpose of reflecting on the motives and ends of human action is Johnson's periodical writing. In *Rambler* 3—the allegory of true and false criticism—he asserts that "the task of an author is, either to teach what is not known, or to recommend known truths, by his manner of adorning them." In this same essay he asserts that there is a false and a true rhetoric. In Johnson's writing, Hoyt Trowbridge remarks, "The words and thoughts arise naturally from the intellectual and moral character of the implied speaker, and have added force because of it." This "naturally" has nothing to do with any supposed natural connection or *naturalité du signe* between words as articulated sounds and the moral values we agree that, however imprecisely, they represent. The words and thoughts, signifier and thing signified—the unit of the sign itself— arise naturally because the speaker believes those values and exemplifies them by action.[29]

The art of rhetoric brings the idea of *mimesis* full circle. As imitation may depict what Priestley (and later Hazlitt) calls the "principles of human actions," the end of rhetoric is to move readers and hearers to appreciate, to decide, and to act.[30] So conceived, literature is bound up with our every choice and experience, from polemics to simple pastimes to nursery rhymes (often first read as satires). The motives of writing and of criticism become the motives of human action at large.

**NOTES**

1. For general studies, see Wilbur Samuel Howell, *Eighteenth-Century British Logic and Rhetoric* (441–691), and George A. Kennedy, *Classical Rhetoric and Its Christian Secular Tradition from Ancient to Modern Times* (220–41).

2. For "theory," see, for example, George Campbell, *The Philosophy of Rhetoric* (I: 25–83). Campbell refers to "the theory now laid down and explained" (83). Howell (616–33) treats Lawson "as much . . . for the new rhetoric as for the old" (630). For Ward and Lawson, see Kennedy, *Classical Rhetoric* (228–29). Vincent M. Bevilacqua and Richard Murphy, editing Joseph Priestley's, *A Course of Lectures on Oratory and Criticism*, refer to Ward and Lawson as "the culmination of classical rhetoric in the eighteenth century" (xxii). For background, see Victor Anthony Rudowski (683–90). Studies of eighteenth-century semiotics and rhetoric have tended to cluster around Germany and France: e.g., David E. Wellbery, *Lessing's Laocoon: Semiotics and Aesthetics in the Age of Reason*; Tzvetan Todorov, "Esthétique et sémiotique au XVIIIe siècle"; and Wolfgang Bender, "Rhetorische Tradition und Asthetik im 18. Jahrhundert."

3. Adam Smith, *Lectures on Rhetoric and Belles Lettres . . . Reported by a Student in 1762–63* (23). The manuscript is not in Smith's hand; some lectures may have been recorded partly from memory. On the persistent view of rhetoric as mere terminology, see Wayne C. Booth, "The Scope of Rhetoric Today" (94), and Jonathan Culler, *Structuralist Poetics* (179).

4. See also Campbell's *Philosophy*, ed. Lloyd F. Bitzer, which reprints the 1850 London edition. By 1912 *Philosophy* had entered eleven editions. In New York it was reprinted nineteen times between 1845 and 1887 (Bitzer xxx–xxxi). The first edition (1776) is quoted here.

5. See Karl R. Wallace, "The Fundamentals of Rhetoric" (II).

6. Hans Aarsleff states (*Language in England* 53) that Horne Tooke conceived of language *as* thought, not merely as that which makes thought possible. For general background, see also Murray Cohen.

7. This seems to concern what Susan Sontag calls an erotics of art.

8. Recall T. S. Eliot's remark that communication alone does not explain poetry; or Coleridge's, that poetry is most enjoyed when *im*perfectly understood.

9. For example see Hugh Blair, *Lectures* (I: 94–95), on the difference between describing and actually imitating nature; also Samuel Johnson in *Rambler* 36, where he says the effects of nature on the ear and eye are "incapable of much variety of description."

10. For another view, see M. H. Abrams, *The Mirror and the Lamp* (53–54).

11. See Gibbons, *Rhetoric* (392); Campbell, *Philosophy of Rhetoric* (I: 242–48); James Beattie, *Essays on Poetry and Music as They Affect the Mind* (194). See also Beattie, *Dissertations Moral and Critical* (166–190).

12. See Morton W. Bloomfield, "Personification-Metaphors," and Earl R. Wasserman, "The Inherent Values of Eighteenth-Century Personification."

13. Gibbons, *Rhetoric* (95–96); Campbell, *Philosophy of Rhetoric* (I: 306–9, 314–38); Kames, *Elements of Criticism* (I: 104–27); see also Abrams, *Mirror and Lamp* (270–71, 324–25). Erasmus Darwin emphasized this power of pleasing illusion and

ideal presence in poetry, and his view may have influenced Coleridge in the 1790s. See also Wallace Jackson, *Immediacy,* chap. 3.

14. Campbell, *Philosophy of Rhetoric* (I: 207), offers an interesting defense and definition of the "rather modern" term, "the *sentimental.*"

15. See also Damrosch, "William Warburton as 'New Critic'" (249–265).

16. Bishop Lowth also discussed the Song of Deborah in his *Lectures on the Sacred Poetry of the Hebrews.*

17. For another view of the stress on natural language, see Abrams, *Mirror and Lamp* (16, 288).

18. See Aarsleff, *From Locke to Saussure* (42–83, 120–45), on Locke's reputation in the nineteenth century. An acute view of the philosophical context is provided by James G. Buickerood, "The Natural History of the Understanding," which traces the evolution of semiotics and logic as related concepts in Locke's thinking during the 1670s and 1680s. For additional background, see Nancy S. Struever, "The Conversable World." For words, ideas, and things, see, e.g., Thomas Gunter Browne, *Hermes Unmasked; or, The Art of Speech Founded on the Association of Words and Ideas* (1795), and the earlier, anonymous *The Way to Things by Words, and to Words by Things* (1766).

19. See also Campbell (II: 112; I: 342); Blair, *Lectures* (I: 105); Jonathan Culler, *Ferdinand de Saussure* (10–15).

20. Wordsworth's phrase appears not only in *The Prelude* but also in his 1815 Preface to *Lyrical Ballads.*

21. Quoted by Gibbons, *Rhetoric* (69), from John Ward, *A System of Oratory* (1759) (II: 25–26). Harold Bloom makes metaleptic imagination a central act in his own new rhetoric of the psychology of poetic imagination.

22. Compare Aarsleff, *Study of Language* (53, 20–25).

23. For Addison's treatment of nature (things), description (signs), and the activity of mind involved with them, see *Spectator* 416.

24. *Rambler* 202 uses "vehicle" similarly, as does Blair (*Lectures* I: 98, 289). In Johnson's *Dictionary* the second definition of "tenour" is "sense contained; general course or drift," and the illustration is from Locke: "Reading it must be repeated again and again with a close attention to the *tenor* of the discourse, and a perfect neglect of the divisions into chapters and verses." Under the third definition of "vehicle," Johnson quotes L'Estrange: "The gaiety of a diverting word, serves as a *vehicle* to convey the force and meaning of a thing."

25. Compare Campbell, *Philosophy of Rhetoric* (I: 39).

26. Edward P. J. Corbett, in "John Locke's Contributions to Rhetoric," remarks: "The expansion of the province of rhetoric in the schools [in the 18th and 19th centuries] is probably due mainly to the influence of George Campbell, who proposed that the purposes of discourse were 'to enlighten the understanding, to please the imagination, to move the passions, or to influence the will,' or to the influence of Alexander Bain, who propagated the notion of the four modes of discourse—narration, description, exposition, and argumentation. It is clear, however, that the impetus for that expansion comes from Locke's *Essay*" (75). Bain stressed the psychological basis of such figures as metonymy and synecdoche, not so much from the point of view of the writer, but of the reader. See also Winifred Bryan Horner, "Rhetoric in the Liberal Arts"; Gerald P. Mulderig, "Nineteenth-Century Psychology"; and Nan Johnson, "Three Nineteenth-Century Rhetoricians."

27. For theoretical discussion, see Campbell, *Philosophy of Rhetoric,* "Of the different sources of Evidence, and the different subjects to which they are respectively adapted" (I: 103–63).

28. Howell, *Logic and Rhetoric* (547), says Smith "made rhetoric the general theory of all branches of literature—the historical, the poetical, the didactic or scientific, and oratorical."

29. For discussion of Johnson's rhetoric, see Hoyt Trowbridge, "The Language of Reasoned Rhetoric in *The Rambler*" (200–216). Trowbridge ably discusses the use and limits of logic in Johnson's rhetoric.

30. Wallace, "The Fundamentals of Rhetoric" (19 n.7), cites Everett Hunt in *The Rhetorical Idiom* (4): "If we can keep as basic our conception that the humanities embrace whatever contributes to the making of free and enlightened choices, whether it be knowledge scientific, sociological, or poetic, and that in addition to adequate knowledge of all the alternatives there must be imagination to envision all the possibilities and sympathy to make some of the options appeal to the emotions and powers of the will, we can see that rhetoric is an essential instrument for the enterprises of the human spirit."

# XV

# THE CONVERSABLE WORLD
## EIGHTEENTH-CENTURY TRANSFORMATIONS OF THE RELATION OF RHETORIC AND TRUTH

*Nancy S. Struever*

A perfectly ordinary reaction to Jane Austen's novels is to remark that they seem "true," historically correct. The reaction is in large part due to the manner in which Austen "accounts for" the fictional events she gives an "account of"; the reader senses, for example, the diagnostic power of her descriptions of conversation. Austen's skill is a capacity both to epitomize and to analyze a broad shift in the English cultural program in the eighteenth century. Further, her skill is necessarily a skill in discursive critique, because this revisionary moment is primarily a transformation of traditional rhetorical programs.

The core of the classical rhetorical program had been constituted by the integration of three tasks—*docere, delectare, movere:* rhetoric as discipline regulated a discourse of instruction, delight, and persuasion. We note in the eighteenth-century program not only the persistence of each of the original interests but the reassertion of the strategy of integration as well. The program, while it serves new orientations and new goals, retains classical rhetorical premise and procedure: significant truth is still defined by locating it in a pragmatic domain of use, of political and social utility, and the procedure for the definition of truth still requires the assumption that moral and aesthetic values are at once hegemonous and conjoint. Thus, for example, the philosopher David Hume's *Enquiry concerning the Principles of Morals* presents a rhetorical program:

> The end of all moral speculations is to teach us our duty; and, by proper representations of the deformity of vice and beauty of virtue, beget correspondent habits, and engage us to avoid the one, and embrace the other. (*Principles of Morals* 172)[1]

Here speculation on moral truth precedes and produces discursive engagement; Hume's definition of moral work is the classical definition of epideictic task. Furthermore, Hume retains the strict rhetorical connection between affect and rational persuasion; the domain of moral judgment can be mapped by the tactics of aesthetic judgment:

> in many orders of beauty, particularly those of the finer arts, it is requisite to employ much reasoning, in order to feel the proper sentiment; and a false relish may frequently be corrected by argument and reflection. There are just grounds to conclude, that moral beauty partakes much of this latter species, and demands the assistance of our intellectual faculties, in order to give it a suitable influence on the human mind. (*Principles of Morals* 173)

For Hume, then, the domain of moral truth is an empirical realm of specific facts and sentiments, a domain pervaded by contingency, and one that requires very specific tactics of investigation and argument: the very domain presumed by Ciceronian and Quintilianesque treatises on argument. Hume's reworking of *A Treatise on Human Nature* as "enqueries," even his preference for inductive as opposed to deductive modes, acknowledges the value of critique governed by rhetorical and inclusive as opposed to formal and exclusive logical rules. The *Enquiries,* indeed, is a summary rejection of doctrinal truth defined by systematic methods in favor of practical truth characterized by informal methods, a truth that, as practical, requires persuasive discourse.[2]

The pragmatic nature of the eighteenth-century program exemplified by Hume's *Enquiries* helps explain its practical force; the program both shapes intellectual discipline and invests social behavior. The ability to engage in pleasant and informal, "polite," argument and in the argumentative development of moral and aesthetic judgment, "taste," constitutes a general receptive competence, an accomplishment in the discovery of true propriety, "truth." Rhetorical discipline is reassembled as a new skill that is the duty, property, and talent of a new social elite; the faculties to be developed in education and social intercourse enhance and give meaning to status and connection: taste, for example, is a mode of social communication, the hegemonous social competence.[3]

But a precise description of Austen's skill requires more than a general reference to Austen as both beneficiary and critic of this program; it demands a specific focus on the peculiar alliance of rhetorical skills and aesthetic interests forged in the eighteenth century, a union of argumentative modes and aesthetic topics that intervened directly in the reorganization of investigative roles as social roles. This reorganization underwrites the perspicacity of Austen's account of her society by assuring the coherence of social and investigative rules. To describe this alliance I shall appeal to a limited range of texts. I shall begin with the works of Anthony Ashley Cooper, Third Earl of Shaftesbury, turning to his "Advice to an Author" for a description of the discourse of inquiry and to his *Second Characters* for his definition of aesthetic value. I shall focus next on Hume's eight essays on aesthetic topics, where his strongly empiricist treatment of the reception (rather than the production) of art redefines and authenticates the new discourse of taste, and then on Hume's *Enquiry concerning the Principles of Morals,* which projects a receptive ethics, a new moral critique. Finally, I shall examine Austen's novels, which translate Hume's philosophical project into a literary project and in the process become powerfully descriptive of the new social-discursive rules—descriptive, in short, of the essential constraints of "gentlemanlike behavior."

Shaftesbury's confection of the role of critic is a key event in the transformation of rhetoric into criticism, a criticism that retains an argumentative cognitive strategy, a rhetorical theory of truth, to discipline reception. Shaftesbury substitutes "rhetorical" argument for "philosophical" system; recall his stricture that "the most ingenious way of becoming foolish is by a system" (Cooper, *Characteristics* 1: 189). But it is a highly privatized notion of discipline; aesthetic truth is defined in argument, but the argument that is both paradigmatic and preparatory is a typically Renaissance argument, the interior dialogue. Just as Petrarch developed the genre of interior dialogue as a mode of inquiry, so Shaftesbury takes the position in "Advice to an Author" that soliloquy—discourse requiring the dividing of oneself into two persons, and thus a dialogue with the self—originates insight (*Characteristics* 1: 105–6).[4] Shaftesbury projects a notion of discipline as an internal self-discipline; his dialogic introspection is a kind of private empiricism where the rules of discourse are the rules of inquiry: "'Tis the hardest thing in the world to be a good thinker without being a strong self-examiner and thorough-paced dialogist in this solitary way" (*Characteristics* 1: 112).

This dialogue with the self generates an awareness of the values of harmony, order, and proportion, which mark good moral performance as well as aesthetic production (*Characteristics* 1: 228, 279). Shaftesbury represents these values not in a "systematic" fashion as preexisting armatures but as qualities attached to, and to be derived from, the disciplined exercise of verbal and visual skills. His "Advice to an Author" admits the necessity of transferring to public discussion the attribution of value but presents the rules of this investigational public exchange as no other than the social rules that acknowledge a reciprocity and symmetry of sincere intention. The exchange that develops and communicates values is, moreover, remarkably untrammeled, even irreverent and combative, certainly neither pious nor genteel. Shaftesbury's stance against enthusiasm is also a stance pro wit; in the essay "Freedom of Wit and Humor," he states that "truth, 'tis supposed, may bear all lights; and one of those principal lights, or natural mediums, by which things are to be viewed, in order to a thorough recognition, is ridicule itself, or that manner of proof by which we discern whatever is liable to just raillery in any subject" (*Characteristics* 1: 44). A free-ranging wit is the preserver of virtue and wisdom, and there can be no exemptions by "custom or national opinion" from its critique (*Characteristics* 1: 9, 15). Furthermore, free access to the argumentative domain is a guarantee of personal development: "All politeness is owing to liberty. We polish one another, and rub off our corners and rough sides by a sort of amicable collision" (*Characteristics* 1: 46). Enthusiasm, or intolerance, is marked by a refusal to abide by the "fair laws of combat by wit and argument" (*Characteristics* 1: 47).

Accessibility does not entail slackness, however; Shaftesbury's discipline is a tight discipline, and he makes a strong distinction between "control, debate, argument" and "uncontrolled harangue" (*Characteristics* 1: 111). Furthermore, aesthetic truth is not a matter of simple sensuous reaction, "false relish," but of reflection and processing (*Second Characters* 61, 43). He regards his own skill as discursive and asserts that his science is "no better than that of a language master, or a logician" (*Characteristics* 1: 104)—indeed, he emphasizes his discipline as "trivial," of the trivium—yet his posture is not masterful: a strong cooperative model obtains, the kind of eloquent equity characteristic of gentlemanly debate as opposed to the authoritarian and ungenerous maneuvers of learned discourse. The preface to *Second Characters* shows that while the genre group he aspires to seems modest and informal enough—"*noctes atticae,* evening conversations, hours, virtuoso-amusement, plastic-entertainments, *Deliciae elegantiae artis*" (*Second Characters* 6)—he is obviously taking great pains to place himself precisely as an author and to place his book in a framework that will ensure its proper reception. Thus he reminds himself: "And even the *we, us, ours,* never used but in a sense as it were, taking in the reader, cooperating with the writer, and discovering, investigating, as a party himself" (*Second Characters* 12).[5] He knows that the skill he would impart must seem easy, so that he must write in such a way that his mixed audience "may comprehend, or be persuaded that they comprehend"—an important qualification—"what is there written in the text" (*Second Characters* 8–9).

Shaftesbury, then, takes very seriously the array of approved roles for his audience—amateur, dilettante, virtuoso. Perfectly aware of the fun and security of collecting, he is less interested in the role of patron-collector than of virtuoso-critic; his method of criticism and self-criticism is used not only to allow liberation from the errors of taste, of expensively misplaced patronage, but also to make the roles of patron-collector and virtuoso-critic independent and richly "respectable" (*Characteristics* 1: 174, 214; *Second Characters* 12–13). His anxiety to modify roles reshapes the Shaftesburian forms of discourse. Here again we see continuity with Renaissance motives: recall the development between Petrarch's letters and Montaigne's essays—the development of a discursive form that permits a personal view of a large variety of topics; wholeness, unity of vision, is the goal of an extending, stretching exercise.[6] In the essay form which both Shaftesbury and Hume employ, variety of topic evidences coherent individual achievement, and a hungry introspective empiricism nourishes omnicompetence, inclusive control.

Ernst Cassirer has argued the importance for the history of aesthetics of Shaftesbury's basic requirement that the critic have intuitive sympathy with, and penetration of, the intentions of the producers of art (313–14); I would claim that Shaftesbury saw sympathy and penetration as a social duty of a social class. It is not the hackneyed postulate of the coherence of beauty and truth that is the guide for his project but the thesis that beauty grants access to a defensible social role, a true vocation. A privileged access open to the privileged, it requires that great pains be taken to construct an enabling discourse, a discourse that makes possible a response to the "finer and more delicate imitations of art," for, he claims, it is by the "nicest slightest touches ... and not by exaggeration, amplification, straining, tightening, overcharging" that art instructs (*Second Characters* 100). Delicacy, then, is an important constraint—requiring an uncommon, probably classbound investment—a constraint that permits the intuition of unity, a common enough intellectual goal. Since "the unity and equality of life [are] made by the unity of object," which is in turn the attribute of true art, the life of an artist is "worthy even of a liberal and noble born youth." If, that is to say, he is a genius, and if he does not slight his first, "economic," duty to family and public (*Second Characters* 174–75). But discursive practice is Shaftesbury's stated priority; where even the vulgar can feel and recognize, only the virtuoso of reception can prove, demonstrate. Shaftesbury's hero is the critic, whose talent is first formed by interior dialogue, then exercised by the critic "giving voice and accent" to obscure and implicit thought; finally it begins to act in public dialogue to improve the reception of the arts, and therefore the production of the arts, of the nation (*Second Characters* 22–23, 93, 112, 156–57, 177, 234).

In contrast with Shaftesbury, Hume's avowedly philosophical competence presents the tasks of the critical construction of taste and the analysis of virtue as interconnected in the most explicit and strong manner: moral sentiment is the taste for virtue, and the discourse of edification is necessarily a discourse of pleasure, delectation.

Hume's essays on aesthetic issues resume Shaftesbury's empiricist attack on system and retain Shaftesbury's empiricist emphasis on the reception, not the production, of art. At the same time, Hume places more stress on the accessibility of the canons of good taste, which are discovered by exercising the skills of public argument in the exploration of shared experience. Hume, of course, is constrained by the intransigence of his empiricism; the effect of his radical skepticism is to force the discussion onto the ground of the common language of common sentiment.[7] This intransigence also expresses itself in discursive tact: Hume's pronouncements on discourse in the essays call for a general lowering of sights—another kind of accessibility. Hume praises contemporary eloquence as Attic, that is to say, as "calm, elegant, and subtle" speech that "never raised its tone above argument or common discourse" (*Essays* 109).[8] The harangue, for Hume as well as Shaftesbury, is out: "The merit of delivering true general precepts in ethics is indeed very small" (*Essays* 223). And consider the modesty of the verb in this sentence: the intent of the essay as form, he claims, "is to *mingle* [emphasis added] some light of the understanding with the feelings of sentiment" (*Essays* 239).[9] To mingle finely, perhaps, because in the essays as a whole, "to refine" is the crucial verb, the relevant illocutionary act; and his coordinate noun, "delicacy," connotes the values of precision, refinement, decorum (*Essays* 240). Yet the exercise of delicacy of taste is subject to dispute and submits to the rules of argument; the authors "must produce the best arguments that their invention suggests to them; they must acknowledge a true and decisive standard to exist somewhere ... and they must have indulgence to such as differ from them in their appeals to this standard" (*Essays* 248).

The essays on aesthetics appeal to the philosopher, concerned with the structure of thought, and to any self-defined moralist, concerned with the nature of society. The operative postulates are, first, that aesthetic issues are necessarily serious issues to the staunch empiricist, and second, that aesthetic competence is both a social competence and a social duty. In the essay "Of the Delicacy of Taste and Passion," Hume's distinction is that delicacy of passion is a captive in the domain of chance, *fortuna,* while delicacy of taste acts in the domain of *virtù;* taste is not only a capacity to discriminate the works of genius, which proceeds by clarifying and rendering sentiment distinct (discovering the conformity of object and organ), but also a competence that enhances the other activities and attitudes of a civilized life (*Essays* 6–7, 234, 242). Hume contrasts the stability of the law, which "is the slow product of order and liberty" but is easily preserved (*Essays* 124), to the vulnerability and fragility of the arts, which depend on a refined taste or sentiment for preservation. The more vulnerable, the more need for cherishing. Luxury— "great refinement in the gratification of the senses" (*Essays* 275)—and delicacy represent two levels of social value; furthermore, of the three areas of achievement—industry, knowledge, and humanity—humanity is the particular concern of the arts: "The more these refined arts advance, the more sociable men become: nor is it possible, that, when enriched with science, and possessed of a fund of conversation, they should be contented to remain in solitude, or live with their fellow-citizens in that distant manner, which is peculiar to ignorant and barbarous nations" (*Essays* 278).

It is the elision of boundaries between refinement, sociability, and conversation that is intriguing. Certainly the vindication of conversation as humanizing must sound endearingly familiar to the historian of rhetoric: "beside the improvements which [men] receive from knowledge and the liberal arts," Hume claims, "it is impossible but they must feel an increase of humanity, from the very habit of conversing together" (*Essays* 278).[10] Hume's "Of Essay Writing" is a social manifesto of the eighteenth century, lightly proffered, doggedly received; it makes a distinction between the "learned world," the preserve of scholars, and the "conversable world," presided over by the ladies, asserting, in the neat language of irony, a functional differentiation between the two domains:

> The conversable world joins to a sociable disposition, and a taste for pleasure, an inclination for the easier and more gentle exercises of the understanding,

## The Conversable World

for obvious reflections on human affairs, and the duties of common life, and for observation of the blemishes or perfections of the particular objects that surround them. Such subjects of thought furnish not sufficient employment in solitude, but require the company and conversation of our fellow-creatures, to render them a proper exercise for the mind; and this brings mankind together in society, where every one displays his thoughts in observations in the best manner he is able, and mutually gives and receives information, as well as pleasure. (*Essays* 568)[11]

Hume's justification of the conversable world is in two rather simple senses an aesthetic one: first, the conversable world is the agreeable, pleasurable domain; and second, domestic aesthetic objects, the decorative arts, are claimed as a serious interest and pertinent environment.[12] But more important, the discourse of the conversable world is socially redemptive: his contrast between learned and conversable is a contrast between the solitude of learning and the conviviality of conversation, between the passivity of knowledge and the activity of exchange (*Essays* 278). Conversation liberates, since good conversation is distinguished by its facility, its freedom of expression (*Essays* 569). Even its exclusive nature is of use; eloquence, public oratory, is unfortunately constrained by the need to appeal to the general populace (*Essays* 108; cf. *Principles of Morals* 241). When Hume specifies three pleasures in life—ambition, study, and conversation (*Essays* 276)—he overvalues conversation as a disinterested social act: the rules of conversation are ethical rules. You are civil, or you are not conversing:

> Among the arts of conversation, no one pleases more than mutual deference or civility, which leads us to resign our own inclinations to those of our companion, and to curb and conceal that presumption and arrogance so natural to the human mind. A good-natured man, who is well-educated, practices this civility to every mortal, without premeditation or interest. (*Essays* 127–28)

The rules of conversation are premised on equality, deference, generosity; social refinement expresses itself in a compensatory tactic: "to throw the bias on the opposite side" (*Essays* 132).

But Hume is not only claiming that equity is the ruling convention of conversation; he is also maintaining that the discursive experience of equity generates the sense of common interest that is the sense of "humanity." If we turn to *An Enquiry concerning the Principles of Morals*, we see that the constructs which invest the conversable world can modify those of the learned world; indeed, Hume stipulates the conversable world as the site of serious investigative projects. Recall that Hume defined the work of the moralist as the task of epideictic discourse; all moral speculations must be pragmatic, must produce speech acts of praise and blame. But it is the moralist's immersion in conversation and social intercourse that is the source of his moral standards:

> General language, therefore, being formed for general use, must be moulded on some more general views, and must affix the epithets of praise and blame,

in conformity to sentiments, which arise from the general interest of the community. (*Principles of Morals* 228)[13]

The more we converse, the more we learn of the principles of humanity and universal moral sentiment. Discourse is the privileged domain of benevolence—a virtue that is "cherished by society and conversation" (*Principles of Morals* 275)—a domain where the classical canons of the useful and agreeable, "utile et dulce," are the criteria of value (*Principles of Morals* 268).

The learned world, in sum, must both recruit and prove itself in the conversable world. Hume as moral philosopher is concerned with uniting a plausible psychological story with his moral principles, and he deplores the fact that philosophers have ignored the psychological dimension, that is, the passions, in their systems of ethics (*Principles of Morals* 213).[14] They ignored, then, the absolutely basic fact that "social virtues . . . have a natural beauty and amiableness" (*Principles of Morals* 214). And conversely, they were blind to the fact that an aesthetic value, the sublime, is nothing but "the echo or image of magnanimity," a moral value (*Principles of Morals* 252). The passions, as Alasdair MacIntyre has so convincingly argued, furnish the bridge concept between "is" and "ought"; for Hume, any account of moral competence must consider sentiment as well as reason, feeling as well as circumstantial fact: moral action is passionate action.[15]

But the learned world has hitherto produced implausible and unnatural moral accounts:

> Theories of abstract philosophy, systems of profound theology, have prevailed during one age: in a successive period these have been universally exploded: their absurdity has been detected: other theories and systems have supplied their place, which again gave place to their successors: and nothing has been experienced more liable to the revolutions of chance and fashion than these pretended decisions of science. (*Essays* 248)

While Hume's antisystematic bias recalls a classical rhetorical bias, his critique pushes far beyond classical moral tradition. Hume presents a morality, as well as an aesthetics, of reception. For Hume, virtue is *"whatever mental action or quality gives to a spectator the pleasing sentiment of approbation"* (*Principles of Morals* 289).[16] Pleasure, in sum, is not simply the mode of edification; pleasure is the sign of truth. Just as there is no architectural beauty till a spectator appears who can evaluate the structure—"from his sentiments alone arise its elegance and beauty"—so there is no particular "fact" of crime; rather "crime" arises entirely "from the sentiment of disapprobation" (*Principles of Morals* 289). Still, any emphasis on reception requires some emphasis on production; it is significant that Hume employs Cicero's orations to illustrate his notion of receptive ethics: the full panoply of Cicero's epideictic eloquence is required to elicit the response "crime" (*Principles of Morals* 292).

But the conversable world of Hume's essays, of course, offers simple, durable rules and undemanding opportunities; after all, Hume points out, belles lettres, which d'Alembert places in the domain of reflective discussion, has not prospered under the complex rules and unnerving demands that obtain in the cloisters of the learned world, and he suggests the return of literary territory to the dominion of conversation. Hume indeed embarks on an extended diplomatic metaphor, very droll, in which he casts himself in the role of ambassador from the world of learning to the domain of ladies, sovereigns of the realm of conversation, asking for an offensive-defensive league against the enemies of reason and liberty (*Essays* 569–70). What is quite clear is that "aesthetic" qualifies not simply topic but also function and criterion: because they possess delicacy, the ladies are sovereigns; the fundamental law of the conversable realm is the standard of taste. Hume has described the maneuver whereby peripheral interests capture the center; the decline of rhetoric as discipline and training must not obscure for us the fact that the new pervasive control, the taste which is a social competence, represents a reorganization of old rhetorical concerns. For in this way antisystematic discursive modes with strong aesthetic-empiricist premises reconstruct general, serious investigative moments as social instrumentalities: the primary, central domain where criticism functions is the conversable world. Where Shaftesbury had developed the role of the adult (male) virtuoso critic, Hume describes the resources and constraints of community. To be sure, Hume is frankly horrified at the thought of the ladies as sovereigns of both worlds, the "public" republic of letters as well as the intimate realm of conversation, as was certainly the case in the French salons (*Essays* 571). But it is precisely Hume's restricted realm of the feminine, domestic, and conversable that Austen will appropriate (*Essays* 135).

In "Of Essay Writing" Hume has specified the boundaries, rules, and goals of the domain of the conversable, and in so doing, has specified the program for Jane Austen, whose novels are the literary fulfillment, the fleshing out, of this program, and an ingenious use of an ironic suggestion. Austen takes up Hume's thesis that the conversable world is a site of serious inquiry but rejects his satiric description of "female sovereigns." The maneuver accomplished is not so much the cession of literary territory to the conversable world as the deft and thorough amalgamation of the critical and conversable polities.

That conversation is the site and mode of discovery of character and plot, of insight and issue, is the premise not only of Austen's rapid and efficient dialogue, but also of the series of set pieces, the neatly demarcated debates dispersed throughout her novels. These debates have the particular literary purpose of clarification of plot and solidification of character, as well as the more general, perfectly serious purpose of clarification of issue and attitude. But further, an examination of these debates, which are guided by Hume's canons of "calmness, elegance, and subtlety," but which vary in topic from the solemn to the consummately light, shows that a significant number of the arguments turn on aesthetic issues. For Austen's purposes, conversation is the perfect form, aesthetics is the perfect topic; she employs the argumentative occasions to depict a well-motivated experience as the precise definition of pure aesthetic experience: every display of taste is a display of social form; conversation is an exercise of social tact, true taste. The debates thus not only orient the protagonists to the nature of experience but also orient the reader to the nature of the protagonists' social competence and moral intelligence.[17] Aesthetic choices precede moral choices; aesthetic judgments prepare future events.

The aesthetic arguments spring readily enough to mind. Recall the discussion of the nature of the picturesque in *Northanger Abbey:* a leisurely meeting with Henry and Eleanor Tilney taking place in the picturesque landscape surrounding Bath, a meeting achieved only by the most dogged perseverance on the part of young Catherine Morland. The charm of the dialogue lies in Austen's cheerful acceptance of the social reality that not every match is an even match, in either marriage or debate; the literary clarification is the reader's insight into the naturalness and simplicity of Catherine's character, conveyed by means of Austen's very sophisticated, ironic exposure of contemporary aesthetic pretension to taste in painting and in novels, an exposure made by means of attributing *lack* of pretension to all the protagonists (1.14.10–15).[18]

The arguments on aesthetic issues in *Pride and Prejudice,* in contrast, are much more truly arguments, engaging the formidable talents of Elizabeth Bennet and Darcy, and stipulating proper argumentative tasks of definition and distinction. The sharper exchanges assert the power of rules. The argument on music at Lady Catherine de Bourgh's, which includes Elizabeth, Darcy, and his cousin Colonel Fitzwilliam, has the major function of clarification of plot: it illumines the completely unmutual regard of Darcy and Elizabeth. But it also performs the minor task of relegating the miserable Lady Catherine "out of the discussion" into self-imposed exile. Here a badly placed discursive role defines a failed social role (2.8.174–76). Furthermore, Elizabeth's attempts to put Darcy out of the discussion anticipate her later rejection of his proposal as "ungentlemanlike" in form and repulsive in fact, a rejection that achieved its powerful effect because of her emphasis on faulty discursive form (2.11.189).

There are, of course, two extended debates on aesthetic issues in *Mansfield Park:* the general discussion of the improvement of Rushworth's estate, Sotherton, and the prolonged arguments over the choice of play for the Mansfield Park theatricals. By far the most complicated of Austen's set pieces is the many-jointed argument that emerges from the series of dialogues Fanny Price has with a series of protagonists during an afternoon spent in the gardens of Sotherton, most of the dialogues beginning with, or turning on, issues of the aesthetics and morality of landscape. This complex series must serve the double literary function of definitively orienting Fanny to both the Crawfords and the Bertrams and of preparing the reader for the inevitable turns of plot generated by the various future combinations of the two families: all of this is extracted from sympathetic or callous reactions to avenues and fences, prospects and landscapes (1.10.97–106).

Certainly *Mansfield Park* is the most literal expression of the axiom that aesthetic experience is the site of discovery; the environmental contexts—the parsonage shrubbery for Fanny Price and Mary Crawford's somewhat dysfunctional dialogue, the ramparts of Portsmouth for Fanny's issueless encounter with Henry Crawford, the gardens of Mansfield Park for her late new understanding with Edmund Bertram—all serve to make the dialogue easier: opaque moral situations can be referred back to the simpler structures of aesthetic reaction. Then, much of the dialogue in the early novel *Sense and Sensibility* is forthrightly organized around the constructs of "genius" and "taste." Elinor Dashwood's admiration for innate propriety and simplicity of taste (1.4.19) is contrasted with the enthusiasm of her sister Marianne's pursuit of aesthetic genius. For Marianne, reciprocal love is marked by conformity of aesthetic judgment (1.10.47) or by reciprocity of genius and taste: in an excess of sisterly feeling she cheers Elinor with the notion that in a long courtship Edward Ferrars would at least have time to develop a taste for Elinor's genius (1.4.22).

The evidence for moral competence in judgment is largely displayed in discursive practice. Discursive sensitivity is the source of moral sensitivity for author, reader, and protagonist. Thus, while of all Austen's heroines Marianne Dashwood is the most explicit and most assertive in her claims to aesthetic competence, her social performance is beset by verbal incompetence: on one hand, she concedes that much of the current discourse on the picturesque is pure jargon; on the other hand, she herself is reduced to silence in a situation that rules out enthusiasm (1.18.97). To be sure, through the protagonists in *Mansfield Park* Austen furnishes straightforward discussion of *pronuntiatio*—in sermons, in the reading aloud of Shakespeare, and in theatrical productions. But *pronuntiatio* is not a serious discursive issue for Austen; Henry Crawford's delivery of Shakespearean lines is described as compelling, but at the same time it is placed firmly in the context of adolescent exercise: learning to read aloud well is part of a boy's education (3.3.336–38).[19] *Mansfield Park* also proffers some easy alignments of judgment and language: when both Edmund Bertram and the Crawfords give Fanny Price necklaces for her brother William's amber cross, the reader may join Fanny in contrasting the simplicity and decorum of Edmund's plain gold chain and his transparent manly prose with the more elaborate necklace and positively Byzantine discourse of the intriguing Crawfords (2.8.258–60).

*Northanger Abbey,* on the other hand, contains not only extensive ironizing of aesthetic discourse but also the most prolonged and self-conscious critique of discursive practice, a critique in which Austen's diagnostic skill in rhetorical analysis makes the link between faulty discourse and moral incompetence explicit. The contrast between Catherine Morland and Isabella Thorpe is a contrast between well- and ill-motivated substandard discourse; "truth" is at stake in the comparisons of Catherine's naïve and candid formulations with

Isabella's verbal overkill. Isabella is fundamentally sloppy and imprecise, so careless that the most perfidious betrayal has no name. The self-deceptive exaggerations of Isabella and James Thorpe—those two loose cannons on the deck of society—both complement and underline the selfish deceptions of General Tilney and his eldest son.

What is *always* at stake in the Austenian text is the accurate description of the competence to make moral judgment. Virtuous or proper perception is defined by Hume's "warmth" and "delicacy" (*Principles of Morals* 225); furthermore, the definition stipulates a union of warmth and delicacy: Catherine Morland's warmth, for example, can support the easy correction of her unrefined Gothic sensibility. The archetypal embodiment of this harmony of warmth and delicacy is, of course, Anne Elliot, the heroine of Austen's last novel, *Persuasion*. As its title would imply, *Persuasion* has an obvious and explicit rhetorical interest, and has the most direct movement from issues of aesthetic response to the process of describing and classifying feeling as emotion and the basis of a personal bond. Anne's argument with Captain Benwick about the most "useful" genres of literature is a direct confrontation between Benwick, who represents strong feelings that recognize no frame, and Anne, who represents that Humean and Austenian project—strong feelings contained within a polite frame. The dialogue looks back to the discussion between Captain Wentworth and Louisa Musgrove on the attraction of strength of feeling and anticipates the discussion between Anne and Captain Harville on the definition of virtuous strong feelings. The argument also serves the literary function of plot orientation, clarifying for the hero, Frederick Wentworth, his strong feelings for Anne; he is enlightened not by means of the views she expresses but by means of his perception of the debate as a close male-female encounter, a discursive intimacy (1.11.100–1). *Persuasion* presents a complicated tissue of differences of opinion and contrasts in judgmental capacity: of Anne and Wentworth; of Anne, Wentworth, and Louisa; of Anne, Mary, and Elizabeth Elliot; of Sir Walter and William Elliot—a web in which Lady Russell functions as a kind of inadequate center and thus a focus for the illumination of bad judgment: as a protagonist in argumentative exchange, she makes persuasive cases for the wrong point of view.

Where *Persuasion* offers strong contrasts of good and bad judgment, *Sense and Sensibility* heavily illustrates flaws, either misalignments of aesthetic and moral choice or overextensions of aesthetic taste to moral judgment. Marianne Dashwood's reactions to character range from her enthusiasm for Willoughby's pursuits, talents, and genius to her decided opinion that Colonel Brandon has neither genius, taste, nor spirit: "his understanding has no brilliancy, his feelings no ardour, and his voice no expression" (1.19.43; 1.10.51). When the villainous Willoughby passes her tests, while Edward Ferrars, a hero, fails them, it is clear that it is Marianne's testing capacity that is at fault. The determined selfishness of the John Dashwoods is attributed to neither Mrs. Dashwood nor Marianne, yet both err in the overextension of aesthetic competence, which makes Marianne, in particular, fail in benevolence,

Hume's most "pleasing" virtue. In *Emma,* on the other hand, Austen indicates deficiency, not surplus: Emma's lack of interest in aesthetic matters seems diagnostic of the series of blunders she makes in the discrimination of character; Emma, in short, is morally tone deaf. Thus the debates in *Emma*—which are often negative in tone and function—turn less on aesthetic issues, on positive positions on matters of taste, than on the false enterprises undertaken by protagonists deficient in social delicacy whose activities are stigmatized and excluded in debate.

Delicacy most assuredly characterizes Austen's tactics of definition. The texts contain strong commonsense oppositions, but oppositions that are, in an interesting way, subservient to the "minute distinctions" which Hume had stipulated as the moralist's concern *(Principles of Morals* 225). One could contrast the refining motives of Austen with the reductive ones of Thomas Peacock. While the victims of Austenian irony share qualities with the victims of Peacock's burlesque, Austen confects an "integrated" male-female community of serious domestic commitment, whereas Peacock, through satiric strategies, generates only a ludic situation, a masculine game. The total effect of her minute discriminations is to perfect the definition of a society with extraordinary capabilities for both control and encouragement, discipline and motivation. Austen's domestic domain of moral competence is not the realm of the "lesser morality" of good manners, the sphere of "company" ruled by "politeness," which is subsumed by Hume under the domain of "society" ruled by "justice" *(Principles of Morals* 209, 261).[20] This is condescension, and Austen does not condescend. The boundaries and rules of her domestic conversable world exploit those of Hume's nourishing "general conversation," and her results improve on Hume's results: where Hume drew ideal pictures of domestic peace, Austen describes the tough-minded precision that creates an elegant social economy.[21]

She improves on Hume by employing Shaftesburian modes; Austen is a virtuoso critic with Shaftesburian flashes of wit and irreverence. Shaftesburian also is the exploration of the private or personal origins of useful truth: whereas the Shaftesburian critic begins with interior dialogue, the Austenian heroine corrects and revises general debate by means of interior debate, contention with the self.[22] But like Hume, Austen places much less emphasis on the transfer of receptive virtue, the achievements of taste, to the production of the fine arts; the vital transfer is to the social domain of moral action. And all—Hume, Austen, Shaftesbury—agree that discursive accessibility or liberty is the condition of intellectual work; all are engaged in refining the rules of discursive equity that make discovery possible. For Austen, domestic discourse improves on Hume's general conversation as the best provider of ruled liberty; conversation is not simply an idle, leisurely preoccupation but the purposeful construction of life and attitude and value, a project with socially redemptive values. Domestic peace is more than the reward of professional—naval or ecclesiastical—excellence. Without at all advocating carelessness toward duty or profession—even Mr. Bennet is observant of his hay and his horses—

Austen portrays not action as generating leisure, but leisure as the frame for activity. But leisure is domestic; the virtues of both hero and heroine are primarily domestic virtues: the respectability of Sir Thomas Bertram, displayed in his horror of amateur theatricals, is a commitment to domestic virtue, a commitment which the accomplished Henry Crawford, for all his zeal for his own country house and landscape, lacks.

We have moved, then, from a theoretical treatise that claimed that belles lettres is in the province of argument and that taste, aesthetic truth, is established by debate to a belletristic project, a series of argumentative novels that employ set debates on taste to orient the protagonists, and thus the reader, to the nature of true experience. This is truly sophisticated empiricism. From Shaftesbury's description of the member of society as having primarily an economic duty but also a spiritual obligation to be receptive to, even to participate in, art; to Hume's description of conversation, a refined art, as a social template that patterns discovery; to Austen's use of fictional debates to describe social forms: in all we find a rich interconnection that entwines aesthetic interest, a dialogical or rhetorical discovery of truth, and social-moral value. Aesthetics provides the entrée to a general consideration of the goals, texture, and rules of life of a leisured elite; one moves easily from the theory of aesthetic truth to the theory of true behavior. The dominance of the argumentative mode obtains not simply in aesthetic inquiry or inquiry in general but in the formation of a matrix of linguistic and social rules governing persuasion, a rule matrix that invests the general strategy of a hegemonous social group. The argumentative mode that invested aesthetic inquiry comes to dominate the discussion of propriety and pleasure. The hegemony of conversation and the onmicompetence of rules governing conversation are shown in the fact that mastery of the rules is tantamount to social mastery.

Some of the rules are old rules, Renaissance rules, to be sure; but there is a shift, for example, from the valorization of negligence, a courtieresque *sprezzatura,* to the valorization of precision and refinement. The informality that masks precision still preserves its restraint by requiring ordinary exchanges to produce endless small discriminations, explicit taste. But the primary competence that marks both discursive and social skill is a persuasive, argumentative one; what keeps the practitioners "honest" is the rules of the debate, the necessity of submitting to argument, to patterns of concession and closure, offering and riposte. Here rhetorical commitment is not simply a persistent, mild, English interest in *elocutio,* or style, but rather a serious and central preoccupation with discursive enlightenment, with affective or rhetorical edification. Austen's project epitomizes the eighteenth-century transformation of the classical rhetorical tasks of *docere, movere, delectare;* it reasserts the connection of truth and pleasure within a pragmatic frame.

Austen's rhetorical analysis of the conversable world describes a critical competence that controls a manageable social space; the confected dialogues and debates furnish a precise account of the variety of successful and unsuccessful appropriations of the Shaftesburian critical task by a social elite. In

Austen's modest domain of conversation, the rules for determining success and failure put in place a decorum of equity, a decorum that generates as well as reflects equity. Austen, like Shaftesbury and Hume, stresses that good argument is accessible argument; the Austenian novels give us a strong account of equitable access for women. Her heroines argue well. They initiate exchanges that are nontrivial and interesting as theory—exchanges where failure defines as surely as success. And the debates point to another layer of accessibility: the heroines have access to rules as well as performance; they not only experience failure, but they may stipulate failure. In the Austenian text the exploration of "pure," that is, aesthetic, experience assumes and confirms an easy introspective empiricism and facilitates critique as self-critique—a strong extension of the equitable impulse to include and discipline the self. The rule that enjoins the conversationalists to start from, or at least take seriously, the experiences of beauty and pleasure is a rule designed to ensure honesty as well as lucidity. Austen's novels enjoin moral work.

## NOTES

1. See Cicero, *De Oratore* (1.9.35), and *De Officiis* (1.4.14). Hume does not specify his Ciceronian inspiration as "rhetorical." In a letter of 1739 to Hutcheson, he claims that throughout book 2 of *A Treatise of Human Nature,* Cicero's *De Officiis* (he might have added *De Finibus*) was "in my Eye in all my reasonings" (*The Letters of David Hume* [1:34]).

2. Hume asserts that ethics presents questions of fact, not of abstract science (*Principles of Morals* 174). In "A Dialogue," appended to *Principles of Morals,* Hume makes some antiphilosophical statements that recall Quintilian, *Institutio Oratoria* (5.14.28–29); see "A Dialogue" (340, 341). Furthermore, it is significant that Hume felt compelled to rewrite *A Treatise of Human Nature* as "enqueries"; in section 1 of *An Enquiry concerning Human Understanding* he claims his own task as a kind of discursive meditation: "Happy, if we can unite the boundaries of the different species of philosophy, by reconciling profound enquiry with clearness, and truth with novelty! And still more happy, if, reasoning in this easy manner, we can undermine the foundations of an abstruse philosophy, which seems to have hitherto served only as a shelter to superstition, and a cover to absurdity and error" (*An Enquiry concerning Human Understanding* 16). On "use" as criterion, recall *Principles of Morals* (179): "In general, what praise is implied in the simple epithet *useful!* What reproach to the contrary!"

3. Elsewhere I have argued that "the possession of taste is the possession of an enabling capacity ..., a social competence that is agile, inclusive, and pleasantly coherent, and that both vivifies and protects social roles." See Nancy S. Struever, "Translation as Taste."

4. See Francesco Tateo, *Dialogo interiore e polemica ideologica nel 'Secretum' del Petrarca.*

5. Thus in "Idea of the Work" Shaftesbury proposes an epistolary form, since the use of "private address" or a "half-general address" to friend and general public enables an intimacy and directness (*Second Characters* 5, 7, 8, 12).

6. See Marc Fumaroli, "Genèse de l'épistolographie classique" (888), and *L'Age de l'éloquence* (154–55).

7. "Common," of course, does not denote "popular"; on Hume's aesthetic empiricism see Ernst Cassirer, *Philosophy of the Enlightenment* (305–6). The relevant essays of Hume are "Of the Delicacy of Taste and Passion," "Of Eloquence," "Of the Rise and Progress of the Arts and Sciences," "Of Simplicity and Refinement in Writing," "Of Tragedy," "Of the Standard of Taste," "Of Refinement in the Arts," and, "Of Essay Writing," all found in Hume, *Essays Moral, Political, and Literary*.

8. See Stephen Toulmin's formal analysis of informal argument in his *Uses of Argument*.

9. On the essay as genre, the remarks of Edward W. Said are perspicuous; see "The Text, the World, the Critic" (186–87). In a letter to Gilbert Elliot written in 1751, Hume claims: "I believe the philosophical Essays contain every thing of Consequence relating to the Understanding, which you would meet with in the Treatise; & I give you my Advice against reading the latter. By shortening & simplifying the Questions, I really render them much more complete" (*Letters* 1: 158).

10. See Hume's *Principles of Morals* (238).

11. In a letter of 1753 to Dr. Clephane, Hume's heavy irony in regard to "the ladies" is inspired, interestingly, by a question of lexical usage (*Letters* 1: 182–83).

12. There are several passages in *Principles of Morals* that elaborate on the importance and pleasure of domestic environment; see, for example, 179, 220.

13. See also *Principles of Morals* (274). Earlier in the same work, Hume claims, in asserting the accuracy of introspective moral reaction, that "the very nature of language guides us almost infallibly in forming a judgement of this nature; and as every tongue possesses one set of words which are taken in a good sense, and another in the opposite, the least acquaintance with the idiom suffices, without any reasoning, to direct us in collecting and arranging the estimable or blameable qualities of men" (174).

14. The appeal to the passions, of course, is regarded as the peculiar competence of the classical rhetorician; see Quintilian, *Institutio Oratoria* Book 6.

15. On reason as no motive to action, see *Principles of Morals* (293–94); the whole of appendix 1 on "Moral Sentiment" is pertinent. See also Alasdair MacIntyre's "Hume on 'Is' and 'Ought.'" He notes that "we could give a long list of the concepts which form such bridge notions between 'is' and 'ought': wanting, needing, desiring, pleasure, happiness, health—and these are only a few" (463). MacIntyre's paper confronts misreadings of Hume; MacIntyre's claim that he was tempted "to retitle this paper 'Against Bourgeois Formalism in Ethics'" (459) should be related to his statement that "the difference between what Hume has been thought to assert and what Hume really asserted is very much the difference between Hare and Toulmin" (466). Here, I believe, MacIntyre is underlining the connection between mode of argument and meaning: Toulmin, of course, is the defender not simply of a naturalistic psychological basis for ethics but of informal modes of argumentation as well.

16. There is a striking analogy with the radical strategies of the Renaissance rhetorician Lorenzo Valla. In his *Repastinatio dialectice et philosophice*, Valla reduces the ten predicaments of Aristotle to two, *actio* and *qualitas*, a tactic that has strong implications for ethical theory (see, in particular, I.c.10, 73–98; I.c.17, 134–39). In *De vero falsoque bono*, one of Valla's major emphases is on the "naturalness" and thus the veracity of pleasure, *voluptas*.

17. The easy movement from taste in the arts to taste in life and manners is, of course, Shaftesburian; see *Characteristics* (1: 192–93) and *Second Characters* (22–23).

18. References to Austen's novels are to section, chapter, and page as found in *The Novels of Jane Austen*, ed. R. W. Chapman (1949 reprint).

19. It is interesting that in the same chapter Edmund Bertram argues that an improvement in reception is in part the cause of an improvement in the production of sermons: "there is more general observation and taste, a more critical knowledge diffused, than formerly; in every congregation, there is a larger proportion who know a little of the matter, and who can judge and criticize" (3:3:340).

*The Conversable World*

20. Austen, of course, is aware of this subordinate domain of accomplishment; good company, Anne Elliot claims, is "the company of clever, well-informed people, who have a great deal of conversation" (*Persuasion* 2.4.150).

21. See, for example, Hume, *Principles of Morals* (220); but this work is permeated with evocations of domestic tranquillity.

22. Fanny Price makes the point of the interior guide's authority: "We have all a better guide in ourselves, if we would attend to it, than any other person can be" (*Mansfield Park* 3.11.412; cf. Hume, *Principles of Morals* 174). Gilbert Ryle too has argued that Austen is Shaftesburian, in "Jane Austen and the Moralists."

# XVI

# JEANIE DEANS AND THE NATURE OF TRUE ELOQUENCE

*Marie Secor*

This essay attempts to negotiate between two different but related approaches to the fiction of Sir Walter Scott: the nineteenth-century tradition that regarded him as the heir of Shakespeare, creator of eloquent characters of high and low station, and the more recent perspective that has tended to regard him as a historical novelist, one who explores in fiction how the force of events shapes personality and how personalities get caught up in events. Its approach is ultimately historicist, assuming we can understand the eloquence of Scott's characters by placing them in their own historical and fictional context and that we can understand that history (at least partly) by investigating its ideas, both articulated and assumed, about what constituted eloquence. My focus here will be on one novel, *The Heart of Midlothian,* and I will try to indicate, briefly, how the contemporary reader's response to it is enriched by awareness of its highly conscious adumbration of its rhetorical and linguistic frames, ranging from the immediate rhetorical context of discursive acts of eloquence committed within the text to the novel's historical function as a document contributing to the late eighteenth-century debate about the nature of eloquence.

Scott's readers have long noted that the Waverley novels are filled with high rhetoric—with narrators who run on before they get to the main story, long-winded lawyers, garrulous servants, bardic seers, fiery preachers, smooth politicians, and colorful, crafty peasants. Scott himself, though systematically effaced as actual author of the novels, anticipates the reader's reaction to his discursive manner and, with typical self-consciousness about narrative and language, allows discussion of his characteristic talkiness to arise at the beginning of *The Bride of Lammermoor.* There Dick Tinto, a painter who expresses his own preference for a more scenic method of composition, accuses Peter Pattieson, the fictive author of Tales of my Landlord and fictionalized surrogate of Scott, of making "too much use of the gob box"; your characters, he says, "patter too much, . . . there is nothing in whole pages but mere chat and dialogue." Tinto accuses Pattieson of "indulging in prolonged scenes of mere conversation until the course of your story has become chill and constrained, and you have lost the power of arresting the attention and exciting the imagination" (24). No subsequent critic of Scott has ever indicted the actual author more precisely; indeed, many readers—both casual and professional—have reinforced Tinto's accusation, complaining about the elaborate frames and leisurely pace of Scott's novels. But as a literary artist (and like most artists), Scott's weaknesses are inseparable from his strengths; in his historicized fictions and fictionalized histories, the most compelling revelations of character and the most significant historical events often conjoin at high points of eloquence.

Such a high point occurs in *The Heart of Midlothian,* when Jeanie Deans pleads to Queen Caroline for the life of her sister Effie, who has been unjustly sentenced to death for the murder of her newborn child. Having refused to save Effie at her trial by bearing false witness, the heroic Jeanie undertakes the arduous journey on foot from Edinburgh to London to appeal to the Queen's compassion and plead for her sister's pardon. Generations of Scott's readers have praised her speech to Queen Caroline as the climax and moral center of the novel and the definitive expression of Jeanie's ethos as a Scottish heroine. Jeanie Dean's speech is short (only about 360 words), so here is its complete text, excluding preliminary dialogue and scene setting:

"If it like you, madam," said Jeanie, "I would hae gaen to the end of the earth to save the life of John Porteous, or any other unhappy man in his condition; but I might lawfully doubt how far I am called upon to be the avenger of his blood, though it may become the civil magistrate to do so. He is dead and gane to his place, and they that have slain him must answer for their ain act. But my sister, my puir sister Effie, still lives, though her days and hours are numbered!—she still lives, and a word of the King's mouth might restore her to a broken-hearted auld man, that never, in his daily and nightly exercise, forgot to pray that his Majesty might be blessed with a long and prosperous reign, and that his throne, and the throne of his posterity, might be established in righteousness. O, madam, if ever ye kend what it was to sorrow for and with a sinning and a suffering creature, whose mind is sae tossed that she can be neither ca'd fit to live or die, have some compassion on our misery!—save an honest house from dishonour, and an unhappy girl, not eighteen years of age, from an early and dreadful death! Alas! it is not when we sleep soft and wake merrily ourselves, that we think on other people's sufferings. Our hearts are waxed light within us then, and we are for righting our ain wrangs and fighting our ain battles. But when the hour of trouble comes to the mind or to the body—and seldom may it visit your Leddyship—and when the hour of death comes, that comes to high and law—lang and late may it be yours—O, my Leddy, then it isna what we hae dune for oursells, but what we hae dune for others, that we think on maist pleasantly. And the thoughts that ye hae intervened to spare the puir thing's life will be sweeter in that hour, come when it may, than if a word of your mouth could hang the haill Porteous mob at the tail of ae tow. (404–5)[1]

At the end of the speech, the Queen responds, simply, "This is eloquence," summarizing her own reaction and that of subsequent generations of readers. And indeed it is. Rhetorical analysis can reveal how Jeanie's speech persuades and moves its hearer within the text and how it functions within its fictional context. But such analysis itself must be conducted within a context of shared assumptions and definitions; the reader's response to this passage depends not only on our response to its internal ethical, logical, and pathetic appeals and its mobilization of certain kinds of arguments, but also on our historical knowledge about eighteenth-century attitudes toward language and rhetoric. Certain questions, then, become relevant: what resonance did the term *eloquence* have for Scott and his readers in the early decades of the nineteenth century? What political and cultural conditions affected their judgment of what could be considered eloquent? To answer such questions, it is necessary to attempt to relate critical commentary to cultural, linguistic, and rhetorical history. To that end, this study will examine first the late eighteenth-century rhetorical tradition that Scott was both heir to and participant in, then discuss his invocation of the special kind of language of eloquence expressed in the Scottish dialect of Jeanie's speech, and finally examine the speech in its immediate fictional and historical rhetorical contexts.

In addition to its setting in immediate rhetorical, dramatic, and linguistic contexts, Jeanie's speech can also be understood as a product of the broader rhetorical tradition in which Scott himself wrote, as both a child of the Scottish Enlightenment and a contemporary of the English Romantic poets. We might expect that he would have been influenced by ideas about eloquence drawn from both his contemporaries, the Romantic poets, and from the Scottish rhetoricians he studied at Edinburgh University. His depiction of eloquence in *The Heart of Midlothian* can, in fact, be seen as a confluence of both streams of influence.

Though never a theoretical rhetorician, Scott was conventionally educated in rhetoric at Edinburgh High School and University, where he studied law with David Hume, the nephew of the philosopher, and was so impressed by his brilliance that he recopied his lecture notes several times. He was also a participating member of the Edinburgh Literary and Speculative societies, which were elocution and debating clubs whose members produced essays on topics of current interest and presented them for discussion at meetings. Scott engaged actively in the work of both societies: his essays on antiquarian subjects were well received by the Literary Society, and later he served the Speculative Society as librarian, secretary, and treasurer in addition to taking part in debates on such forensic issues as the authenticity of Ossian's poems, whether permanent support ought to be provided for the poor, whether there ought to be an established religion, and whether the slave trade should be abolished—all standard debate topics (Lockhart 150–51).

As a lawyer too, Scott was perforce a practical rhetorician, as his education would require. We can get some idea of Scott's awareness of the rhetorical skills needed by a young lawyer in the portrait of young Alan Fairford in

*Redgauntlet* when he pleads his first case at the bar. The hitherto unimpressive Fairford surprises his audience by marshaling all the arts of reason and eloquence in defense of his unfortunate client. He modestly but effectively introduces his speech by disposing his audience favorably toward himself as a replacement for a more experienced advocate: "he spoke of himself as he really was, and of young Dumtoustie as what he ought to have been, taking care not to dwell on either topic a moment longer than was necessary." In good classical form he follows this introduction with an exposition of the facts of his case, carefully disentangling "those complicated formalities with which it had been loaded." Only upon the completion of all this attitude building and exposition does he set forth his defense of his client, whom he presents feelingly as a dupe, "a simple-hearted, honest, well-meaning man, who during a co-partnership of twelve years had gradually become impoverished, while his partner . . . had become gradually more and more wealthy." His speech, structured like a classical oration, is a rhetorical triumph in its convincing employment of the appeals of ethos, pathos, and logos; appropriately, it impresses its audience, who respond to the young lawyer with "murmurs of approbation" and "hands of gratulation" (149).

Thus both biographical and fictional evidence bespeak Scott's rhetorical sophistication. What rhetoric he would have known and what ideas about eloquence would have affected his thinking and his readers' reactions to his characters can best be determined by sampling some relevant concepts from the best-known Scottish rhetoricians of the last half of the eighteenth century, David Hume, George Campbell, and Hugh Blair, and suggesting points of convergence between their theories and those articulated by the English poet Scott most admired, William Wordsworth.

The term *eloquence* has always been slippery, in its broadest sense encompassing the whole of rhetoric, but usually implying special emphasis on oral utterance and application to writing that has the attributes of good oratory. In the eighteenth-century usage familiar to Scott and his readers, it suggests a further component: emphasis on moving an audience, on stirring the emotions of hearers. The nature of true eloquence was a subject of lively interest to the eighteenth-century Scottish rhetoricians, beginning with Hume, whose short tract "Of Eloquence" (1743, rpt. *Essays Moral, Political and Literary* 102) breaks no new theoretical ground but does raise some issues later elaborated by the more systematic rhetorics of Campbell and Blair. In his essay, Hume expresses great admiration for the classical orator, interest in the sublime, dismay at the inferiority of present-day British eloquence to classical, and exhortation to more passionate utterance. He defines the purpose of eloquence in relation to its emotional appeal: "To inflame the audience, so as to make them accompany the speaker in such violent passions, and such elevated conceptions: And to conceal, under the torrent of eloquence, the artifice, by which all this is effectuated" (166). (That second element in Hume's definition, the concealing of artifice, surfaces later in a nineteenth-century reviewer's response to Jeanie's speech; more of that later.)

George Campbell's *Philosophy of Rhetoric* (1776) takes up the subject of eloquence plainly under Hume's influence. Beginning with a definition of eloquence broad enough to take in all rhetoric as "that art of talent by which discourse is adapted to its end" (1), Campbell contrasts logic and eloquence and relates the latter firmly to audience: "Pure logic regards only the subject, which is examined solely for the sake of information. Truth, as such, is the proper aim of the examiner. Eloquence not only considers the subject, but also the speaker and the hearers, and both the subject and the speaker for the sake of the hearers, or rather for the sake of the effect intended to be produced in them" (33). In its distrust of syllogistic reasoning and emphasis on the heart as spring of action, Campbell's notion of eloquence anticipates an attitude explored more fully in the poetics of the next century, the idea that eloquence always springs from the heart.

In his project of relating rhetoric to the study of human nature, Campbell defends the legitimacy of the emotional appeal, indeed promotes it to the highest level in persuasion. A speaker who aims to move not only can but must appeal to the passions:

> [When] persuasion is the end, passion must also be engaged. If it is fancy which bestows brilliancy on our ideas, if it is memory which gives them stability, passion doth more, it animates them. Hence they derive spirit and energy. To say that it is possible to persuade without speaking to the passions, is but at best a kind of specious nonsense. The coolest reasoner always in persuading others addresseth himself to the passions some way or other. This he cannot avoid doing, if he speak to the purpose. To make me believe it is enough to show me that things are so; to make me act, it is necessary to show that the action will answer some end.... So far therefore is it from being an unfair method of persuasion to move the passions, that there is no persuasion without moving them. (122)

Although Campbell never explores the practical implications of this conviction on imaginative literature, plainly its application extends to fiction and even poetry as well as formal argumentation: the literary genres can depict dignified and legitimate passion in persuasive circumstances; indeed, the available and appropriate subject matter for fiction is extended if such passion is viewed as natural to us all, not available only to trained orators.

More popular and more accessible than Campbell's *Philosophy of Rhetoric* was the Reverend Hugh Blair's *Lectures on Rhetoric and Belles Lettres,* which he published in the year of his retirement from Edinburgh University, 1783— the same year that Scott began his course of study there. A less systematic and original thinker than Campbell, Blair was a popular pedagogue who won wide admiration for his soundness and moderation in both religion and rhetoric. Echoing Hume, Blair laments the decline of eloquence in Great Britain and compares British eloquence, which he characterizes as temperate and cool, unfavorably with that of the French, who, he claims, excel in animation (Schmitz 1).[2] A similar critique of Scottish emotional coolness also finds its way into Scott's fiction. Listening to a preacher in Glasgow's Laigh Kirk, Frank Osbaldistone in *Rob Roy* comments: "The Scotch, it is well known, are more remarkable for their exercise of their intellectual powers than for the keenness of their feelings; they are, therefore, more moved by logic than by rhetoric, and more attracted by acute and argumentative reasoning on doctrinal points, than influenced by the enthusiastic appeals to the heart and to the passions by which popular preachers in other countries win the favour of their hearers" (187). There too is the dissociation between head and heart: if eloquence cannot be found in religion and lawyers are hemmed in by technicalities, we evidently must look elsewhere—perhaps even to the less educated and sophisticated—for it.

Like Campbell, Blair connects eloquence with passion and identifies its source as nature rather than instruction: "Eloquence is no invention of the schools. Nature teaches every man to be eloquent when he is much in earnest." If we can have faith in nature to teach us eloquence in appropriate circumstances, it follows that the emotional appeal has legitimacy—even primacy. Blair argues that we are most eloquent when inspired by passion, "that state of the mind in which it is agitated, and fired by some object it has in view" (161–63).

A subject mentioned briefly by Hume and Campbell but elaborated by Blair is the identification of the three great scenes of eloquence, the three forums that call for its exercise: Parliament, the law, and the pulpit (corresponding generally to the Aristotelian venues of the deliberative, forensic, and epideictic). As we might expect, Blair is convinced that British eloquence has declined in all three: in Parliament because ministerial influence presently prevails over debate; in law because knowledge of it has become so technical; and in the pulpit because of the English practice of reading sermons rather than repeating them from memory. With the demise of its independent Parliament after the Union of 1707, Scotland lost one of its primary forums for the display of eloquence, leaving only the law and the pulpit, which were indeed the two most prominent institutions of eighteenth-century Scotland, attracting men of highest ability, among them, of course, Blair, Campbell, and Scott. Readers aware of the historical context of Scottish rhetoric will recognize within *The Heart of Midlothian* the depiction of all three institutional scenes of eloquence in their decline: the Duke of Argyle, more effective in his ministerial than any legislative role, where his coolness and tact rather than oratorical power lend him influence; lawyers throughout the text who debate overlearnedly or semi-learnedly, but ineffectually; even an English preacher whose service Jeanie attends on the road to London and whose delivery she faults because he reads instead of reciting his sermon.

Blair also discourses on the necessary connection between virtue and eloquence: "In order to be a truly eloquent or persuasive speaker," he writes, "nothing is more necessary than to be a virtuous man" (289). Of course, Scott's heroine excels as a brave woman, her virtue of the highest order, acquired not through the kind of schooling available to men of higher social standing, but by nature and, we might add, the nurture of her righteous father. Thus Jeanie Deans embodies all the principles that her age regarded as necessary for the cultivation and exercise of eloquence: virtue, passion, naturalness, and (at least partly because she is a woman) isolation from the influences that have corrupted modern eloquence.

Concern for eloquence can thus be seen as extending from Hume, through Campbell and Blair, to Scott and even Wordsworth. Their sense of British decline, their distrust of reason, their justification of pathos in argument, and their turn to nature as the source of passion and hence eloquence support the arguments of Wordsworth's Preface to *Lyrical Ballads,* with its call for a poet who chooses "incidents and situations from common life" and uses "a selection of language really used by men." Indeed, at the beginning of *The Antiquary* Scott openly proclaims his allegiance to Wordsworthian principles and his conviction that the language of the peasantry is powerful not only because of its simplicity but also because of its eloquence: "the lower orders are less restrained by the habit of suppressing their feelings, and . . . I agree with my friend Wordsworth, that they seldom fail to express them in the strongest and most powerful language. That is, I think, peculiarly the case with the peasantry of my own country, a class with whom I have long been familiar. The antique force and simplicity of their language, often tinctured with the oriental eloquence of Scripture, in the mouths of those of elevated understanding, give pathos to their grief, and dignity to their resentment" (5). One difference between Wordsworth and Scott is that Wordsworth purifies the language of his peasants, as he says, "from what appear to be its real defects, from all lasting and rational causes of dislike and disgust" (that is, he does not use dialect in his poetry), while in his fiction Scott allows his peasants to speak in "unpurified" language, imparting to it the eloquence inspired by virtue and passion.

In addition to occurring within the context of Scott's audience's awareness (however general) of an ongoing cultural conversation about the nature of true eloquence, Jeanie's speech also occurs within a significant linguistic context. In eighteenth-century Scotland, people spoke that northern dialect of English we call Scots, but the prestige dialect of educated people was Augustan English, the standard of the south. Although even educated people spoke Scots informally, they wrote a standard English that they tried to render indistinguishable from the English of the south: no Scotticisms adorn (or disfigure, depending on your politics) the prose of David Hume or Adam Smith. The result was a linguistic double standard, with English the language of public discourse, of educated and successful people, and Scots the language of the heart, spoken in private by the poor and powerless. English was the standard for serious literature and philosophy, Scots used for low subjects and humor.

Evidence of this linguistic split appears throughout the discourse embedded in Scott's fiction, and sensitivity to the politics of dialect enables the contemporary reader to place characters and their mode of speaking into an appropriate context. The discourse of Scott's fiction ranges between the formal, correct, standard English and the homely Scots, the English (predictably) spoken by the framing narrators of the novels, the heroes, the heroines, and all characters of high social station (except when they address their students), the Scots spoken by the folk—the servants, farmers, gypsies, beggars, fanatics—the whole underclass of the Waverley novels. Although Scott has often been criticized for his pasteboard ladies and gentlemen and praised for his depiction of Scots speakers, the actual powerlessness of the latter is revealed in their habitation of the underplots of the novels. There they speak irreverent truths and common sense: wild seers possess knowledge of past events hidden from the consciousness of soft refined ladies and gentlemen, and clever servants (like Andrew Fairservice and Calem Balderstone) save their skins and sometimes those of their masters. The antics of the Scots speakers set off, parody, and facilitate the actions of their social betters in the main plot, who court, fight, perform heroics, and establish their true and noble lineages in pure (though undeniably stiff) English. Thus to the extent that Scott's low characters speak dialect, his fiction illustrates—indeed, it perpetuates—the linguistic double standard of his day. To whatever extent these low characters are able to shape events, however, his fiction can also be seen as subverting the implication of the superiority of the English and the English speaking. Only in *The Heart of Midlothian* does he present to his readers a Scots-speaking heroine, one who is neither young nor beautiful, but still one whose speech does not invite patronization. Here Scott rescues the dialect from lowliness and triviality by exploiting its rhetorical possibilities. By occupying the center rather than the periphery of the action of the novel, the discursive practices of Davie and Jeanie Deans embody a notion of eloquence that invites readers to take seriously Scots-speaking characters and their values.

It is thus accurate to say that Jeanie's speech functions as the rhetorical and moral centerpiece of a novel that might be thematized as a study of the nature of true eloquence. In praising it in his introduction to the Holt edition, David Daiches shrewdly observes that it "comes near enough to formal rhetoric to be supremely effective *as* rhetoric, but is saved by the rhythms and expressions of folk speech from sounding either artificial or sentimental" (21). I would argue that we can extend Daiches's observation and claim that this speech does more than "come near to" formal rhetoric; it *is* formal rhetoric—not to be regarded suspiciously, neither artificial nor sentimental in its appeals, but intricately wrought and legitimately affecting—and in its rhetoricity is its strength, capturable only by awareness and acceptance of such rhetoricity. Its language (interestingly) is only intermittently that of folk speech; its rhythms, tropes, figures, and arguments are describable by formal rhetoric.

Jeanie's speech uses elements of the vocabulary of Lowland Scots, but what gives her plea distinction is its rhetoric more than its diction. Among its most obvious figures, the speech employs many tropes and schemes described by classical rhetoric: antithesis worthy of John F. Kennedy ("it is not what we hae dune for oursells, but what we hae dune for others"); hyperbole ("I would hae gaen to the end of the earth to save the life of John Porteous");

litotes ("it is not when we sleep soft and wake merrily ourselves, that we think on other people's sufferings"); polyptoton and ploche ("save an honest house from dishonour", "my sister, my puir sister Effie, still lives . . . she still lives"); parallelism and rhyme ("we are for righting our ain wrangs and fighting our ain battles"); as well an many instances of parenthesis, apostrophe, apposition, alliteration, anaphora, polysyndeton, metaphor, and metonymy. The heavy figurative texture might result in artificiality if not for the simple, largely monosyllabic diction. In fact, the whole speech contains only thirty words of more than two syllables, and most of those are drawn from the common lexicon: *pleasantly, merrily, dishonour, exercise, prosperous, establishes, righteousness.*

Interestingly, a contemporary reviewer of *The Heart of Midlothian* noticed the Queen's attribution of eloquence to Jeanie's speech and disputed it, judging the speech "too rhetorical for the person and occasion" and the Queen's reply as "still worse," for "had it been eloquence, it must necessarily have been unperceived by the Queen" (cited in Whately 151–52). Such a response suggests a high degree of public rhetorical sophistication to begin with; it joins the popular and recurring argument that rhetorical art should be completely invisible because its use is morally suspect. Even notable rhetoricians—including Richard Whately in the nineteenth century—have subscribed to this view, which recurs as part of the long tradition of suspiciousness of rhetoric as amoral manipulation of *techne*. The problem is as old as Plato. An opposing position might argue that as readers of fictional rhetorical discourse, we are aware in this situation of the great imbalance of power and control over the rhetorical situation that exists between Jeanie the rhetor and both her textual and extratextual audience. Rhetor and audience (whether textual or extratextual) need not both preserve innocence of artifice; it is only necessary that the speaker herself be moved and not be manipulative from her own position of power (though she may certainly intend to move), but the reader and the audience may be both aware and moved or unaware and moved, depending on their sophistication in relation to the rhetor. In this instance, Jeanie never claims eloquence for herself, is never self-consciously manipulative, and her rhetorical art can be seen as natural for one who, though not formally educated, has been steeped in Biblical eloquence. It is also plausible that the Queen, a much more sophisticated listener than Jeanie is speaker, be impressed even while she is moved.

Not only does Jeanie's speech occur in a context in which eloquence is directly thematized; the discourse of the entire novel resounds with claims to eloquence and exemplifications of it by characters possessing varying degrees of ethical plausibility and political effectuality. Jeanie is, first of all, the daughter of Douce Davie Deans, a man described as vain "of his own talents for expounding hidden truths," one who unstintingly "poured forth his eloquence upon the controversies and testimonies of the day" (96). Speaking in the rhythms and metaphors of the Bible, Davie Deans remains, in spite of the political turmoil and controversy surrounding him, religious, puritanical, and full of old-fashioned eloquence uniting Biblical phrases with the local landscape and idiom, as the following description of his lost daughter Effie illustrates:

> "She went out from us, my bairn, because she was not of us," replied David. "She is a withered branch will never bear fruit of grace—a scape-goat gone forth into the wilderness of the world, to carry with her, as I trust, the sins of our little congregation. The peace of the warld gang wi' her, and a better peace when she has the grace to turn to it. If she is one of His elected, His ain hour will come. What would her mother have said, that famous and memorable matron, Rebecca M'Naught, whose memory is like a flower of sweet savor in Newbattle, and a pot of frankincense in Lugton?" (446)

Contrasting with Davie Deans's archaic puritanism, one who strains for eloquence but falls short of it, is the self-appointed legal expert, Bartoline Saddletree, whom the narrator wryly describes as having "a considerable gift of words, which he mistook for eloquence, and conferred more liberally upon the society in which he lived than was at all times gracious and acceptable" (39). Laboring under the illusion that he is learned in law, Saddletree fills his speeches with snatches of legal jargon, half-understood precedents, and mangled Latin, parodying the eloquence of courtroom lawyers. True to his own creed and conscience, which inserts Scripture into the local landscape ("pot of frankincense in Lugton"), Davie Deans suspects Saddletree's pseudo-learned and "foreign" brand of eloquence; to him Saddletree's garbled Latin is "the language of the Antichrist" (127).

Appearing briefly and lending neither luster nor credibility to official legal eloquence is the lawyer Fairbrother, who defends Effie in court. There he plays shamelessly on the jury's automatic sympathy for "a creature so young, so ingenuous, and so beautiful" (236) and tries to gain sympathy for Effie not by sound argument but by appeals to his hearers' belief in the "facility and pliability of the female sex" (237). Though superficially eloquent, the lawyer is only a clever and opportunistic manipulator who exploits stereotypes of gender and culture but does not respond to real feeling; at one point, when Effie cries out in distress, he dramatically seizes the occasion to exclaim, "in that piteous cry you heard the eloquence of maternal affection, far surpassing the force of my poor words" (238). But his cheap theatrics fail and Effie is condemned for the murder of her child.

A fourth, more positive model combining eloquence and effectuality is the Duke of Argyle, who occupies a space between the archaic moral rigidity of Davie Deans, who makes his daughter an outcast, and the slipperiness or ignorance of the lawyers. A cautious and politic mediator between England and Scotland, Argyle is capable of discussing with equal grace policy with the Queen and cheeses with Jeanie. He is presented as one who, though tactful and decorous in his immediate accommodations to audience, has been known to soar above politics, has been willing to raise his voice "whether in office or opposition, for those measures which were at once just and lenient" (377).

For example, when the Queen's pardon of Porteous was followed by a veritable lynching, Argyle saved Edinburgh from the crown's reprisal by "the animated and eloquent opposition which he had offered to the severe measures which were about to be adopted toward the city" (377), thus proving his ability to temper the public consequences of the larger historical action that frames the narrative of Jeanie's private tale. With typical prodigality of verbal and rhetorical detail, Argyle's parliamentary speech, a defense of his honor against charges of partisanship, is presented:

> I appeal . . . to the House—to the notion, if I can be justly branded with the infamy of being a jobber or a partisan. Have I been a briber of votes?—a buyer of boroughs?—the agent of corruption for any purpose, or on behalf of any part?—Consider my life; examine my actions in the field and in the cabinet, and see where there lies a blot that can attach to my honor. (378)

Thus *The Heart of Midlothian* resounds with high rhetoric, with people passionately discussing political, ecclesiastical, and personal issues, pleading in court, defending their honor, preaching from the pulpit, and debating in Parliament, characters educated (often only half-educated) in the highly rhetoricized professions of law, religion, and politics. Against all this official, partisan, and sectarian rhetoric, Jeanie's speech gains plausibility because it combines "natural" sincerity with "naturally acquired" rhetorical appeals.

Of course, Jeanie's speech does not persuade in an immediate contextual vacuum any more than it persuades in a vacuum of total fictional context. It is placed within a series of events that establish her own high moral character and the political, moral, and rhetorical contexts that determine what pleas can and should succeed. As we might expect from a novelist as historically sophisticated as Scott, the domestic drama of the Deans family unfolds against a thoroughly detailed historical backdrop.

To create that backdrop the novel's early pages abound with the talkiness Dick Tinto deplored, with patriotic reminders of Scotland's history, with legalistic arguments of varying precision and expertise, with clerical admonitions, and with perorations that help the Edinburgh mob work itself into frenzy after the Porteous pardon. But in the aftermath of the infamous Porteous pardon, talk is ineffectual; preachers offer little comfort to men condemned to death on petty charges, especially in a context within which the Queen has arbitrarily pardoned institutionalized violence. In the contextualized historical world of the novel, law and clergy exercise their eloquence without impact on the political sphere. The novel thematizes the moral efficacy of rhetoric: of what use is religious faith when preachers counsel people to tolerate injustice or create factions among the oppressed? What good are lawyers who make speeches but are helpless to get justice administered? When is a plea for mercy, an appeal to the heart, legitimately and genuinely moving? All these issues arise in the framing historical narrative long before Jeanie sets out on foot for London to plead her private case.

Just as rhetorical activity is conducted within a historical context, so also is it conducted within a specific dramatic context. As expert stage manager for Jeanie, Argyle attempts to control this context. Both politician and patriot, he has maintained his own access to the Queen, but he has not flattered her at the expense of conscience. In fact, his defense of the Edinburgh mob was "the more gratefully received in the metropolis, as it was understood that the Duke's interposition had given personal offense to Queen Caroline." That Argyle has displayed this degree of integrity is essential, since Jeanie herself displays the highest personal honor and disdain for expediency. It is also important that Argyle not function as a favorite of the Queen, because Jeanie's intercession for her sister must win assent on its own merit. Still, although Argyle must not tell Jeanie what to say, he can provide her with one rhetorical necessity she lacks on her own—decorum. She may have righteousness, plainness, and goodness on her side, but she does not know what is enough and what is too much to say. Therefore, he offers to signal when she should say no more on a subject; the point is that honest spontaneity may need courtly restraint and sensitivity to audience in order to move. As Hugh Blair admonishes those who address public assemblies, though the great rule is to follow nature, "we must still set a guard on ourselves, not to allow impetuosity to transport us too far; keeping audience in mind, we must always preserve regard to what the public ear will bear."

Reinforcing the significance of Jeanie's speech is the Queen's initial reluctance to grant pardon; she must be moved. After the riots following the Porteous pardon, she has understandably "had enough of Scotch pardons" (379), and she is known to be contentious, "rather fond . . . of an argument," we are told. Indeed, once she has ascertained Argyle's personal disinterestedness in the case, she is ready to engage in legal disputation about the grounds of Effie's conviction, but Argyle has wit to avoid such direct argumentative confrontation. To argue would simply harden her conviction "until she became obliged, out of mere respect to consistency, to let the criminal suffer" (401). Here again, Argyle's tact, his sense of *kairos*, prepares the way for Jeanie's effective emotional appeal while calling into question the efficacy of direct argumentation at this time and place.

In its handling of the dramatic context of Jeanie's speech, the novelistic rendering makes many delicate rhetorical and moral discriminations. It is, for instance, important that Effie's innocence remain unproved until the end. A matter for emotional appeal is not one in which the facts are obvious, but one in which rhetoric could affect the disposition of the issue. With legal principle insufficiently compelling, humanity and common sense come into play. Or, to put the point rhetorically, where logos is indecisive (as it so often is), ethos and pathos make the difference. Pathos—the emotional appeal of Jeanie's speech, its plea for pity and its identification with suffering victims—is obvious enough, her ethical advantage less so. But if we define ethos as the persuasive value of the character of the writer or speaker, Jeanie's behavior and demeanor embody the highest ethical standards. First, she seeks no personal benefit; she pleads disinterestedly for her sister, "for whose sake she was willing to sacrifice all but truth and conscience" (401). Furthermore, she appears before the Queen in honest simplicity, uninhibited because unaware to whom she speaks, dressed in her natural attire, her plaid, and "speaking in her broad northern accent" (401). Earlier she had contemplated writing out and memorizing her speech, but the rhetorically sophisticated Argyle counseled naturalness, suggesting that a written speech "would be like reading a sermon, you know, which we good Presbyterians think has less unction than when spoken without book" (349). Thus she speaks from a consistent and religious standpoint, without affectation in dress or artifice in manner.

To reinforce her ethical power, Jeanie places her listeners, the Queen and Lady Suffolk, at a moral disadvantage—though she accomplishes this unwittingly and unmanipulatively so that they cannot take offense at any imputation of her own moral superiority over them. For instance, early in their confrontation, the Queen casually insults Scotland by questioning "what sort of a barbarous people your countryfolk are, where child-murder is become so common as to require the restraint of laws like yours." Bridling at this imputation of Scottish barbarity, Jeanie tartly replies that "there are many places beside Scotland where mothers are unkind to their ain flesh and blood," unaware of the strained relations between Caroline and her son Frederick, the prince of Wales. Then Jeanie discomposes Lady Suffolk, the Queen's companion and the King's mistress, by referring innocently to the "cutty stool" as "the stool of repentance . . . for light life and conversation and for breaking the seventh commandment" (402). With both ladies unable to respond to such indirect but telling moral barbs, Jeanie gains the upper hand rhetorically.

In addition to being a model of stylistic devices and a triumph of ethos, Jeanie's speech reveals much about the nature and relevance of emotional appeals. Itself a rhetorical artifact, it functions simultaneously as a rhetorical tract. It suggests that emotional appeals need not be dishonest, but they are most effective when disinterested; they do not contradict reason or evidence, but they do aid in moving people to action when reason offers no certain direction; the more genuine and spontaneous the appeal, the more moving. Most important (and rhetorical theorists from Quintilian to Blair remind us of this, as well as the most skilled rhetorical practitioners), we cannot hope to move others if we are ourselves unmoved or hope to arouse in others emotion we do not feel ourselves. Unlike the courtroom lawyer who merely exploits his audience's prejudices, Jeanie is a compassionate woman who identifies with her sister's situation and is genuinely moved by it, as her actions, her words, and her tears attest. Therefore she is able to transfer her own compassion to the Queen.

Of course, the eloquence of Jeanie Deans is ultimately the creation of Scott's literary and rhetorical art, not necessarily a record of reality, regardless of how much historicized and rhetoricized context is invoked to surround the immediate drama. We cannot know whether Scottish peasants were really as eloquent as Scott painted them, although we might suspect that he heightens and purifies their speech just as much as he does the speech of his ladies and gentlemen. As readers, we are aware at some level that their eloquence is ultimately their creator's. Unfortunately, we do not even know for certain whether virtue and passion inspire elevated expression, although most of us would like to consider such a connection appropriate and inevitable. Even for highly conscious rhetoricians, where reason is uncertain, passion and emotion come into play, as we have seen in the novel. We can be fairly certain, however, that Scott believed that virtue and simplicity inspired eloquence, and we can be fairly certain that in so believing he followed and illustrated the principles of both Wordsworth and his own age's best rhetoricians. Scott's fiction, especially *The Heart of Midlothian*, illustrates these principles and reveals how decisions about the language characters use have recoverable rhetorical dimensions, which in turn have recoverable moral, historical, and political implications.

## NOTES

1. This and subsequent references to the novel, incorporated within the text, are from the 1963 Holt edition of *The Heart of Midlothian*, introduction by David Daiches.

2. Blair was well known as the most popular preacher of his day. Scott's hero in *Guy Mannering*, for instance, on a visit to Edinburgh expresses eagerness to hear "some of your Scottish preachers whose talents have done such honour to your country—your Blair, your Robertson, or your Henry" (311).

# APPENDIX
## WORDSWORTH AND THE RHETORICAL TRADITION IN ENGLAND (1944)

*Klaus Dockhorn*
*Translated by Heidi I. Saur-Stull*

### Translator's Note

Klaus Dockhorn's 1944 article "Wordsworth und die rhetorische Tradition in England," originally published in *Nachrichten der Akademie der Wissenschaften in Göttingen, Philologisch-Historische Klasse* (no. 11), was received with considerable interest by Wordsworth scholars everywhere. In fact, it almost seemed during the following decades that no Wordsworth bibliography was considered complete unless it included this article, and no research paper was written that did not agree or disagree with Dockhorn's findings.

Through careful examination and analyses of the poet's lyrical and critical writings, Dockhorn had concluded that Wordsworth, rather than introducing a revolutionary new tradition based on feelings and emotions, follows the mainstream of European thought, which in turn was based on the traditional rhetorical sources adopted from antiquity. In addition to numerous examples drawn from Wordsworth's writings, Dockhorn provides carefully chosen examples from other English as well as from French and German (especially Lessing's) critical writings, in which, according to his judicious philological analyses, the concept and teachings of "manners and passions" are the core not only of rhetoric but also of poetry. Accordingly, the real novelty in Wordsworth's writings was his debunking of prevailing traditions in order to reexamine their true and unadulterated sources (namely Aristotle's and Quintilian's writings), to draw his own conclusions, and to construct his own body of aesthetic criticism and poetry on this solid foundation.

Dockhorn served on the faculty of the English Department at the Georg August Universität Göttingen from 1942 to 1949. His research interest focused primarily on rhetoric and the rhetorical tradition and its impact on literary production from the Carolingian Renaissance to the twentieth century (see also Dockhorn's "Die Rhetorik als Quelle des vorromantischen Irrationalismus in der Literatur und Geistesgeschichte" [Rhetoric as the source of pre-Romantic irrationalism in literature and intellectual history], published in

1949). Other publications examine the relationship between British and German intellectual histories.

Scholars generally agree that Dockhorn's research is always meticulous and solid, albeit at times sententious and long-winded (the first four sentences in his opening paragraph, for example, contain 176 words—not counting the German composites). While eliminating most references to literary practices on the Continent, it is hoped that this considerably shortened version of the translation has retained all of Dockhorn's main ideas and conclusions pertaining to Wordsworth, giving Wordsworth students and scholars access to this important work.

Ever since Legouis established the basis for modern Wordsworth research by dispersing in his book *La Jeunesse de Wordsworth* the myth of Wordsworth as a natural genius (so eagerly promoted by the poet himself), research has tried to determine which literary traditions had affected Wordsworth.... Scholars looked to a surprising extent at philosophical traces within the texture of his poetic world view and asked whether Wordsworth built upon the genuinely English philosophical traditions—following Locke's sensual empiricism, to be found in particular in Hartley's associational psychology—or whether he was touched more profoundly by the teachings of transcendental idealism, with which his friend Coleridge had familiarized him.[1] Even studies that went beyond the tracing of philosophical patterns and recognized, for example, in aesthetic criticism such influences as the "connoisseurs" or the "School of Taste," emphasized again and again philosophical thoughts and categories because they were the basis for the aesthetic values and deductions established by a Blair, a Reynolds, an Alison. With this approach, researchers overlooked the fact that the aesthetic values of the eighteenth century had led a life of their own far removed from contemporary philosophy and long before they entered the arena of philosophical considerations, a life nurtured by a series of concepts arising from a totally different constellation of intellectual history, a situation initially alien to contemporary philosophy. This is what constitutes the continuing tradition of classical rhetoric with its initially purely pragmatic intention of persuading, the πείθειν, the "persuasio," as it evolved in antiquity in the city council with its theories on categories of speech, genres, figures of speech, with its critique of poets and above all its theories on the emotions.... We can observe the powerful influence the rhetorical tradition exerted on Wordsworth through his preoccupation with its formulas. As a point of departure for this examination we will choose what I would like to call the ἤθη-πάθη formula. This formula, the "moeurs et passions" of the French, the "manners and passions" of the English, the "Sitten und Leidenschaften" of the Germans, derives its unmistakable character from the position it occupies in the system of rhetoric since Aristotle's time. The purpose, the "opus" of the art of rhetorics—and every consideration of any art starts in antiquity with the element of pragmatic purpose—is persuasion,

# Appendix

captivating a listener. For this end, there are two main means that dominate as basic categories the disposition of classical rhetorics: the appeal to reason, the "docere," which is accomplished through proofs, πίστεις, probations, enthymeme, and secondly, the arousing of emotions, the awakening of affects, the "movere," accomplished through two artificial means, through the λόγος παθητικός and λόγος ἠθικός; through the πάθη and the ἤθη. . . .

The coupling of πάθη and ἤθη, as the two means through which the speaker does not convince by reason but touches and moves the emotions, was—as we know—already considered problematic in antiquity, but this did not cause the formula to lose any of its effectiveness. It was practically always clear what the πάθη were: since Aristotle's time, they have usually been defined as "perturbationes mentis," troubled aberrations, for which fear, rage, hatred, and ambition were quoted as examples. . . .

In the concept ἤθη however, . . . elements, already brought together by Aristotle, make it impossible for us to accept the German equivalents "Sitten" or "Charakter" whose contradictoriness and multiplicity of meaning had led in early German aestheticism (for example with Lessing) to concepts such as "Moralen" and "Gesinnungen." Aristotle is talking about ἦθος as a disposition with reference to passions, habits (virtuous or vicious), age and fortune such as birth and riches, i.e., social standing. The ἦθος thus contains first through its connection to πάθος the element of moving and exciting; it can be presented objectively and is apparent, and is consequently not merely an attitude; it contains furthermore quite explicitly the concepts of the habitual and valid and of the appropriate, which we do not necessarily experience in the concept of character; it is furthermore related to social behavior, since it varies according to age and position in the community; it consequently lacks the element of conscience, which we associate with the term *ethos*. For the moment we remember as the most important designation its formulalike relationship to πάθος, because it not only constitutes a connection with the main body of rhetoric but since antiquity it also constitutes a connection with poetics; in other words, it generates an affect by exciting and moving the emotions.

It is due to this terminological uncertainty surrounding the Greek concept ἦθος that the Romans, when they had to come to terms with the πάθη-ἤθη formula (for which they had no immediate and suitable equivalent), attached to ἦθος the meaning of a weaker, moderate, even pleasant and mild passion. . . .

The difficulty to come to terms with the ἦθος within the dual term πάθη-ἤθη can be clearly seen with Quintilian. He recognizes two kinds of emotions: one is the actual "affectus," the πάθος, the other is ἦθος: "Alteram Graeci πάθος vocant, quam nos recte vertentes ac proprie affectum dicimus: alteram ἦθος cuius nomine, ut ego quidem sentio, caret sermo Romanus; mores appellantur . . . " and then he continues in this sense: "mores" does not exactly express what the Greek meant. ἦθος is more a "morum proprietas," an attribute, an idiosyncrasy of the customs, a characteristically moral behavior. Discerning individuals "who are more concerned with the meaning than with the word" see it still differently; and in that respect Quintilian joins them and thus determines the course of the further development of the meaning: "Affectus igitur hos concitatos, illos mites atque compositos esse dixerunt: in altero vehementer commotos, in altero lenes: denique hos imperare, illos persuadere; hos ad perturbationem, illos ad benevolentiam praevalere" (*Institutio Oratoria* vi.2). Here it can be understood quite clearly: πάθος and ἦθος, belonging to the general term of the "affectus," are functions of the "movere," πάθη affecting the excited, vehement, disquieting emotions, while ἤθη touches the gentle, sensitive, well-intentioned ones. And Quintilian clarifies it even better: the ἦθος is "blandum et humanum, et audientibus amabile atque iucundum." It prevails in the sociable, in the relationships within the family and friendship: "quod est sine dubio inter conunctas maxime personas, quoties perferimus, ignoscimus, satisfacimus, monemus, procul ab ira, procul ab odio. Sed tamen alia patris adversus filium, tutoris adversus pupillum, mariti adversus uxorem moderatio est." The strongly excited passion and the gentle, humane emotion, "perturbatio" and "benevolentia," are with Quintilian πάθη and ἤθη, subsumed under the general term of the "affectus," destined to move passionately or to touch gently. . . .

The rhetoric of late antiquity sees in πάθη and ἤθη in increasing measure the real art and task of speech; to teach them is the task of rhetoric. The theory of the πάθη and the ἤθη, the rhetorical theory about emotions, is becoming the core not only of rhetoric but also of poetics. In Περὶ ὕψους Longinus establishes πάθος as the actual and essential characteristic of the elevated, at about the same time Quintilian establishes the theory about emotions as the core of rhetorics. To draw the judges into the desired state of anger, of compassion, to move them—that is the most important element in the courtroom. Proof is great, but emotion is more powerful: "Huc igitur incumbat orator, hoc opus eius, hic labor est . . . velut spiritus operis eius atque animus est in affectibus."

And now to Wordsworth. For the moment, one passage may speak for itself without any analysis. It is quite obvious that it belongs to the problem of the πάθη-ἤθη formula with the separation "docere" or "probare" in the background on one hand and "movere" on the other:

>             Methinks
> It were a pleasant pastime to construct
> A scale and table of belief—as thus—
> Two columns, one for *passion,* one for *proof;*
> Each rises as the other falls: and first,
> Passion a unit and against us—proof—
> Nay, we must travel in another path,
> Or we're stuck fast for ever;—passion, then,
> Shall be a unit for us; proof, no, passion!
> We'll not insult thy majesty by time,
> Person, and place—the where, the when, the how,
> And all particulars that dull brains require

> To constitute the spiritless shape of Fact,
> They bow to, calling the idol, Demonstration.
> (*The Borderers* III, lines 55ff.)

Just as Wordsworth's examination of the specifically rhetorical problem of persuasion under the viewpoint of "proof" and "passion" is here quite obvious, his preoccupation with the rhetorical concept of emotions will be shown in an even more instructive round-about way in his examination of the πάθη-ἤθη formula as the more subtle subcategory of "passion."

First of all, it is worth noticing that the πάθη-ἤθη formula appears with Wordsworth several times and in totally different contexts in a three-link string, which, as we shall see, is in its sequence and evaluation of its links so typical for the eighteenth century that it must be regarded as a conventional cliché, as a critical formula. With Wordsworth too it is connected to an expansion of the interrelationship of meanings and a clarification of the relationship of its links as they appear in a frequently recurring pattern and always coupled together. In the 1798 Advertisement to the *Lyrical Ballads* Wordsworth indicates that his poetic attempts are addressing (1) "human passions," (2) "human characters," and (3) "human incidents." ...

In the 1800 Preface the enumeration is repeated, even though at first glance it does not appear with the same formulalike clarity. Upon closer examination, especially when compared with the 1798 enumeration in the Advertisement, it is clearly recognizable: first the poet wants to present the "maternal passion," then the emotions of age and youth when confronted with death; then, however—and this strange formulation is especially important, because in it the emotional content of the "moral" comes close to the concept of "passion"—he wants to show the "fraternal, or, to speak more philosophically, the moral attachment."[2] These are to be followed by "moral sensations"—here again the element of the touching and sentimental, of the "moral" becomes obvious—as in the "Incident of Simon Lee," followed by "characters of less impassioned feelings," "characters which from their constitution may be distinctly and profitably contemplated." This is a series of steps of "passions" in decreasing intensity, i.e., already related to Quintilian's separation of the emotions from the content. However, it also seems to approach the dual meaning of the ἤθος concept insofar as "fraternal or moral attachment" are clearly separated from "passion," touching on Quintilian's meaning of ἤθος = "mores": "alia patris adversus filium, alia tutoris adversus pupillum, alia mariti adversus uxorem est moderatio," meaning those feelings arising from companionship, while "less impassioned feelings" correspond to the other component of the Quintilian ἤθος = "affectus": "affectus mites atque compositi." The "incident," too, resurfaces ... with the mentioning of the "Incident of Simon Lee" because this thought process of "passions" and "characters" or "less impassioned feelings" concludes for Wordsworth obviously and habitually with "incidents." ...

[It is interesting to see that, again in a three-link sequence whose] parts are clearly separated from each other with the conjunction "or," the sequence "passions, characters, incidents" reappears factually, even though slightly differently formulated when the old "mores" appears as "manners" in the place of "characters," presenting the ἤθη-πάθη formula in its pure meaning. One even is tempted to see at this point a special closeness to the rhetorical tradition in the reversed presentation of the qualities of true poetry through exaggeration, which was a favorite method of classical rhetoric when it attempted to better characterize the "genera dicendi" with its "vitia" by exaggeratedly designating, for example, "grande" with "turgidum" and the "tenue" with "frigidum." Wordsworth states: "The qualities of writing best fitted for eager reception are either such as startle the world into attention; *or* they are chiefly of the superficial kind, lying upon the surfaces of manners; *or* arising out of a selection and arrangement of incidents, by which the mind is kept upon the stretch of curiosity and the fancy amused without the trouble of thought" (Essay Supplementary to the Preface, 1815). Here we have quite distinctly and at first glance the "manners" of the second and the "incidents" of the third link of the by now familiar links "characters" and "incidents," while the still missing "passions" of the first link is not difficult to recognize, since "to startle the world into attention by audacity and extravagance" is the hyperbolic mark of "passionate language" whose hallmark—at all times recognized by all criticism influenced by antiquity—was the bold and daring metaphor. The appearance of "manners" and "incidents" at the end of an obvious clearly three-link string permits the only possible conclusion, that "passions," supported by the content analogy "to startle into attention by audacity and extravagance," rounds it out formally.

However, it can be shown that the ἤθη-πάθη formula surfaces on an even more profound level in Wordsworth's contemplation about the essence of poetry, leaving its mark and placing the poet therefore more than ankle deep in the stream of the rhetorical tradition that this concept attests to. To do this, we are starting with a concept that is added to explain the difficulty surrounding the ἤθος formula, the concept of "circumstances."[3] ... Starting now with the concept of "circumstances," we discover via a short but all the more revealing detour proof of further influence on Wordsworth through the ἤθη-πάθη formula. First of all, the "circumstances" appear quite clearly in the passage of the monologue that deals with the relationship of "proof" and "passion" in *The Borderers*—this first and fundamental division of the disposition in all rhetorics:

> proof, no, passion!
> We'll not insult thy majesty by time,
> Person, and place—the where, the when, the how,
> And all particulars that dull brains require
> To constitute the spiritless shape of Fact ... (III, 55)

Here the rhetorical recollection becomes especially clear, when "time, person, and place" (tempus, persona, locus) are paraphrased by "the where, the when, the how, and all particulars" ("aut ubi aut quando aut quo modo") in the same manner in which Quintilian and Fortunat Rhetor had paraphrased them. This passage from *The Borderers* tells us that Wordsworth was quite familiar with the problems of rhetoric.

Then, however—and this will get us considerably further—Wordsworth knows and formulates the differentiation of "pathos" and the "sublime," which he develops upon the use of the concept of "circumstances."

> As the Pathetic participates of an animal sensation, it might seem that if the springs of this emotion were genuine, all men, possessed of competent knowledge of the facts and *circumstances,* would be instantaneously affected. But there are emotions of the pathetic that are simple and direct, and others—that are complex and revolutionary; some—to which the heart yields with gentleness; others—against which it struggles with pride: these varieties are infinite as the combinations of *circumstance* and the constitutions of *character.* Remember also, that the medium through which in Poetry the heart is to be affected—is language. There is also a meditative, as well as a human pathos; an enthusiastic as well as an ordinary sorrow; a sadness that has its seat in the depths of reason, to which the mind cannot sink gently of itself—but to which it must descend by treading the steps of thought. And for the sublime—if we consider what are the cares that occupy the passing day, and how remote is the practice and the course of life from the sources of sublimity in the soul of man? (Essay Supplementary to the Preface, 1815)

Before proceeding to show how, with the help of the ἤθη-πάθη formula, we are led to the more profound and for Wordsworth the more decisive poetic concerns, we must first note that this question of "manners" is by no means peripheral for Wordsworth.... "Characteristic and circumstantial," those, as we have seen, explanatory *accretions* of the "manner" concept of the ἤθος, are for him important requirements for poetic output. They appear time and again: the Spenser stanza, he tells us in another passage, does not recommend itself for "circumstantial narrative."[4] On the occasion of the imitation of Chiabrera's Epitaphs he states: "His epitaphs are characteristic and circumstantial, so have I endeavoured to make this of mine."[5] After all that we have shown, we must regard the ἤθη-πάθη formula, the "manners and passions," as the vision that prompted him to praise Ovid's and Pope's "characteristic and impassioned epistle" (Preface to the Edition of 1815). From this partiality for the "pastoral describing manners" we encounter his preferential differentiating of the pathetic from the sublime; in the same Preface we encounter the conventional dividing of the poetic genres according to "characters, manners, and sentiments," which really is nothing else but a string of concepts for the problematic ἤθος concept. Quite clearly and with the same modifications like "particular thoughts," "circumstances of age, occupation, manner of life, etc.," he describes in the text (without referring to it by name) the unmistakably recognizable pathetic element, contrasting it with the sublime (and also not referring to it by name, but just as obviously recognizable) by means of such determinants as "sinking into the heart," "uttered strikingly." . . . "The first requirement, then, in an Epitaph is, that it should speak, in a tone which shall sink into the heart, the general language of humanity ('general and obvious' in Webb: the 'Sublime' is 'general'!) as connected with the subject of death. . . . This general language may be uttered so strikingly ('to strike' is the first requirement of the 'sublime') as to entitle an epitaph to high praise; yet it cannot lay claim to the highest praise unless other excellencies be superadded." Thus far, the epitaph is merely sublime. Only when ἦθος is added, represented by "particular thoughts" and "circumstances," does the epitaph—according to the Webb-Wordsworth antitheses—acquire the properties of pathos: "This general sympathy ought to be quickened, provoked, and diversified, by particular thoughts, actions, images,—circumstances of age, occupation, manner of life, prosperity which the deceased had known, or adversity to which he had been subject; and these ought to be bound together and solemnised into one harmony by the general sympathy. The two powers should temper, restrain and exalt each other" (On Epitaphs, I, *Prose Works* II: 150).

This thought, that the pathetic evolves, as it were, when ethos enters general and—what constitutes pathos par excellence—sublime thought in order to tune it down again from the regions of the sublime to true pathos, this thought, considering the initial and apparent opposites of ἦθος and πάθος, appears at first paradoxical. But we have shown that this, too, was present in antiquity: τὸ ἐν τῇ λέξει μέτριον καὶ ἐπιεικὲς ἦθος ἔχον εὔνουν ποιεῖ τὸν ἀκροατὴν, καὶ παθητικὸν ἀπεργάξεται λόγον (Ulpian docet ad Demosthen. Olynth. I sub initio, in Ernesti, Lex. Rhet. Graec. Techn., 150). Indeed, the differentiation of the sublime and the pathetic, which goes back to the ἤθη-πάθη formula, was an ever-present thought for Wordsworth. He tied it time and again directly to poetic endeavor, in which he sees, poetically speaking, the human element. The critical formula reaches down to the depths of the ongoing poetic concern: "Paul and David may be called the two Shakespearean characters in the Bible; both types, as it were, of human nature in its strength and weakness. Moses is grand, but then it is chiefly from position, from the office he had entrusted to him. We do not know him as a Man, as a brother man" (*Prose Works* III: 455, ed. Grosart). What else is this, if not the statement that Paul and David are of pathetic nature, Moses, however, is sublime. The contrast is "Shakespearean characters . . . of human nature in its strength and weakness" on one hand, and "grand . . . not as a Man, a brother man" on the other. It is nothing else and follows Quinitilian's identical thought processes when the latter paraphrases the ἦθος with "blandum et humanum" and as "quod est sine dubio inter coniunctas maxime personas, quoties perferimus, satisfacimus, monemus, procul ab ira, procul ab odio," differentiating it as the mild and human emotion (Wordsworth's "Man, brother man") from the majestic πάθος (Wordsworth's "grand," the sublime per se) as a noble, heroic emotion that transcends the human. As "moral and tender-hearted" (notice the pairing: it is not natural, but at first rather the exact opposite) versus "lofty," i.e., "grand" or "sublime") we discover the same contrast of the pathetic as the "human-gentle" versus the sublime as the "greatness-grandeur," i.e., the ἦθος versus the πάθος, in the following extremely enlightening passage: "Simonides, it is related, upon landing in a strange country, found the corpse of an unknown person lying by the sea-side; he buried it, and was honoured throughout Greece for the piety of the act. Another ancient philosopher, chancing to fix his eyes upon a dead body, regarded the same with slight, if not with contempt, saying, 'See the shell of the flown bird!' But it is not to be supposed that the moral and tender-hearted Simonides was incapable of the lofty movements of thought, to which that other Sage gave way at the moment while his soul was intent only upon the indestructible being, ... each of these sages was in sympathy with the best feelings of our nature; feelings which, though they seem opposite to each other, have another and a finer connection than that of contrast" (Upon Epitaphs I, *Prose Works* II: 129–30). Consequently the basically human, gentle attitude characterizes the pathetic—here separated from the "sublime"—while the "sublime," the "lofty," is suprahuman, lofty, divine, and elevates the human being beyond its human state. Another paraphrase of the by now already familiar differentiation ... attributes to the pathetic "peculiarity in the situation," "specific indications of Manners and Passions" while attributing to the sublime "obvious and general indications of passion": "the profound and the exquisite in feeling, the lofty and universal in thought and imagination; or, in ordinary language, the pathetic and sublime;—are neither of them, accurately speaking, objects of a faculty which could ever without a sinking in the spirit of Nations have been designated by the metaphor—Taste."[6] All these passages show clearly that each of these differentiations is based on the same antithetical formulalike thought process, and the epithets "moral and tenderhearted" on one hand and "lofty" on the other point conclusively to ἦθος, "mores," and to πάθος, the "grand," the "sublime."

After providing these proofs, our working thesis about the effectiveness of the ἦθη-πάθη formula should not have appeared as beating a dead horse, especially if we believe it confirmed in the end in the most important passage of Wordsworth's aesthetic criticism and if we are now attempting to discover behind the continuously inspiring character of this formula its system-building impact. The aesthetic intent, initially set in motion by the originally rhetorical formula, the planning framework and determining of values set in motion by the formula are evolving into a program whose—as we shall see—Rousseauesque basic tenor turns out be time and again the old ἦθη-πάθη formula used as a developing basis, as its catalyst. Wordsworth does apply the "manners" concept ... in such a way that rhetoric formula and world view/revolutionary experience overlap and complement each other. In the aesthetic writings of the seventeenth and eighteenth centuries, "manners" does not only take its objective meaning of "Sitten" or "more gentle affects" or "character" from the synonymous usage of ἦθος and ἠθικὸς λόγος, from ἦθος and ἠθοποιία, but also the dynamic meaning of "description of manners or milder affects," "presentations according to character," this "being able to put oneself from the point of view of the narrator in the true condition of any person," the way Lessing did. Rhetoric consequently does not only mean that the speaker presents "manners" but that he have "manners," which means nothing else but that he has the ability to present "manners." ...

Ultimately and with every semblance of probability, we can thus suppose that Wordsworth has in mind this dynamic usage of the word "manners" when in a letter addressed to Coleridge from the year 1797, comparing Bürger with Burns, he laments "Bürger's lack of manners" (ἀήθης), "whereas in Burns you have manners everywhere" (*Early Letters of William Wordsworth* 229).

That in this Bürger-Burns criticism, in which ἦθος appears as "manners," the ἤθη-πάθη formula has established itself as leitmotif is acknowledged by Coleridge himself, who varies and even synonymizes the same thought in his answer to Wordsworth by substituting Wordsworth's "lack of manners" with a lack of "presence of character in his personages" and describing this now as the source of "delicate and minute feelings." It is precisely these "delicate and minute feelings" that Wordsworth connects with the concept of "manners": "the profound and exquisite in feeling" he considers in 1815 the mark of pathos, which, as we have seen above in detail, is the "sublime" modified by ἦθος, i.e., by "manners" or "character." Coleridge says: "Bürger is one of those authors I like to have in my hand, but when I have laid down the book I do not think about him. I remember a hurry of pleasure, but I have few distinct forms that people my mind, nor any recollection of delicate or minute feelings which he has either communicated to me, or taught me to recognise. I do not perceive the presence of character in his personages. I see everywhere the character of Bürger himself; and even this, I agree with you, is no mean merit. But yet I wish him sometimes at least to make man forget himself in his creations. It seems to me that in poems descriptive of human nature, however short they may be, character is absolutely necessary etc., incidents are among the lowest allurements of poetry" (*Letters of Coleridge* 273). Here we have again, as above, "incidents" coupled with "manners." Here one almost seems to hear, in the antithesis "character is absolutely necessary"–"incidents are among the lowest allurement of poetry," Aristotle explicitly opposed: ἄνευ μὲν πράξεως οὐκ ἄν γένοιτο τραγῳδία, ἄνευ δὲ ἠθῶν γένοιτ ἄν. Wordsworth, however, seems to deny the dynamic, i.e., the specifically rhetorical coloration of the "manner" concept almost immediately, lapsing completely into the Rousseau mood of his time when he continues: "Not transitory manners reflecting the wearisome, unintelligible obliquities of city life, but manners connected with the permanent objects of nature, and partaking of the simplicity of these objects." That the ἤθη part of the ἤθη-πάθη formula is at work in these lines can be seen with absolute conviction in a key passage that takes up the ἤθη-πάθη formula in the Preface of 1800, written two years after this letter: "Low and rural life was generally chosen, because, in that condition, the essential *passions* of the heart find a better soil in which they can attain their maturity, are less under restraint, and speak a plainer and more emphatic language; because in that condition of life our *elementary feelings* co-exist in greater simplicity, and consequently, may be more accurately contemplated; because the *manners* of rural life germinate from those elementary feelings, and from the necessary character of rural occupation, are more easily comprehended, and are more durable; and lastly, because in that condition the passions of men are incorporated with the beautiful and permanent forms of nature." The passage of the letter from 1797: "In Burns you have manners everywhere . . . manners connected with the permanent objects of nature, and participating of the simplicity of these objects"; the 1800 Preface: "manners of rural life germinating from those elementary feelings" and "passions incorporated with the beautiful and permanent forms of nature"— these are not merely rhapsodic-sentimental Rousseauisms in the Romantic manner, not mere "sentimentality"—although, of course, they qualify for that, too—these are, if considered in connection with our quest, just as much formulations based on a preoccupation with a rhetorical concept, a preoccupation influenced by multifaceted aesthetic currents, formulations which, despite an attempt at paraphrasing elements, continue to remain within the constraints of the system of the formula using it time and again as a planning outline. Thus we finally come back to the ἤθη-πάθη formula, the most important point as an expression of the poet's valid object of poetry at large, exactly the way Lessing had expressed it at the end of the *Hamburgische Dramaturgie,* his lifetime preoccupation with the "manners and passions" as the object of poetry: "It is apprehended, that the more conversant the reader is with our elder writers, and with those in modern times who have been the most successful in painting manners and passions, the fewer complaints of this kind will he have to make" (Advertisement to *Lyrical Ballads,* 1798). This is taken up again in 1815, here too in a most important passage: "Invention—by which characters are composed out of materials supplied by observation, whether of the Poet's own heart and mind, or of external life and nature; and such incidents and situations produced as are most impressive to the imagination, and most fitted to do justice to the characters, sentiments, and passions, which the Poet undertakes to illustrate" (Second Preface to the Edition of 1815). This represents, after all we have shown, not merely a conventional and meaningless phrase using the "manners and passions" or "characters, sentiments, passions" as they had been used as the object of poetry throughout the entire seventeenth and eighteenth centuries, but a programmatic and well-considered usage of the old ἤθη-πάθη formula, a commitment to a poetic program that sees in the representation of the emotions, and only in it, the essence of poetry.

An examination like this would make little sense if it added another and possibly peripheral influence to the many literary influences that are supposed to help us understand the personality of a poet according to its individuality and its position in literary history. The validity of our findings can only be proved if they can serve to clarify other problems or to help shed new light on them. If the thesis of this essay is to have any validity, does it shed new light upon the poet, possibly upon a central point in his work, possibly also upon his time? Is the ἤθη-πάθη formula, i.e., the assessment of the rhetorical theory of the emotions with its differentiation between the general and vehement passions and the humane, more tender and less passionate emotions, are those inclinations and friendly attitudes as they evolve from human relationships suitable for interpretation, and do they reveal further affinities?

Already a brief overview of Wordsworth's poetic work shows that the poet harbored a slight dislike of heroic and vehement passions (something also apparent in his choice of subjects), that he preferred to describe the ἤθη that are not "sublime" and "grand" and "lofty"—"sublime" and "lofty" being his favorite epithets for nature, the majestic cosmic manifestations, meditations about the highest things like immortality, duty, God—but on the contrary just "pathetic" in the sense of the word as we specified above, the lasting and persistent gentle emotions flowing from the lasting, natural, and characteristically human situations, "maternal passion," "fraternal, or to speak more correctly, moral attachment," "passion of property," etc. Garrod has shown, in his fine series of Wordsworth lectures, how Wordsworth, after the crisis of his youth, attains the heights of his poetic power and the perfection *(Vollendung)* of his philosophical assessment of the world.[7] He attains human maturity and moral stability by going beyond the passionate, sensualistic, nature experiences to arrive at a new sense of the world sublimated through the "affections," the experiences of the human condition, that no longer know the excitement of the youthful "passion," but a more profound view transmitted through the experiences of the human being, "the still sad music of humanity":

> She gave me eyes, she gave me ears,
> And humble cares, and delicate fears;
> A heart,—the fountain of sweet tears—
> And love, and thought, and joy . . .

> Thanks to the human heart by which we live,
> Thanks to its tenderness, its joys and fears,
> To me the meanest flower that blooms can give
> Thoughts that do often lie too deep for tears . . .

What here constitutes objectively the difference between the "passions" and the "humble cares and delicate fears," is shown even clearer with the terminology: in addition to "passions," Wordsworth knows the "affections," and he values them higher:

> And if the vulgar joy by its own weight
> Wearied itself out of the memory,
> The scenes which were a witness to that joy
> Remained in their substantial lineaments

# Appendix

> Depicted on the brain, and to the eye
> Were visible, a daily sight; and thus,
> By the impressive discipline of fear,
> By pleasure and repeated happiness, and by force
> Of obscure feelings representative
> Of things forgotten, these same scenes so bright,
> So beautiful, so majestic in themselves
> Though yet the day was distant, did become
> Habitually dear, and all their forms
> And changeful colours by invisible links
> Were fastened to the affections.

Just as the distinction between the "sublime" and the "pathetic" is here again taken up by transforming the "beautiful and majestic" of nature through the emotions of "fear," "pleasure," and "happiness" to "habitually dear" and therefore "affection," in the same way the "habitual" is seen as the counter- or corresponding concept to "passions" and is added to it in a quasi-formula:

> Sometimes it suits me better to invent
> A tale from my own heart, more near akin
> To my own passions and habitual thoughts,
> Some variegated story, in the main
> Lofty.[8]

That (according to our considerations) the "affections" have something in common with the "manners," the "mores," or Quintilian's ἦθος, becomes quite obvious in a passage in which Wordsworth attempts to portray that condition of "passionate" experiencing where passion has not been allayed to "affection." At that time he was "to the moral power, / The affections and the spirit of the place / Insensible." Confronted with such passages, one is tempted to assume that he had Quintilian's definition of the ἦθος as "blandum et humanum" in mind when he wrote that he had learned "To look on Nature, not as in the hour / Of thoughtless youth, but hearing oftentimes / The still sad music of humanity," and when he warned a friend not to imitate Shelley, known already by his generation as the poet of the "sublime," that attempting "to outsoar the humanities" was detrimental to poetry (*Prose Works*, III:489, ed. Grosart). If one compares such passages with such clearly formulalike strings as "intellectual instincts, affections, and passions" (*Letters of the Wordsworth Family* I:58), which appear several times, the proximity of "affections" and "manners" becomes quite obvious.

From all that has been said, the following corresponding string for the differentiation of "passions" from "manners" can be established: passions/manners, sublime/pathetic, general and vague ideas/happiness in the circumstances peculiar to the situation and character, sources of sublimity remote from the cares of life/human nature in its strength and weakness, lofty and universal in thought and imagination/profound and exquisite in feeling, lofty movements of thought/moral and tender-hearted, beautiful and majestic/habitually dear, passions/affections. In view of this corresponding string, it is quite plausible that the frequent use of the epithet "habitual" as a description of the "affections" in contrast to the "passions," goes back to the popular discussion of the ἦθος—or the "manners"— concept that undoubtedly had evolved from interpretations of Aristotle. Twining's famous translation of the *Poetics* had appeared in 1789 in Cambridge. Wordsworth was surely familiar with it. It attempted to clarify the concept as follows: "The word ἦθος, taken in its utmost extent, includes everything that is habitual and characteristic, but it is often used in a limited sense for the habitual temper or disposition."[9]

Looking at it this way and pointing to the rhetorical formulas of the theory of emotions in Wordsworth's work . . . they are beginning to have consequences within intellectual history. For if one is ready to accept the still prevailing strength of such a tradition, the question arises whether additional critical concepts—until now considered to be expressions of Wordsworth's new, specifically Romantic attitude toward life—do not, in reality, emanate from older currents of traditions and hence need to be understood from thence. I am thinking about expressions such as "emotion recollected in tranquillity" and "overflow of spontaneous feelings." It is known that Wordsworth was profoundly influenced by Burke's separation of the "Sublime" and the "Beautiful" and adopted from it many antitheses like "love and fear" and the frequent mentioning of "fear" as the motif of the feeling of the sublime. But it seems likely that—starting with the presence of rhetorical formulas in Wordsworth's work—many other proofs will turn up pointing to his participation in the tradition of classical rhetoric and his serious preoccupation with it, proofs which then will go beyond Burke to others who transmitted it and possibly revealing the sources themselves. . . .

One could, with a further strengthening of our thesis, conceivably arrive at a Wordsworth picture that does not put him as much at the beginning of the modern, i.e., subjective-romantic, poetry in England (that sees in the confession of the poet's personality, in the expression, and in the symbol the essence of poetic expression), but rather at the end of the objective-classical writings based, in the last analysis, upon the classical attitudes which, while postulating the excitement of the emotions as the poet's greatest task, attribute to him an essentially moral function of guiding the soul, the psychagogy, which, considered in its intellectual and stylistic development, belongs with its manifestions for the continuation of Antiquity to the Renaissance and the Baroque era and therefore not to the Romantic one. Nor would the poet then belong to the Romantic category of the natural genius, but in a very specific sense to that of the consciously creating artist who, finding himself under the influence of critical thought processes, adjusts his writing accordingly and who, when writing, wants to give these critical outlines conscious poetic expression. . . .

## NOTES

1. See A. E. Beatty, *William Wordsworth*, Madison, 1922; A. C. Bradley, *English Poetry and German Philosophy in the Age of Wordsworth*, Manchester, 1904; W. P. Stallknecht, "Wordsworth and Philosophy," *PMLA* 44:116–43; Melvin Rader, *Presiding Ideas in Wordsworth's Poetry*, Seattle, 1931; O. J. Campbell, *Sentimental Morality in Wordsworth's Narrative Poetry*, Wisconsin, 1920.

2. The affective content, the emotional moment of the concept "moral," is very obvious in Shaftesbury: "By the word moral are understood in this place all sorts of judicious representations of the human passions." Quoted by Weiser in *Shaftesbury und das deutsche Geistesleben* (Shaftesbury and the German intellectual life), 111.

3. "Circumstances," too, is a specifically rhetorical terminus technicus. It actually belongs to the teaching about πίστεις: characters as well as actions can—according to their motives—be determined by circumstances. Quintilian writes (*Institutio Oratoria* V, 10, 104): "hoc genus argumentorum sane dicamus ex circumstantia, quia πρίστασιν dicere aliter non possumus." Circumstances surrounding the actions, "accidentia," are, according to Quintilian, causa, tempus, locus, occasio, instrumentum, modus et cetera (V, 10, 23); for persons: natio, patria, sexus, aetas, educatio et disciplina, habitus corporis, fortuna, condicio, animi natura, victus, studia, quid adfectet quisque, commotio, nomen. This enumeration shows the proximity to the ἦθος theory most clearly. In yet another passage Quintilian paraphrases the "rerum accidentia" with "aut quare aut ubi aut quando aut quo modo aut per quae" (V, 10, 32). All this is taken directly from the practice of court speech and transfers easily from the theory of testimony into the theory of emotions, where it was particularly easy to couple them with the "mores." In the rhetoric of the late classical period "septem circumstantiae" become canonical, cf. Ernesti, Lex. Rhet. Techn. Lat.: Fortun. Rhetor, 2, 1, 102, 1: "Reperto statu quid consideremes? totam materiem per septem circumstantias ... quae sunt circumstantiae? persona, res, causa, tempus, locus, modus, materia." The item "Umstand" (circumstances) in Grimm's *Wörterbuch* is quite revealing in regard to this entire problem. In it "circumstances" is given three different meanings as, among others: "in the beginning demonstrated by speech." From the court speech and by way of rhetoric, the theory about "circumstances" shifts to the theory of confessions: "this I will show now that we may learn what is meant by a circumstance, being understood in the Bible generally and by all circumstances. ... 'Circumstances' are: where, how, when, and person, time, what kind of person or against whom" (Zwingli, *Freiheit der Speisen*). It is interesting to find in this context of the application of rhetorical terminology to theological problems also the pertinent ethopoiie in Zwingli. In this way he differentiates the ethopoiie as it appears in passages like John 12: 32 and 3: 13, from the figure of speech of the alloeose occurring in other passages in the Bible. "Poetry of manners, in which manners are assigned to a person, manners that do not come naturally, such a kind of poetry that Paulus needed from Christ to much greater extent" (Loofs, *Lehrbuch der Dogmengeschichte*, 365). That God, in order to adjust the words of the revelation (which human beings are incapable of comprehending) to the human being and its manner of speech (the so-called συγκατάβασις of God), carried on ethopoiie in a big way is one of the oldest teachings of the Fathers of the Church.

4. *Letters of the Wordsworth Family* II:403, ed. Knight, Boston.

5. *Prose Works*, II:183, ed. Knight.

6. Essay Supplementary to the Edition of 1815. Within the framework of this study (which is devoted exclusively to the "manners-passions" formula), it is impossible to pursue any further proofs contained in the two last mentioned passages regarding Wordsworth's concept of the "sublime" and his sources. This will be reserved for later studies of the "elevated and beautiful" in Wordsworth. Such studies will not be able to get around examining most carefully the classical conceptuality of these notions.

Burke's "love and fear," as the twin sources of the beautiful and the elevated, are by far not the only notions Wordsworth entertained.

7. H. W. Garrod, *Wordsworth*, Oxford, 1927.

8. Here, by the way, in "some variegated story in the main lofty," the "dignified and variegated" is taken up again, whose classical provenance we have shown at the beginning of this examination. "Variegated, in the main lofty" is the stylistic characteristic of the epic and reappears in similar formulations hundredfold in the aesthetic criticism of the sixteenth through eighteenth centuries.

9. Buckley, *The Rhetoric of Aristotle*.

# Select Bibliography

Aarsleff, Hans. *From Locke to Saussure; Essays on the Study of Language and Intellectual History*. Minneapolis: U Minnesota P, 1982.
———. *The Study of Language in England 1780–1860*. Princeton: Princeton UP, 1967.
Abbey, Lloyd. *Destroyer and Preserver: Shelley's Poetic Skepticism*. Lincoln: U of Nebraska P, 1979.
Abrams, M. H. *The Mirror and the Lamp*. New York: Oxford UP, 1953.
———. "Structure and Style in the Greater Romantic Lyric." In *Romanticism and Consciousness*. Ed. Harold Bloom. New York: Norton, 1970. 201–29.
Addison, Joseph. *The Works of the Right Honourable Joseph Addison*. Ed. Henry G. Bohn. 6 vols. London: Henry G. Bohn, 1856.
*Ad C. Herennium (Rhetorica ad Herennium)*. Trans. Harry Caplan. London: Heinemann, 1954.
Aeschines. "The Oration of Aeschines *Against Ctesiphon*." *Orations of Demosthenes Pronounced to Excite the Athenians against Philip, King of Macedon; and on Occasions of Public Deliberation*. Trans. Thomas Leland. Rev. ed. New York: Colonial, 1900. 281–349.
Alter, Robert. *The Art of Biblical Poetry*. New York: Basic, 1985.
Altick, Robert. *The English Common Reader*. Chicago: U of Chicago P, 1957.
*The Arabian Nights' Entertainments*. Trans. M. Galland. 14th ed. 4 vols. London: T. Longman, 1778.
Arac, Jonathan. *Critical Genealogies: Historical Situations for Postmodern Literary Studies*. New York: Columbia UP, 1987.
Arieti, James A., and John M. Crossett, trans. [Longinus.] *On the Sublime*. Texts and Studies in Religion. Vol. 21. New York: Mellen, 1985.
Aristotle. *The "Art" of Rhetoric*. Trans. John Henry Freese. Cambridge: Harvard UP, 1959.
———. *Politics*. Trans. H. Rackham. London: Heinemann, 1959.
———. *Rhetoric*. Ed. Lane Cooper. Englewood Cliffs, N.J.: Prentice, 1932.
———. *On Rhetoric*. Trans. George A. Kennedy. New York: Oxford UP, 1991.
Auerbach, Erich. "Dante's Addresses to the Reader." *Romance Philology* 7 (1953–54): 268–78.
———. *Literary Language and Its Public in Late Latin Antiquity and in the Middle Ages*. Trans. Ralph Manheim. Bollingen Series 74. New York: Pantheon, 1965.
Augustine. *The Confessions of Saint Augustine*. Trans. Edward B. Pusey. New York: Modern Library, 1949.
Austen, Jane. *Mansfield Park*. *The Novels of Jane Austen*. Ed. R. W. Chapman. 3d ed. Oxford: Clarendon, 1933. Reprint 1949.
———. *Northanger Abbey*. *The Novels of Jane Austen*. Ed. R. W. Chapman. 3d ed. Oxford: Clarendon, 1933. Reprint 1949.
———. *Persuasion*. *The Novels of Jane Austen*. Ed. R. W. Chapman. 3d ed. Oxford: Clarendon, 1933. Reprint 1949.
———. *Pride and Prejudice*. *The Novels of Jane Austen*. Ed. R. W. Chapman. 3d ed. Oxford: Clarendon, 1933. Reprint 1949.
———. *Sense and Sensibility*. *The Novels of Jane Austen*. Ed. R. W. Chapman. 3d ed. Oxford: Clarendon, 1933. Reprint 1949.

Bahti, Timothy. "Figures of Interpretation, the Interpretation of Figures: A Reading of Wordworth's 'Dream of the Arab.'" *Studies in Romanticism* 18 (1979): 601–20.
———. "Wordsworth's Rhetorical Theft." In *Romanticism and Language*. Ed. Arden Reed. Ithaca: Cornell UP, 1984. 86–124.
Barilli, Renato. *Rhetoric*. Trans. Giuliana Menozzi. Minneapolis: U of Minnesota P, 1989.
Barnouw, Jeffrey. "Peirce and Derrida: 'Natural Signs' Empiricism versus 'Originary Trace' Deconstruction." *Poetics Today* 7 (1986): 73–94.
Barth, J. Robert. S. J. "The Poet, Death, and Immortality: The Unity of *The Prelude*, Book V." *Wordsworth Circle* 10 (1979): 69–75.
Barthes, Roland. *Image-Music-Text*. London: Fontana, 1977.
Bateson, F. W. *Wordsworth: A Re-Interpretation*. 2d ed. London: Longmans, 1956.
Beattie, James. *Dissertations Moral and Critical*. London: Strahan, 1783.
———. *Essays on Poetry and Music As They Affect the Mind*. Edinburgh: William Creech, 1778.
Beer, John B. "Blake and Augustine." *Times Literary Supplement* July 2, 1970, 726–27.
Behrendt, Stephen C. *Shelley and His Audiences*. Lincoln: U of Nebraska P, 1989.
Bender, John, and David E. Wellbery, eds. *The Ends of Rhetoric: History, Theory, Practice*. Stanford: Stanford UP, 1990.
Bender, Wolfgang. "Rhetorische Tradition und Asthetik im 18. Jahrhundert." *Zeitschrift für deutsche Philologie* 99 (1980): 481–506.
Bernhardt-Kabisch, Ernest. "The Stone and the Shell: Wordsworth, Cataclysm, and the Myth of Glaucus." *Studies in Romanticism* 23 (1984): 455–90.
Bewell, Alan. *Wordsworth and the Enlightenment: Nature, Man, and Society in the Experimental Poetry*. New Haven: Yale UP, 1989.
Bialostosky, Don. *Making Tales: The Poetics of Wordsworth's Narrative Experiments*. Chicago: U of Chicago P, 1984.
———. *Wordsworth, Dialogics, and the Practice of Criticism*. Cambridge: Cambridge UP, 1992.
Bitzer, Lloyd, and Edwin Black. *The Prospect of Rhetoric*. Englewood Cliffs, N.J.: Prentice, 1971.
Bizzell, Patricia, and Bruce Herzberg, eds. *The Rhetorical Tradition*. Boston: St. Martin's, 1990.
Blackwell, Thomas. *An Enquiry into the Life and Writings of Homer*. 1736. New York: George Olms Verlag, 1976.
Blair, Hugh. *Lectures on Rhetoric and Belles-Lettres*. 3 vols. London: Strahan, 1783.
———. *Lectures on Rhetoric and Belles Lettres*. 1783. Ed. Harold F. Harding. Foreword by David Potter. 2 vols. Carbondale: Southern Illinois UP, 1965.
———. *Lectures on Rhetoric and Belles Lettres*. Philadelphia: Robert Aitken, 1784.
———. *Lectures on Rhetoric and Belles Lettres*. Philadelphia: S. C. Hayes, 1860.
Blake, William. *The Book of Urizen*. *The Complete Poetry and Prose of William Blake*. Ed. David V. Erdman. New York: Doubleday, 1988.
———. *The Complete Poetry and Prose of William Blake*. Ed. David V. Erdman. Garden City, N.Y.: Anchor, 1982.
———. *The Illuminated Blake*. Ed. David V. Erdman. Garden City, N.Y.: Doubleday, 1974.
Bloom, Harold. *The Anxiety of Influence*. New York: Oxford UP, 1973.
———. *Blake's Apocalypse: A Study in Poetic Argument*. 1963. New York: Anchor, 1965.
———. *The Visionary Company*. Ithaca: Cornell UP, 1971.
———. *Wallace Stevens: Poems of Our Climate*. Ithaca: Cornell UP, 1977.
Bloomfield, Morton W. "Personification-Metaphors." *Chaucer Review* 14 (1980): 287–97.
Blount, Thomas. *The Academy of Eloquence*. 1654. Menston: Scolar P, 1971.

Bonner, S. F. *Roman Declamation in the Late Republic and Early Empire.* Berkeley: U of California P, 1949.
Booth, Wayne C. "The Scope of Rhetoric Today: A Polemical Excursion." In *The Prospect of Rhetoric.* Ed. Lloyd F. Bitzer and Edwin Black. Englewood Cliffs, N.J.: Prentice, 1971.
Bornstein, George. *Transformations of Romanticism in Yeats, Eliot and Stevens.* Chicago: U of Chicago P, 1976.
Bourdieu, Pierre. *Outline of a Theory of Practice.* Trans. Richard Nice. Cambridge: Cambridge UP, 1977.
Boyer, James. "Liber Aureus." British Museum, Ashley MS. 3506.
Brett, R. L., and A. R. Jones, eds. *"Lyrical Ballads": Wordsworth and Coleridge.* London: Methuen, 1963.
Brisman, Leslie. *Milton's Poetry of Choice and Its Romantic Heirs.* Ithaca: Cornell UP, 1973.
———. *Romantic Origins.* Ithaca: Cornell UP, 1978.
Brooks, Cleanth. "Coleridge as Metaphysical Poet." In *Romanticism: Vistas, Instances, Continuities.* Ed. David Thorburn and Geoffrey Hartmann. Ithaca: Cornell UP, 1973. 143–54.
———. *The Well-Wrought Urn: Studies in the Structure of Poetry.* 1947. New York: Harcourt, 1975.
Brown, Marshall. Forum. *PMLA* 99 (1984): 997.
Browne, Thomas Gunter. *Hermes Unmasked; or, The Art of Speech Founded on the Association of Words and Ideas.* London: T. Payne, 1795.
———. *The Way of Things by Words, and to Words by Things.* London: Davies and Reymers, 1766.
Bruns, Gerald L. *Inventions: Writing, Textuality, and Understanding in Literary History.* New Haven: Yale UP, 1982.
Buchan, David. *The Ballad and the Folk.* London: Routledge, 1972.
Buickerood, James G. "The Natural History of Understanding: Locke and the Rise of Facultative Logic in the Eighteenth Century." *History and Philosophy of Logic* 6 (1985): 157–90.
Burgess, Theodore C. "Epideictic Literature." *U of Chicago Studies in Classical Philology* 3 (1902): 89–261.
Burwick, Frederick. Introduction. *Selected Essays on Rhetoric by Thomas De Quincey.* Carbondale: Southern Illinois UP, 1967.
Butler, Marilyn. *Romantics, Rebels, and Reactionaries.* New York: Oxford UP, 1981.
Byron, George Gordon, Lord. *Byron.* Ed. Jerome J. McGann. Oxford: Oxford UP, 1986.
———. *The Complete Poetical Works.* Ed. Jerome J. McGann. 6 vols. Oxford: Clarendon, 1980–90.
———. *Don Juan. The Poetical Works of Lord Byron.* Ed. Humphrey Milford. London: Oxford UP, 1921.
———. *The Works of Lord Byron with his Letters and Journals and his Life.* Ed. Thomas Moore. London, 1832.
Campbell, George. *The Philosophy of Rhetoric.* 2 vols. London: Strahan, 1776.
———. *The Philosophy of Rhetoric.* Ed. Lloyd F. Bitzer. Carbondale: Southern Illinois UP, 1963.
Carrino, Elnora. "Conceptions of Dispositio in Ancient Rhetoric." Ph.D. dissertation. Ann Arbor: University Microfilms, 1959.
Cassirer, Ernst. *The Philosophy of the Enlightenment.* Boston: Beacon, 1955.
Cervantes. *Historia del Famosa Cavallero Don Quixote de la Mancha.* Ed. Rev. D. J. Bowle. London and Salisbury: B. White, P. Elmsley, 1781.
———. *The Ingenious Gentleman Don Quixote de la Mancha.* Trans. Samuel Putnam. 2 vols. New York: Viking, 1949.

Chandler, James K. *Wordsworth's Second Nature: A Study of the Poetry and Politics.* Chicago: U of Chicago P, 1984.

Chase, Cynthia. *Decomposing Figures: Rhetorical Readings in the Romantic Tradition.* Baltimore: Johns Hopkins UP, 1986.

Christensen, Jerome. *Coleridge's Blessed Machine of Language.* Ithaca: Cornell UP, 1981.

Cicero, Marcus Tullius. *Ad C. Herennium (Rhetorica ad Herennium).* Trans. Harry Caplan. London: Heinemann, 1954.

———. *De Inventione.* Trans. H. M. Hubbell. London: Heinemann, 1976.

———. *De Officiis.* Trans. Walter Miller. London: Heinemann, 1961.

———. *De Oratore.* Trans. H. Rackham. 2 vols. London: Heinemann, 1942.

———. *De Oratore. Cicero on Oratory and Orators.* Trans. J. S. Watson. Introduction by Ralph A. Micken. Carbondale: Southern Illinois UP, 1970.

———. *Orator.* Trans. H. M. Hubbell. London: Heinemann, 1939.

———. *Selected Works.* Trans. Michael Grant. Harmondsworth: Penguin, 1971.

Clarke, C. C. *Romantic Paradox: An Essay on the Poetry of Wordsworth.* Westport: Greenwood, 1962.

Cohen, Murray. *Sensible Words: Linguistic Practice in England, 1670–1785.* Baltimore: Johns Hopkins UP, 1977.

Coleman, Deirdre. "Re-living Jacobinism: Wordsworth and the Convention of Cintra." *Yearbook of English Studies* 19 (198): 144–61.

Coleridge, Samuel Taylor. *Aids to Reflection, in the formation of a manly character on the several grounds of prudence, morality and religion.* London: Taylor and Hessey, 1825.

———. *Biographia Literaria, or Biographical Sketches of my Literary Life and Opinions.* 1817. Ed. James Engell and W. Jackson Bate. 2 vols. Princeton: Princeton UP, 1983.

———. *Coleridge's Miscellaneous Criticism.* Ed. Thomas Middleton Raysor. Cambridge: Harvard UP, 1936.

———. *Collected Letters of Samuel Taylor Coleridge.* Ed. Carl Leslie Griggs. 6 vols. Oxford: Clarendon, 1956–71.

———. *The Collected Works of Samuel Taylor Coleridge.* Princeton: Princeton UP, 1969–.

———. *Essays on His Times.* Ed. David V. Erdman. 3 vols. London: Routledge, 1978.

———. [Essay Written at Christ's Hospital.] *Illustrated London News,* April 1, 1893, 398.

———. *The Friend.* Ed. Barbara E. Rooke. 2 vols. Princeton: Princeton UP, 1969.

———. *Lay Sermons.* Ed. R. J. White. *The Collected Works of Samuel Taylor Coleridge.* Princeton: Princeton UP, 1972.

———. *Lectures 1795 on Politics and Religion.* Ed. Lewis Patton and Peter Mann. *The Collected Works of Samuel Taylor Coleridge.* Princeton: Princeton UP, 1971.

———. *Lectures 1808–1819 on Literature.* 2 vols. Ed. R. A. Foakes. Princeton: Princeton UP, 1987.

———. *The Notebooks of Samuel Taylor Coleridge.* Ed. Kathleen Coburn. Vols. 1 and 2, New York: Bollingen/Pantheon, 1957, 1961. Vol. 3, Princeton: Princeton/Bollingen, 1973.

———. *On the Constitution of the Church and State.* Ed. John Colmer. Vol. 10. *The Collected Works of Samuel Taylor Coleridge.* Princeton: Princeton UP, 1976.

———. *The Poems of Samuel Taylor Coleridge.* Ed. E. H. Coleridge. 1912. London: Oxford UP, 1960.

———. *Shakespearean Criticism.* Ed. Thomas Middleton Raysor. 2 vols. London: Constable, 1930.

———. *The Statesman's Manual. Lay Sermons.* Ed. R. J. White. Princeton: Princeton UP, 1972.

———. *Table Talk*. (Recorded by Henry Nelson Coleridge and John Taylor Coleridge.) 2 vols. Ed. Carl Woodring. Princeton: Princeton UP, 1990.
———. *The Watchman*. Ed. Lewis Patton. *The Collected Works of Samuel Taylor Coleridge*. Princeton: Princeton UP, 1970.
*College Examination Book*. 2 vols. College Archives MS. C.15.6, St. John's College, Cambridge.
Colmer, John. *Coleridge: Critic of Society*. Oxford: Clarendon, 1959.
Connors, Robert. "Greek Rhetoric and the Transition from Orality." *Philosophy and Rhetoric* 19 (1986): 38–65.
Cooke, Michael G. *Acts of Inclusion*. New Haven: Yale UP, 1979.
Cooper, Anthony Ashley, Third Earl of Shaftesbury. *Characteristics of Men, Manners, Opinions, Times, Etc.* Ed. John M. Robertson. 2 vols. London: G. Richards, 1900.
———. *Second Characters or the Language of Forms*. Ed. Benjamin Rand. New York: Greenwood, 1969.
Cooper, Lane. *A Concordance to the Poems of William Wordsworth*. London: Smith, Elder, 1911.
Corbett, Edward P. J. "John Locke's Contributions to Rhetoric." In *The Rhetorical Tradition and Modern Writing*. Ed. James J. Murphy. New York: MLA, 1982. 73–84.
Cousin, Jean. *Etudes sur Quintilian*. 1935. Rpt. Amsterdam: P. Schippers, 1967.
Covino, William. "Thomas De Quincey in a Revisionist History of Rhetoric." *Pre/Text* 4 (1983): 121–36.
Coward, Harold. "The Spiritual Power of Oral and Written Scripture." *Silence, the Word, and the Sacred*. Waterloo: Wilfred Laurier UP, 1989.
Culler, Jonathan. "Changes in the Study of the Lyric." In *Lyric Poetry: Beyond New Criticism*. Ed. Chaviva Hosek and Patricia Parker. Ithaca: Cornell UP, 1985. 38–54.
———. *Ferdinand de Saussure*. New York: Penguin, 1976.
———. *On Deconstruction*. Ithaca: Cornell UP, 1982.
———. *The Pursuit of Signs: Semiotics, Literature, Deconstruction*. Ithaca: Cornell UP, 1981.
———. "Reading Lyric: The Lesson of Paul de Man." *Yale French Studies* 69 (1985): 98–106.
———. *Structuralist Poetics: Structuralism, Linguistics, and the Study of Literature*. Ithaca: Cornell UP, 1975.
Curran, Stuart. "*Multum in Parvo*: Wordsworth's *Poems, in Two Volumes of 1807*." In *Poems in Their Place*. Ed. Neil Fraistat. Chapel Hill: U of North Carolina P, 1986.
———. "Wordsworth and the Forms of Poetry." In *The Age of William Wordsworth: Critical Essays on the Romantic Tradition*. Ed. Kenneth R. Johnston and Gene W. Ruoff. New Brunswick: Rutgers UP, 1987.
Curtis, Jared R., ed. *Poems, in Two Volumes, and Other Poems, 1800–1807 by William Wordsworth*. Ithaca: Cornell UP, 1983.
———. "William Wordsworth and English Poetry of the Sixteenth and Seventeenth Centuries." *Cornell Library Journal* 1 (1966): 28–39.
———. *Wordsworth's Experiments with Tradition: The Lyric Poems of 1802*. Ithaca: Cornell UP, 1971.
Curtius, Ernst R. *European Literature and the Latin Middle Ages*. Trans. Willard R. Trask. 1953. Princeton: Princeton UP, 1973.
Daiches, David. *The Paradox of Scottish Culture: The Eighteenth-Century Experience*. London: Oxford UP, 1964.
Damrosch, Leopold. "The Significance of Addison's Criticism." *SEL* 19 (1979): 430.
———. "William Warburton as 'New Critic.'" In *Studies in Criticism and Aesthetics:*

Essays in Honor of Samuel Holt Monk. Ed. Howard Anderson and John S. Shea. Minneapolis: U of Minnesota P, 1967.
Danby, John F. *The Simple Wordsworth: Studies in the Poems 1797–1807.* London: Routledge, 1960.
D'Angelo, Frank. "The Evolution of the Analytic Topoi." In *Essays on Classical Rhetoric and Discourse.* Ed. Robert J. Connors, Lisa S. Ede, and Andrea Lunsford. Carbondale: Southern Illinois UP, 1984. 50–68.
Darbishire, Helen, ed. *Wordsworth: "Poems in Two Volumes."* 1914. Oxford: Clarendon, 1952.
Daubuz, Charles. *A Perpetual Commentary on the Revelation of St. John.* London, 1720.
Day, Angel. *A Declaration of al such Tropes, Figures or Schemes. The English Secretary.* London, 1599.
DeLacy, P. H. "Cicero, Marcus Tullius." In *The Encyclopedia of Philosophy.* Ed. Paul Edwards. New York: Macmillan, 1967. 2: 113–14.
De Man, Paul. *Blindness and Insight: Essays in the Rhetoric of Contemporary Criticism.* 2d ed. Introduction by Wlad Godzich. Minneapolis: U of Minnesota P, 1983.
———. *The Resistance to Theory.* Foreword by Wlad Godzich. Minneapolis: U of Minnesota P, 1986.
———. *The Rhetoric of Romanticism.* New York: Columbia UP, 1984.
DeNeef, A. Leigh. "Epideictic Rhetoric and the Renaissance Lyric." *Journal of Medieval and Renaissance Studies* 3 (1973): 203–31.
De Quincey, Thomas. *The Collected Writings of Thomas De Quincey.* Ed. David Masson. 14 vols. Edinburgh: Adam and Charles Black, 1889–90.
———. *Confessions of an English Opium-Eater and Other Writings.* Ed. Grevel Lindop. New York: Oxford UP, 1985.
———. *Recollections of the Lakes and the Lake Poets.* Ed. David Wright. Harmondsworth: Penguin, 1970.
———. *Reminiscences of the English Lake Poets.* Introduction and notes by John E. Jordan. Rev. ed. London: Dent, 1961.
Demosthenes. *Demosthenes' On the Crown: A Critical Case Study of a Masterpiece of Ancient Oratory.* Ed. James J. Murphy. Trans. John J. Keaney. New York: Random, 1976.
———. *The Oration of Demosthenes On the Crown."* Trans. Francis P. Simpson. Rhetorical Commentary by Francis P. Donnelly, S.J. New York: Fordham UP, 1941.
Derrida, Jacques. *Of Grammatology.* Trans. Gayatri Chakravorty Spivak. Baltimore: Johns Hopkins UP, 1974.
———. *The Post Card: From Socrates to Freud and Beyond.* Trans. Alan Bass. Chicago: U of Chicago P, 1987.
———. "White Mythology: Metaphor in the Text of Philosophy." Trans. F. C. T. Moore. *New Literary History* 6 (1974): 5–74.
———. *Writing and Difference.* Trans. Alan Bass. Chicago: U of Chicago P, 1978.
Dickstein, Morris. "Coleridge, Wordsworth, and the 'Conversation Poems.'" *Centennial Review* 16 (1972): 367–83.
Doddridge, Philip. *The Family Expositor: or, A Paraphrase and Version of the New Testament.* 6 vols. London, 1792.
Downey, James. *The Eighteenth-Century Pulpit: A Study of the Sermons of Butler, Berkeley, Secker, Sterne, Whitefield and Wesley.* Oxford: Clarendon, 1969.
Downing, Richard. "Blake and Augustine." *Times Literary Supplement,* June 18, 1970, 662.
Dyck, Andrew R. "The Function and Persuasive Power of Demosthenes' Portrait of

## Select Bibliography

Aeschines in the Speech *On the Crown*." *Greece and Rome* 2d ser. 32 (1985): 42–48.
Eagleton, Terry. *Literary Theory: An Introduction.* Minneapolis: Minnesota UP, 1983.
Eisenstein, Elizabeth. *The Printing Press as an Agent of Change.* New York: Cambridge UP, 1980.
Ellis, David. *Wordsworth, Freud, and the Spots of Time: Interpretation in "The Prelude."* Cambridge: Cambridge UP, 1985.
Ellis, George. *Specimens of the Early English Poets.* Vol. 3. London: Henry Washbourne, 1845.
Emerson, Ralph Waldo. "The American Scholar." *Essays & Lectures.* New York: Library of America, 1983. 53–71.
———. *The Collected Works of Ralph Waldo Emerson.* Vol. 3. Ed. Joseph Slater et al. Cambridge: Harvard UP, 1983.
Erdman, David V. "*America*: New Expanses." In *Blake's Visionary Forms Dramatic.* Ed. David V. Erdman and John E. Grant. Princeton: Princeton UP, 1970. 92–114.
Fénelon, François de Salignac de la Mothe. *Dialogues on Eloquence in General.* Trans. William Stevenson. London, 1808.
Fenner, Dudley. *The Artes of Logike and Rhetorike.* N.p., 1584.
Ferguson, Frances. *Wordsworth: Language as Counter-Spirit.* New Haven: Yale UP, 1977.
Ferry, David. *The Limits of Mortality: An Essay on Wordsworth's Major Poems.* Middletown: Wesleyan UP, 1959.
Findlay, L. M. "Culler and Byron on Apostrophe and Lyric Time." *Studies in Romanticism* 24 (1985): 335–53.
Fine, John V. A. *The Ancient Greeks: A Critical History.* Cambridge: Harvard UP, 1983.
Fineman, Joel. *Shakespeare's Perjured Eye: The Invention of Poetic Subjectivity in the Sonnets.* Berkeley: U of California P, 1986.
Foerster, Donald M. *Homer in English Criticism: The Historical Approach in the Eighteenth Century.* New Haven: Yale UP, 1947.
Fowler, Alistair. *Kinds of Literature.* Cambridge: Harvard UP, 1982.
Fox, Susan. *Poetic Form in Blake's Milton.* Princeton: Princeton UP, 1976.
Fraunce, Abraham. *The Arcadian Rhetoric.* 1588. Menston: Scolar, 1969.
Freimarck, Vincent. Introduction to *Lectures on the Sacred Poetry of the Hebrews* by Robert Lowth. Trans. G. Gregory. St. Paul's Church Yard: J. Johnson, 1787. Rpt., Hildesheim: George Olms, 1969.
Friedman, Michael H. *The Making of a Tory Humanist: William Wordsworth and the Idea of Community.* New York: Columbia UP, 1979.
Frosch, Thomas R. "Wordsworth and the Matrix of Romance: *The Prelude*, Book V." *CUNY English Forum.* Ed. Saul N. Brody and Harold Schechter. Vol. 1. New York: AMS, 1985. 179–97.
Frost, Robert. *Complete Poems of Robert Frost.* London: Cape, 1951.
Fry, Paul H. *The Poet's Calling in the English Ode.* New Haven: Yale UP, 1980.
Frye, Northrop. *Fearful Symmetry: A Study of William Blake.* Princeton: Princeton UP, 1947.
Fumaroli, Marc. *L'Age de l'éloquence: Rhetorique et "res literaria" de la Renaissance au seuil de l'époque classique.* Geneva: Librarie Droz, 1980.
———. "Genèse de l'épistolographie classique: rhétorique humaniste de la lettre, de Petrarque à Juste Lipse." *Revue d'historie littéraire de la France* 78 (1978): 886–900.
Gallant, Christine, ed. *Coleridge's Theory of Imagination Today.* New York: AMS, 1989.

Galperin, William H. "Authority and Deconstruction in Book V of *The Prelude*." *Studies in English Literature* 26 (1986): 613–31.
Gardner, John. *The Life and Times of Chaucer*. New York: Vintage, 1978.
Gatta, John, Jr. "Coleridge and Allegory." *MLQ* 38 (1977): 62–77.
Genette, Gérard. *Figures in Literary Discourse*. Trans. Alan Sheridan. Oxford: Blackwell, 1982.
Gibbons, Thomas. *Rhetoric; Or a View of Its Principal Tropes and Figures*. 1767. Menston: Scolar, 1969.
———. *Rhetoric*. London: Oliver, 1767.
Giddens, Anthony. *Central Problems in Social Theory*. Berkeley: U of California P, 1979.
———. "Structuration Theory: Present, Past and Future." In *Giddens' Theory of Structuration*. Ed. Christopher G. A. Bryant and David Jary. New York: Routledge, 1991. 201–21.
Gill, John. *An Exposition of the Old Testament*. 6 vols. 1748–63. Philadelphia, 1818.
Gill, Stephen. *William Wordsworth: A Life*. Oxford: Clarendon, 1989.
Gillham, D. G. "Wordsworth's Hidden Figures of Speech." In *Generous Converse: English Essays in Memory of Edward Davis*. Ed. Brian Green. Cape Town: Oxford UP, 1980. 79–87.
Glen, Heather. *Vision and Disenchantment: Blake's "Songs" and Wordsworth's "Lyrical Ballads."* Cambridge: Cambridge UP, 1983.
Godwin, William. *Enquiry concerning Political Justice, and Its Influence on Morals and Happiness*. 1793. 3d ed., 1798. Ed. F. E. L. Priestley. 3 vols. Toronto: U of Toronto P, 1946.
Gomme, A. H. "Some Wordsworthian Transparencies." *Modern Language Review* 68 (1973): 507–20.
Graff, Harvey. *The Legacies of Literacy*. Bloomington: Indiana UP, 1987.
Graham, William A. *Beyond the Written World: Oral Aspects of Scripture in the History of Religion*. Cambridge: Cambridge UP, 1987.
Graver, Bruce Edward. "Wordsworth's Georgic Beginnings." *Texas Studies in Language and Literature* 33 (1991): 137–59.
Gray, Thomas. *The Complete Poems of Thomas Gray*. Ed. H. W. Starr and J. R. Hendrickson. Oxford: Clarendon, 1966.
Grob, Alan. *The Philosophic Mind: A Study of Wordsworth's Poetry and Thought 1797–1805*. Columbus: Ohio State UP, 1973.
Guthrie, W. K. C. *A History of Greek Philosophy*. Cambridge: Cambridge UP, 1969.
Hagstrum, Jean. "Blake and the Sister-Arts Tradition." In *Blake's Visionary Forms Dramatic*. Ed. David V. Erdman and John E. Grant. Princeton: Princeton UP, 1970. 82–91.
Hammond, Henry. *A Paraphrase and Annotations Upon All the Books of the New Testament*. London, 1681.
Haney, David P. "The Emergence of the Autobiographical Figure in *The Prelude*, Book I." *Studies in Romanticism* 20 (1981): 33–63.
Harding, Anthony John. "Coleridge's College Declamation, 1792." *Wordsworth Circle* 8 (1977): 361–67.
Hardison, O. B., Jr. *The Enduring Monument: A Study of the Idea of Praise in Renaissance Literary Theory and Practice*. Chapel Hill: U of North Carolina P, 1962.
Hartley, David. *Observations on Man, His Frame, His Duty, And His Expectations*. 1749. 2 vols. Facsimile. Gainesville: Scholars' Facsimiles & Reprints, 1966.
Hartman, Geoffrey H. *Criticism in the Wilderness: The Study of Literature Today*. New Haven: Yale UP, 1980.
———. *The Fate of Reading*. Chicago: U of Chicago P, 1975.
———. *The Unremarkable Wordsworth*. Foreword by Donald G. Marshall. Minneapolis: U of Minnesota P, 1987.

*Select Bibliography* 289

———. *Wordsworth's Poetry 1787–1814*. New Haven: Yale UP, 1964.
Havelock, Eric. *Preface to Plato*. Cambridge: Harvard UP, 1963.
Havens, Raymond Dexter. *The Mind of a Poet*. 2 vols. Baltimore: John Hopkins UP, 1941.
Hazlitt, William. *The Complete Works of William Hazlitt*. Ed. P. P. Howe. New York: Dent, 1930–34.
Heath, William. *Wordsworth and Coleridge: A Study of Their Literary Relations in 1801–1802*. Oxford: Clarendon, 1970.
Heffernan, James A. W. *Wordsworth's Theory of Poetry*. Ithaca: Cornell UP, 1969.
Hepworth, Brian. *Robert Lowth*. Boston: Twayne, 1978.
Hertz, Neil. "Wordsworth and the Tears of Adam." *Studies in Romanticism* 7 (1967): 15–33.
Hill, Alan G. "New Light on *The Excursion*." *Ariel* 5 (1974): 37–47.
Hill, Henry, ed. *Euclid's Elements*. London: William Pearson, 1724.
Hoagwood, Terence Allan. *Skepticism and Ideology: Shelley's Political Prose and Its Philosophical Context from Bacon to Marx*. Iowa City: U of Iowa P, 1988.
Hodgson, John A. "'Was It for This ...?': Wordsworth's Virgilian Questionings." *Texas Studies in Literature and Language* 33 (1991): 125–59.
———. *Wordsworth's Philosophical Poetry, 1797–1814*. Lincoln: U of Nebraska P, 1980.
Hogg, James. *De Quincey and His Friends*. London, 1895.
Hollander, John. "Originality." *Raritan* 2 (1983): 24–44.
Holman, C. Hugh. *A Handbook to Literature*. 4th ed. Indianapolis: Bobbs-Merrill, 1983.
Holmes, John. *The Art of Rhetoric Made Easy; Or, The Elements of Oratory*. London, 1766.
Hooper, Finley. *Greek Realities: Life and Thought in Ancient Greece*. New York: Scribner, 1967.
Horace. *The Ars Poetica of Horace*. Ed. Augustus S. Wilkins. Basingstoke and London: Macmillan Education Limited, 1939.
Horner, Winifred Bryan. "Rhetoric in the Liberal Arts: Nineteenth-Century Scottish Universities." In *The Rhetorical Tradition and Modern Writing*. Ed. James J. Murphy. New York: MLA, 1982. 85–94.
Horsley, Samuel. *Critical Disquisitions on the Eighteenth Chapter of Isaiah in a Letter to Edward King, Esq*. 1799. Philadelphia, 1800.
Hoskins, John. *Directions for Speech and Style*. 1599. Ed. Hoyt H. Hudson. Princeton: Princeton UP, 1935.
Howell, Wilbur Samuel. "De Quincey on Science, Rhetoric, Poetry." In *Readings in Rhetoric*. Ed. Lionel Crocker and Paul Carmack. Springfield: Charles C. Thomas, 1965. 409–28.
———. *Eighteenth-Century British Logic and Rhetoric*. Princeton: Princeton UP, 1971.
Howes, Thomas. "Doubts Concerning the Translation and Notes of the Bishop of London to Isaiah, vindicating Ezekiel, Isaiah, and other Jewish Prophets from Disorder in Arrangement." *Critical Observations on Books, Antient and Modern*. Vol. 2. 1776–1813. New York: Garland, 1972. 109–449.
Hudson, Hoyt H. "De Quincey on Rhetoric and Public Speaking." In *Historical Studies of Rhetoric and Rhetoricians*. Ed. R. F. Howes. Ithaca: Cornell UP, 1961. 198–214.
Hume, David. "A Dialogue." Appended to *An Enquiry concerning the Principles of Morals. Enquiries concerning Human Understanding and concerning the Principles of Morals*. Ed. L. A. Selby-Bigge. 3d ed. Oxford: Clarendon, 1975.
———. *An Enquiry concerning Human Understanding. Enquiries concerning Human*

*Understanding and concerning the Principles of Morals.* Ed. L. A. Selby-Bigge. 3d ed. Oxford: Clarendon, 1975.

———. *Essays Moral, Political, and Literary.* London: Grant Richards, 1903.

———. *The Letters of David Hume.* Ed. J. Y. T. Greig. 2 vols. Oxford: Clarendon, 1932.

———. *The Philosophical Works.* Vol. 1. Ed. Thomas Hill Green and Thomas Hodge Grose. Scientia Verlag Aalen, 1964.

———. *A Treatise of Human Nature.* Ed. L. A. Shelby-Bigge. Oxford: Clarendon, 1888.

Hunt, Everett. "Herbert A. Wichelns and the Cornell Tradition of Rhetoric as a Humane Study." In *The Rhetorical Idiom.* Ed. Donald Bryant. Ithaca: Cornell UP, 1958. 1–4.

Hunt, Leigh. *Autobiography.* Ed. J. E. Morpurgo. London: Cresset, 1949.

Hurd, Richard. *An Introduction to the Study of the Prophecies Concerning the Christian Church.* 2d ed. Warburtonian Lectures, No. 1. London: 1772.

Huxley, Aldous. *Texts and Pretexts: An Anthology with Commentaries.* London: Chatto & Windus, 1932.

Jackson, J. R. de J. *Coleridge: The Critical Heritage.* New York: Barnes, 1970.

———. *Method and Imagination in Coleridge's Criticism.* Cambridge: Harvard UP, 1969.

Jackson, Wallace. *Immediacy: The Development of a Critical Concept from Addison to Coleridge.* Amsterdam: Rodopi, 1973.

Jacobus, Mary. "Apostrophe and Lyric Voice in *The Prelude.*" In *Lyric Poetry: Beyond New Criticism.* Ed. Chaviva Hosek and Patricia Parker. Ithaca: Cornell UP, 1985. 167–81.

———. "The Art of Managing Books: Romantic Prose and the Writing of the Past." In *Romanticism and Language.* Ed. Arden Reed. Ithaca: Cornell UP, 1984. 215–46.

———. *Romanticism, Writing and Sexual Difference.* New York: Oxford UP, 1989.

———. "Wordsworth and the Language of the Dream." *English Literary History* 46 (1979): 618–44.

Jakobson, Roman. *Language in Literature.* Ed. Krystyna Pomorska and Stephen Rudy. Cambridge: Harvard UP, 1987.

Jauss, Hans Robert. *Question and Answer: Form of Dialogic Understanding.* Ed. and trans. Michael Hays. Minneapolis: U of Minnesota P, 1989.

Jaye, Michael C. "The Artifice of Disjunction: Book V, *The Prelude.*" *Papers on Language and Literature* 14 (1978): 43–50.

Jeffrey, Francis. "*The Excursion* by William Wordsworth." Book Review. Edinburgh Review 48 (1814):1–30.

———. Review of Poems by George Crabbe. *Edinburgh Review* 12 (1808): 131–51.

Johnson, Barbara. *A World of Difference.* Baltimore: Johns Hopkins UP, 1987.

Johnson, Karl R. *The Written Spirit: Thematic and Rhetorical Structure in Wordsworth's "The Prelude."* Salzburg: Institut für Englische Sprache und Literatur, 1978.

Johnson, Lee M. *Wordsworth and the Sonnet.* Copenhagen: Rosenkilde and Bagger, 1973.

———. *Wordsworth's Metaphysical Verse: Geometry, Nature, and Form.* Toronto: U of Toronto P, 1982.

Johnson, Nan. "Three Nineteenth-Century Rhetoricians: The Humanist Alternative to Rhetoric as Skills Management." In *The Rhetorical Tradition and Modern Writing.* Ed. James J. Murphy. New York: MLA, 1982. 105–17.

Johnston, Kenneth. *Wordsworth and "The Recluse."* New Haven: Yale UP, 1984.

Jones, Alun R., ed. *Wordsworth's Poems of 1807.* Atlantic Highlands, N.J.: Humanities, 1987.

# Select Bibliography

Jones, John. *The Egotistical Sublime: A History of Wordsworth's Imagination.* London: Chatto & Windus, 1954.
Joseph, Sister Miriam. *Shakespeare's Use of the Arts of Language.* New York: Columbia UP, 1947.
Josephus, Flavius. *The Genuine Works of Flavius Josephus.* Trans. William Whiston. 3 vols. London: W. Bowyer, 1737.
Kaestle, Karl. "The History of Literacy and the History of Readers." In *Perspectives on Literacy.* Ed. Eugene R. Kintgen et al. Carbondale: Southern Illinois UP, 1988.
Kames, Henry Home, Lord. *Elements of Criticism.* 3 vols. Edinburgh: Millar, 1762.
Kant, Immanuel. *Critique of Judgment.* Trans. J. H. Bernard. New York: Hafner, 1951.
Keach, William. *Shelley's Style.* New York: Methuen, 1984.
Keats, John. *The Fall of Hyperion. Complete Poems.* Ed. Jack Stillinger. Cambridge: Harvard UP, 1978.
Kelley, Theresa M. "'Fantastic Shapes': From Classical Rhetoric to Romantic Allegory." *Texas Studies in Language and Literature* 33 (1991): 225–60.
———. "Spirit and Geometric Form: The Stone and the Shell in Wordsworth's Arab Dream." *Studies in English Literature* 22 (1982): 563–82.
———. *Wordsworth's Revisionary Aesthetics.* Cambridge: Cambridge UP, 1988.
Kennedy, George A. *The Art of Persuasion in Greece.* Princeton: Princeton UP, 1963.
———. *The Art of Rhetoric in the Roman World.* Princeton: Princeton UP, 1972.
———. *Classical Rhetoric and Its Christian and Secular Tradition from Ancient to Modern Times.* Chapel Hill: U of North Carolina P, 1980.
———. *Quintilian.* New York: Twayne, 1969.
Kneale, J. Douglas. *Monumental Writing: Aspects of Rhetoric in Wordsworth's Poetry.* Lincoln: U of Nebraska P, 1988.
Kroeber, Karl. "Graphic-Poetic Structuring in Blake's *Book of Urizen.*" *Blake Studies* 3 (1970): 7–18.
Kroll, Richard. *The Material Word.* Baltimore: Johns Hopkins UP, 1991.
Kugel, James L. *The Idea of Biblical Poetry: Parallelism and Its History.* London: Yale UP, 1981.
Lanham, Richard. *A Handlist of Rhetorical Terms.* Berkeley: U of California P, 1968.
LeFevre, Karen Burke. *Invention as a Social Act.* Carbondale: Southern Illinois UP, 1987.
Lerner, L. D. "The Miltonic Simile." *Essays in Criticism* 4 (1954): 297–308.
Lessenich, Rolf. *Aspects of English Preromanticism.* Cologne: Bohlau Verlag, 1989.
Lewalski, Barbara Kiefer. *Donne's "Anniversaries" and the Poetry of Praise: The Creation of a Symbolic Mode.* Princeton: Princeton UP, 1973.
Lindenberger, Herbert. *On Wordsworth's "Prelude."* Princeton: Princeton UP, 1963.
Liu, Alan. "The Power of Formalism." *ELH* 56 (1989): 721–71.
Lockhart, John Gibson. *Memoirs of Sir Walter Scott.* Vol. 1. London: Macmillan, 1900.
Longinus. *On the Sublime.* Trans. James A. Arieti and John M. Crossett. New York: Mellen, 1985.
Lord, Albert. *The Singer of Tales.* Cambridge: Harvard UP, 1960.
Lowth, Robert, trans. *Isaiah: A New Translation with a Preliminary Dissertation, and Notes, Critical, Philological, and Explanatory.* 1778. Albany, N.Y., 1794.
———. *Lectures on the Sacred Poetry of the Hebrews.* Trans. G. Gregory. 2d ed. 2 vols. London, 1816.
———. *Lectures on the Sacred Poetry of the Hebrews.* Trans. G. Gregory. St. Paul's Church Yard: J. Johnson, 1787. Rpt., Hildesheim: George Olms, 1969.
Lukits, Steven. "Wordsworth Unawares: The Boy of Winander, the Poet, and the Mariner." *Wordsworth Circle* 19 (1988): 156–60.
Lyon, Judson. *"The Excursion": A Study.* New Haven: Yale UP, 1950.
McCall, Marsh H., Jr. *Ancient Rhetorical Theories of Simile and Comparison.* Cambridge: Harvard UP, 1969.

McCarthy, John F. "The Conflict in Books I–II of *The Prelude.*" *Modern Language Quarterly* 30 (1969): 370–75.
McConnell, Frank. *The Confessional Imagination: A Reading of Wordsworth's "Prelude."* Baltimore: Johns Hopkins UP, 1974.
McFarland, Thomas. *Originality and Imagination.* Baltimore: Johns Hopkins UP, 1985.
———. "Wordsworth's Hedgerows: The Infrastructure of the Longer Romantic Lyric." In *The Age of William Wordsworth.* Ed. Kenneth R. Johnston and Gene W. Ruoff. Rutgers UP, 1987. 239–58.
McGann, Jerome J. *The Romantic Ideology: A Critical Investigation.* Chicago: Chicago UP, 1983.
MacGillvray, J. R. "The Three Forms of *The Prelude.*" In *Wordsworth, The Prelude: A Casebook.* Ed. W. J. Harvey and Richard Gravil. London: Macmillan, 1972.
MacIntyre, Alasdair. "Hume on 'Is' and 'Ought.'" *Philosophical Review* 68 (1959): 451–68.
McLachlan, H. *English Education under the Test Acts.* Manchester: Manchester UP, 1931.
Magnuson, Paul. "'The Eolian Harp' in Context." *Studies in Romanticism* 24 (1985): 3–20.
Manning, Peter. *Reading Romantics.* New York: Oxford UP, 1990.
Martin, Wallace. "Floating on Issue of Tropes." *Diacritics* 12 (1982): 75–83.
Marx, Karl. "Money." *Early Writings.* Trans. T. B. Bottomore. New York: McGraw, 1964.
"Mathematics." *Encyclopaedia Britannica.* 3d ed. 1797.
Matlak, Richard E. "Classical Argument and Romantic Persuasion in 'Tintern Abbey.'" *Studies in Romanticism* 25 (1986): 97–129.
Mede, Joseph. *The Key of the Revelation.* Trans. Richard More. London, 1643.
Meisenhelder, Susan. *Wordsworth's Informed Reader.* Nashville: Vanderbilt UP, 1988.
Mellor, Anne Kostelanetz. *Blake's Human Form Divine.* Berkeley: U California P, 1974.
Mileur, Jean-Pierre. *Vision & Revision: Coleridge's Art of Immanence.* Berkeley: U California P, 1982.
Mill, John Stuart. *Essays on Poetry.* Ed. F. Parvin Sharpless. Columbia: U of South Carolina P, 1976.
Miller, J. Hillis. "The Stone and the Shell: The Problem of Poetic Form in Wordsworth's Dream of the Arab." *Mouvements premiers.* Paris: Librarie Jose Corti, 1972. 125–47.
Milton, John. *Complete Poems and Major Prose.* Ed. Merritt Y. Hughes. New York: Odyssey, 1957.
Mitchell, W. J. T. "Blake's Composite Art." In *Blake's Visionary Forms Dramatic.* Ed. David V. Erdman and John E. Grant. Princeton: Princeton UP, 1970. 57–81.
———. "Influence, Autobiography, and Literary History: Rousseau's *Confessions* and Wordsworth's *Prelude.*" *English Literary History* 57 (1990): 643–64.
———. "Poetic and Pictorial Imagination in *The Book of Urizen.*" In *The Visionary Hand: Essays for the Study of William Blake's Art and Aesthetics.* Ed. Robert N. Essick. Los Angeles: Hennessey and Ingalls, 1973. 337–80.
Modiano, Raimonda. *Coleridge and the Concept of Nature.* Tallahassee: Florida State UP, 1985.
Monboddo, Lord [James Burnet]. *Of the Origin and Progress of Language.* 6 vols. 1774–92. Menston: Scolar, 1967.
Morkan, Joel. "Structure and Meaning in *The Prelude,* V." *PMLA* 87 (1972): 246–54.
Morton, Lionel. "Books and Drowned Men: Unconscious Mourning in Book V of *The Prelude.*" *English Studies in Canada* 8 (1982): 23–37.
Mulderig, Gerald P. "Nineteenth-Century Psychology and the Shaping of Alexander

## Select Bibliography

Bain's *English Composition and Rhetoric*." In *The Rhetorical Tradition and Modern Writing*. Ed. James J. Murphy. New York: MLA, 1982. 95–104.

Murphy, James J., ed. *The Rhetorical Tradition and Modern Writing*. New York: MLA, 1982.

Murray, Roger N. *Wordsworth's Style: Figures and Themes in the "Lyrical Ballads" of 1800*. Lincoln: U of Nebraska P, 1967.

Nabholtz, John R. *"My Reader My Fellow-Labourer."* Columbia: U of Missouri P, 1986.

———. "Romantic Prose and Classical Rhetoric." *Wordsworth Circle* 11 (1980): 119–26.

Newcome, William, trans. *An Attempt Towards an Improved Version, a Metrical Arrangement, and an Explanation of The Prophet Ezekiel*. Dublin, 1788.

Newton, Thomas. *Dissertations on the Prophecies*. 1754. Northampton, Mass., 1796.

Nicholson, Kathleen. *Turner's Classical Landscapes: Myth and Meaning*. Princeton: Princeton UP, 1990.

Nielsen, Eduard. "The Role of Oral Tradition in the Bible." In *Old Testament Issues*. Ed. Samuel Sandmel. New York: Harper, 1968.

Ochs, Donovan J. "Aeschines' Speech *Against Ctesiphon*" (an abstract). In *Demosthenes' On the Crown: A Critical Case Study of a Masterpiece*. Ed. James J. Murphy. Trans. John J. Keaney. New York: Random, 1967. 48–58.

Ong, Walter J. *Orality and Literacy*. London: Methuen, 1982.

———. "The Writer's Audience is Always a Fiction." *PMLA* 90 (1975): 9–21.

Onorato, Richard J. *The Character of the Poet: Wordsworth in "The Prelude."* Princeton: Princeton UP, 1971.

Ostriker, Alicia. *Vision and Verse in William Blake*. Madison: U of Wisconsin P, 1965.

Ovidius Naso, Publius. *The Fifteen Books of Publius Ovidius Naso entytuled Metamorphoisis*. 1576. Trans. Arthur Golding. Ed. John Fredrick Nims. New York: Macmillan, 1976.

Paine, Thomas. *The Rights of Man*. 1791. London: Pelican, 1969.

Parker, Patricia. *Literary Fat Ladies: Rhetoric, Gender, Property*. London: Methuen, 1987.

Parker, Reeve. *Coleridge's Meditative Art*. Ithaca: Cornell UP, 1975.

Pater, Walter. "Coleridge." *Appreciations*. London: Macmillan, 1898.

Patrick, J. Max, ed. *The Complete Poetry of Robert Herrick*. New York UP, 1963.

Patterson, Annabel M. *Hermogenes and the Renaissance: Seven Ideas of Style*. Princeton: Princeton UP, 1970.

Peacham, Henry. *The Garden of Eloquence*. London, 1593.

Pearce, Zachary. *A Review of the Text of Twelve Books of Milton's* Paradise Lost: *In which the Chief of Dr. Bentley's Emendations are Consider'd; And several other Emendations and Observations are offer'd to the Public*. London: John Shuckburgh, 1733.

Pease, Arthur S. "Things without Honor." *Classical Philology* 21 (1926): 27–42.

Peckham, Morse. "Poet and Critic: or, the Damage Coleridge Has Done." *Romanticism and Behavior*. Columbia: U of South Carolina P, 1976.

Perkins, David. "How the Romantic Poets Recited Their Poetry." Paper delivered at 1990 MLA convention.

Phinney, A. W. "Wordsworth's Winander Boy and Romantic Theories of Language." *Wordsworth Circle* 18 (1987): 66–72.

Plato. *Phaedrus. Plato: The Collected Dialogues*. Ed. Edith Hamilton and Huntington Cairns. Princeton: Princeton UP, 1961.

Poirier, Richard. *Poetry and Pragmatism*. Cambridge: Harvard UP, 1992.

Pope, Alexander. *The Complete Poetical Works of Alexander Pope*. Ed. Henry W. Boynton. Cambridge: Houghton, 1903.

Pöschl, Viktor. *The Art of Vergil: Image and Symbol in* The Aeneid *(Die Dichtkunst Virgils)*. 1950. Trans. Gerda Seligson. 1962. Ann Arbor: U of Michigan P, 1970.
Potts, A. F. *The Elegiac Mode: Poetic Form in Wordsworth and Other Elegists*. Ithaca: Cornell UP, 1967.
Prickett, Stephen. *Words and the Word*. New York: Cambridge UP, 1986.
Priestley, Joseph. *A Course of Lectures on Oratory and Criticism*. Ed. Vincent M. Bevilacqua and Richard Murphy. Carbondale: Southern Illinois UP, 1965.
———. *A Course of Lectures on the Theory of Language, and Universal Grammar*. Warrington: W. Eyres, 1762.
*Princeton Encyclopedia of Poetry and Poetics*. Ed. Alex Preminger. Princeton: Princeton UP, 1974.
Pulos, C. S. *The Deep Truth: A Study of Shelley's Skepticism*. Lincoln: U of Nebraska P, 1954.
Puttenham, George. *The Arte of English Poesie*. London, 1589.
Quintilian. *Institutio Oratoria*. Trans. H. E. Butler. 4 vols. London: Heinemann, 1921.
Ragussis, Michael. "Language and Metamorphosis in Wordsworth's Arab Dream." *Modern Language Quarterly* 36 (1975): 148–65.
———. *The Subterfuge of Art: Language and the Romantic Tradition*. Baltimore: Johns Hopkins UP, 1978.
Rajan, Tilottama. "Displacing Post-Structuralism: Romantic Studies after Paul de Man." *Studies in Romanticism* 24 (1985): 451–74.
———. *Lyric Poetry: Beyond New Criticism*. Ed. Chaviva Hosek and Patricia Parker. Ithaca: Cornell UP, 1985. 194–207.
———. "Romanticism and the Death of Lyric Consciousness." *Dark Interpreter: The Discourse of Romanticism*. Ithaca: Cornell UP, 1980.
Ramsay, Roger. "The Structure of De Quincey's *Confessions of an English Opium-Eater*." *Prose Studies* 5 (1978): 20–28.
Raysor, T. M. "Unpublished Fragments in Aesthetics by S. T. Coleridge." *Studies in Philology* 22 (1925): 529–37.
Reed, Arden. *Romantic Weather: The Climates of Coleridge and Baudelaire*. Hanover: UP of New England, 1983.
Reed, Mark L. *Wordsworth: A Chronology of the Early Years: 1770–1799*. Cambridge: Harvard UP, 1967.
———. *Wordsworth: A Chronology of the Middle Years: 1800–1815*. Cambridge: Harvard UP, 1975.
Regueiro, Helen. *The Limits of Imagination: Wordsworth, Yeats, and Stevens*. Ithaca: Cornell UP, 1976.
Rehder, Robert. *Wordsworth and the Beginnings of Modern Poetry*. London: Croom Helm, 1981.
Reiman, Donald H., ed. *The Romantics Reviewed*. New York: Garland, 1972.
Riffaterre, Michael. "Prosopopeia: The Lesson of Paul de Man." *Yale French Studies* 69 (1985): 107–23.
Robertson, Mary F. "Deconstructive 'Contortion' and Women's Historical Practice." *Poetics Today* 7 (1986): 705–28.
Rosenfield, Lawrence W. "The Practical Celebration of Epideictic." In *Rhetoric in Transition*. Ed. Eugene E. White. University Park: Pennsylvania State UP, 1980. 131–55.
Roston, Murray. *Prophet and Poet: The Bible and the Growth of Romanticism*. London: Faber, 1965.
Rouse, W. H. D. *A History of Rugby School*. London, 1898.
Royle, Edward, and James Walvin. *English Radicals and Reformers, 1760–1848*. Lexington: UP of Kentucky, 1982.
Rudowski, Victor Anthony. "The Theory of Signs in the Eighteenth Century." *Journal of the History of Ideas* 35 (1974): 683–90.

Russell, D. A., and N. G. Wilson, eds. *Menander Rhetor.* Oxford: Clarendon, 1981.
Ryle, Gilbert. "Jane Austen and the Moralists." *Oxford Review* 7 (1966): 5–18.
Said, Edward. "The Text, the World, the Critic." In *Textual Strategies: Perspectives in Post-Structuralist Criticism.* Ed. Josué V. Harari. Ithaca: Cornell UP, 1979. 161–88.
Saintsbury, George. *A History of English Prosody, from the Twelfth Century to the Present Day.* Vol. 3. London: Macmillan, 1910.
Sanderson, David. "Coleridge's Political 'Sermons': Discursive Language and the Voice of God." *Modern Philology* 70 (1973): 319–30.
Schmitz, Robert Morell. *Hugh Blair.* New York: King's Crown P, 1945.
Schneider, Ben Ross, Jr. *Wordsworth's Cambridge Education.* Cambridge: Cambridge UP, 1957.
Scott, Sir Walter. *The Antiquary.* London: George Rutledge & Sons, 1880.
———. *The Bride of Lammermoor.* London: George Rutledge & Sons, 1879.
———. *Guy Mannering.* London: George Rutledge & Sons, 1880.
———. *The Heart of Midlothian.* New York: Holt, 1963.
———. *Redgauntlet.* London: George Rutledge & Sons, 1880.
———. *Rob Roy.* Ed. Edgar Johnson. Boston: Houghton, 1957.
Scoular, Kitty W. *Natural Magic: Studies in the Presentation of Nature in English Poetry from Spenser to Marvell.* Oxford: Clarendon, 1965. 38–117.
Scrivener, Michael Henry. *Radical Shelley: The Philosophical Anarchism and Utopian Thought of Percy Bysshe Shelley.* Princeton: Princeton UP, 1982.
Segal, Charles Paul. "Nature and the World of Man in Greek Literature." *Arion* 2 (1963): 19–53.
Shakespeare, William. *Sonnets.* Ed. Martin Seymour-Smith. London: Heinemann, 1963.
Shakir, Evelyn. "Books, Death, and Immortality: A Study of Book V of *The Prelude.*" *Studies in Romanticism* 8 (1969): 156–67.
Shaver, Chester L. and Alice C. *Wordsworth's Library: A Catalogue.* New York: Garland, 1979.
Shawcross, John. "Coleridge's Marginalia." *Notes and Queries* 4 (1905): 341–42.
Sheats, Paul. "Wordsworth's 'Retrogrades' and the Shaping of *The Prelude.*" *JEGP* 71 (1972): 477.
Shell, Marc. *Economy of Literature.* Baltimore: Johns Hopkins UP, 1978.
Shelley, Mary Wollstonecraft. *Frankenstein, or The Modern Prometheus (The 1818 Text).* Ed. James Rieger. Chicago: U of Chicago P, 1982.
———. *The Journals of Mary Shelley, 1814–1844.* Ed. Paula R. Feldman and Diana Scott-Kilvert. 2 vols. Oxford: Clarendon, 1987.
Shelley, Percy Bysshe. *The Complete Works of Percy Bysshe Shelley.* Ed. Roger Ingpen and Walter E. Peck. 10 vols. London: Ernest Benn, 1926–28.
———. *The Letters of Percy Bysshe Shelley.* Ed. Frederick L. Jones. 2 vols. Oxford: Clarendon, 1964.
———. *Shelley's Poetry and Prose.* Ed. Donald H. Reiman and Sharon B. Powers. New York: Norton, 1977.
"Shells." *Encyclopaedia Britannica.* 3d ed. 1797.
Sheridan, Thomas. *A Course of Lectures on Elocution.* 1762. London: Dodsley, 1787.
Sherry, Richard. *A Treatise of Schemes and Tropes.* 1550. Intro. Herbert W. Hildebrandt. Gainesville: Scholars' Facsimiles and Reprints, 1961.
Shullenberger, William. "'Something' in Wordsworth." In *Ineffability: Naming the Unnamable from Dante to Beckett.* Ed. Peter S. Hawkins and Anne Howland Schotter. New York: AMS, 1984.
Shuster, George N. *The English Ode from Milton to Keats.* New York: Columbia UP, 1940.
Slotkin, J. S. *Readings in Early Anthropology.* Chicago: Aldine, 1965.

Smith, Adam. *Lectures on Rhetoric and Belles Lettres . . . Reported by a Student in 1762–63*. Ed. John M. Lothian. London: Nelson, 1963.
Smith, John [of Montague Close]. *The Mysterie of Rhetorique unvail'd*. London, 1657.
Smith, Olivia. *The Politics of Language, 1791–1819*. Oxford: Clarendon, 1984.
Smyser, Jane Worthington, "Wordsworth's Dream of Poetry and Science: *The Prelude*, V." *PMLA* 7 (1956): 269–75.
Spector, Stephen J. "Wordsworth's Mirror Imagery and the Picturesque Tradition." *ELH* 44 (1977): 85–107.
Stafford, William. *Socialism, Radicalism, and Nostalgia: Social Criticism in Britain, 1775–1830*. Cambridge: Cambridge UP, 1987.
Stallknecht, Newton. *Strange Seas of Thought: Studies in Wordsworth's Philosophy of Man and Nature*. Bloomington: Indiana UP, 1966.
Stillinger, Jack. *Multiple Authorship and the Myth of Solitary Genius*. New York: Oxford UP, 1991.
Struever, Nancy S. "The Conversable World: Eighteenth-Century Transformations of the Relation of Rhetoric and Truth." William Andrews Clark Memorial Library Seminar Papers No. 65.
———. "Translation as Taste." *The Eighteenth Century: Theory and Interpretation* 22 (1981): 32–46.
Swinburne, Algernon Charles. *William Blake: A Critical Essay*. 1868. Lincoln: U of Nebraska P, 1970.
Tateo, Francesco. *Dialogo interiore e polemica ideologica nel "Secretum" del Petrarca*. Florence: Le Monnier, 1965.
Tenneman, Wilhelm Gottlieb. *Geschicte der Philosophie*. Leipzig: 1798–1819.
Tetreault, Ronald. *The Poetry of Life: Shelley and Literary Form*. Toronto: U of Toronto P, 1987.
Thomas, Gordon Kent. *Wordsworth's Dirge and Promise: Napoleon, Wellington, and the Convention of Cintra*. Lincoln: U of Nebraska P, 1971.
Thomas, W. K., and Warren Ober. *A Mind For Ever Voyaging: Wordsworth at Work Portraying Newton and Science*. Edmonton: Alberta UP, 1989.
Thompson, T. W. *Wordsworth's Hawkshead*. Ed. with introduction, notes, and appendices by Robert Woof. London: Oxford UP, 1970.
Thornton, Percy M. *Harrow School and Its Surroundings*. 1885.
Todorov, Tzvetan. "Esthetique et semiotique au XVIIIe siècle." *Critique* 29 (1973): 29–39.
Toulmin, Stephen. *The Uses of Argument*. Cambridge: Cambridge UP, 1958.
Trimpi, Wesley. "The Ancient Hypothesis of Fiction: An Essay on the Origins of Literary Theory." *Traditio* (1971): 1–78.
———. "The Quality of Fiction: The Rhetorical Transmission of Literary Theory." *Traditio* (1974): 1–118.
Trowbridge, Hoyt. "The Language of Reasoned Rhetoric in *The Rambler*." In *Greene Centennial Essays*. Ed. Paul J. Korshin and Robert K. Allen. Charlottesville: UP of Virginia, 1984.
Vaihinger, Hans. *The Philosophy of 'As If': A System of the Theoretical, Practical and Religious Fictions of Mankind*. Trans. C. K. Ogden. 1924. London: Routledge, 1949.
Valla, Lorenzo. *De vero falsaque bono*. Ed. Maristella Lorch. Bari: Adriatica, 1970.
———. *Repastinatio dialectice et philosophice*. Ed. Gianni Zippel. Padua: Antenone, 1982.
Venn, John, and J. A. Venn. *Alumni Cantabrigienses: A Biographical List of All Known Students, Graduates and Holders of Office at the University of Cambridge, from the Earliest Times to 1900*. 2 pts. 10 vols. Cambridge: Cambridge UP, 1922–54.
Vickers, Brian. *Classical Rhetoric in English Poetry*. London: Macmillan, 1970.

———. "Epideictic and Epic in the Renaissance." *New Literary History* 14 (1983): 497–537.
———. *In Defence of Rhetoric*. Oxford: Clarendon, 1988.
Virgil. *Georgics*. Ed. Richard Thomas. 2 vols. Cambridge: Cambridge UP, 1988.
Vogler, Thomas A. *Preludes to Vision: The Epic Venture in Blake, Keats, Wordsworth, and Hart Crane*. Berkeley: U of California P, 1971.
Walker, John. *A Rhetorical Grammar*. Boston: Cummings and Hilliard, 1822.
Wall, Adam. *Ceremonies Observed in the Senate House of the University of Cambridge*. Ed. Henry Gunning. 2d ed. 1828.
Wallace, Karl R. "The Fundamentals of Rhetoric." In *The Prospect of Rhetoric*. Ed. Lloyd F. Bitzer and Edwin Black. Englewood Cliffs, N.J.: Prentice, 1971. 3–20.
Wallerstein, Ruth. *Studies in Seventeenth-Century Poetic*. Madison: U of Wisconsin P, 1965.
Ward, John. *A System of Oratory*. London: Printed for John Ward, 1759.
Ward, Patricia. "Coleridge's Critical Theory of the Symbol." *TSLL* 8 (1966): 15–32.
Warminski, Andrzej. "Facing Language: Wordsworth's First Poetic Spirits." In *Romantic Revolutions: Criticism and Theory*. Ed. Kenneth Johnston, Gilbert Chaitin, Karen Hanson, and Herbert Marks. Bloomington: Indiana UP, 1990. 26–49.
———. "Missed Crossing: Wordsworth's Apocalypses." *MLN* 99 (1984): 983–1006.
Wasserman, Earl R. "The English Romantics: The Grounds of Knowledge." *Studies in Romanticism* 4 (1964):17–34.
———. "The Inherent Values of Eighteenth-Century Personification." *PMLA* 65 (1950): 435–63.
Watson, J. R. *Wordsworth's Vital Soul: The Sacred and the Profane in Wordsworth's Poetry*. London: Macmillan, 1982.
*The Way to Things by Words and Words by Things*. London: Davies and Reymers, 1766.
Webb, Timothy. *Shelley: A Voice Not Understood*. Atlantic Highlands, N.J.: Humanities, 1977.
Weiner, David. "Wordsworth, Books, and the Growth of a Poet's Mind." *JEGP* 74 (1975): 209–20.
Weinsheimer, Joel. *Imitation*. Boston: Routledge, 1984.
Wellbery, David E. *Lessing's Laocoon: Semiotics and Aesthetics in the Age of Reason*. London: Cambridge UP, 1984.
Wellek, René. "De Quincey's Status in the History of Ideas." *Philological Quarterly* 23 (1944): 248–72.
Wesley, John. *Explanatory Notes Upon the New Testament*. 2d American ed. 2 vols. New York, 1806.
Wesling, Donald. *The Chances of Rhyme: Device and Modernity*. Berkeley: U of California P, 1980.
Whaler, James. "The Miltonic Simile." *PMLA* 46 (1931): 1034–74.
Whalley, George. "Simile." In *Princeton Encyclopedia of Poetry and Poetics*. Ed. Alex Preminger et al. Princeton: Princeton UP, 1974.
Whately, Richard. *Elements of Rhetoric*. 7th ed. Louisville: John P. Morton, 1853 (?).
Whiston, William, trans. *The Elements of Euclid*. Ed. Andrew Tacquet. London: J. Senex, 1727.
White, Newman Ivey. *Shelley*. 2 vols. New York: Knopf, 1947.
White, Samuel. *A Commentary on the Prophet Isaiah*. London, 1709.
Willey, Basil. *Samuel Taylor Coleridge*. London: Chatto & Windus, 1972.
Wilson, Thomas. *Wilson's Arte of Rhetorique*. 1560. Ed. G. H. Mair. Oxford: Clarendon, 1919.
Wimsatt, W. K., Jr. "The Structure of Romantic Nature Imagery." *The Verbal Icon: Studies in the Meaning of Poetry*. Lexington: U of Kentucky P, 1954. 103–16.

Wittreich, Joseph Anthony, Jr. *Angel of Apocalypse: Blake's Idea of Milton*. Madison: U of Wisconsin P, 1975.

———. "'The Crown of Eloquence': The Figure of the Orator in Milton's Prose Works." In *Achievements of the Left Hand: Essays on the Prose of John Milton*. Ed. Michael Lieb and John T. Shawcross. Amherst: U of Massachusetts P, 1974. 3–54.

———. "Opening the Seals: Blake's Epics and the Milton Tradition." In *Blake's Sublime Allegory*. Ed. Stuart Curran and Joseph Anthony Wittreich, Jr. Madison: U of Wisconsin P, 1973. 23–58.

———. "'A Poet Amongst Poets': Milton and the Tradition of Prophecy." In *Milton and the Line of Vision*. Ed. Joseph Anthony Wittreich, Jr. Madison: U of Wisconsin P, 1975. 97–142.

Wolfson, Susan J. "The Illusion of Mastery: Wordsworth's Revisions of 'The Drowned Man of Esthwaite,' 1799, 1805, 1850." *PMLA* 99 (1984): 917–35.

———. "The Language of Interpretation in Romantic Poetry: 'A Strong Working of the Mind.'" In *Romanticism and Language*. Ed. Arden Reed. Ithaca: Cornell UP, 1984. 22–49.

———. "Romanticism and the Measures of Meter." *Eighteenth-Century Life* (November 1992): 221–46.

Woodring, Carl. *Politics in English Romantic Poetry*. Cambridge: Harvard UP, 1970.

———. ed. *Prose of the Romantic Period*. Boston: Houghton, 1961.

———. "Road Building: Turner's *Hannibal*." *Studies in Romanticism* 30 (Spring 1991): 19–36.

Wooten, Cecil W. "The Nature of Form in Demosthenes' *De Corona*." *Classical World* 72 (1979): 321–27.

Wordsworth, Christopher. *Scholae Academicae: Some Account of the Studies at the English Universities in the Eighteenth Century*. 1877. New York: A. M. Kelly, 1969.

Wordsworth, Jonathan. *The Music of Humanity*. London: Nelson, 1969.

———. "The Two-Part *Prelude* of 1799." In *The Prelude: 1799, 1805, 1850*. Ed. Jonathan Wordsworth et al. New York: Norton, 1979.

———, and Stephen Gill. "The Two-Part *Prelude* of 1798–99." *JEGP* 72 (1973): 503–25.

Wordsworth, William. *The Excursion*. Ed. Jonathan Wordsworth. Oxford: Woodstock, 1991.

———. *The Fourteen-Book Prelude*. Ed. W. J. B. Owen. Ithaca: Cornell UP, 1985.

———. *The Letters of William and Dorothy Wordsworth*. Ed. Ernest de Selincourt. Rev. 2d ed. 7 vols. *The Later Years, 1821–1853*. Ed. Alan G. Hill. 4 parts. Oxford: Oxford UP, 1978–88.

———. *The Poems*. Ed. John O. Hayden. 2 vols. New Haven: Yale UP, 1981.

———. *Poems, in Two Volumes, and Other Poems, 1800–1807*. Ed. Jared Curtis. Ithaca: Cornell UP, 1983.

———. *The Poetical Works of William Wordsworth*. Ed. Ernest de Selincourt and Helen Darbishire. 5 vols. Oxford: Oxford UP, 1959.

———. *The Prelude*. Ed. Ernest de Selincourt and Helen Darbishire. 2d ed. rev. Oxford: Clarendon, 1959.

———. *The Prelude: 1799, 1805, 1850*. Ed. Jonathan Wordsworth, M. H. Abrams, and Stephen Gill. New York: Norton, 1979.

———. *The Prose Works of William Wordsworth*. Ed. W. J. B. Owen and J. W. Smyser. 3 vols. Oxford: Oxford UP, 1974.

———. *The Ruined Cottage and The Pedlar*. Ed. James Butler. Ithaca: Cornell UP, 1979.

Worthington, Jane. *Wordsworth's Reading of Roman Prose*. New Haven: Yale UP, 1946.

## Select Bibliography

Wu, Duncan. "A Chronological Annotated Edition of Wordsworth's Prose and Poetry, 1785–1790." Dissertation, Oxford U, 1990.

———. *Wordsworth's Reading 1770–1799.* Cambridge: Cambridge UP, 1993.

Yates, Frances. *The Art of Memory.* Chicago: U of Chicago P, 1966.

Young, Michael C. "'The True Hero of the Tale': De Quincey's *Confessions* and Affective Autobiographical Theory." In *Thomas De Quincey Bicentenary Studies.* Ed. Robert L. Snyder. Norman: U of Oklahoma P, 1985. 54–71.

Zall, Paul M., ed. *Literary Criticism of William Wordsworth.* Lincoln: U of Nebraska P, 1966.

Zumthor, Paul. *Oral Poetry: An Introduction.* Trans. Kathryn Murphy-Judy. Minneapolis: U of Minnesota P, 1990.

# CONTRIBUTORS

**Stephen C. Behrendt** is Professor of English at the University of Nebraska. He has published extensively on the public dimension of Romantic literature and visual art and is the author of *Shelley and His Audiences* (University of Nebraska Press, 1989) and *The Moment of Explosion: Blake and the Illustration of Milton* (University of Nebraska Press, 1983). He also is editor of *Approaches to Teaching Shelley's* Frankenstein (Modern Language Association, 1990).

**Don H. Bialostosky** is Professor of English at Pennsylvania State University. Having published extensively on Bakhtin and rhetoric, he is also author of two books on the arts of discourse and Romanticism: *Making Tales: The Poetics of Wordsworth's Narrative Experiments* (University of Chicago Press, 1984) and *Wordsworth, Dialogics, and the Practice of Criticism* (Cambridge University Press, 1991).

**Jerome Christensen** is Professor of English at Johns Hopkins University. He has published extensively on rhetoric, authorship, and the Romantic literary career, including work on Coleridge and Byron. His books include *Coleridge's Blessed Machine of Language* (Cornell University Press, 1981) and *Lord Byron's Strength* (Johns Hopkins University Press, 1993).

**Richard W. Clancey** is Professor of English at John Carroll University. He has written on Romantic poetry and the classical tradition and currently is writing a book on Wordsworth's classical education.

**James Engell** is Professor of English and Comparative Literature at Harvard University. He has published extensively on the eighteenth-century background to Romantic aesthetic and critical principles, including two books: *Forming the Critical Mind: Dryden to Coleridge* (Harvard, 1989) and *The Creative Imagination: Enlightenment to Romanticism* (Harvard, 1981). He also is the co-editor of *Teaching Literature: What Is Needed Now* (Harvard, 1988), the editor of *Johnson and His Age* (Harvard, 1984), and co-editor of *Biographia Literaria* (Princeton, 1983).

**David Ginsberg** has written on Wordsworth and the epideictic tradition, demonstrating the continuity of the rhetorical tradition from the classical period through the Renaissance to the Romantic period. He is an Assistant Professor of English at Nassau Community College.

**Bruce E. Graver** has published several articles on Wordsworth and translation, and he currently is editing Wordsworth's translations of Latin poetry for the

Cornell Wordsworth series. He teaches in the Department of English at Providence College.

**Scott Harshbarger** has written about eighteenth-century theories of "natural," expressive language and the sublime, especially as they relate to Romantic writing. He also has published on Hawthorne. He is an Assistant Professor of English at Hofstra University.

**Theresa M. Kelley** is Professor of English at the University of Texas, Austin. She has published widely on Romanticism and the sublime, and is author of *Wordsworth's Revisionary Aesthetics* (Cambridge University Press, 1988).

**J. Douglas Kneale** is Associate Professor of English at the University of Western Ontario. He has written on narrative voice and rhetoric and is the author of *Monumental Writing: Aspects of Rhetoric in Wordsworth's Poetry* (University of Nebraska Press, 1988).

**John R. Nabholtz** is Professor of English at Loyola University. He has published articles on rhetoric and Romanticism and is the author of a book on Romantic prose and reader response, *"My Reader My Fellow-Labourer"* (University of Missouri Press, 1986).

**Lawrence D. Needham** has published articles on rhetoric and Romanticism, including work on the prose prefaces of De Quincey and Wordsworth. He is an Assistant Professor of English at Lakeland Community College and an Affiliate Scholar at Oberlin College.

**Marie Secor** is Associate Professor of English at Pennsylvania State University. The co-author of *A Rhetoric of Argument* (Random House, 1982), she has published articles on logic and argument as well as on nineteenth-century theories of style.

**Nancy S. Struever** is Professor, Humanities Center, Johns Hopkins University. She has published numerous articles on ethics and the arts of discourse in the Italian Renaissance. She has written, as well, on the eighteenth-century English rhetorical tradition. She is the author of *The Language of History in the Renaissance: Rhetoric and Historical Consciousness in Florentine Humanism* (Princeton, 1970).

**Leslie Tannenbaum** has written on the influence of the Bible on Romantic literature and is the author of *Biblical Traditions in Blake's Early Prophecies* (Princeton, 1982). He teaches at Ohio State University.

**Susan J. Wolfson** is Professor of English at Princeton University. She has published numerous articles on Romantic discourse and interpretation, as well as essays on Romantic literature and feminism. She is the author of *The Questioning Presence: Wordsworth, Keats, and the Interrogative Mode in Romantic Poetry* (Cornell University Press, 1986).

# INDEX

Aarsleff, Hans, 220, 225, 230n6, 231n18, 231n22
Abbey, Lloyd, 180n13
Abrams, M. H., 1, 156, 196n1, 196n3, 196n5, 199–200, 230n10, 230n13, 231n17
accumulation, 37
Addison, Joseph, 46n11, 224
address, 150, 154–56, 161, 163n14
adoxography, 112, 119n8
*Aeneid,* 107n21
aesthetics, 237
   and language, 224
   and rhetoric, 223
   of the sublime, 41
affections, 276, 278
allegory, 31, 33, 42–43, 45n2, 46n4
Alter, Robert, 213n12
Altick, Robert, 214n15
amplification, 112, 114
analogy, 29, 34–35, 39, 46n13, 47n22
   analogical argument, 39
   analogical reading, 39
anaphora. *See under* figures and tropes
anthropology, rhetorical, 200, 206, 208, 210, 212
aporia. *See under* figures and tropes
apostrophe. *See under* figures and tropes
appeals, rhetorical, 71–72, 252, 253, 260, 267
   Ciceronian, 71–72
   conscious and unconscious, 207
   emotional, 73, 253–55, 261, 262
Arac, Jonathan, 1, 164n21
Arendt, Hannah, 121n16
argument, 33, 235
   *a fortiori,* 74
   analogical, 39
   and belles lettres, 246
   classical genres of, 66
   efficacy of, 261
argumentation, Euclidian, 76
Arieti, James A., 162n3
Aristotle, 14, 27n8, 28, 32–33, 47n6, 50, 66, 69–71, 110–11, 116, 267
arrangement, 73, 188–89
   poetic, 188
artifice, rhetorical, 258
asyndeton. *See under* figures and tropes
audience, 169, 177, 258
   invoked, 152
   sensitivity to, 261

Auerbach, Erich, 1, 150, 197n13
Augustine, 126, 190, 197n13
Austen, Jane, 4, 233, 234, 241–47
   *Emma,* 245
   *Mansfield Park,* 242–43
   *Northanger Abbey,* 242, 243–44
   *Persuasion,* 244
   *Pride and Prejudice,* 242
   *Sense and Sensibility,* 234, 244
   use of conversation, 241–47
authority
   Biblical, 69, 70, 71, 75
   cultural, 8
   of the poet, 86
   of the written word, 211
authorship, 48–49, 134
Averroes, 110
aversio. *See under* figures and tropes: apostrophe

Bahti, Timothy, 131, 137n16, 139, 147n7
Barilli, Renato, 175
Barnouw, Jeffrey, 137n18
Barth, J. Robert, 128, 164n21
Barthes, Roland, 47n15
Bateson, F. M., 164n21
Beattie, James, 106n12, 222, 223, 224, 230n11
Beatty, A. E., 279n1
beautiful, the, 40
Beer, John B., 197n13
Behrendt, Stephen C., 180n18
belief, 207
Bender, John, 1, 6, 7, 123
Bender, Wolfgang, 230n2
Bengel, Johannes Albrecht, 191
Bentley, Richard, 47n19
Bernhardt-Kabisch, Ernest, 164n21
Bevilacqua, Vincent M., 230n2
Bewell, Alan, 200
Bialostosky, Don, 127, 200
Bible, the, 36, 75, 130, 185–96, 202, 204–205, 211, 279n3
Biblical
   criticism, 187
   form, 185–96
   poetry, 185–91
Bitzer, Lloyd F., 230n4
Bizzell, Patricia, 1, 123
Blackwell, Thomas, 202

302

# Index

Blair, Hugh, 106n7, 106n12, 125, 209–10, 221, 222, 224, 228, 254–56, 261
  *Lectures on Rhetoric and Belles Lettres,* 152, 177, 200, 208, 209–10, 218, 219, 230n9, 231n19
Blake, William, 4, 32, 46n5, 185–96, 212, 213
Bloom, Harold, 124, 125, 137n12, 198n28, 211, 214n17, 231n21
Bloomfield, Morton W., 230n12
Blount, Thomas, 162n9
Bonner, S. F., 51, 60n4, 61n9
Booth, Wayne C., 230n3
Bourdieu, Pierre, 124, 136
Bowles, W. L., 28, 29, 37, 45n2
Boyer, James, 77n7
Bradley, A. C., 279n1
Brett, R. L., 46n11, 164n19
Brisman, Leslie, 164n21
Brooks, Cleanth, 42, 47n20, 47n22
Brown, Marshall, 137n5
Browne, Thomas Gunter, 231
Bruns, Gerald, 123, 127, 137n9
Buchan, David, 209
Buickerood, James G., 231n18
Burgess, T. C., 118n6
Burke, Edmund, 52, 53
  influence on Wordsworth, 81, 278
Burke, Kenneth, 87
Burwick, Frederick, 49
Butler, James, 106n6
Butler, Marilyn, 59
Butler, Samuel, 218
Byron, George Gordon, Lord, 37, 103, 213
  *Childe Harold,* 226
  *Don Juan,* 37, 107n18, 169, 227
  rhetorical education of, 67

Campbell, George, 221, 223, 227, 228, 254
  *The Philosophy of Rhetoric,* 177, 218, 220, 225, 226, 230n2, 230n4, 230n11, 230n13, 231n14, 231n25, 231n27
Campbell, O. J., 279n1
Carlyle, Alexander, 229
Carrino, Elnora, 141
Cassirer, Ernst, 236, 248n7
casuistry, 55
Cervantes, 133–34, 137n15
Chandler, James, 81, 91n2, 210
Chase, Cynthia, 128, 137n7, 162n2, 163n15, 164n21
Chaucer, 116, 120n15
chiasmus. *See under* figures and tropes
Christ, 4, 168–69, 178–79
Christ's Hospital, 66–67, 68
Cicero, 4, 51, 53–54, 60n5, 66, 94, 102, 125–26, 167–79, 240
  *De Inventione,* 70, 71
  *De Natura Deorum,* 101, 170
  *De Officiis,* 247n1
  *De Oratore,* 2, 94–95, 96–97, 99–100, 126, 129, 167–68, 174, 175–76, 180n1, 247n1
  orations, 171
  *Orator,* 203–204
Clancey, Richard W., 106n8
Clarke, C. C., 164n21
Cohen, Murray, 230n6
Coleman, Deirdre, 80, 81, 91n2
Coleridge, E. H., 45
Coleridge, Samuel Taylor, 3, 4, 11–28, 28–45, 65–66, 68–76, 156, 213, 222, 223, 227, 230n8, 274
  *Aids to Reflection,* 27n4, 31, 33, 36, 76
  *Biographia Literaria,* 11, 18, 28, 76, 220, 224
  *Christabel,* 34
  "Dejection," 34
  *Essays on His Times,* 68
  *Essays on Method,* 6
  *Friend, The,* 11–27, 33, 40, 47n20
  *Lectures,* 33, 41, 46n8
  *Notebooks,* 27n2, 31, 39, 45
  *On the Constitution of the Church and State,* 76
  *On the Principles of Genial Criticism,* 76
  plagiarism, 77n8
  rhetorical education of, 67, 77n4
  *Rime of the Ancient Mariner, The,* 34–35
  *Shakespearean Criticism,* 162n6
  *The Statesman's Manual,* 31, 68, 73–76
  *The Watchman,* 76
Colmer, John, 78n17
colors, of rhetoric, 53, 55
commonplaces, classical, 124–31
comparison, 28–45
  ancient theories of, 46n6
  comparative power, 41
composition, manuals of, 67
conceit, poetic, 120n12
Connors, Robert, 8, 214n13
controversiae, 56
  and suasoriae, 51–52
conversation, art of, 4, 238–39, 241–46
  in Jane Austen, 241–47
Cooke, Michael G., 116, 139
Cooper, Anthony Ashley. *See* Shaftesbury, Earl of
Cooper, Lane, 107n2
copiousity, 54, 55
Corbett, Edward P. J., 231n26
Cousin, Jean, 141
Covino, William, 60n2
Coward, Harold, 214n16
critic, the, 235, 237
critical orientations, 1
criticism, 236
  Biblical, 187
  literary, of the Renaissance, 110
  and psychology, 220
Crossett, John M., 162n3

Culler, Jonathan, 135, 146, 148n10, 149, 154–55, 161n1, 218, 230n3, 231n19
Curran, Stuart, 109, 112, 118n4
Curtis, Jared, 109–10, 112, 118n1, 118n4, 118n5, 119n9, 119n10, 119n11, 121n18
Curtius, Ernst R., 2, 118n6, 141, 147n3

Daiches, David, 257
Damrosch, Leopold, 224, 231n15
Danby, John J., 164n21
D'Angelo, Frank, 202
Darbishire, Helen, 110, 112, 118n4
Daubuz, Charles, 190, 191, 197n14, 197n16
Day, Angel, 152, 158
de Man, Paul, 2, 31, 42, 125, 137n7, 153, 154–56, 160, 163n13
De Quincey, Thomas, 3, 5, 48–60, 65, 159
  and Aristotle, 50
  and Cicero, 53–54
  *Confessions of an English Opium Eater*, 3, 48–60, 76
  "Conversation," 6, 77n2
  criticism of, 49
  "Language," 6, 55
  "On Knocking at the Gate in Macbeth," 56
  "On Rhetoric," 5, 6, 49, 55, 57
  rhetorical education of, 66
  rhetorical sources of, 50–54
  rhetorical theories of, 50–56
  "Story of a Libel, The," 55
  "Style," 6, 55
declamation, 3, 50, 51–57
  essential parts of, 52–53
deconstruction, 2, 5, 32, 33, 42, 135
decorum, 34, 146, 238, 261
DeLacy, P. H., 171
Demetrius, 39
Demosthenes, 3, 51, 66, 67, 82, 86, 89–90
  *On the Crown*, 82, 87–88
DeNeef, A. Leigh, 111, 114–15, 118n3, 118n6, 120n13
Derrida, Jacques, 31, 33, 42, 44, 46n6, 135, 149, 153, 154, 166n32
Descartes, René, 123
dialect, 256–57
dialectic, 12, 99, 101
  of absence and presence, 43
  negative, 43
dialogue, 235, 237
  Ciceronian, 95, 105n3
Dickstein, Morris, 164n21
diction, 257–58
digression, 143, 145, 193
discipline, 235–36
discourse, 240
  deliberative, 69, 70, 100
  and dialect, 256
  epideictic, 3, 4, 108–18, 239
  forensic, 33, 71, 100
  public
    decline of, 175
    and private, 256–57
  rules of, 235
discourse community, 4
discursive practice, as evidence of moral competence, 243
dispositio, 3–4, 68, 147n3
  and *The Prelude*, 139–46
dissimilia, 33
divisio, 53
Doddridge, Philip, 191, 197n16
Downey, James, 169
Downing, Richard, 197n13
doxa, and episteme, 50
dream narrative, 132
Drummond, Sir William, 173
Dyck, A. R., 88

Eagleton, Terry, 123
Eaton, Daniel Isaac, 171–72
ecphonesis. *See under* figures and tropes
education
  and eloquence, 104–105
  and the polity, 104–105
  of an orator, 95
  rhetorical, of an orator
    at Christ's Hospital, 77n6, 77n8
    at Eton, 77n9
    at Harrow, 77n9
    at Rugby, 77n9
    at St. John's College, Cambridge, 83–84
  classical curriculum for, 102–103
  of Romantic writers, 66–67, 82
Eichhorn, Johann Gottfried, 191, 197n15, 197n21
Eisenstein, Elizabeth, 214n15, 214n19
Eliot, T. S., 230n8
Ellis, David, 164n21
eloquence, 94–105, 250–63
  decline of, 254–55
  and emotional appeal, 253–55
  forums for, 255
  and moral vision, 95
  parody of, 259
  and passion, 254–56
  and power, 176
  responsible uses of, 176–77
emblem, 37
Emerson, Ralph Waldo, 212, 227
emotion
  appeals to, 72, 253–55, 261, 262
  as the core of rhetoric, 267–68
  and poetry, 109
  as the source of eloquence, 97
encomium, 70
Enlightenment, Scottish, 252
epanaphora. *See under* figures and tropes
epic, classical, 110
episteme, 50

Erdman, David V., 194, 198n28
ethics, 101
  and oratorical power, 176
  and oratory, 100
  receptive, 240
ethos, 115, 251, 261, 267–78
Euclid, 131
excellence, artistic, 55
exclamatio. *See under* figures and tropes
excursio, 95
exordium, 141

fancy, 33
Fénelon, François de Salignac, 190, 197n11
Fenner, Dudley, 152
Ferguson, Frances, 164n21
Ferry, David, 164n21
figures
  hierarchy of, 32
  rhetorical, 38
  visual, 38
figures and tropes, 68, 221–22, 257–58
  anaphora, 70
  aporia, 142, 144
  apostrophe, 4, 5, 29, 140–41, 146, 149–61, 164n18, 166n30
    as distinct from prosopopoeia, 154, 155–56
    confused with address, 154–55
    definitions of, 150–53
    function of, 151
    in *The Prelude,* 143
    misunderstood, 163n17
  asyndeton, 71
  chiasmus, 12, 23–25, 39, 43
  ecphonesis, 150, 153
  epanaphora, 224
  epiphonema, 73
  exclamatio, 154, 158
    as distinct from apostrophe, 151
    definitions of, 153
  hyperbole, 36
  metaphor, 33, 46n6, 69, 71, 165n23, 221, 223
  paralipsis, 72
  personification, 222–23
  prosopopoeia, 140, 150, 151, 157, 162n6, 166n30, 222
  in rhetorical education, 66
  simile, 28–45, 46n11, 46n12, 47n19
Findley, L. M., 162n2
Fine, John, 82
Fineman, Joel, 111, 112, 115, 118n6
first-person, in argumentation, 87
Foerster, Donald M., 213n7
form
  Biblical, 185–96
  living, 185
  mathematical, 185
  in oral tradition, 204

organic, 185
poetic, 32
rhetorical, 39
symbolic, 109
verse, 39
*See also* structure
Fowler, Alistair, 147n5
Fox, Susan, 194, 198n22
Frankenstein, 35
*Frankenstein,* 46n11
Fraunce, Abraham, 162n8
Freidman, Michael, 81, 84, 85, 91n2
Freimarck, Vincent, 213n4, 213n5
Frosch, Thomas R., 164n21
Frost, Robert, 166n31, 166n34
Fry, Paul H., 152, 162n4, 162n7, 164n19
Frye, Northrop, 197n17
Fumaroli, Marc, 247n6

Galperin, William, 164n21
Garrod, H. W., 276, 280n7
Gatta, John, Jr., 46n4
Genette, Gérard, 146
genius, 6, 8, 13, 14, 53, 56–57, 122–36, 174, 187, 238, 243
  critiques of, 123–24
  original, 136n3
genre, 3, 4, 8
  and decorum, 146
  of praise, 110
  and *The Prelude,* 139, 146
Gibbons, Thomas, 152, 154, 220, 223, 224, 230n11, 230n13
Giddens, Anthony, 124, 136, 137n6
Gill, John, 190
Gill, Stephen, 81, 128, 147n8
Gillham, P. G., 164n21
Glen, Heather, 164n21
Godwin, William, 175, 180n15
Gomme, A. H., 164n21
Graff, Harvey, 214n15
Graham, William A., 211
Graver, Bruce Edward, 107n19
Gray, Thomas, 161
Greenwood, Robert, 83
Grob, Alan, 118n4
Guthrie, W. K. C., 27n2

Hagstrum, Jean, 193, 197n20
Hammond, Henry, 191, 197n16
Haney, David P., 139, 141, 146, 165n22
Hannibal, as Wordsworth's figure for original genius, 122–23, 125
Hanson, Lawrence, 77n7
Harding, Anthony John, 77n4
Hardison, O. B., Jr., 110, 118n6, 119n7, 120n12, 120n13
Hartley, David, 45n2
Hartman, Geoffrey H., 1, 2, 119n11, 129, 131,

137n9, 139, 140, 159, 164n18, 164n20, 164n21
Havelock, Eric, 202, 206, 214n13
Havens, Raymond Dexter, 128, 131
Hawkshead School, 83
Hazlitt, William, 65, 73, 76n1, 76n2, 78n17, 103, 104, 118n1, 220
  "The Eloquence of the British Senate," 66
  "On Nicknames," 6
  rhetorical education of, 66
Heath, William, 118n5
Hebrew verse, style of, 203–206
Hefferman, James, 120n14
Hepworth, Brian, 200, 213n2, 213n3, 213n9
Hermagoras, 54
Herrick, Robert, 119n11
Hertz, Neil, 130
Herzberg, Bruce, 1, 123
Hill, Alan G., 105n3
Hill, Henry, 137n14
Hoagwood, Terence Allan, 173, 180n13
Hodgson, John, 129, 131
Hogg, James, 66
Hollander, John, 124
Holmes, John, 152
Homer, 4, 35, 46n11
Hooper, Finley, 82
Horace, 3
Horner, Winifred Bryan, 231n26
Horsley, Samuel, 192, 197n17
Hoskins, John, 152, 153, 162n9, 220
Howell, Wilbur Samuel, 1, 49, 197n11, 197n12, 230n1, 230n2, 231n28
Howes, Thomas, 4, 186–91, 196n6, 197n8
Hudson, Hoyt H., 48
Huezet, Jean, 67
Hume, David, 179, 233–34, 237–41, 245, 253
  *Enquiry concerning the Principles of Morals*, 233–35, 239–40, 245
  essays on aesthetics, 237–39, 241
  "Of the Standard of Taste," 219
Hunt, Leigh, 77n6, 77n8
Hurd, Richard, 191, 197n9, 197n14, 197n16
Huxley, Aldous, 164n21
hyperbole. *See under* figures and tropes
hypothesis, 55

identification, 32, 88
ideology, Romantic, 8, 124
imagination, 30, 33, 221
  and eloquence, 99
imitation, and originality, 136
inspiration
  and expression, 206
  opposed to mechanical composition, 187
invention, 37–38
  classical rhetorical, 124–29
  Romantic, 122–36
    and organic unity, 123

as distinct from invention in classical rhetoric, 123
  topics of, 3
  Wordsworth's, 139–46, 124–31
irony, 44

Jackson, J. R. de J., 27n1, 73, 78n17
Jackson, Wallace, 230n13
Jacobus, Mary, 131, 137n7, 137n11, 146, 161n1, 164n21
Jauss, H. R., 32
Jaye, Michael C., 128
Jeffrey, Francis, 94–95, 103–104, 108–109, 118n3, 159
Johnson, Barbara, 161n1
Johnson, Joseph, 189
Johnson, Karl R., 164n21
Johnson, Lee M., 1, 105n3, 105n5, 106n16, 147n1, 164n19
Johnson, Nan, 231n26
Johnson, Samuel, 33, 230n9, 231n24
  *Preface to Shakespeare*, 219
Johnston, Kenneth R., 105n5, 164n21
Jones, Alun R., 46n11, 119n10, 164n19
Jones, John, 164n21
Joseph, Sister Miriam, 152
Josephus, Flavius, 132
journalists, influence of, 177
judgment, moral and aesthetic, 234

Kaestle, Karl, 214n15
*kairos*, 261
Kames, Henry Home, Lord, 33, 46n7, 220, 223, 230n13
Kant, Immanuel, 47n18
Keach, William, 180n12
Keats, John, 95, 213, 222
Kelley, Theresa M., 6, 131, 137n14
Kennedy, George A., 103, 105n3, 106n11, 106n16, 106n17, 118n6, 167, 169, 213n6, 230n1, 230n2
Kneale, J. Douglas, 141, 166n33
Kroeber, Karl, 193, 198n24, 198n25
Kroll, Richard, 213n3
Kugel, James L., 213n5, 213n12

language, 228, 256
  natural, 4, 224–25, 228
  self-referential nature of, 226
  symbolic, 109
  as a synonym for sophistic rhetoric, 16
  and thought, 227
  as vehicle, 227
Lanham, Richard A., 124, 140, 141, 147n6
Lawson, John, 218
LeFevre, Karen Burke, 123
Lerner, L. D., 46n10
Lessenich, Rolf, 203, 213n11
Lewalski, Barbara K., 118n6

# Index

Lindenberger, Herbert, 1, 2, 28–29, 96, 164n21
listener. *See* audience
literacy, and the decline of public discourses, 175
literature
  and rhetoric, separation of, 5
  Romantic
    conservative impulse in, 7
    contexts of, 8
Liu, Alan, 137n17
*loci,* 126, 129
Locke, John, 225–26
Lockhart, John Gibson, 252
*logos,* 261, 267
Longinus, 268
Lord, Albert, 204
Lowth, Robert, 4, 186, 196n4, 199–213, 231n16
  education of, 200
  indebtedness to classical rhetorical tradition, 201
  *Lectures on the Sacred Poetry of the Hebrews,* 199–213
  use of rhetorical vocabulary, 201–202
Lucretius, 94
Lukits, Steven, 164n21
Lyon, Judson, 105n3

McCarthy, John F., 139, 141
McConnell, Frank, 164n21
McFarland, Thomas, 121n16, 124, 136n3, 137n12
McGann, Jerome J., 42–43, 47n21, 123–24
MacGillvray, J. R., 128
MacIntyre, Alasdair, 240, 248n15
McKeon, Richard, 122, 125
McLachlan, H., 66
magnification. *See* amplification
Magnuson, Paul, 47n17
Mahoney, John, 220
man of genius, the, 56–57
manners, 270–79
Manning, Peter, 128
marketplace, literary, 60
Martin, Wallace, 148n11
Marx, Karl, 25
Masson, David, 50
Matlak, Richard E., 1, 3, 147n1
Mede, Joseph, 190, 191, 192, 194
Meisenhelder, Susan, 105n5
Mellor, Ann Kostelanetz, 198n24
memory, 126
Menander, 119n8
metalepsis, 226–27
metaphor. *See under* figures and tropes
method, 11–28
  and chiasmus, 24–27
  as the distinguishing feature of a superior mind, 18

exemplified by characters from Shakespeare
  *Hamlet,* 19–23
  *Henry IV, Part II,* 18–19
  initiative to, 13
  as link between poetry and science, 24–25
  opposed to artifice, 14
  organic metaphor for, 13
  Plato's, power of, 25–26
  and unity, 14
Middleton, Conyers, 170
Mileur, Jean-Pierre, 46n14
Miller, J. Hillis, 131
Milton, John, 35, 47n19, 81, 190
  "Apology for Smectymnus," 172
  "Lycidas," 156
  method of, 26
  *Paradise Lost,* 26, 41, 47n19, 130, 222–23
Mitchell, W. J. T., 125, 193, 197n19, 197n20, 198n24, 198n25
mnemonics, 126
Modernism, 7
Modiano, Raimonda, 47n18
Monboddo, Lord, 44
Morgann, Maurice, 222
Morkan, Joel, 128, 164n21
Morton, Lionel, 164n21
*mousike,* 206
Mulderig, Gerald P., 231n26
Murphy, Richard, 230n2
Murray, Lindley, 177
Murray, Roger N., 164n21
muse, 115

Nabholtz, John R., 82, 147n2
Napoleon, 123
natural philosophy, 101–102
  and oratory, 100
nature, 221
New Criticism, 42, 224
New Historicism, 42
New Rhetoric, 217–30
  and aesthetics, 223
  empirical bias of, 219
  as moral philosophy, 219
  and orality, 210, 212
  and psychology, 219–20
  as semiotics, 225–26
  as system of criticism, 218–20
Newcome, William, 189, 197n7, 197n9
Newton, Thomas, 197n21
Nicholson, Kathleen, 123
Nielsen, Eduard, 213n10

Ober, Warren, 106n15
Ochs, Donovan, 87, 88
Ong, Walter J., 180n18, 214n15
Onorato, Richard, 164n21
oral poetry, 204, 206–207
oral tradition, 202
orality, 201–208

and conservative ideology, 211
and Greek and Hebrew poetry, 201
and Hebrew poetry, 202–208
and literacy in 18th-century Scotland, 210
and religion, 211
as a tool for change, 210
oration, classical, 66, 253
  parts of, 4, 68–69, 71–76, 140–46, 147n3, 150
orator
  and the body politic, 171
  Ciceronian, 3, 8, 167–79
  distinguished from rhetor, 51–52
  education of, 54, 95, 102–103, 106n16
  ideal, 95, 99, 103
  importance of natural talent for, 102–103
  in Milton, 190
  necessary accomplishments of, 172–73
  necessary attributes of, 172
  as political activist, 173–74
  political importance of, 103
  power of, 176
  and public service, 100
  self-fashioning as, 169
  self-presentation of, 175
oratory, 33
  decline of, 51
  and manipulation, 178
  and philosophy, 99–102
  relation between form and content in, 168
  and writing, 175
order. *See* arrangement
Ostriker, Alicia, 195, 198n25, 198n27, 198n28
Ovid, 52
Owen, W. J. B., 80

Paine, Thomas, 27n3
paradox
  epideictic, 120n12
  in the Renaissance, 111
paralipsis. *See under* figures and tropes
Pareus, David, 191, 195
Parker, Patricia, 161n1
Parker, Reeve, 30, 36, 46n13
passion, 221–23, 228, 240, 269
  and eloquence, 254–55
passions, the, 254, 275–77
Pater, Walter, 27n7
pathos, 24, 97, 109, 115, 261, 267–78, 273
  and classical topoi, 129
  and the sublime, 271–73
Patterson, Annabel M., 152, 162n5
Peacham, Henry, 151–52, 153, 154
Peacock, Thomas, 245
Pearce, Zachary, 47n19
Pease, A. S., 119n7, 119n8
Peckham, Morse, 1
Perkins, David, 214n18
personification. *See under* figures and tropes

persuasion, 179, 254, 266–67
  Cicero's three aspects of, 178
Peterloo, 8
philosophy
  as distinct from rhetoric, 12
  and method, 26
Phinney, A. W., 164n21
Pindaric ode, 111
Plato, 14–15, 24
  *Phaedrus,* 179
  Platonic tradition, 39
  and Socrates, 25–26
pleasure, and truth, 240
Plotinus, 28
poet
  as commentator on public life, 86
  cultural role of, 210
  legislative function of, 174
poetry
  ancient connection to music, 204, 208
  of the commonplace, 108–18
  of the English Renaissance, 110
  equated with rhetoric, 110
  Greek and Hebrew
    common oral features of, 201
    functions of, 201, 203
  lyric, 37
    classical, 189
    of the Renaissance, 111
  metaphysical, 42
  more powerful than oratory, 208
  oral, 203–204
  and oratory, 190
  prophetic, 186–96
  true nature of, 206
  and truth, 223
Poirier, Richard, 137n6
polemic, 58
Pope, Alexander, 35, 46n12
Porteous Affair, the, 8
Pöschl, Viktor, 46n10
poststructuralism, 123–25
Potts, A. F., 118n4, 118n5
power
  aesthetic, 32
  comparative, 41
  and ethics, 176, 261–62
  of the orator, 94
  rhetorical, 203
  of sophistic rhetoric, 16
praise
  genres of, 110
  reflexive nature of, 111, 115
preamble, rhetorical function of, 140–41
prefaces, Romantic, 8
presence, 31–32, 42
Prickett, Stephen, 201, 205
Priestley, Joseph, 75, 189, 197n8, 219, 228, 229
primitivism, 199

# Index

print, 49, 212
proemium, 140–41
pronuntiatio, 243
proofs, rhetorical, 267
  enthymeme, 69, 72, 73
  example, 69
property, literary, 7
prophecy
  as argument, 188
  dramatic and visual nature of, 191
  and genre, 191
  rhetorical function of, 188, 190, 191
  structure of, 190–91
  use of human form in, 192
prophet
  Biblical, 8
  as orator, 4, 190
  as poet, 190
propriety, 234
prose
  argumentative, 66
  Romantic, 65–76
prosopopoeia. *See under* figures and tropes
psychology, 220–21
Pulos, C. S., 180n13
Puttenham, George, 111, 162n8, 163n11

Quintilian, 33, 54, 60n5, 66, 67, 69–70, 72–73, 75, 76n2, 103, 106n16, 125, 140, 219, 267–69
  *Institutio Oratoria*, 94, 97–100, 150–51, 247n2, 248, 279n3

Rader, Melvin, 279n1
Ragussis, Michael, 131, 132, 164n21
Rajan, Tilottama, 37, 44, 47n22, 164n21
Ramsey, Roger, 61n11
Raysor, T. M., 47n18
reader response, 250, 252, 258
reading, analogical, 39
reason, and understanding, 31
Reed, Arden, 44
Reed, Mark L., 77n3, 128, 134
Regueiro, Helen, 164n21
Rehder, Robert, 164n21
Reiman, Donald H., 118n1
representation, 32
rhetor, 51–52
rhetoric
  absent from Romantic literature, 7
  as an art of invention, 50, 52
  as distinct from philosophy, 12
  as manipulation, 258
  as the study of language, 218
  classical, 4, 7, 32, 65–76, 201, 228, 233, 257–58, 266
  and addressed speech, 150
  decline of, 6, 7, 95
  offices of, 3
  death, decline, or end of, 1, 5, 50, 124, 241
  deconstructive, 2, 3
  of display, 3, 48–60
  epideictic, 108–18
  forensic, 152, 157, 158
  and form, 156
  formal, 257–58
  Hebrew, 201, 202
  high, 250–52, 260
  and literature, 5
  manuals and treatises on, 5, 111
  misunderstanding of, 150
  natural, 225
  oral, in literate culture, 207
  and poetics, 124, 268
  and poetry, 96
  Renaissance, 111
  Roman, 119n7
  Romantic
    oral dimension of, 208–13
  Scriptural, 4
  sophistic, 3, 57
    as distinct from philosophy, 14
    The Friend's critique of, 14–18
    power of, 16
    traditional character of, 14–18
  traditional histories of, 5
  training in, 95
  transformation into criticism, 235
  vocabulary of
    in Wordsworth, 95, 107n2, 105n5
*Rhetorica ad Herennium*, 66, 151
*rhetorica docens*, 5
*rhetorica utens*, 5
rhetorical analysis, 218–19
rhetorical situation, 8
rhetorical strategies, 6
Richards, I. A., 217–18, 228
Riffaterre, Michael, 153, 155–56
Robertson, Mary, 138n19
Romantic
  ideology, 8
  poetics, 39
  and classical rhetoric, 124
  revisionism, 211
Romanticism
  and composition theory, 123
  in histories of rhetoric, 123
  and literate culture, 212
  oral emphasis of, 211–12
Rosenfield, Lawrence W., 116–18, 118n6, 121n16, 121n17, 121n18
Roston, Murray, 185, 204, 213n4
Rouse, W. H. D., 77n9
Royle, Edward, 173
Rudowski, Victor Anthony, 230n2
Russell, D. A., 118n6
Ryle, Gilbert, 249n22

Said, Edward W., 248n9
Saintsbury, George, 195

Sanderson, David, 78n14, 78n17
Schneider, Ben Ross, 83, 92n5
Scott, Sir Walter, 4, 250–63
Scoular, Kitty W., 112, 119n9, 119n11
Scriptores Romani, 67, 78n9
Scrivener, Michael Henry, 173, 180n18
Sedgwick, William, 23–27
Segal, Charles Paul, 121n17
self-representation, 122
semiology, 228
semiotics, 225
Seneca, 51–53, 94
sermons, 169
Shaftesbury, Earl of, 102, 235–37, 245, 279n2
  "Advice to an Author," 235
  *Characteristics*, 235–36
  "Freedom of Wit and Humor," 235
  *Second Characters*, 236–37
Shakespeare, 130
  *Hamlet*, 19–23
  *Henry IV, Part II*, 18–19
Shakir, Evelyn, 128, 164n21
Shaver, Chester L., 137n15
Shawcross, John, 47n18
Sheats, Paul, 144, 145–46
Shell, Marc, 27n6, 27n8
Shelley, Mary, 35, 46n11
Shelley, Percy Bysshe, 4, 65–66, 167–80, 213, 226
  *Address to the Irish People*, 168, 179
  *Adonais*, 171
  and Christ, 168–69
  and Cicero, 167
  *A Defense of Poetry*, 167, 174, 179, 226
  and dialogic correspondence, 180n4
  education of, 170
  *Essay on Christianity*, 178, 180n11
  Letter to Lord Ellenborough, 171
  oratorical models, 168–69
  political activism, 169, 171
  *Proposal for Putting Reform to the Vote*, 175
  as public speaker, 168
  *Queen Mab*, 170
  readership, 177
  relationship to reader, 170
  and rhetoric, 168
  self-characterization, 170
  skeptical philosophy of, 173
  and Socrates, 168–69
  views on audience, 177–78
Sheridan, Thomas, 221–22
Sherry, Richard, 151–52
Shullenberger, William, 164n21
Shuster, George N., 155
Sidney, Sir Philip, 90, 223
simile. *See under* figures and tropes
Simonides, 126
Smith, Adam, 225
  *Lectures on Rhetoric and Belles Lettres*, 218, 229, 230n3

Smith, John, 153, 162n9
Smith, Olivia, 177
Smyser, Jane Worthington, 82, 92n4, 101, 105n4, 106n14, 131, 132, 147n2
Socrates, 25–26, 168–69
Solon, 15
Sontag, Susan, 230n7
sophistry, 3
  as illusion, 16–18
Sophists, the, 8, 12, 25–26, 50, 54, 61n6
Southey, Robert, 65–66, 80, 81
Spector, Stephen J., 164n21
speech
  addressed, 150
  authority derived from, 95
speeches, Parliamentary, 68
Spenser, Edmund, 119n10
sprezzatura, 246
Stafford, William, 173
Stallknecht, Newton, 102, 131
stasis, 53
Stillinger, Jack, 134, 136
Stoicism, 95, 105n4, 106n14
strategies, rhetorical, 11, 25, 70, 170
Streuver, Nancy S., 231n18, 247n3
structure
  and arrangement, 185–88
  and internal coherence, 186
  and juxtaposition, 185, 189
  and parallelism, 186
  prophetic, 190, 195
    use of multiple genres, 195–96
    use of multiple styles, 195
  rhetorical, 45
  rhetorical function of, 190
  sense as a unit of, 204
style, 177, 223, 228
  of Hebrew poetry, 206
  obscure, 11
  parallelism, 204–205
  and psychology, 220
  and publicity, 48–49
subjects, trivial
  Wordsworth's, 108–18
  works in praise of, 112–18
sublime, the, 40–41, 47n18, 47n20, 271–73, 276–77
  in Hebrew poetry, 205
  in oral tradition, 206
suspense, 40
suspension of disbelief, 32
Swinburne, Algernon Charles, 195
symbol, 38, 42
symbolism, 31–33, 42
symbology, 30–31
sympathy, 222, 225, 237

talent, individual, 124
taste, 218, 234, 236, 237–38, 242–46, 243
  and moral judgment, 242–46

# Index

Tateo, Francesco, 247n4
tautology, 23
Tenneman, Wilhelm Gottlieb, 27n2
  *Geschicte der Philosophie,* 27n2
tenor, and vehicle, 33–39, 45, 228
Tetreault, Ronald, 170
theses, 3, 53
  and hypothesis, 54
Thomas, Gordon, 79, 80
Thomas, W. K., 106n15
Thompson, T. W., 82
Thornton, Percy M., 77n9
Thucydides, 66
Todorov, Tzvetan, 230n2
Tooke, Horne, 225, 230n6
topoi, 3, 71, 72, 74–75, 111, 125–31, 158, 202
Toulmin, Stephen, 248
tradition
  Augustinian, 190, 197n13
  oral, 202, 204
  rhetorical, 50, 112, 200, 266
Trimpi, Wesley, 59n4
Trowbridge, Hoyt, 229, 232n29
truth, 234, 240
  aesthetic, 235–36, 246
  moral dangers of communicating, 11
  and poetry, 223
  properly communicated by obscure style, 11
Turner, J. M. W., 136n2
Tyson, Ann, 83

unity, 2–29, 31, 40, 44, 185–86, 237
  and method, 14
  organic, 128
  and romantic invention, 123

Vaihinger, Hans, 43, 46n3
Valla, Lorenzo, 248n16
values
  absolute, absence of, 173
  traditional, lost authority of, 17
vehicle, 33–39, 227–28
verisimile, 32
Vickers, Brian, 1, 2, 110, 111, 118n6, 120n13
Virgil, 46n11, 127
  *Culex,* 112, 119n9
  *Georgics,* 103, 107n19
virtue, 255–56
*visiones,* 98
Vogler, Thomas, 46n10
voice, 149–50, 156, 164n18, 166n30
  apostrophe as movement of, 154
  poetic, 44
  silencing of, 158
  in Wordsworth, 159–61

Walker, John, 152
Wallace, Karl R., 230n5, 232n30
Wallerstein, Ruth, 197n12, 197n13
Walvin, James, 173

Ward, John, 218, 226–27
Ward, Patricia, 47n20
Warminski, Andrzej, 137n16, 164n21
Wasserman, Earl R., 30, 45n2, 230n12
Watson, J. R., 164n21
Webb, Timothy, 180n18
Weiner, David, 128
Weinsheimer, Joel, 124, 136n3
Wellbery, David E., 1, 6, 7, 123, 230n2
Wellek, René, 49
Wesling, Donald, 124
Whaler, James, 46n7
Whalley, George, 46n10, 46n12
Whately, Richard, 258
White, Samuel, 190
Willey, Basil, 75
Wilson, Thomas, 153
Wimsatt, W. K., 28–29
Wither, George, 113
Wittreich, Joseph Anthony, Jr., 195, 197n12, 197n16, 197n21, 198n26
Wolfson, Susan J., 128, 136n4, 164n21
Woodring, Carl, 73, 110, 123, 136n2
Woof, Robert, 82
Wooten, Cecil, 87
Wordsworth, Christopher, 66, 83
Wordsworth, Dorothy, 126
Wordsworth, Jonathan, 128, 134, 147n8, 214n14
Wordsworth, William, 1–4, 37, 40–41, 47n18, 47n19, 65–66, 76n2, 77n3, 79–91, 94–105, 108–18, 122–36, 149, 157–61, 212, 221, 224, 226
  aesthetic of, 40–41
  apostasy, 80
  Burns-Burger criticism, 274–75
  and Cervantes, 137n15
  classical education of, 82–84, 92n7
  Convention of Cintra, 3, 8, 79–91
  critical theories of, 273–79
  decline of, 80
  essays on epitaphs, 6
  *Excursion, The,* 3, 94–105, 158, 159
  genius of, 18
  intellectual sources, 266–78
  Letter to Lady Beaumont, 117
  *Lyrical Ballads,* 4, 98, 108–109, 164n19
  "Methinks," 268–69
  and passions, 276
  *Poems, In Two Volumes,* 3, 108–18
  political views, 82, 89, 90–91
  *Preface to Lyrical Ballads, The,* 86, 98, 106n12, 121n16, 172, 177, 225, 256, 269, 275
  *Prelude, The,* 40, 82, 96, 122–36, 139–46, 153, 156, 157–61
    as argument, 144, 145
    as classical oration, 140–46
    deluge narrative in, 132–33
    digression in, 143, 145

disposition of, 139–46
  exposition of, 142
  generic classifications of, 139, 146
  *narratio* of, 141–42
  preamble, 140–41
  proposition of, 142–43
  quaestio, 142
  revisions of, 145
 in retirement, 81
 and self-representation, 122
 and symbolic form, 109
 *Tintern Abbey,* 1, 3, 118, 126, 156
 trivial subjects of, 108–18, 274–75
 views on France, 79–80
*Wanderer, The*
  contemporary reactions to, 94–95, 103–105
  Wanderer, the, 3
  education of, 100–105
  eloquence of, 94–105
  as orator, 94–105
  stoic elements of, 95
Worthington, Jane. *See* Smyser, Jane Worthington
Wu, Duncan, 82, 92n5

Yates, Frances, 126
Young, Michael C., 55

Zall, Paul M., 109, 117, 121n16
Zumthor, Paul, 213n1

ADJ 6351